Workplace Democracy
and
Social Change

Workplace Democracy
and
Social Change

Frank Lindenfeld
Joyce Rothschild-Whitt
Editors

Extending Horizons Books
PORTER SARGENT PUBLISHERS, INC.
11 Beacon Street, Boston, MA 02108

©1982 by Frank Lindenfeld and Joyce Rothschild-Whitt
All rights reserved
Manufactured in the United States of America
Library of Congress Catalog Card Number 82-80137
ISBN 0-87558-101-3 (clothbound)
ISBN 0-87558-102-1 (paperback)

Designed by Christopher Leonesio
Composed by Howard Kirshen Printing Corporation,
Boston, Massachusetts

CONTENTS

Introduction
Reshaping Work: Prospects and Problems
of Workplace Democracy   1
Joyce Rothschild-Whitt
Frank Lindenfeld

Part 1
CHARACTERISTICS OF
ORGANIZATIONAL DEMOCRACY

Introduction to Part 1   21

1. The Collectivist Organization:
   An Alternative to Bureaucratic Models   23
   Joyce Rothschild-Whitt

2. Necessary Elements for Effective Worker
   Participation in Decision-Making   51
   Paul Bernstein

Part 2
ORGANIZATIONAL DEMOCRACY
AND THE INDIVIDUAL

Introduction to Part 2   85

3. Workers' Ownership and Attitudes
   Towards Participation   87
   Tove Helland Hammer
   Robert N. Stern
   Michael A. Gurdon

4. The Rewards of Participation
   in the Worker-Owned Firm   109
   Raymond Russell

5. Fears of Conflict in Face-to-Face
   Democracies   125
   Jane J. Mansbridge

6. Collective Work and Self-Identity:
   Working in a Feminist Illegal
   Abortion Collective   139
   Melinda Bart Schlesinger
   Pauline B. Bart

Part 3
LARGE-SCALE WORKERS'
COOPERATIVES: CASE STUDIES

Introduction to Part 3   157

7. The Worker-Owned Plywood Cooperatives   161
   Katrina V. Berman

8. The Mondragón System of Worker
   Production Cooperatives   177
   Ana Gutiérrez Johnson
   William Foote Whyte

9. The Origin, Structure, and Problems of
   Four British Producers' Cooperatives   199
   J. David Edelstein

10. At IGP, It's Not Business as Usual   221
    Daniel Zwerdling

Part 4
SELF-MANAGED COLLECTIVES:
CASE STUDIES

Introduction to Part 4   243

11. Is Anybody There?
    Notes on Collective Practice   247
    Santa Barbara Legal Collective

12. Problems of Power in a Free School   257
    Frank Lindenfeld

- 13. On Structure and Decision-Making   271
    Gary H. Newton

14. Seattle Workers' Brigade:
     History of a Collective   279
     Peg Pearson
     Jake Baker

Part 5
WORKPLACE DEMOCRACY
AND SOCIAL CHANGE

Introduction to Part 5   293

15. On the Legal Structure of
     Workers' Cooperatives   299
     David Ellerman

16. How the Old Coops Went Wrong   315
     Paula Giese

17. Workers' Cooperatives:
     Remedy for Plant Closings?   337
     Frank Lindenfeld

18. The Youngstown Project   353
     Gar Alperovitz
     Jeff Faux

19. Building Participatory Democracy
     within a Conventional Corporation   371
     Rosabeth Moss Kanter
     Barry A. Stein
     Derick W. Brinkerhoff

20. The Labor Movement and
     Worker Management   383
     C. George Benello

21. Workers' Control Is More
     Than Just That   397
     André Gorz

References   413

Index   431

Introduction

Reshaping Work: Prospects and Problems of Workplace Democracy

Joyce Rothschild-Whitt
Frank Lindenfeld

Work in America is not working very well. While satisfying work remains essential for our well-being — and research shows that it is related to health, self-esteem, and even longevity — it is available to progressively fewer and fewer persons. Even official government reports indicate that, among white-collar workers as well as blue-collar workers, job dissatisfaction is at a record high.

It is the perspective of this book that the fundamental source of the problem, and its potential solution, centers on the issue of *control*: control of the conditions of work, the kind and variety of work done, the pace of work, and the product of work — in short, control over the whole labor process. Control may be hierarchical, as when those who manage and those who do the work tasks are permanent and separate sets of people. Or it may be democratic, as when those who do the work of the organization are the same as those who set its goals and policies. Hierarchical control is so much a part of our society it is sometimes difficult to imagine that work could be arranged in an altogether different manner. This book is about people who have managed to create work organizations in a different image. From lawyers to garbage collectors, from free-school teachers to plywood workers, from journalists to insurance workers, many people have seized the opportunity to build democratic workplaces.

The subject of this anthology is *workplace democracy* as found in both large, democratically managed organizations as well as in small worker-collectives. These two types of enterprises differ in their origins, social base, and characteristics, but they are unified in their common effort to structure their workplaces in a democratic fashion.

The grassroots work-collectives have their origin in the counter-culture movements of the 1960s, and almost all have developed since 1970. Most originated as alternative work-organizations established to fulfill social needs not being met by existing institutions. Collective organizations have been generated in almost every domain of social life, especially in the service fields: health collectives, free schools, "new wave" food cooperatives, legal collectives, newspapers, and so forth (pt. 4). Their membership is based primarily on young and middle-class strata. Although each of these organizations may be relatively small, taken as a whole, this contemporary wave of collectivist organizations constitutes the most numerous category of democratic workplaces in the United States today. They are not, however, the only working models we can observe.

Democratic workplaces have also flourished in fields that are light years away from a counterculture, such as International Group Plans, a Washington, D.C., based insurance firm with over 300 workers that is democratizing its ownership and governance structures (chap. 10). Some represent the collective efforts of an underclass in our society, like a producers' cooperative of strawberry growers near Salinas, California, composed chiefly of former field hands (Alvarado-Greenwood et al. 1978, chap. 9). Some worker-owned and worker-managed businesses have been successfully operating for over fifty years in this country, with the refuse-collection cooperatives in the San Francisco area (chap. 4) and the plywood-workers' cooperatives in the Pacific Northwest (chap. 7) being the two most long-standing examples. These larger enterprises generally have a working class membership. Some workers' cooperatives arise when a group of workers pool their savings to start their own enterprise, and some cases of worker ownership emerge when workers face plant shutdowns and subsequent job loss.

The major differences between the larger, democratically managed enterprises and the smaller collectives are associated with differences in size. *Collectives* are small, usually with less than twenty workers and often less than a dozen. Major decisions affecting the whole organization may be made by the entire group in plenary meetings. Authority resides in the collectivity as a whole, and, though it may be delegated to individuals, such persons are subject to recall. Work roles are holistic. They generally combine administrative tasks with performance tasks and intellectual work with manual work. To accomplish these multifaceted work roles, internal education is often stressed. Internal education may be achieved through task-sharing, job rotation, and the demystification of specialized knowledge. Often, there is no clearcut position corresponding to the lower status positions in conventional organizations (secretary, janitor, etc.), for each member is expected to do some secretarial or janitorial work. Collectives are held together by bonds of friendship and by shared commitment to certain values or goals (chap. 1).

Larger democratically managed organizations include up to several hundred workers, and, in some cases, thousands. These complex, democratic work-organizations usually have some specialization, but this is combined with an emphasis on internal education where specialists share knowledge as much as possible with other members. Generally, there is task-sharing and rotation of work roles, though the latter may not be as frequent as in collectives. Large democratic workplaces may have some degree of stratification, insofar as positions are seen as differentially important and are rewarded unequally, but, as in the small collectives, a limit is set on the income ratio between the highest and the lowest paid. For instance, in the cooperative enterprises near Mondragon, Spain, top managers receive no more than three times the income of the lowest-paid workers. In the worker-owned refuse-collection firms in San Francisco, California, the differential is only 2 to 1. In some of the plywood cooperatives, it is more or less equal. By comparison, the income differential tolerated in many United States corporations is 100 to 1. In large democratically managed organizations, authority resides in the membership, and, though it may be delegated, the membership retains the final say in cases of dispute. For example, in the plywood cooperatives, the general manager may fire a worker for cause, but the worker can appeal that decision to the entire membership.

This volume, due to limitations of space, will focus largely on the American experience with workplace democracy, but some ambitious projects elsewhere, particularly those that are less known and quite probably relevant to America, are also included: workers' cooperatives in Britain (chap. 9) and in the Basque region of Spain (chap. 8).

There have been many other experiments in workplace democracy abroad which we will only mention here. The best known perhaps is the case of Yugoslavia where, since the 1950s, the entire economy has been based on principles of self-management (Adizes 1971a). In Republican Spain, during the mid-thirties, many industrial and agricultural enterprises were run by their workers (Dolgoff 1974, chaps. 6-8). A significant attempt to democratize major industrial firms was undertaken by the Allende regime in Chile between 1970 and 1973 (Espinosa and Zimbalist 1978, chap. 4). In Israel, there are numerous democratically organized agricultural and industrial enterprises within the kibbutzim. Other countries that have tried some form of cooperative management include Algeria (Clegg 1971, chaps. 9, 10); Peru (Knight 1975); and China (Bettleheim 1974, chap. 3).

The articles in this volume attempt to convey something of the diversity as well as the commonalities of democratic work organizations. We hope the book will help convince a wider audience of the desirability and relevance of economic democracy for industrial, service, and governmental organizations.

Part 1 identifies the common characteristics of democratic work organizations. Part 2 examines the psychological impact of working within democratically managed organizations. Part 3 brings together case studies of the larger, democratically managed organizations. Part 4 looks at workplace democracy in the small, collectively controlled organizations. The last section, part 5, considers the implementation of economic democracy in the American context and explores the implications of workplace democracy for social change.

LIMITED PARTICIPATION VS. ECONOMIC DEMOCRACY

"Participation," "participative management," and the like have become such popular terms in United States industry today that it is important to distinguish their usage from what we mean by *economic democracy* in this book.

Worker participation may be conceived as a multidimensional continuum. To identify a particular control structure, we must know over what specific issues the workers exercise influence, to what degree they may exercise influence, and at what level of the organization they exercise influence. Thus, worker participation can be treated as a continuum from the most modest levels of participation, employee *consultation* in decision-making, to the wider levels of employee *coinfluence* to *joint management* or *codetermination,* and finally to full *workers' control* over the process and product of labor (Bernstein 1976, pp. 47-48).

How did the current attraction of industry managers to at least modest levels of labor participation come about? In his history of work in the twentieth century, Braverman demonstrates that, despite the growing level of education of the population and the myth that jobs require ever more skill, most jobs in this country have become less, not more, skilled. Industry adopted *Taylorism,* as developed by

Frederick W. Taylor (1947), the ever more detailed division of labor, because it allows for the substitution of unskilled for skilled workers and is therefore cheaper (Braverman 1974, chaps. 3, 4). For every engineer, there are countless unskilled workers; for every computer technician or skilled maintenance person, scores of operatives; for every manager, dozens of clerks and secretaries. Braverman argues that the divorce between hand- and headwork facilitates managerial control. Technology has been selectively adapted and shaped by large firms in the interest of more centralized control over the knowledge and information necessary to run the organization.

As a result, symptoms of job dissatisfaction and alienation are pervasive and getting worse: absenteeism, slowdowns, wildcat strikes, labor turnover, shoddy workmanship or poor service, and, in some cases, outright sabotage of the product. In response, industry has begun to turn away from so-called scientific management toward more participative models of organization.

Here and there, workers are being granted more autonomy and participation, or at least consultation, in management decisions. Assembly lines are giving way to teams; employees may be sharing some of the profits. Ever since the Hawthorne Western Electric experiments, corporate managers have become increasingly aware that treating employees like human beings may be good business. Happy workers might make more productive workers. Thus, humanized versions of nonetheless hierarchical organizations hold out the possibility of greater output and profit, without relinquishing the prerogative of management to set overall organizational policy.

What identifies such participative models is that the permissible level of workers' participation is strictly controlled and limited by management. Employees may be afforded some measure of decisional control over immediate work tasks and environments, but the primacy of managerial control is left intact. Patterns of ownership are not changed, the structure of rewards and the processes of evaluation remain management prerogatives, and the equalization of pay is nowhere on the organizational agenda. In the end, it is top management that has the authority to order and to halt experiments in workers' participation and job enlargement. Managers of corporations have not been known to let employees' participation and employees' development of skills and responsibility grow to the point where they render management itself obsolete. This unspoken limit on participation was revealed when the Polaroid corporation instituted a job enlargement program for a group of 120 machinists on a "crash" production project. In place of the usual eight-hour day routine, the machinists each had one hour's training plus two hours of coordination activities and five hours at the machines. The program was too successful, and worried management reverted to the old system when it found that workers had little need for managers under the new one (Jenkins 1973, chap. 12). A similar retreat from participation evolved during General Foods' experimentation with job redesign in its dog-food plant in Topeka, Kansas (Zwerdling 1980, pp. 19-29)

WORKPLACE DEMOCRACY

Such limited participation is not what the democratic workplaces discussed in this volume mean by *participatory* or *democratic*. Where there is genuine organizational democracy, it is not a matter of a more supportive or employee-centered management, nor of a more humanized relationship between superior and subordinate. While managerial functions may be delegated to some members of democratic work-organizations, there is no binary system of managers and workers. In one way or another, everyone manages and everyone works. Ultimate authority resides in the collectivity as a whole, and responsibility is exercised at all levels in the organization. This is the meaning of *self-management*.

Democratic workplaces are united in their attempt to break down the division between management and labor, planners and workers, so that all who do the work of the organization have an equal voice in its management and a fair share of the fruits of their labor. What they are seeking to alter, then, is nothing short of the structure of power in organizations. The aim is not the simple *transference* of power from one official to another; it is the *abolition* of the pyramid *in toto*. It is an attempt to accomplish organizational tasks cooperatively and democratically, without recourse to hierarchal authority structures or the stratification systems that accompany them.

Following Vanek (1971, chap. 2), the general features of democratically managed organizations are outlined below. The reader should bear in mind that these are ideal features and are not necessarily found together in pure form in existing firms. (More specific structural characteristics of the democratic enterprise are identified in pt. 1 by Rothschild-Whitt and by Bernstein.)

1. Full worker participation in decision-making exists at all levels of the organization. Enterprises are controlled by those who work in them. In small organizations, decisions are generally made by the entire collective in frequent meetings. Larger organizations have some kind of management positions, but managers are elected on the basis of one person, one vote and can be recalled by the members; the workforce as a whole retains ultimate authority.

2. All who work in an organization share in its net income and decide democratically how income and surplus should be distributed. The tendency is toward equality. Often, such systems include some provision for paying workers partly according to need (e.g., number of family members). The net effect is to flatten the stratification pyramid within the enterprise, region, or society as the case may be.

3. The means of production (land, buildings, machinery) are socially owned and kept in trust as community assets. They may be owned either directly by a firm's workers, or by a trust controlled by them, or leased from community organizations or government.

4. The main purpose of each firm is not the maximization of profit, but the maximization of community well-being. This includes fair income for those who work in the enterprise and workers' control of their own work, with jobs as personally rewarding as possible. Community well-being also includes providing goods or services that are socially useful, of high quality, and ecologically sound. Priority would be given to the conservation of energy and natural resources and to the growth of the organization to an appropriate, medium size. In times of trouble, workers are not laid off, but rather share reduced hours or lower incomes.

5. Profit, or surplus after paying overhead and wages, belongs to all who worked to create it. It may be shared in the form of bonuses, or, it may be used for social and community purposes such as education, health clinics, or day-care centers. A vital use of the surplus is for reinvestment within the firm or in other worker-managed enterprises to create new jobs. Labor-managed systems may be able to create more employment than capitalist systems, as the economic growth of Yugoslavia and of the Mondragón network seem to indicate (Vanek 1971, pp. 28-29; 150-151).

6. In democratically managed enterprises, labor hires capital. As long as capital is scarce there may have to be interest paid for its use, but suppliers of capital (e.g., banks) do not exercise control over the enterprise and usually do not share the profits.*

---

*Vanek argues that the worker-managed firms must operate in a free-market system. This is a controversial point, however. Albert and Hahnel (1981) maintain, in

The general features of worker-managed systems described above are no doubt interrelated, as are the structural characteristics of democratic organizations discussed in the first section of this book. Nonetheless, it is an error to treat self-management as a unitary phenomenon. Self-managed enterprises may not in real life realize all of the above criteria (or any set of criteria) in pure form. For this reason, parts 3 and 4 of this book focus on the actual practices of self-managed workplaces. The democratic principle admits of a variety of specific organizational arrangements (contingent upon particular circumstances of the organization such as its size, technology, funding sources, and so forth). It is the purpose of this volume to convey something of the commonalities as well as the diversity of democratic work.

Subcategories of democratically managed organizations include *workers' cooperatives,* also called *producers' cooperatives, self-managed firms,* and *comanaged firms* (Espinosa and Zimbalist 1978, chap. 1). Workers' cooperatives are both owned and managed by their workers. Self-managed and comanaged organizations are democratically managed, though not legally owned, by their workers. In self-managed organizations, ultimate authority is retained by the firm's workers; in comanaged organizations, such authority is shared by workers and representatives of the state or the community.

Other organizations considered in this volume are worker-owned but not necessarily worker-managed. One selection of this type describes a furniture plant in which the ownership structure has been democratized to include the workers, but where the governance structure has not been substantially altered (chap. 3). At Youngstown Sheet and Tube Company (chap. 18), the authors propose a similar conversion to worker-community ownership coupled with a plan for comanagement of the plant.

Both of these selections are germane to the growing phenomenon of worker ownership (or some form of worker-community ownership) emerging out of corporate divestiture situations. The spread of divestitures and plant closings certainly provides a fertile opportunity to move in the direction of worker ownership, and the essay by Lindenfeld (chap. 17) explores the potentialities of this strategy.

---

contrast, that while central government planning may be undesirable, a self-managed economy should be based upon an integration of plans put together from the bottom up, on the local level, revised by higher level regional councils, sent back "down" for further revision, etc.

CHALLENGES TO DEMOCRACY

As the fact and variety of democratic workplaces makes clear, organizational democracy is not impossible to achieve. But neither is it easily created or maintained. Democratic work organizations face challenges almost daily in their efforts to accomplish the job at hand while still retaining a democratic form. The case material in this volume highlights these challenges and indicates how some organizations resolve them in their everyday practices.

Size and Efficiency

Critics of economic democracy often concede that democracy may work well in small alternative organizations, but question how efficient or even relevant democratic management can be for larger firms. After all, the most compelling reason for the advance of bureaucratic forms of work organization has always been their supposed efficiency. To date, only a few systematic studies have been done comparing the productivity or efficiency of the larger worker-managed firms with that of traditionally managed businesses, and surely more studies are needed here.

One study of democratic participation in a sample of thirty-five major Chilean industrial firms during 1970-73 showed that, after these firms were converted to democratic management, they became more efficient. Productivity increased or remained the same in twenty-nine out of thirty-five enterprises. In fourteen of them, productivity increased at more than 6 percent per year. A direct association was found between the degree of increase in democratic participation and the degree of increase in productivity (Espinosa and Zimbalist 1978b, p. 162). Similarly, a comparison between cooperative and managerial decision-making in the kibbutz vs. private-sector industries in Israel showed that the democratically managed organizations were at least as efficient and productive as the traditionally organized firms, and, in some cases, more so (Melman 1969).

As we shall see in some of the case studies reported in this book, the level of productivity and the quality of output in democratically organized firms can be quite high. Generally, there is higher worker morale in democratic enterprises than in hierarchically organized firms, less absenteeism, and fewer strikes (Blumberg 1968, chap. 5). Production in the Mondragón system of worker cooperatives has grown at a remarkable rate, and, at the same time, the cooperative network has expanded employment. One of the firms has become the largest Spanish exporter of refrigerators and other durable consumer goods (chap. 8). In the cooperative plywood plants in this country, wages are generally higher than the union standard, and, at the same time, workers have more job security, because, when sales are low, each pulls in his belt a little so nobody has to be laid off (chap. 7). There is evidence that the worker-owned refuse-collection firms reported on by Russell in chapter 4 provide higher quality services than comparable municipally-run enterprises or privately owned enterprises.

The need for large-size units is often used as a justification for bureaucracy. But the supposed efficiency of large organizations may well be overstated. The profit rates of large corporations may be far more attributable to their market power than to their efficiency. In an excellent review of the literature on size and efficiency, Stein (1974, p. 90) concludes, "large organizations are not, by virtue of their size, inherently superior to smaller ones. Indeed...the reverse is often more nearly the case, at least within certain segments of the economy and above certain very modest limits on smallness."

Further, in attempting to assess models of workplace democracy, it is essential to understand that the minimization of costs and the maximization of output — the calculus of efficiency — may not be of the highest priority. This is especially true of service organizations in the public or private sector where output is difficult to measure. Optimizing the efficiency of an organization is, in some cases, not even a relevant criterion. Alternative gauges of success — for example, the level of democratic control in the organization, the social utility and quality of the goods or services provided, the fulfillment of the human needs of the workers, and the contribution of the enterprise to progressive societal change — may be far more important to the participants in democratically organized firms. To assess these democratic workplaces against bureaucratic standards of efficiency is to judge them against standards they do not necessarily share.

As case studies in this book indicate, democratic work-organizations can function well, at least in size ranges of up to several hundred persons. Nobody really knows what their practical size limits are. This would differ with the function of the organization, its environment, and with the cultural background of its participants. The largest firm in the Mondragón complex, ULGOR, has over 3,000 workers in two plants, but it also has had the most internal conflict of any of the Spanish cooperatives, including one short-lived strike. Some of the people in the Mondragón network speak of the desirability of limiting the size of new cooperatives to 400-500 or so workers

(Campbell et al. 1977, chap. 47). With few exceptions, efficient and productive organizations, even in manufacturing, do not have to be larger than this. Many can be considerably smaller.

Complex, democratically organized firms take a variety of organizational forms; no one form is the best under all circumstances. One structure appropriate to larger democratic work-organizations is a division into cooperating subgroups. The organization may be divided into service or production teams coordinated by representatives elected to a managerial committee. Such a committee may act as the executive of the firm, under its governing board, or the workers as a body may elect a smaller executive group and/or general manager. In a medium-size firm, say 100-300 persons, the managerial committee might consist of a representative or *link-pin* from up to fifteen teams numbering 10-20 persons each. Delegates and managers would be rotated periodically to avoid the tendency toward oligarchy. Representatives and managers are accountable to the work force as a whole, and are subject to recall. The entire body of workers comes together at periodic plenary meetings to review, ratify, or veto major decisions of managers and committees. Where there is a genuine need to have larger organizations, these might be built out of several semiautonomous subunits of several hundred persons each.

The larger the organization, the more difficult it becomes to maintain internal democracy. Organizations numbering in the thousands will probably be less participatory than those numbering in the hundreds. The challenge is to find specific structures and processes of organization which nevertheless maximize workers' participation in large firms.

Institutionalization

A perennial problem for democratic organizations is the drift toward institutionalization. Through various internal and external pressures, nonbureaucratic organizations may become bureaucratic. This may happen when they grow larger and remain as one unit instead of spinning off parallel but autonomous organizations. Or it may happen when the work load becomes so great that members of the firm hire outsiders as wage-laborers. This changes the relationship of workers to the organization, for newcomers no longer have the same rights of ownership and control. As they become ordinary employees, their interests often diverge from those of the full-fledged members. This can be seen in the worker-owned scavenger companies discussed by Russell in chapter 4.

Growing institutionalization can be seen also in the established food cooperatives where managers may feel a vested interest in the continuation of the organization to insure their own jobs and where a split develops between unpaid members and paid organization employees (chap. 16). As the old-style consumer coops grew, they became increasingly bureaucratized in spite of formal mechanisms for their boards of directors to be elected by the membership. Members "owned" the coop, but practical control rested largely with professional managers hired by the boards of directors. For such managers, like the managers of chain supermarkets, the primary motivation became the expansion of sales. "Profits" were channeled into higher wages for managers and other employees, and to member patronage dividends. In practice, the members of some large consumer coops have had little more say in their operation than small stockholders of any major corporation.

Bureaucratization may also be externally generated. For example, a free high school may begin with an emphatic policy of no records, but find that, if it is to help students who want to transfer back into the public schools or go on to college, then it must begin keeping or inventing documents and records. The preoccupation of other organizations with records (in this case, public schools) may thus force record-keeping on a reluctant free-school (chaps. 1, 12). Other outside pressures, such as the presence of a stream of government communications and inspectors (health, building, fire, etc.) may push the organization into creating special jobs to handle correspondence and personal visits of officials.

Oligarchization

Oligarchization, like institutionalization, is no new problem to social scientists. The organizational literature is replete with case studies that show that, despite the best of intentions, democratic control often yields to oligarchic control. This happens so often that it is regarded as an "iron law" (Michels 1959, pt. 6). How can democratic work organizations avoid this process? We know that oligarchization is favored by certain factors, like membership apathy, large size, and inability to move toward original organizational goals. Conversely, structural factors that militate against oligarchization are identified by Rothschild-Whitt (1976a).

If worker-managed organizations wish to avoid the concentration of power, they must prevent the monopolistic use of expertise. Toward this end, they often stress internal education, job rotation, task-sharing, apprenticeship programs or any plan they can devise that will successfully diffuse the knowledge needed to perform the organization's tasks. Such efforts at knowledge diffusion require considerable energy and, while essential for collective control, they, too, have their tensions and dilemmas. Should a person be taken off a task, although very good at it, to make room for another person who wants to learn to do it? How much time can be devoted to apprenticeships and other forms of internal education without sacrificing the quality of the product or service that the organization provides? Are there certain skills (or arts) that cannot be taught to more than a few organizational members? These are some of the challenges that democratic work organizations must face in their everyday practices.

Worker vs. Community Interests

Worker-owned enterprises may in many respects be better places for the worker-owners to work, but one criticism of such enterprises is that they may overlook the general needs and interests of the community in favor of the particular interests of their members. The fact that workers in a self-managed firm may not always make decisions that are in the interest of the community at large is an issue of considerable debate in Yugoslavia. Self-managed firms, for instance, may charge prices higher than necessary or produce inferior products or services. However, because workers are also community members and consumers, this is not as likely in the self-managed firm as in the standard corporation.

To insure the responsiveness of such organizations to the community and the society, some form of comanagement is often preferable to pure worker-self-management. In comanaged systems, consumer, community, or government representatives may also be appointed or elected to governing boards alongside worker representatives. For example, the organizational structure for the worker/community-owned steel plant proposed as a successor to the factory shut down in Youngstown, Ohio, provides for a board of directors with two-fifths of its members selected by the workers, one-fifth by members of the community, and two-fifths by outside investors. While not a "pure" example of democratic management, such a structure does attempt to provide for representation of community-wide interests (chap. 18). This is a general problem which affects any self-managed enterprise and, in each case, the best mix of worker, government, community, and consumer representation needs to be found.

Auxiliary Institutional Supports

Worker-owned and -governed enterprises face many problems in the United States which derive from the fact that they are, as yet, isolated examples of economic democracy in an otherwise bureaucratic and capitalist context.

Isolated democratically-managed firms may run into difficulties with financing, marketing, and so forth. For this reason, cooperation among democratic firms will be critical for their survival. There have been many efforts in the United States to develop federations that would provide mutual aid to cooperative enterprises on a regional or industrial basis (for an example of a federative effort in Seattle, see chap. 14). In some cases, worker collectives and cooperatives have come together on a local level to help provide mutual benefits for each other, such as group health insurance; in other instances, they have come together nationally on the basis of industry type (e.g., alternative newspapers, food coops, law collectives) to provide various forms of material and moral support for each other. However, the attempts to develop federated networks in the United States have so far not been nearly as broad in scope as the infrastructure of financial, educational, and other supporting institutions that have developed in the Mondragón network of cooperatives.

First, there is a great need for educational institutions in which people could learn the skills of effective democratic management. While democratically run enterprises may have very positive effects on participants' self-identities and on their opportunities to develop new competencies (as the Bart and the Russell articles in pt. 2 make clear), we also know that other members may, for a variety of reasons, avoid participating in the democratic arena (chaps. 5, 10). Further, Hammer, Stern, and Gurdon show in chapter 3 that worker ownership alone may not be sufficient to bring profound changes in workers' attitudes toward participation. This underlines the practical need for education in the democratic method.

The New School for Democratic Management was founded in San Francisco in the late 1970s with the express aim of teaching business skills and particularly the skills of democratic management to the people who are involved in such organizations. In its first years of operation, it held sessions in a number of American cities attracting many hundreds of participants from community enterprises around the country.

In addition to educational requirements, democratic enterprises also have financial needs that are not ordinarily met by the mainstream institutions in our society. Without their own credit unions or other lending institutions, it may be difficult for democratic firms to acquire the financial independence they need. If it survives, the National Cooperative Bank will help to meet the needs of consumer coops, and, to a lesser extent, of producer cooperatives, for investment capital, but it cannot, of course, provide cooperative enterprises with financial autonomy. For autonomy, they would have to follow the Mondragón model in the development of their own savings and investment institutions.

The need for democratic enterprises to federate in the creation and use of their own support organizations presents a major challenge to these enterprises.

Legal Forms

The development of democratic enterprises is sometimes inhibited by the particular legal form that they take. For instance, worker-owned firms arising out of divestiture situations have usually taken the form of stock ownership by the employees (among others), who are then either entitled or not entitled to vote their stock, depending upon its type. This means that unequal share-ownership brings with it unequal weight in voting power, if there is worker voting at all.

Two main deficiencies are built into this particular legal structure. In the first place, there is the temptation of workers to sell their shares either when the price of the stock rises sufficiently or when they reach retirement age and want to cash in their accumulated stock earnings. This problem is most acute with financially successful firms. For example, the price of shares in some of the cooperative plywood factories rose so dramatically that, when older workers neared retirement, it was difficult for younger workers to come up with the funds to buy their stock; the only ones that could afford to do so were major lumber corporations. In this way, some of the most successful worker-owned plants were converted to corporate subsidiaries. At Vermont Asbestos Group, workers purchased the asbestos mine when GAF, the corporate owner, threatened to shut it down. Mine workers from rural Vermont had to dig into their savings to purchase an average of six shares apiece at $50 per share to save the mine and their jobs. After only a few years, due primarily to increases in the world price of asbestos, the stock jumped in value to nearly $2,000, and it is not surprising that, at this point, many workers decided to sell. The mine was never democratically managed; it may soon no longer be democratically owned.

The use of standard, corporate, stock-ownership plans usually allows for unequal ownership, and, therefore, unequal voting rights. Even in cases where the worker-owners do have equal voting rights, such as the scavenger and the plywood companies discussed in this book, they may hire wage laborers who are not partners and who do not have a vote. A more desirable legal form might place a nominal value on voting stock and limit ownership of voting stock to one share for each working member, or it might place the stock in a trust controlled by the working members on the basis of one worker, one vote (chap. 15). A successful example of the latter legal structure was put into practice by a collectively-run newspaper studied by Rothschild-Whitt (chap. 1).

The Movement for Economic Democracy

The movement for workplace democracy in the United States is still in its formative stages. A few examples of large, democratically managed firms are beginning to appear, such as International Group Plans (IGP), a Washington, D.C., based insurance company (chap. 10). Unlike the situation in Europe, there has been little pressure in the United States for industrial democracy by the trade unions; by and large, union leadership has emphasized bread-and-butter issues rather than shop-floor and workplace democracy (chap. 20). Continued plant closings, however, may make industrial democracy a timely and relevant issue, as workers struggle to save their jobs; one way to prevent the layoffs that accompany plant closings is for workers to buy and run the productive facilities with the aid of friends, community organizations, and government loans. That was the reaction in Youngstown, Ohio, for example, when 4,100 steel workers learned that their factory was to be closed (chaps. 17, 18).

The struggle by workers to cope with corporate decisions to close plants and deprive them of their employment may help to popularize the idea of economic democracy in the United States. As companies announce such closings, workers, in cooperation with their unions and state and local governments, may attempt to buy up the productive facilities to preserve their jobs. Similar occurrences in Europe have led to sit-in strikes and the occupation of workplaces. Corporate decisions to close plants and to relocate in other regions of the United States or in other areas of the world could lead to greater union militance and gradual acceptance of the issue of workers' ownership and control.

The increasing frequency of corporate divestitures may well put economic democracy on the political agenda for the next decade. We are already witnessing political and social support for national legislative action, such as the establishment of the National Cooperative Bank, and the Kostmeyer legislation, which would provide technical and financial support to worker/community efforts to buy and run their own workplaces. (See the discussion by Whyte [1978b] who was instrumental in developing the latter piece of legislation.)

One national opinion poll shows that the American public is already ahead of its leaders on the issue of economic democracy. When presented with the alternative of working for a government-owned company, an employee-owned and -controlled one, and a stockholder corporation, two out of three respondents in a 1977 Hart poll said they would prefer to work where employees own and control the firm. Fifty-six percent of the people polled said that they would vote for a presidential candidate who favored employee control of United States companies (Rifkin 1977, pp. 45-57). Tom Hayden, running for the Senate on a platform of economic democracy, attracted a significant minority of California voters in 1976.

Democratically managed organizations are sometimes criticized for their supposed tendency to be nonpolitical. However, there are several different meanings of the term *political*. We may identify not only a *politics of struggle,* but also a *politics of function* (Dennison 1972). The former is what is usually meant by politics — the direct confrontation and struggle against the powers that be. But, by the latter, we mean that an organization is political if, in its very form, it exemplifies the sort of democratically run, community-based organization that could provide a model for a new society. Insofar as worker-managed organizations fulfill vital social needs (for food, housing, health care, education, etc.) in a democratic manner, they are engaged in a politics of function.

The overriding political message of worker-managed organizations will reside, we believe, in their ability (or inability) to demonstrate that democratic organizations can work, that they can accomplish the tasks heretofore reserved for hierarchical organizations. To the extent that they accomplish tasks that need doing in this or any society, in equalitarian organizational settings, they begin to convince the nonbelieving public that work organizations can be democratically managed. They begin to break down the hegemony of the prevailing ideology which says that hierarchical authority structure and corresponding stratification systems are necessary incentives to get people to do their jobs.

A goal implicit in the movement for economic democracy is the creation of regionally based networks of mutually supporting democratic enterprises, and, eventually, the emergence of a democratically managed sector of the economy. The growth of such a sector would reflect a gradual change in power relationships in our society leading to a more complete implementation of the democratic ideal. It remains to be seen whether democratic enterprises can accomplish their goals, operating as they do in the context of the presently existing society, or whether they will be forced to make too many accommodations to their environment. The full potential of economic democracy may not be realized without the growth of a parallel political movement that can help to democratize the hierarchical organizations that presently control most of this society's resources. The development of social and political momentum for economic democracy is perhaps the largest challenge facing this movement today.

It is hoped that the selections in this book, and the research and discussion they generate, will help us to anticipate and to resolve the kinds of social, political, and organizational issues that confront democratic workplaces.

Part 1

CHARACTERISTICS OF ORGANIZATIONAL DEMOCRACY

Introduction to Part 1

Both selections below attempt to isolate the essential characteristics of participatory-democratic organizations. Implicitly or explicitly, both use bureaucratic organizations as a comparative reference point.

Organizations may be seen as consisting of *workers, managers, and mandators.*[1] The latter, in principle, retain ultimate authority for organizational policy and are responsible for appointing and dismissing the chief executive. In rational-bureaucratic organizations, there is a clear distinction among workers, managers, and mandators. The mandators in a private corporation, for example, may be its major stockholders and its board of directors. In comanaged organizations, mandators may include both workers and community members or representatives of the state. In the workers' cooperatives and self-managed organizations discussed here by Rothschild-Whitt and Bernstein, the workers are also the mandators and often the managers.

By grounding her model in a comparative study, Rothschild-Whitt is able to identify generic and defining features of organizational democracy. Her approach underscores the importance of assessing collectivist-democratic organizations not as failures to achieve bureaucratic standards they do not share, but as attempts to realize wholly different values. In their attempts to create genuinely democratic organizations, coops and collectives face structural constraints and social costs, and these are discussed in the latter half of the Rothschild-Whitt paper.

Bernstein's work also employs a comparative design, enabling him to isolate additional elements that appear to be essential for organizational democracy. Bernstein approaches the issue as a political scientist; Rothschild-Whitt, from the point of view of sociology and organizations theory. Fundamentally, they are asking the same question in these two papers: What essential organizational properties must democratic workplaces have? Their answers tend to highlight different, though complementary, properties.

In the first two selections in this book, Rothschild-Whitt and Bernstein focus on the internal features of organizational democracy. In other work, they have identified some of the external factors that make a difference.[2] For our purposes here, we will mention only two external factors: the presence of a culture and of institutions that support democratic participation and cooperation, and the occurrence of political-economic crises and social movements which point to the failures of present institutional arrangements.

The history of cooperation in America from 1790 to the present reveals a clear pattern. Cooperatives have arisen (and fallen) in waves, and these waves follow social protests about current institutional arrangements. The post-1970 wave of cooperative development is no exception. Like earlier waves, its origins are in social movement activity of the 1960s. For a variety of reasons, however, the contemporary wave of coops and collectives is more prolific than all those in American history combined.

If institutional failures and subsequent social movements are a precondition that help the seeds of organizations germinate, the existence of a culture that supports cooperation and democratic decision-making is fertile soil to sustain workers' cooperatives. As Bernstein argues, a participatory-democratic consciousness among members is one of the conditions that contributes to workplace democracy, and, as Rothschild-Whitt points out, a sense of community is an important component of organizational democracy. Some cultures, however, are more conducive than others to the development of participatory habits and a sense of community. This is at least one factor that helps to account for the success of the network of workers' cooperatives in the Basque area of Spain (chap. 8).

Finally, the existence of various kinds of institutional support is crucial if democratically organized workplaces are to grow and prosper. With the development of a number of cooperative workplaces in given geographical areas, we are now witnessing the growth of credit unions, educational programs, economic cooperation among the enterprises, and other forms of mutual support. Similarly, democratic workplaces may be fostered through external institutional support such as laws that permit favorable taxation, as, for example, the Employee Stock Ownership legislation, or the provision of loans to coops, as exemplified in the National Consumer Cooperative Bank.

NOTES

1. See Bengt Abrahamsson, *Bureaucracy or Participation: The Logic of Organization* (Beverly Hills, Sage Publications, 1977).
2. On external factors, see Joyce Rothschild-Whitt, "Conditions for Democracy: Making Participatory Organizations Work," in *Coops, Communes and Collectives,* ed. J. Case and R. Taylor (New York: Pantheon Books, 1979), pp. 215-244.

1

The Collectivist Organization: An Alternative to Bureaucratic Models

Joyce Rothschild-Whitt

For many decades, the study of organizations has been, in effect, the study of bureaucracy and its many variations. This decade, however, has given rise to a wide array of organizations that self-consciously reject the norms of rational-bureaucracy and identify themselves as *alternative institutions* or *collectives*. The emergence of these counter-bureaucratic organizations calls for a new model of organization that can encompass their alternative practices and aspirations. What type of organization do these alternative institutions create in place of bureaucracy? This paper represents the first approach to a model of collectivist-democratic organization, a model that is premised on the logic of *substantive rationality* rather than *formal rationality*.

The tension between substantive and formal rationality was recognized long ago by Max Weber. For Weber, formal rationality — an emphasis on instrumental activity and procedural regularity — would have its main locus of expression in bureaucracy, and, as such, would come to dominate modern society. But it would come into inevitable conflict with the desire to realize substantive goals and values, what Weber called substantive or *value-rationality*. Modern bureaucracy would be built on the procedural regularity of formal law. But, in Weber's view, it could never eliminate all moral, subjective concerns (Bendix 1962, pp. 391-438). Nevertheless, in his classic statement on bureaucracy (1946, pp. 196-244), Weber sets forth the characteristics of bureaucracy as if it could eliminate all substantive, moral considerations, and contrasts this ideal-typical conception of bureaucracy with patrimonial administration. The polar opposite of

This article originally appeared in *American Sociological Review* 1979, 44 (Aug.): 509–527. It is reprinted here, with changes, by permission of the author.

the monocratic, formal bureaucracy drawn by Weber would be a fully collectivized democracy which turned on principles of substantive rationality.

Just as the ideal of bureaucracy, in its monocratic pure type, is probably not attainable (Mouzelis 1968), so the ideal of democracy, in its pure and complete form, is probably never achieved. In practice, organizations are hybrids.

The purpose of this paper is to develop an ideal-typical model of collectivist-democratic organization. It is an attempt to delineate the form of authority and the corresponding mode of organization that follow from value-rational premises. It is grounded in extensive study of counter-bureaucratic organizations which aspire to being collectives or *participatory-democracies*. The ideal-typical approach allows us to understand these new forms of organization not only in terms of bureaucratic standards they do not share, but in terms of the alternative values they do hold (cf. Kanter and Zurcher 1973). Further, the use of an ideal-type permits us to locate actual organizations along a continuum.

Constraints and social costs that inhibit the realization of organizational democracy will be taken up in the latter half of this paper.

RESEARCH SETTINGS AND METHODS

During the 1970s, the United States has witnessed an impressive proliferation of what have popularly come to be termed *alternative institutions*. Alternative institutions may be defined in terms of their members' resolve to build organizations which are parallel to, but outside of, established institutions and which fulfill social needs (for education, food, medical aid, etc.) without recourse to bureaucratic authority.

Parallel, oppositional organizations have been created in many service domains — e.g., free medical clinics, free schools, legal collectives, alternative media collectives, food cooperatives, research collectives, communes. Grassroots cooperative businesses are proliferating as well, especially in fields with relatively low capitalization needs such as restaurants, bookstores, clothing manufacture and retail, auto repair, housing construction, alternative-energy installation, newspapers, and so forth. They are burgeoning at a remarkable rate. For instance, in 1967, there were about 30 free schools in the United

States. By 1973, there were over 800 documented free schools (*New Schools Exchange Directory* 1967; 1973). A 1976 directory locates some 5,000 alternative organizations nationwide, and does not even claim to be exhaustive (Gardner 1976). These collectively owned and managed work enterprises represent one of the enduring legacies of the antiauthority movements of the 1960s.[1]

Little social-scientific research has been devoted to this social development. Some research studies describe one or another of these alternative work organizations, but few point to commonalities which link them. This paper identifies some of the structural commonalities and attempts to develop a general organizational framework of collectivist-democracy in which specific cases may be understood.

The organizational properties formulated in this paper are grounded in comparative data from different types of collectivist organizations. Glaser and Strauss (1967) have argued that theory generated from data, namely, grounded theory, will have more power to predict and explain the subject at hand than will theory arrived at through speculation or logical deduction.

Following the comparative research strategy of Glaser and Strauss (1967), I selected for study five collectivist work-organizations that were as varied as possible: a free medical clinic, a legal collective, a food cooperative, a free school, and an alternative newspaper.[2] All are located in a medium-sized city in California. Although they differ greatly as to the type of product or service they provide, organizational size, funding sources, technology utilized, and so forth, they are unified by the primacy each gives to developing a collectivist-democratic form of organization.

Participant observation was conducted in each of the research settings ranging in duration from six months to two years per organization. Observational material was amplified by structured interviews with selected members of each of the organizations, with a mean interview time of 2¼ hours. This was followed by questionnaire surveys to the membership of three of the organizations under study.

Each theoretical point in the paper is grounded in numerous instances from the empirical material. I have tried to select those few that seem most characteristic of the data. Of course, no number of illustrations can ever constitute a "proof." The theoretical formulations in this work should be assessed for their logical consistency, clarity, integration, and especially for the extent to which they are found to be generic properties of collectivist organizations.

THE COLLECTIVIST-DEMOCRATIC ORGANIZATION: CHARACTERISTICS

Collectivist-democratic organizations can be distinguished from bureaucratic organizations along at least eight dimensions. Each of these characteristics will be taken up in turn, and are summarized in table 1-1.

Authority

> When we're talking about collectives, we're talking about an embryonic creation of a new society.... Collectives are growing at a phenomenal rate all over this country. The new structures have outgrown the science of analyzing them. Sociology has to catch up with reality.... Collectivism is an attempt to supplant old structures of society with new and better structures. And what makes ours superior is that the basis of authority is radically different. (Staff member, Alternative Paper)

The words of this activist get right to the heart of the matter: authority. Perhaps more than anything else, it is the basis of authority that distinguishes the collectivist organization from any variant of bureaucracy. The collectivist-democratic organization rejects rational-bureaucratic justifications for authority. Here authority resides not in the individual, whether on the basis of incumbency in office *or* expertise, but in the collectivity as a whole.

This notion stems from the ancient anarchist ideal of "no authority." It is premised on the belief that social order can be achieved without recourse to authority relations (Guerin 1970). Thus it presupposes the capacity of individuals for self-disciplined, cooperative behavior. Indeed, collectivist organizations routinely emphasize these aspects of human beings. Like the anarchists, their aim is not the transference of power from one official to another, but the abolition of the pyramid in toto: organization without hierarchy.

An organization cannot be comprised of a collection of autonomous wills, each pursuing its own personal ends. Some decisions must be binding on the group.

Decisions become authoritative in collectivist organizations to the extent that they derive from a process in which all members have the right to full and equal participation. This democratic ideal, however, differs significantly from conceptions of "democratic bureaucracy" (Lipset et al. 1962), "representative bureaucracy"

(Gouldner 1954), or even representative democracy. In its directly democratic form, it does not subscribe to the established rules of order and protocol. It does not take formal motions and amendments, it does not usually take votes, majorities do not rule, and there is no two-party system. Instead, there is a *consensus process* in which all members participate in the *collective* formulation of problems and negotiation of decisions.[3] All major policy issues, such as hiring, firing, salaries, the division of labor, the distribution of surplus, and the shape of the final product or service, are decided by the collective as a whole. Only decisions which appear to carry the consensus of the group behind them, carry the weight of moral authority. Only these decisions, changing as they might with the ebb and flow of sentiments in the group, are taken as binding and legitimate. These organizations are collectively controlled by their members or workers; hence the name *collectivist* or *collectivist-democratic* organization.

In Weberian terms, we are concerned here with organizations which aspire and claim to be free of *Herrschaft*.[4] They are organizations without domination in that ultimate authority is based in the collectivity as a whole, not in the individual. Individuals, of course, may be delegated carefully circumscribed areas of authority, but authority is delegated and defined by the collectivity and subject to recall by the collectivity.

Rules

Collectivist organizations also challenge the bureaucratic conception that organizations should be bound by a formally established, written system of rules and regulations. Instead, they seek to minimize rule use. But, just as the most bureaucratic of organizations cannot anticipate, and therefore cannot circumscribe, *every* potential behavior in the organization, so the alternative organization cannot reach the theoretical limit of *zero* rules. Collectivist organizations, however, can drastically reduce the number of spheres of organizational activity that are subject to explicit rule governance.

In the most simple of the collectivist organizations in this study, the free high school, only one explicit organizational rule was formulated: no dope in school. This rule was agreed upon by a plenary meeting of the school's students and staff primarily because its violation was perceived to threaten the continued existence of the school. Other possible rules also were discussed at the free school, rules that might seem self-evident in ordinary schools, such as "each student should take X number of classes" or "students are required to attend the courses for which they are registered." These did not receive the consensual backing of the school's members, however.

In place of the fixed and universalistic rule use which is the trademark of bureaucracy, operations and decisions in alternative organizations tend to be conducted in an ad hoc manner. Decisions generally are settled as the case arises and are suited to the peculiarities of the individual case. No written manual of rules and procedures exists in most collectives, though norms of participation clearly obtain. While there is little attempt to account for decisions in terms of literal rules, concerted efforts are made to account for decisions in terms of substantive ethics. This is like Weber's (1968, pp. 976-8) *Kadi* justice and far removed from the formal justice that informs rational-bureaucratic action.

One of the chief virtues of extensive rule use in bureaucracy is that it permits predictability and appeal of decisions. The lack of universalistic standards in prebureaucratic modes of organization invited arbitrary and capricious rule. In bureaucracy, decisions could be calculated and appealed on the basis of their correspondence to the written law. In collectivist organizations, however, decisions are not necessarily arbitrary. They are based on substantive values (e.g., equality) applied consistently, if not universally. This permits at least some calculability on the basis of knowing the substantive ethic that will be invoked in a particular situation.

Social Control

This issue of social control is critical in any bureaucracy. From a Weberian point of view, organizations are tools. They are instruments of power for those who head them. But what means does the bureaucracy have of ensuring that lower-level personnel, people who are quite distant from the centers of power, will effectively understand and implement the aims of those at the top? Perrow (1976) examines three types of social-control mechanisms in bureaucracies: direct supervision, standardized rules, and selection for homogeneity. The first type of control, direct supervision, is the most obvious. The second is far less obtrusive but no less effective: standardized rules, procedures, and sanctions. Gouldner (1954) showed that rules can substitute for direct supervision. This allows the organization considerable decentralization of everyday decision-making and even the appearance of participation, for the *premises* of those decisions have been carefully controlled from the top. Decentralized decision-making, when decisional premises are set from the top via standardized rules, may be functionally equivalent to centralized authority (cf. Blau 1970; Bates 1970; Perrow 1976).

Collectivist organizations generally refuse to legitimate the use of centralized authority *or* standardized rules to achieve social control. Instead, they rely upon personalistic and moralistic appeals to provide the primary means of control, as Swidler (1979) demonstrates in her examination of free schools. In Etzioni's (1961) terms, compliance here is chiefly normative. One person appeals to another: "Do X *for me*," "Do X in the interest of equality," and so forth.

The more homogeneous the group, the more such appeals can hold sway. Thus, where personal and moral appeals are the chief means of social control, it is important, perhaps necessary, that the group select members who share their basic values and world view. All five of the alternative organizations in this study tried to do that. At the Law Collective, for instance, I asked how they decide whether to take in a new member, and was told:

> They have to have a certain amount of past experience in political work...[,] something really good and significant that checks out ....Secondly, they have to share the same basic assumptions as far as politics goes and they have to be willing to accept the collective way of doing things...

Such recruitment criteria are not at all uncommon or hidden in alternative work organizations.

In Perrow's (1976) terms, alternative organizations eschew first- and second-level controls, but accept third-level controls. Third-level controls are the most subtle and indirect of all: selection of personnel for homogeneity. On this level, social control may be achieved by selecting for top managerial positions only people who "fit in" — people who read the right magazines, go to the right clubs, have the right style of life and world view. This is also true in collectivist organizations. Where people are expected to participate in major decisions (this means *everyone* in a collective and high-level managers in a bureaucracy), consensus is crucial, and people who are likely to challenge basic assumptions are avoided. A person who reads the *Wall Street Journal* would be as suspect in applying for a position at the Law Collective as a person who reads the *New Left Review* would be at ITT. Both kinds of organizations utilize selection for homogeneity as a mechanism for social control.

Social Relations

Impersonal social relations are key features of the bureaucratic model. Personal emotions are to be prevented from distorting rational judgments. Relationships between people are to be role-based, segmental, and instrumental. Collectivist organizations, on the other hand, strive toward the ideal of community. Relationships are to be holistic, affective, and of value in themselves. The search for community may even become an instance of goal displacement, as when, for example, a free school comes to value community so highly that it loses its identity as a school and becomes a commune (see, e.g., Kay 1972).

Recruitment and Advancement

Bureaucratic criteria for recruitment and advancement are resisted in the collectivist organization. Here employment is not based on specialized training or certification, nor on any universal standard of competence. Instead, staff are generally recruited and selected by collectives on the basis of friendship and social-political values. Personality attributes that are seen as congruent with the collectivist mode of organization, such as self-direction and collaborative styles, also may be consciously sought in new staff (see, e.g., Torbert 1973).

Employment does not constitute the beginning of a career in collectivist organizations in the usual sense, for the collective does not provide a lifelong ladder to ever higher positions. Work may be volunteer or paid, and it may be part-time or full-time or even sixty hours per week, but it is not conceptualized as a career. Bureaucratic career advancement (based on seniority and/or achievement) is not a meaningful concept in collective work-organizations, for there is no hierarchy of offices. Therefore, there can be no individual *advancement* in positional rank (though there may be much change in positions).

Collectivist work organizations generally recruit competent and skilled personnel even though their selection criteria explicitly emphasize friendship networks, political values, and personality traits. To illustrate, during the year in which the free clinic was observed, four full-time staff positions were filled, and between nine and sixty-five applications were received for each position. Yet each of the four positions went to a friend of present staff members. The relevant attributes cited most frequently by the staff making these decisions were: articulation skills, ability to organize and mobilize people, political values, self-direction, ability to work under pressure, friendship, commitment to the organization's goals, cooperative style, and relevant experience. These selection criteria are typical of alternative organizations. In spite of their studied neglect of *formal* criteria of competence (e.g., certification), alternative organizations often attract highly qualified people.[5] In many ways, their selection criteria are well suited to their needs for multitalented and committed personnel who can serve a variety of administrative and task-oriented functions and who are capable of comanaging the organization in cooperation with others.

Incentive Structures

Organizations use different incentive structures to motivate participation. Most bureaucratic workplaces emphasize remunerative incentives, and few employees could be expected to donate their services if their paychecks were to stop. Collectivist organizations, on the other hand, rely primarily on purposive incentives (value fulfillment), secondarily on solidary incentives such as friendship, and only tertiarily on material incentives (Clark and Wilson 1961). According to Etzioni (1961), this kind of normative compliance system tends to generate a high level of moral commitment to organization. Specific structural mechanisms which produce and sustain organizational commitment are identified by Kanter (1972a). Because collectivist work organizations require a high level of commitment, they tend to utilize some of these mechanisms as well as value-purposive incentives to generate it. Indeed, work in collectives is construed as a labor of love, and members may pay themselves very low salaries and may expect each other to continue to work during months when the organization is too poor to afford their salaries.

Alternative organizations often appeal to symbolic values to motivate people to join and to participate actively. The range of these values is considerable. At the free clinic, for instance, a member describes motivation:

> Our volunteers are do-gooders.... They get satisfaction from giving direct and immediate help to people in need. This is why they work here.

At the alternative newspaper, the following is more illustrative:

> Our motives were almost entirely political. We were moving away from a weathermen type position, toward the realization that the revolution will be a very gradual thing.... We wanted to create a base for a mass left. To activate liberals and open them up to left positions. To tell you the truth, the paper was conceived as a political organ.

At the food coop, it is the value of community that is most stressed, and the coop actively helps to create other community-owned and -controlled institutions in its locale.

However, we should guard against an overly idealistic interpretation of participation in alternative organizations. In these organizations, as much as any, there exists an important *coalescence of material and ideal interests*. Even volunteers in these organizations, whose motives on the face of it would appear to be wholly idealistic, also have material incentives for their participation.

For example, staff members at the free clinic suspect that some volunteers donate their time to the clinic "only to look good on their applications to medical school." Likewise, some of the college students who volunteered to teach at the free school believed that, in a tight market, this would improve their chances of getting a paid teaching job. And, for all the talk of community at the food coop, many members undoubtedly joined simply because the food was cheaper. Because material gain is not part of the acceptable vocabulary of motives in these organizations, public discussion of such motives is suppressed.

Nonetheless, for staff members as well as for volunteers, material incentives coalesce with moral incentives. At the law collective, for instance, legal workers often used their experience there to pursue the bar, since California law allows eligibility for the bar through the alternative means of apprenticing under an attorney for three years. At the alternative newspaper, a few staff members confided that they had entered the paper to gain journalistic experience.

Yet members of alternative institutions often deny the existence of material considerations and accept only the idealistic motivations. In the opinion of one longtime staffer at the alternative paper:

> I don't think anyone came for purely journalistic purposes, unless they're masochists. I mean it doesn't pay, the hours are lousy, and the people are weird. If you want professional journalistic experience you go to a straight paper.

In many ways, she is right. Alternative institutions generally provide woefully inadequate levels of remuneration by the standards of our society. But it does not impugn the motives of participants to recognize that these organizations must provide some material base for their members if they are to be alternative places of employment at all.

At the free clinic, full-time staff were all paid $500 per month during 1974-1975; at the law collective, they were paid a base of $250 per month plus a substantial supplement for dependents; and, at the alternative paper, they received between $150 and $300 per month, in accordance with individual "needs." These pay levels were negotiated in open discussion of the collectives as a whole, as were decisions regarding the entire labor process. If these wage levels appear exploitative, it is a case of self-exploitation. It is the subsistence wage levels which permit the young organization to accumulate capital and to reinvest this surplus in the organization rather than paying it out in wages. This facilitates the growth of the organization and hastens the day when it may be able to pay higher salaries.[6]

Many collectives have found ways to help compensate for the meager salaries they pay their members. The law collective stocked food so that members could eat at least a meal or two per day at the office for free. The collective also maintained a number of cars that its members could share, thereby eliminating the need for private automobile ownership. Free-clinic staff decided to allow themselves certain fringe benefits to compensate for what they regarded as underpaid work: two weeks of paid vacation time each year, plus two additional weeks of unpaid vacation (if desired); one day off every other week; and the revised expectation that staff would regularly work a twenty-eight to thirty- rather than forty-hour week. But these are compensations or supplements for a generally poor income, and, like income, they do not motivate people to work in alternative organizations. They only make work there possible.

First and foremost, people come to work in an alternative organization because it offers them substantial control over their work. Collective control means that members can structure both the product of their work and the work process in congruence with their ideals. Hence, the work is purposeful to them. It is not infrequently contrasted with alienating jobs that they have had, or imagine, in bureaucracies:

> A straight paper would have spent a third of a million dollars getting to where we are now and still wouldn't be breaking even. We've gotten where we are on the sweat of our workers. They've taken next to no money when they could have had $8,000 to $15,000 in straight papers doing this sort of job.... They do it so they can be their own boss. So they can own and control the organization they work in. So they can make the paper what *they* want it to be.... (interview, member of alternative newspaper)

Social Stratification

In the ideal-type bureaucracy, the dimensions of social stratification are consistent with one another. Specifically, social prestige and material privilege are to be commensurate with one's rank, and the latter is the basis of authority in the organization. Thus, a hierarchical arrangement of offices implies an isomorphic distribution of privilege and prestige. In this way, hierarchy institutionalizes (and justifies) inequality.

In contrast, egalitarianism is a central feature of the collectivist-democratic organization. Large differences in social prestige or privilege, even where they are commensurate with level of skill or authority in bureaucracy, would violate this sense of equity. At the free clinic, for instance, all full-time staff members were paid equally, no matter what skills or experience they brought to the clinic. At the law collective and alternative newspaper pay levels were set "to each according to his need." Here, salaries took account of dependents and other special circumstances contributing to need, but explicitly excluded considerations of the worth of the individual to the organization. In no case I observed was the ratio between the highest pay and the lowest pay greater then two to one.

In larger, more complex, democratic organizations, wages are still set, and wage differentials strictly limited, by the collectivity. For example, in the sixty-five production cooperatives that constitute the Mondragón system in Spain pay differentials are limited to a ratio of 3 to 1 in each firm (Johnson and Whyte 1977). In the worker-owned and managed refuse collection firms in San Francisco, the differential is only 2 to 1 or less (chap. 4; Perry 1978). Schumacher (1973, p. 276) reports a 7 to 1 ratio between the highest and the lowest paid at Scott Bader, a collectively-owned firm in England. The cooperatively-owned plywood mills in the Pacific Northwest pay their members an equal wage (Bernstein 1976, pp. 20-21). By comparison, the wage differential tolerated today in Chinese work organizations is 4 to 1; in the United States it is about 100 to 1.

Prestige, of course, is not as easily equalized as is pay. Nonetheless, collectivist organizations try in a variety of ways to indicate that they are a fraternity of peers. Through dress, informal relations, task sharing, job rotation, the physical structure of the workplace, equal pay, and the collective decision-making process itself, collectives convey an equality of status. As Mansbridge (1977) observes of collectives, reducing the sources of status inequality does not necessarily lead to the magnification of trivial differences. Likewise, decreasing the material differentials between individuals in a collectivist organization does not ordinarily produce a greater emphasis on status distinctions.

Differentiation

A complex network of differentiated, segmental roles marks any bureaucracy. Where the rules of scientific management hold sway, the division of labor is maximized: jobs are subdivided as far as possible. Specialized jobs require technical expertise. Thus, bureaucracy ushers in the ideal of the specialist-expert and defeats the cultivated, renaissance man of an earlier era (Weber 1946, pp. 240-44).

In contrast, differentiation is minimized in the collectivist organization. Work roles are purposefully kept as general and holistic as possible. They aim to eliminate the division of labor that separates intellectual workers from manual workers, administrative tasks from performance tasks. Three means are commonly utilized toward this end: role rotation, teamwork or task sharing, and the diffusion or demystification of specialized knowledge through internal education.

Ideally, universal competence (of the collective's members) would be achieved in the tasks of the organization. It is the *amateur-factotum,* then, who is ideally suited for the collectivist organization. In the completely democratized organization, everyone works. This may be the most fundamental way in which the collectivist mode of organization alters the social relations of production.[7]

This alteration in the division of labor is perhaps best illustrated by the free school, an organization in which administrative functions were quite simple and undifferentiated. The free school had no separate set of managers to administer the school. Whenever administrative tasks were recognized, "coordination meetings" were called to attend to them; these were open to all interested teachers and students. Coordinators were those who were willing to take responsibility for a particular administrative task (e. g., planning curriculum, writing a press release, organizing a fund-raiser). A coordinator for one activity was not necessarily a coordinator for another project. Further, the taking on of administrative tasks was assumed to be a part-time commitment which could be done alongside of one's other responsibilities. Coordinators, then, were *self-selected, rotated,* and *part-time.* No one was allowed to do administration exclusively. By simplifying administration and opening it up to the membership-at-large, the basis and pretense of special expertise was eliminated.

The school even attempted to break down the basic differentiation between students and staff, regarding students not as clients but as members with decision-making rights and responsibilities. The free clinic also tried to integrate its clients into the organization. For instance, it created spaces on its board of directors for consumers of medical care and recruited many of its volunteers from the ranks of its patients.

Most alternative organizations are more complex than the free school. They cannot assume that everyone in the organization knows how (or would want to know how) to do everything. Thus, they must develop explicit procedures to achieve universal competence. Such procedures, in effect, attack the conventional wisdom of specialized division of labor and seek to create more integrated, multifaceted work roles.

The alternative newspaper, for example, utilizes task-sharing (or teamwork), apprenticeships, and job rotations toward this end. Instead of assigning one full-time person to a task requiring one person, they would be more likely to assign a couple of people to the task part-time. Individuals' allocations of work often combine diverse tasks, such as fifteen hours writing, fifteen hours photography, and ten hours production. In this way, the distribution of labor combines satisfying tasks with more tedious tasks and manual work with intellectual work. People do not enter the paper knowing how to do all of these jobs, but the emphasis on task-sharing allows the less experienced to learn from the more experienced. Likewise, if a task has few people who know how to perform it well, a person may be allocated to apprentice with the incumbent. Internal education is further facilitated by occasional job rotations. Thus, while the alternative paper must perform the same tasks as any newspaper, it attempts to do so without permitting the usual division of labor into specialities or its concomitant monopolization of expertise.

Minimizing differentiation is difficult and time-consuming. The alternative paper, for instance, spent a total of fifteen hours and forty minutes of formal meeting time and many hours of informal discussion in planning one systematic job rotation. Attendance at the planning meetings was 100 percent. The time and priority typically devoted to internal education in collectivist organizations makes sense only if it is understood as part of a struggle against the division of labor. The creation of an equitable distribution of labor and holistic work roles is an essential feature of the collectivist organization.

Table 1.1 summarizes the ideal-type differences between the collectivist mode of organization and the bureaucratic.[8] Democratic control is the foremost characteristic of collectivist organization, just as hierarchal control is the defining characteristic of the smoothly-

TABLE 1.1 COMPARISONS OF TWO IDEAL TYPES OF ORGANIZATION

DIMENSIONS	BUREAUCRATIC ORGANIZATION	COLLECTIVIST-DEMOCRATIC ORGANIZATION
1. Authority	1. Authority resident in individuals by virtue of incumbency in office and/or expertise; hierarchal organization of offices. Compliance is to universal fixed rules as these are implemented by office incumbents.	1. Authority resident in the collectivity as a whole; delegated, if at all, only temporarily and subject to recall. Compliance is to the consensus of the collective which is always fluid and open to negotiation.
2. Rules	2. Formalization of fixed and universalistic rules; calculability and appeal of decisions on the basis of correspondence to the formal, written law.	2. Minimal stipulated rules; primacy of ad hoc, individuated decisions; some calculability possible on the basis of knowing the substantive ethics involved in the situation.
3. Social control	3. Organizational behavior subject to social control, primarily through direct supervision or standardized rules and sanctions, tertiarily through the selection of homogeneous personnel especially at top levels.	3. Social controls primarily based on personalistic or moralistic appeals and the selection of homogeneous personnel.
4. Social relations	4. Ideal of impersonality; relations are to be role-based, segmental, and instrumental.	4. Ideal of community; relations are to be holistic, personal, of value in themselves.
5. Recruitment and advancement	5.a. Employment based on specialized training and formal certification. 5.b. Employment constitutes a career; advancement based on seniority or achievement.	5.a. Employment based on friends, social-political values, personality attributes, and informally assessed knowledge and skills. 5.b. Concept of career advancement not meaningful; no hierarchy of positions.
6. Incentive structure	6. Remunerative incentives primary.	6. Normative and solidarity incentives primary; material incentives, secondary.
7. Social stratification	7. Isomorphic distribution of prestige, privilege, and power; i.e., differential rewards by office; hierarchy justifies inequality.	7. Egalitarian; reward differentials, if any, strictly limited by the collectivity.
8. Differentiation	8.a. Maximal division of labor: dichotomy between intellectual work and manual work and between administrative tasks and performance tasks. 8.b. Maximal specialization of jobs and functions; segmental roles. Technical expertise exclusively held: ideal of the specialist-expert.	8.a. Minimal division of labor: administration combined with performance tasks; division between intellectual and manual work reduced. 8.b. Generalization of jobs and functions; holistic roles. Demystification of expertise: ideal of the amateur-factotum.

running bureaucracy. Thus, collectivist-democratic organization would transform the social relations to production. Bureaucracy maximizes formal rationality precisely by centralizing the locus of control at the top of the organization; collectives decentralize control so that it may be organized around the alternative logic of substantive rationality.

IMPERFECT DEMOCRACY: CONSTRAINTS AND SOCIAL COSTS

Various constraints limit the actual attainment of democracy, and, even to the extent that the collectivist-democratic ideal is achieved, it may produce social costs that were unanticipated. This section outlines some of the more important of these constraints and social costs.

Judgments about the relative importance of the listed social costs are intricately tied to cultural values. Alternative organizations may be mistakenly assessed when seen through the prism of the norms and values of the surrounding bureaucratic society.

Time

Democracy takes time. This is one of its major social costs. Two-way communication structures may produce higher morale, the consideration of more innovative ideas, and more adaptive solutions to complex problems, but they are undeniably slow (Leavitt 1964, pp. 141-50). Quite simply, a boss can hand down a bureaucratic order in a fraction of the time it would take a group to decide the issue democratically.

The time absorbed by meetings can be extreme in democratic groups. During the early stages of the alternative newspaper, for instance, three days out of a week were taken up with meetings. Between business meetings, political meetings, and "people" meetings, very little time remained to do the tasks of the organization. Members quickly learn that this is unworkable. Meetings are streamlined. Tasks are given a higher priority. Even so, constructing an arrangement that both saves time and ensures effective collective control may prove difficult: Exactly which meetings are dispensable? What sorts of decisions can be safely delegated? How can individuals still be held accountable to the collectivity as a whole? These sorts of questions come with the realization that there are only twenty-four hours in a day.

There is a limit, however, to how streamlined collectivist meetings can get. In the end, commitment to decisions and their implementation can only be assured in collectives through the use of the democratic method. Unilateral decisions, albeit quicker, would not be seen as binding or legitimate. With practice, planning and self-discipline, groups can learn to accomplish more during their meeting time. But once experience is gained in how to conduct meetings, time given to meetings appears to be directly correlated with level of democratic control. The free clinic, for instance, could keep its weekly staff meetings down to an average of one hour and fifteen meetings only by permitting individual decision-making outside the meeting to a degree that would have been unacceptable to members of the alternative paper, where a mean of four hours was given over to the weekly staff meeting.

Homogeneity

Consensus, an essential component of collectivist decision-making, may require from the outset substantial homogeneity. To people who would prefer diversity, this is a considerable social cost.

Bureaucracy may not require much homogeneity, partly because it does not need the moral commitment of its employees. Since it depends chiefly on remunerative incentives to motivate work, and since, in the end, it can command obedience to authority, it is able to unite the energies of diverse people toward organizational goals. But in collectives, where the primary incentives for participation are value-purposive and the subordinate-superordinate relation has been delegitimated, moral commitment becomes necessary. Unified action is possible only if individuals substantially agree with the goals and processes of the collective. This implies a level of homogeneity (in terms of values) unaccustomed and unnecessary in bureaucracy.[9]

Consequently, collectivist organizations also tend to attract a homogeneous population in terms of social origins. At the alternative paper, full-time staff members came from families where the mean parental income was about $29,000. A random sampling of the general membership of the food coop (consisting of 1,100 people) reveals an average parental income of $19,500, while the most active members of the coop, the staff and board, show a mean parental income of $46,000. In addition to being of financially privileged origins, people in alternative organizations tend to come from well-educated families. In both of the above organizations, over half of the mothers had at least some college education; fathers, on the average, had acquired some graduate or professional training beyond the B.A. Thus, the need for substantial agreement on the values, goals, and processes of the collective, in effect, has limited their social base. This is an important constraint to members who would like to broaden the base of their social movement.

This is also an important constraint in organizations with heterogeneous populations of employees. For example, International Group Plans, a Washington, D.C. insurance company, is in the process of trying to democratize its ownership and governance structure (chap. 10). To many of its employees who do not share collectivist values, democratization may only mean added time and responsibility, and they may wish to retain the traditional separation of managers and workers.

To guard against this problem and to ensure that all members profess collectivist values, alternative organizations tend to recruit very selectively. The law collective, for instance, instituted a probationary period of six months on top of its careful selection procedures.

In sum, cultural homogeneity makes reaching and abiding by a consensus easier, but it may constrain the social base of collectivist organization.

Emotional Intensity

The familial, face-to-face relationships in collectivist organizations may be more satisfying than the impersonal relations of bureaucracy, but they are also more emotionally threatening. The latter may be experienced as a social cost of participatory organization.

Interpersonal tension is probably endemic in the directly democratic situation, and members certainly perceive their workplaces to be emotionally intense. At the law collective, a member warns that "plants die here from the heavy vibes." At the alternative newspaper, I observed headaches and other signs of tension before meetings in which devisive issues would be raised. A study of the New England town meeting found citizens reporting headaches, trembling, and even fear of heart attacks as a result of the meetings. Altogether, a quarter of the people in a random sample of the town spontaneously suggested that the conflictual character of the meetings disturbed them (Mansbridge, 1973; chap. 5).

To allay these fears of conflict, townspeople utilize a variety of protective devices: criticism is concealed or at least softened with praise, differences of opinion are minimized in the formulation of a consensus, private jokes and intimate communications are used to give personal support during the meetings. Such avoidance patterns have the unintended consequence of excluding the member not fully-integrated, withholding information from the group, and violating the norms of open participation. Further, these same fears of conflict and avoidance patterns are in evidence even in groups which are highly sensitive to these issues and in which many members have been trained in group process (chap. 5).

The constancy of such feelings in all of the groups I observed suggests that they are rooted in the structure of collectivist decision-making. Although participants generally attribute conflict and avoidance to the stubborn, wrongheaded, or otherwise faulty character of others, it may be an inherent cost of participatory democracy.

Structural tensions inherent in collectivist organization render conflict difficult to absorb. First, the norm of consensual decision-making in collectives makes the possibility of conflict all the more threatening because unanimity is required (where a majoritarian system can institutionalize and absorb conflicting opinions). Second, the intimacy of face-to-face decision-making personalizes the ideas that people espouse and thereby makes the rejection of those ideas harder to bear. A more formal bureaucratic system, to the extent that it disassociates an idea from its proponent, makes the criticism of ideas less interpersonally risky.

Nondemocratic Individuals

Due to prior experiences, many people are not very well-suited for participatory democracy. This is an important constraint on its development.

The major institutions of our society, such as educational institutions, combine to reinforce ways of thinking, feeling, and acting that are congruent with capitalist-bureaucratic life and incompatible with collectivist orientations. For example, Jules Henry (1965) has shown how the norms of capitalist culture become the hidden curriculum of the school system. Even at the preschool level, the qualities of the bureaucratic personality are unconsciously, but nevertheless consistently, conveyed to children (Kanter 1972b). In fact, Bowles and Gintis (1976) argue that the chief function of the entire educational apparatus is to reproduce the division of labor and hierarchal authority of capitalism.

In the face of these behavior-shaping institutions, it is very difficult to sustain collectivist personalities. It is asking, in effect, that people in collectivist organizations constantly shift gears, that they learn to act one way inside their collectives and another way outside. In this sense, the difficulty of creating and sustaining collectivist attributes and behavior patterns results from a cultural disjuncture. It derives from the fact that alternative work organizations are as yet isolated examples of collectivism in an otherwise capitalist-bureaucratic context. Where they are not isolated, that is, where they are part of an interlocking network of cooperative organizations, such as the Mondragón system in Spain (Johnson and Whyte 1977; chap. 8) this problem is mitigated.

In their present context, the experience of the alternative institutions has shown that selecting people with collectivist attitudes does not guarantee that these attitudes will be effectively translated into cooperative behavior (e.g., Swidler 1976; Taylor 1976; Torbert 1973).

Nevertheless, a number of recent case studies of democratic workplaces, one of the worker-owned refuse collection companies (chap. 4; Perry 1978) and one of a women's health collective (chap. 6), reveal that the experience of democratic participation can alter people's values, the quality of their work, and, ultimately, their identities. In a comparative examination of many cases of workers' participation, Bernstein (1976, pp. 91-107) finds democratic consciousness to be a necessary element for effective workers' control to take place.

Fortunately, the solution to this problem of creating democratic consciousness (and behavior) may be found in the democratic method itself. In this vein, Pateman has amassed a considerable body of evidence from research on political socialization in support of the classical arguments of Rousseau, Mill, and Cole. She concludes:

> We do learn to participate by participating and . . . feelings of political efficacy are more likely to be developed in a participatory environment . . . . The experience of a participatory authority structure might also be effective in diminishing tendencies toward non-democratic attitudes in the individual. (1970, p. 105).

Elden (1976) provides further empirical support for Pateman's position that participation enhances feelings of political efficacy. If bureaucratic organizations thwart the sense of efficacy that would be needed for active participation in democracy (Blumberg 1973, pp. 70-138), then collectivist-democratic organizations must serve an important educative function, if they are to expand beyond their currently limited social base.[10]

Environmental Constraints

Alternative organizations, like all organizations, are subject to environmental constraints. Because they often occupy an adversary position vis-à-vis mainstream institutions, such external pressures may be more intense. Extra-organizational constraints on the development of collectivist organizations may come from legal, economic, political, and cultural realms.

It is generally agreed among free schoolers, for instance, that building and fire codes are most strictly enforced for them (Kozol 1972; Graubard 1972). This is usually only a minor irritant, but, in extreme cases, it may involve a major disruption of the organization, requiring them to move or close down. One small, collectively-run, solar-power firm was forced to move its headquarters several times because of this sort of legal harrassment. At one site, the local authorities charged over a hundred building "violations" (Etzkowitz 1978). An even more far-reaching legal obstacle is the lack of a suitable statute for incorporating employee-owned and controlled firms. The alternative newspaper, for example, had to ask an attorney to put together corporate law in novel ways in order to ensure collective control over the paper.[11]

The law can be changed, but the more ubiquitous forces against collectivism are social, cultural, and economic. In fact, alternative organizations often find that bureaucratic practices are thrust on them by established institutions. The free school, for example, began with an emphatic policy of absolutely no evaluative records of students. In time, however, it found that, in order to help its students transfer back into the public schools or gain entrance into college, it had to begin keeping or inventing records. The preoccupation of other organizations with records and documents may thus force record-keeping on a reluctant free school. In another free school, the presence of a steady stream of government communications and inspectors (health, building, etc.) pushed the organization into creating a special job to handle correspondence and personal visits of officials (chap. 12).

Alternative organizations often strive to be economically self-sustaining, but, without a federated network of other cooperative organizations to support them, they cannot. Often they must rely on established organizations for financial support. This acts as a constraint on the achievement of their collectivist principles. For instance, in order to provide free services, the free clinic needed and received financial backing from private foundations as well as from county revenue-sharing funds. This forced them to keep detailed records on expenditures and patient visits and to justify their activities in terms of outsiders' criteria of cost-effectiveness.

In less fortunate cases, fledgling democratic enterprises may not even get off the ground for failure to raise sufficient capital. Two recent attempts by employee groups to purchase and collectively manage their firms reveal the reluctance of banks to loan money to collectivist enterprises, even where these loans would be guaranteed by the government. From the point of view of private investors, collective ownership and management may appear, at best, an unproven method of organizing production and, at worst, a dangerous method.[12]

For a consistent source of capital, collectivist enterprises may need to develop cooperative credit unions as the Mondragón system has done (Johnson and Whyte 1977; chap. 8) or an alternative investment fund. In many collectives, the unpaid (or poorly paid) labor of the founders forms the initial capital of the organization, enabling some measure of financial autonomy. In any case, the larger issue of organization-environment relations remains problematic, particularly when we are considering collectivist-democratized organizations in a capitalist-bureaucratic context.[13]

Individual Differences

All organizations, democratic ones notwithstanding, contain persons with very different talents, skills, knowledge, and personality attributes. Bureaucracies try to capitalize on these individual differences, so that ideally, people with a particular expertise or personality type will be given a job, rewards, and authority commensurate with it. In collectives such individual differences may constrain the organization's ability to realize its egalitarian ideals.

Inequalities in influence persist in the most egalitarian of organizations. In bureaucracies, the existence of inequality is taken for granted, and, in fact, the exercise of power is built into the opportunity structure of positions themselves (Kanter 1977). However, in collectivist organizations, this may be less true. Here, precisely because authority resides in the collectivity as a unit, the exercise of influence depends less on positional opportunities and more on the personal attributes of the individual. Not surprisingly, members who are more articulate, responsible, energetic, glamorous, fair, or committed carry more weight in the group.[14] John Rice, a teacher and leader of Black Mountain (a group that "seceded" from the educational system and anticipated the free-school movement), argued that Black Mountain came as close to democracy as possible: the economic status of the individual had nothing to do with community standing. But, beyond that, "the differences show up . . . [;] the test is made all day and every day as to who is the person to listen to" (Duberman 1972, p. 37).

Some individual differences are accepted in the collectivist organization, but not all, particularly not differences in knowledge. In bureaucracy, differences of skill and knowledge are honored. Specialized jobs accompany expertise. People are expected to protect their expertise. Indeed, this is a sign of professionalism, and it is well known that the monopolization of knowledge is an effective instrument of power in organizations (Weber 1968; Crozier 1964). For this very reason, collectivist organizations make every attempt to eliminate differentials in knowledge. Expertise is considered not the sacred property of the individual, but an organizational resource. In collectives, individually held skills and knowledge are demystified and redistributed through internal education, job rotation, task sharing, apprenticeships, or any plan they can devise toward this end.[15]

The diffusion or demystification of knowledge, while essential to help equalize patterns of influence, involves certain trade-offs. Allowing a new person to learn to do task X by rotating her/him to that job may be good for the development of that person, but it may displace an experienced person who had received a sense of satisfaction and accomplishment in job X. Further, encouraging novices to learn by doing may be an effective form of pedagogy, but it may detract from the quality of goods or services that the organization provides, at least (theoretically) until universal competence in the tasks of the organization is reached.

Even in the collectivist organization that might achieve universal competence, other sources of unequal influence would persist (e.g., commitment level, verbal fluency, social skills).[16] The most a democratic organization can do is to remove the bureaucratic bases of authority: positional rank and expertise. The task of any collectivist-democratic workplace, and it is no easy task, is to eliminate all bases of individual power and authority save those that individuals carry in their person.

CONCLUSION

The organizations in this study are admittedly rare and extreme cases. To the extent that they reject received forms of organization, they present an anomaly. For precisely this reason, they are of great theoretical significance. By approaching the polar opposites of bureaucracy, they allow us to establish the limits of organizational reality. The parameters appear to be far wider than students of organizations have generally imagined. Once the parameters of the organizational field have been defined, concrete cases can be put into broader perspective. Professional organizations, for example, while considerably more horizontal than the strictly hierarchical bureaucracy (Litwak 1961), are still far more hierarchal than the collectivist-democratic organization. Thus, we may conceive of the range of organizational possibilities illustrated in figure 1.1.

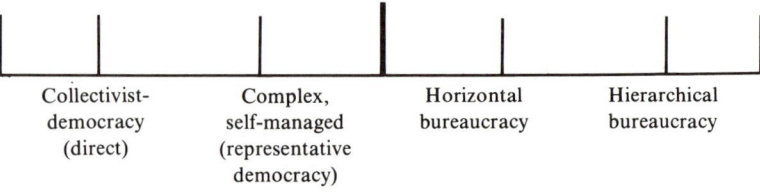

| Collectivist-
democracy
(direct) | Complex,
self-managed
(representative
democracy) | Horizontal
bureaucracy | Hierarchical
bureaucracy |

FIG. 1.1 RANGE OF ORGANIZATION FORMS

By contrasting collectivist democracy and rational bureaucracy along eight continuous dimensions, this paper has emphasized the quantitative differences between the two. In many ways, this understates the difference. At some point, differences of degree produce differences of kind. Fundamentally, bureaucracy and collectivism are oriented to qualitatively different principles. Where bureaucracy is organized around the calculus of formal rationality, collectivist-democracy turns on the logic of substantive rationality.

If, in the Weberian tradition, we take the basis of authority as the central feature of any mode of organization, then organizations on the right half of figure 1.1 empower the *individual* with authority (on the basis of office or expertise), while organizations on the left side grant ultimate authority only to the *collectivity* as a whole unit. Moreover, if, following Marx's lead, we take the division of labor as the key to the social relations of production, organizations on the right side of the diagram in figure 1.1 maintain a sharp division between managers and workers, while organizations on the left side are integrative: those who work also manage. Departures of this magnitude from established modes of organization may be considered a "social invention" (Coleman 1970).

Organization theory has for the most part considered only the right half of this spectrum, and, indeed, the vast majority of organizations in our society do fall on the right side of the continuum. Still, we gain perspective on these organizations by putting them into a broader frame of reference. With the proliferation of collectivist organizations both in this society and in others (e.g., China, Spain, Yugoslavia), we will need an alternative model of organization, one which they themselves aspire toward, by which to assess their impact and success. To wit, collectivist organizations should be assessed not as failures to achieve bureaucratic standards they do not share, but as efforts to realize wholly different values. It is in the conceptualization of alternative forms of organization that organizational theory has been weakest, and it is here that the experimentation of collectives will broaden our understanding.

NOTES

1. Gardner (1976) estimates that about 1,000 new alternative institutions are being created annually in the United States. This is his best estimate, but the kind of evidence that would be needed to compute actual rates of creation and of dissolution is not yet available. However, the historical record is instructive. The nineteenth century and the first third of the twentieth century saw at least 700 cases of producers' cooperatives (Aldrich and Stern 1978). These were in many ways the forerunners of the contemporary wave of collectives and cooperatives discussed in this paper. Historically, cooperatives have come in distinct waves — the 1840s, the 1860s, the 1880s and the 1920s-1930s. Their longevity has varied widely between industries (Aldrich and Stern 1978). Those of the nineteenth century had a median duration of less than ten years, while more than half of the worker cooperatives of the 1920s and 1930s (particularly in the plywood industry and in the refuse collection industry) are still in operation today (Jones 1979). Since the current wave of collectives is largely a post-1970 phenomenon and is still on the rise, it is too early to say how long it will last.

2. All persons and organizations have been given fictitious names in this paper. For a more detailed account of the research sites and methods, see Rothschild-Whitt (1976; 1978).

3. As organizations grow beyond a certain size, they are likely to find purely consensual processes of decision-making inadequate, and may turn to direct voting systems. Other complex, but nevertheless democratic, work-organizations may sustain direct democracy at the shop-floor level, while relying upon elected representative systems at higher levels of the organization (cf. Edelstein and Warner 1976).

4. Actually, Weber did recognize the possibility of directly democratic organization, but he dealt with this only incidentally as a marginal-type case (Weber 1968;

pp. 948-52, 289-92). Although Weber's three types of legitimate domination were meant to be comprehensive both in time and in substance as Mommsen (1974; pp. 72-94) points out, it is difficult to find an appropriate place for modern plebiscitarian leader-democracy in Weber's scheme. Weber did come to advocate the "plebiscitarian leader-democracy," but this was a special version of charismatic domination (Mommsen 1974; p. 113). He did not support "democracies without leadership" *(fuererlose Demokratien)* which try to minimize the domination of the few over the many, because organization without *Herrschaft* appeared utopian to him (Mommsen 1974; p. 87). Thus, it is difficult to identify the acephalous organizations of this study with any of Weber's three types of authority.

5. A dissertation conducted in the San Francisco area found that free-school teachers there have higher degrees from more prestigious universities than their public-school counterparts (McCauley 1971; p. 148).

6. The self-exploitation common in collectivist organizations and the justifications for it (e.g., autonomy, control over the workplace, self-expression in work) are similar to that of the small entrepreneur. It may be that as economic concentration and oligopolistic control over markets renders traditional enterpreneurial activity obsolete, collectively-owned enterprises may grow. For, in many ways, collectivist efforts evoke the old entrepreneurial spirit, but today it may require the intense work and self-sacrifice of many people rather than just one to make a fledgling enterprise viable.

7. Industrial organizations in China have implemented similar changes in the division of labor. These were considered an essential part of transforming the social relations of production. Their means for reducing the separation of intellectual work from manual work and administration from performance tasks were similar to those used by the alternative work organizations reported in this paper: team work, internal education, and role rotation. For specific points of comparison, see Bettelheim (1974) and Whyte (1973).

8. The eight dimensions discussed here are clearly interrelated, a point not explored herein. However, there is evidence from bureaucracies that they are also somewhat independent (Hall 1963). That is, an organization may be highly collectivist on one dimension but not so on another. The interrelationships between these variables may be elusive. For instance, of seven propositions offered by Hage (1965) in an axiomatic theory of organizations, six could be supported by the organizations in this study. One, however, that higher complexity produces lower centralization, was contradicted by the evidence of this study, although it has received empirical support in studies of social service bureaucracies (Hage 1965; Hage and Aiken 1970). Hage suggests that relationships in organizational theory may be curvilinear: when organizations approach extreme scores, the extent of relationships may no longer hold or may actually be reversed. This is an important limitation to bear in mind, especially as we begin to consider organizations, such as the ones in this study, that are by design extreme on all eight continua proposed in this model.

9. Organizations which are homogeneous in this sense probably register substantial agreement over organizational goals (or what Thompson and Tuden [1959] call "preferences about outcomes"), but register considerable disagreement about how to get there ("beliefs about causation"). In such cases, Thompson and Tuden predict that organizations will reach decisions by majority judgment. A collegium type of organization, they maintain, is best suited for solving judgmental problems. This would require that all members participate in each decision, route per-

tinent information about causation to each member, have equal influence over the final choice, give fidelity to the group's preference structure, and designate as ultimate choice the judgment of the majority. On all but the last point, Thompson and Tuden correctly describe collectivist work organizations. Further, as they point out, the social science literature does not contain models of this type of organization as it does for bureaucracy (Thompson and Tuden 1959; p. 200).

10. To Pateman (1970), the theory of participatory democracy rises or falls on this educative function. But other social scientists (see especially Argyris 1974) remain unconvinced that participation in collectivist-democratic processes of organization can produce the desired changes in people's behavior. For Argyris, unilateral, defensive, closed, mutually protective, nonrisk-taking behavior, what he calls *model I behavior,* is nearly universal: it permeates not only western bureaucracies but also counterbureaucracies such as alternative schools, as well as collectivist organizations in contemporary China and Yugoslavia. Change in organizational behavior cannot be expected to follow from fundamental change in the mode of production; for model I behavior is rooted in the pyramidal values of industrial culture and in the finiteness of the human mind as an information-processing machine in the face of environmental complexity.

Contrarily, I am arguing that, where people do not have participatory habits, it is because they generally have not been allowed any substantive control over important decisions. Nondemocratic (pyramidal) habits are indeed a problem for democratic groups, but they are not a problem that a redistribution of power could not resolve. Admittedly, the evidence is not yet conclusive on this issue, but much of it does indicate that the practice of democracy itself develops the capacity for democratic behavior among its participants (see especially Blumberg 1973; Pateman 1970).

11. The result of this effort was a two-tiered structure: the paper was incorporated as a general corporation and a trust, which owns all the stock in the paper. Each six months of full-time work is worth one voting share in the trust. This grants ultimate control of the paper to the staff, past and present. Immediate control is exercised by the board of directors of the corporation, which consists of the currently working staff. As a member of the paper said, "the structure is neither graceful nor simple, but it...guarantees that the working staff will maintain editorial control, and makes it nearly impossible ever to sell the paper."

12. See the abortive attempts to raise capital for employee-ownership at Kasanof's Bakery, "How the Workers Almost Pulled It Off," *The Boston Phoenix,* 26 April 1977, and at the Colonial Press in Clinton, Massachusetts.

13. Organization-environment relations are always reciprocal. In part, the low wages, hard work, and intense personal involvement that make collectivist organizations seem so costly may be due to costs imposed by the environment. Conversely, collectivist organizations rely upon goods and services produced by the surrounding bureaucratic organizations, e.g., light bulbs, fast food chains.

14. Swidler (1976) vividly describes the extent to which members of a free school will literally ransack their private lives to locate sources of glamour that will enhance their sense of worth and influence in the group.

15. A case study of the demystification of skills in a collectivist work organization is provided by Bart (1979; chap. 6).

16. Mansbridge (1977) observes that even the most genuinely democratic organization will accept some measure of inequality of influence in order to retain individual liberties.

2

Necessary Elements for Effective Worker Participation in Decision-Making

Paul Bernstein

For many decades, conventional managerial practice relied on strict hierarchical and authoritarian relationships to direct and coordinate a smooth flow of production. Managers' personal predilections for strict control were supported by Weberian views of the *rational* administrative system, which held that the most efficient performance of subordinates would be obtained by increasing the organization's degree of standardization, impersonality, specialization, routine, formal regulations, and promotion through levels of hierarchy to create a career (Weber 1947, pp. 330-40).

Beneath this administrative apparatus, the tenets of *scientific management* were applied to the production line. This approach assumed that the greatest efficiency would be obtained by fragmenting the overall production assignment into smaller and smaller operations, each to be performed by an individual repeating a simple task hundreds of times a day. Most important, job tasks were devised not by workers themselves but by trained industrial engineers, on the premise that all "brainwork" and all physical labor must be separated into different strata of the firm (Taylor 1947, pp. 98-99). These job design engineers followed mechanical, rather than human, principles of efficiency, seeking to mesh the work of laborers with their machines and the time clocks that set the pace. Later these principles (and increased automation) came to play a crucial role in office tasks also, with the result that many white-collar workers now experience

Paul Bernstein is Assistant Professor of Sociology, Boston College. He is currently involved in developing a Ph.D. program on Social Economy which has a special focus on self-management.

Reprinted from the *Journal of Economic Issues* (June 1976) by special permission of the copyright holder, the Association for Evolutionary Economics.

fragmentation and routinization of work similar to industrial workers (HEW 1973, pp. 38-40). The office has, in many instances, become much like a factory (Fromm 1968, p. 33).

Although these practices produced much output for industrial societies, they also produced much dissatisfaction, and not only among workers (HEW 1973, chap. 2). The search for an alternative to managerialism has led to many different political movements, scientific experiments, and autonomous trial-and-error experiences. Each of these efforts has operated from at least one of the following perspectives: (1) an attempt to change *how the employee experiences* his/her work situation (for example, the human relations school, T-group, or sensitivity sessions); (2) an attempt to *reverse the prevailing trend toward extreme division of labor and specialization* (for example, by job "enlargement"); and (3) an attempt to *change the power relations between worker and manager* from the strict authoritarianism of the ideal-type bureaucracy and from the extreme separation of physical from mental labor that Taylorism had encouraged.

So far, most attempts by United States scientists to create an alternative to conventional workplace relations have involved job enlargement or job enrichment (Jenkins 1973, chaps. 10, 12). Minimally, these procedures introduce more variety into the employee's life, expanding his or her job from the repetition of a simple operation hundreds of times a day to the completion of several tasks in the overall production-cycle. In its more ambitious form, job enrichment also grants the worker some autonomy over his/her pace of work and over the distribution of tasks among his/her coworkers. As such, it introduces an element of workers' control — although that concept has rarely, if ever, been articulated in this context. Instead, the managerial literature refers to this innovation merely as the "autonomous workgroup technique" (Emery and Trist 1969).

Yet, such forms of job enrichment do involve employees in participative decision-making, perhaps for the first time in their working careers, and thus are a qualitative departure from traditional authoritarian administration. Ironically, too, almost every time this participative element has crept into the practice of job enrichment, even when unintended, both worker satisfaction and productivity have increased dramatically (Blumberg 1973, pp. 123-38; Jenkins 1973, pp. 188-235).

The present article is written from the premise that a much greater degree of participation by employees is feasible in the modern economy, without necessarily going to the extreme of first creating a political revolution to change the national regime. In order to be most successful in implementing greater worker participation in the present situation, research can make use of the experience of advanced cases of workers' control in several countries of the world, including overlooked cases in the United States. Table 2.1 lists all the cases the present research was based on — both successes and failures — and the published sources in which their experiences were described. Earlier works leading to the present research presented some of these cases in detail (Bernstein 1974; 1976, chaps. 2, 3), and their experiences were integrated and analyzed in a separate paper, focusing on their *internal* dynamics (Bernstein 1975).[1] Here the essential conclusions of that analysis will be presented and applied to the search for an alternative, democratic model of decision-making for United States workplaces.

DISCRIMINATING AMONG VARIOUS KINDS OF PARTICIPATION

Much confusion can be avoided when considering worker participation if it is kept in mind that each individual case can be distinguished along three dimensions: (1) the *degree* of control employees enjoy over any particular decision; (2) the *issues* over which that control is exercised; and (3) the organizational *level* at which their control is exercised.

For example, French law requires that one or two workers serve on company director boards, but worker participation at levels below this is not simultaneously guaranteed (dimension 3). As a result, the average employee's participation directly in the shop or office is hardly changed (Sturmthal 1964). By the same token, many job enrichment cases allow worker decision-making *only* in their immediate shop or office task, retaining traditional managerial prerogatives at all levels above that (Jenkins 1973, chap. 12). An effective plan for democratization must take into account the need for worker influence at many levels of the organization. Participation at the top can protect and broaden participation on the plant floor. Participation at the bottom increases the interest and support workers give to their representatives on the top director boards and strengthens the representatives' positions vis-a-vis directors.

The significance of the second dimension, the range of issues over which workers may decide, becomes apparent when one examines collective bargaining as it is generally conducted by United States

TABLE 2.1 CASES OF DEMOCRATIZATION EXAMINED

Case and Country	Sources

TYPE I. AUTONOMOUS FIRMS

Case and Country	Sources
Worker-owned plywood companies — United States	1. Personal on-site investigation (Bernstein 1974) 2. (Berman 1967) 3. (Bellas 1972)
Scott-Bader Commonwealth — United Kingdom	1. (Blum 1968) 2. (Farrow 1965)
American Cast Iron Pipe Co. — United States	1. (Bentley 1925) 2. (Employee's Manual n.d.) 3. (Zwerdling 1974)
John Lewis Partnership — United Kingdom	1. (Farrow 1964) 2. (Flanders et al. 1968)
Bat'a Boot & Shoe Co. — Czechoslovakia	1. (Dubreuil 1963) 2. (International Labor Office 1930) 3. (Sprague 1932) 4. (Cekota 1964) 5. (Hindus 1947)
Scanlon Plan companies — United States	1. (Lesieur 1958) 2. (Frost et al. 1973)
Works councils — (1919–1930s) United States	1. (Derber 1970) 2. (National Industrial Conference Board 1919, 1922) 3. (Douglas 1921)
Polish works councils[1] Democratization experiments — Norway	(Kolaja 1960) 1. (Blumberg 1968) 2. (Jenkins 1973) 3. (Gustavsen 1973)
Participation, work redesign and job enrichment experiments — United States	1. (HEW 1973) 1. (Blumberg 1968) 3. (Gouldner 1954) 4. (O'Toole 1973)
British job redesign (Tavistock experiments)	(Emery and Trist 1960)
Histradrut Union Enterprises — Israel	1. (Fine 1973) 2. (Tabb and Goldfarb 1970)
Imperial Chemical Industries — United Kingdom	(*Business Week* 1971)

TYPE II. COMMUNITARIAN

Case and Country	Sources
Spanish anarchist collectives (1936–1939)	(Dolgoff 1974)
Israeli kibbutzim and moshavim	1. Personal interview 2. (Fine 1973) 3. (Tabb and Goldfarb 1970)

TABLE 2.1— CONTINUED

Case and Country	Sources
Nineteenth-century U.S. communes	1. (Nordhoff 1972) 2. (Holloway 1966)
TYPE III. STATE AUTHORIZED	
Czechoslovak mines (1920–1939)	1. (Papanek 1946) 2. (Bloss 1938)
Most Czechoslovak industry (1945–1948) (1968–1969)	(Hindus 1947) 1. Personal interview 2. (Remington 1969) 3. (Stradal 1969)
British nationalized industries	1. Personal interview 2. (Schumacher 1973)
Codetermination in coal and steel industries — West Germany	1. (Blumenthal 1956) 2. (McKitterick and Roberts 1953) 3. (Sturmthal 1964) 4. (Schuchman 1957)
French works councils and worker directors	(Sturmthal 1964)
Works councils — Belgium	(Potvin 1958)
Works councils — Germany	(Sturmthal 1964)
Works councils — Norway	1. (*agenor* 1969) 2. (Blumberg 1968)
Yugoslav self-management	1. (Sturmthal 1964) 2. (Hunnius 1973) 3. (Blumberg 1968) 4. (Rus 1973) 5. (Kolaja 1965) 6. (Flaes 1971) 7. (Gorupić and Paj 1971) 8. (Obradovic 1970) 9. (Adizes 1973)
Swedish industrial democracy	1. (H. Bernstein 1974) 2. (Karlsson 1972) 3. (Therborn 1974) 4. (Norcross 1975)
U.S. labor unions[2]	1. (Derber 1970) 2. (Sturmthal 1970) 3. Personal interviews
Canadian provincial enterprises	1. (Shearer 1974) 2. (*Business Week* 1975) 3. (*NDP News*) 4. (Wilson 1974)

TABLE 2.1— CONTINUED

Case and Country	Sources
Soviet industry	1. (Brinton 1970)
	2. (Mallet 1972)
	3. Personal interviews
Chinese enterprises	1. (Richman 1967)
	2. (Myrdal 1970)
	3. (Macciocchi 1972)
	4. (Bettelheim 1974)
Algerian workers' councils	(I. Clegg 1971)

1. These were autonomously initiated by the firms' employees, although later restricted by the state (Type III).
2. This case is state-*enabled*, but is not required by law.

unions. Issues relating to safety, dismissals, wages, and fringe benefits are fought for fiercely, but such issues as choice of product, company investments, and selection of managers are explicitly left to management, by terms of the same collective bargaining contract (Lynd 1974). By contrast, in certain worker-owned plywood cooperatives in the Northwest, workers decide not only on their pay rate and safety questions, but also on the annual distribution of the company's profits and the selection of management personnel (Bernstein 1974; Berman 1967; chap. 7). Figure 2.1 illustrates the general range of issues available for decision-making in the modern firm, conceived as extending along a continuum from the worker's own immediate sphere of activity (issues 1-7) to the company's overall goals (issues 15-16). In between these poles are the issues which arise as part of the company's means to achieve its goals.[2]

It is perfectly possible for participation to begin at the lower end of the scale and to expand to broader and higher company questions. Some early cases of worker participation in United States firms exhibited this kind of development (NICB 1922, pp. 40-43), and a few contemporary advocates of workers' control argue for this as a strategy (Craft 1974, p. 4; Gorz 1967). By a clear understanding of the interrelatedness of these issues, present-day unions could facilitate worker control by expanding their collective bargaining demands from what they now consider "workers' issues" into the realm they have usually abdicated under the rubric "management issues."

FIG. 2.1 DIMENSION 2: RANGE OF ISSUES OVER WHICH CONTROL MAY BE EXERCISED

	[Economic relations if this is a subsidiary]*
To company's goals	16. Raising capital; economic relations to other firms, banks, governments
	[Economic relations if this is a subsidiary]*
	15. Division of the profits — allocation of net earnings to reserves, investment, distribution to employees, outside stockholders, and so forth
	14. Investments in new buildings
	13. Investments in new machinery
Through	12. [Economic relations with company's other divisions,* if this is headquarters]
organization's	11. Promotion of executives
means	10. Choice of products, markets, pricing
	9. Research and development
	8. Setting salaries; management bonus plans and stock options
	7. Job security, layoffs; setting wages
	6. Fringe benefits; collective-welfare income (for example, medical, housing)
	5. Promotions
	4. Hiring; training
From worker's	3. Placement in particular jobs; discipline; setting work standards and pace — how the job is done
own work	2. Safety rules and practices
	1. Physical working conditions

*Economic relations with company's other divisions as a factor is ranked according to whether the establishment in question is the headquarters or a subsidiary. If the latter, there may be conflict about whether its relations with the home office should be ranked first or third, particularly in multinational corporations [Vernon 1971].

The one dimension remaining to be presented concerns the degree of control employees exercise over any given decision (dimension 1), leaving aside the specific issue and level of organization at which the decision is to be made. It is here that many common labels are sometimes confused and used in overlapping ways: *consultation, joint management, codetermination,* and so forth. In order to clarify the situation, the various kinds of participative decision-making have been arranged in figure 2.2 along a continuum from least to greatest control by workers, describing the actual process of decision-making in each case in the left-hand column, paralleling the list of common, broader labels on the right-hand side of the chart.

ACTUAL FORMS AND PROCESSES

GENERAL LABELS

7. *WORKERS'* Council or Assembly *SUPERIOR* to managers[1] (and if outside constituencies have representatives in this body, they must be approved by the workers).[2]

FULL WORKERS' CONTROL or "SELF-MANAGEMENT" (WORKERS' AUTONOMY)

6. Joint Power or *PARTNERSHIP* (workers and managers codecide on joint board)

many different { 50–50[4]
voting proportions { 3–4[3]
exist { 1–2[4]

JOINT MANAGEMENT or "CODETERMINATION"

5. Workers wait until management has decided; then may *VETO OR APPROVE*; if veto then management submits modifications.[5]

"Collective bargaining"[6]

4. *MANAGER DELEGATES* some decisions generally to workers, reserving ultimate veto which is rarely used.[7]

(borderline form)

3. Workers initiate *CRITICISMS AND SUGGESTIONS* and discuss them face-to-face with managers. Latter still have sole power to decide, but usually adopt workers' proposals.[8]

COOPERATION or "COINFLUENCE"

Threshold of → democratic participation

2. Same as immediately above, but managers usually reject workers' proposals.

1. Managers give *PRIOR NOTICE* of a change, workers have chance to voice their views and perhaps stimulate reconsideration.[9]

"CONSULTATION"

Threshold of → regular participation

0. Impersonal *SUGGESTION BOX System*; managers accept or reject without giving reasons.[10]

Illustrative cases: 1. U.S. plywoods; 2. Czechoslovak state-owned enterprises 1968–1969; 3. Czechoslovak mines 1921–1938; 4. West German coal and steel industry 1947; 5. Schuchman (1957); 6. U.S. labor unions; 7. Heller and Rose (1973); 8. Most Scanlon Plan firms, United States, and safety rules committee in Gouldner's Gypsum Company; 9. Likert (1967); 10. Lesieur (1958)

An example of the most minimal form of participation is the suggestion box, common in conventional work situations. Because it lacks face-to-face communication and frequently does not include even a response by management, this form has been placed below the threshold of regular participation. (It is included at all because it is considered by many managing personnel to be a form of soliciting worker input into company policy, and indeed it is, in its very limited way.) Above this threshold lies the realm of "consultation," where managers seek the opinion of a group of employees on certain questions and may be influenced by the workers' collective recommendation as in Rensis Likert's System 3 type of management (1961, pp. 13-29). However, since managers are still the ones who initiate these consultations and because they retain full power to accept or reject the employees' decision, this form of participation is placed below the threshold of what we consider truly democratic participation.

Above the second threshold, employees initiate criticisms and suggestions on company policy, most of which actually are incorporated. In this realm are all the more advanced degrees of worker participation in decision-making: joint management or codetermination and full self-management. The structure usually relied upon in this realm is a representative council or committee elected by the workers, in whole or in part, from among their own number. Members of the council continue to serve in their regular jobs and generally receive no extra pay unless their council meetings are scheduled after regular working hours. The council meets, often with professional managers, at a frequency that varies from weekly to monthly. In addition, the entire workforce of a shop, office, or department may assemble frequently to discuss matters appropriate to its own unit, with or without the supervisor. In some companies, a general assembly of all employees convenes once or twice a year to consider overall, long-term matters (Berman 1967; chap. 7; Sturmthal 1964; Lesieur 1958).

Collective bargaining is included above the threshold of truly democratic participation because, through it, unions exercise real power over decisions basic to the firm, decisions which, at one time, were the sole prerogative of the employer (Derber 1970; Sturmthal 1964). The argument occasionally raised against considering collective bargaining as a form of worker participation in decision-making either must refer to the bureaucratization of unions or to the restricted number of issues commonly decided on through this mechanism. The latter reflects dimension 2, not the present dimension, which measures only the degree of influence over any single decision.

For greater clarity it is possible to bring these two dimensions together graphically, capturing the simultaneity at issue. Figure 2.3 is one such graph. There it can be seen that although United States unions exert less influence than the employees of a fully worker-owned plywood cooperative, they still exert a great deal more influence over several issues than do workers in an average nonunionized shop.

FIG. 2.3 A SIMULTANEOUS COMPARISON OF CASES ALONG TWO DIMENSIONS

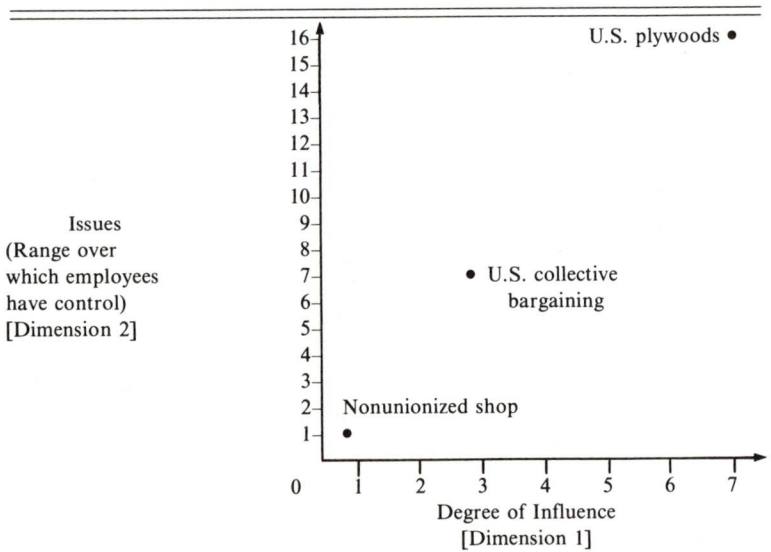

Below collective bargaining and other forms of joint management lies a complex area of *de facto* but not *de jure* workers' control (form 3 in fig. 2.2). Here the vast majority of employee suggestions and criticisms do become company policy, although managers retain a formal right to reject any of these decisions. Cases with this degree of influence are several of the Scanlon Plan firms (Lesieur 1958, p. 49). When, in any particular case, *de facto* conversion of employee recommendations into a company policy falls below 50 percent in frequency, that case has crossed below the threshold of democratic participation (has moved from form 3 to form 2 in fig. 2.3).

These three dimensions seem to identify the main characteristics of any structure of worker participation in decision-making. The methodology of this research was not designed to find one best system for all occasions, but to identify what caused certain systems to fail and others to succeed.[3] In so doing, it was discovered that participation covering any combination of the three main dimensions was usually adequate as a start to more advanced degrees of worker control, so long as it began above the democratic threshold on dimension 1. However, several other components were found to be necessary for the bare structure of participation to become an ongoing, self-reinforcing system of employee power.

Before discussing those other components, it will be useful to clear up one question often posed about the degree of democracy in workplaces, namely: Is it necessary for *all* employees to participate in decision-making for a system to be democratic? Obviously, different ideologies will present different standards. The concrete cases examined for this research (representing several ideological traditions) suggest that active participation by each and every worker is not necessary for the rank and file to exercise real accountability over company decisions. Nevertheless, striving for full participation is likely to add benefits to the personal development of individual members, thereby accomplishing the overall goal of humanization of the work experience.

Sometimes overparticipation has occurred. In these cases, workers noticed the general efficiency of their firm to be declining and discovered the cause to be too many interruptions of the administrative process on minor details, or too much time spent by the collective on decisions better delegated to individuals. The group therefore chose to reduce participation on some issues and at some levels of the organization, while reserving its power for overall policy decisions and monitoring — but not frequently interrupting — the performance of appointed supervisors and department heads (Berman 1967; chap. 7). The lesson, apparently, is that for maximum benefit to the collective there is a particular mix of *managerial authority* and *democratic control,* the precise proportions of which have to be found by each case through its own experience.

THE OTHER NECESSARY COMPONENTS

As stated earlier, the data show that, for participation to be maintained, other components are necessary. This research was guided by the customary scientific principle of parsimony, so the least number of additional elements that seemed to explain success and failure of participation was selected. Elements that did not prove absolutely essential, although in some cases they enhanced the system marginally, were left aside. In subsequent research, those latter elements may be added to the model established here.[4]

Five elements emerged from the comparison of case histories as minimally necessary to support participation: (1) employee access to and sharing of management level information; (2) guaranteed protection of the employee from reprisals for voicing criticisms (plus certain other rights); (3) an independent board of appeals to settle disputes between those holding managing positions and those being managed; (4) a particular set of attitudes and values (type of consciousness); and (5) frequent return to participating employees of at least a portion of the surplus they produce (above their regular wage).

These five elements or components are necessary not only individually, but they also depend on each other cybernetically to feed back and reinforce the whole system. This is why the search for a minimal list resulted in no less than five (plus participation itself, which represents a sixth distinct component). Any empirical case of workplace democratization with less than this minimal group failed to sustain itself for more than a few years. (Explanation of such failures will be presented later; see also Bernstein 1976, chap. 3 and pt. 2).

First Additional Component:
Sharing Management-Level Information

Obviously, if employees are to decide on issues extending beyond their immediate tasks, they need information on those more distant areas. Technical information that heretofore only the company engineers were familiar with must now be available to them. Economic information that previously only the accounting and finance departments were concerned with must be made available as well. If such information is not forthcoming when employees feel the need for it, not only is frustration on that issue likely to result, but also employee confidence in the entire comanagement system may disappear. This is what occurred in the Belgian attempt to create meaningful works councils after World War II. When the crucial component of management-level information was withheld from workers by reluctant managers, workers withdrew from further attempts at participation, and the system essentially died (Potvin 1958).

To be supportive of democratization, it was found the amount of information available to employees must be *at least* what they feel they need for adequate decision-making. (This is why demands raised by unions such as the United Auto Workers for corporate books to be open to employees by right make sense in a strategy for democratization.) But firms committed to democratization go beyond this. Rather than passively *allowing* worker participants to find out crucial information, they actively establish mechanisms to keep all participants informed and to assist their utilization of this information. Written reports on the performance of each department and the state of the whole enterprise are distributed, as are written reminders on issues approaching a decision point (Flanders et al. 1968; Blum 1968; Bernstein 1974). Also, those occupying manager positions remain available for frank questioning by other participants, not only in formal meetings set aside for that purpose, but also as an accepted custom whenever chance encounters arise.

Up to this point, we have been discussing the *availability* of information. Just as consequential a factor is the employees' *ability* to handle the necessary information. Obviously, in the beginning stage of democratization, many employees may be, or may feel themselves to be, ill-prepared for handling all the requisite data. This fact points to the need for specific training to precede, or at the least to accompany, any consciously implemented plan of democratization. Swedish unions have established such training courses as their country moves toward greater worker participation (*Business Week* 1970), as has Yugoslavia (Gorupić and Paj 1971). Besides on-the-job training, changes within the basic educational system will probably be necessary to facilitate workplace democratization in the United States, for there is evidence that school experience deeply affects how young people later approach their jobs and careers, including how they approach authority figures at work (Behn et al. 1976; Freire 1970). In addition, the experience of democratization itself can develop participants' abilities to deal intelligently with requisite complex information (National Industrial Conference Board 1922; Jenkins 1973). Just how well this occurs in any particular case seems to depend in part on how committed are the workers' own leaders and the firms' managers to developing all employees' business expertise and participatory skills. (Such a commitment by leadership is considered here to be part of the necessary component of consciousness, discussed below.)

Serious problems can arise in the practical implementation of the informational component. Space permits only identification and brief presentation of possible solutions to these difficulties (more extended discussion can be found in Bernstein [1975, chap. 6]). One problem is that of industrial secrecy, at least whenever workers' control is implemented in a market economy.[5] In such a situation, firms may still need to prevent certain technical data and financial plans from being released to other firms if they are to retain a competitive advantage. Swedish unions and employers have designed a clever solution that allows managers to request the withholding of disputed information, but leaves ultimate release power in the hands of workers' elected representatives (Bergnéhr 1975). By contrast, systems which allow managers to retain this ultimate power are likely to weaken democratization, as the German codetermination firms have found (Blumenthal 1956).

A second problem in the operation of the informational component is that employees may not make use of available information on issues of less than immediate, personal interest to them, that is, on issues besides wages and physical working conditions (Gorupić and Paj 1971). This is a problem of citizen participation common to all democracies, societal as well as intraorganizational. One means for solution in the workplace is for managers and the workers' own elected leaders to make clear to participants how the areas they have been ignoring do relate directly to the areas of their immediate concern. This kind of communication was observed to be effective in several of the United States plywood cooperatives (Bernstein 1974).

A third problem in information sharing can be the reluctance of some managers to abandon their former habits of prerogative and secrecy. This is especially likely where democratization has been forced on them (as by national law) or in the early stages of democratization when old habits and fears are still governing a great deal of the behavior of managers and others. Although much information may be circulating to participants, certain crucial bits may be imparted only vaguely or held back entirely by individual managers, and this may reduce the overall effectiveness of the participation system. Here again, part of the solution lies in the consciousness of those occupying managerial posts, a topic dealt with below (see table 2.3).

Finally, there is the problem of managers' continually greater expertise on certain issues in contrast to the managed, even when full information is provided. This is an inevitable situation flowing from the division of labor and time inherent in any complex group endeavor. Although there seems to be no neat, final solution to this problem, certain experiences in workers' control are worth noting. *Rotation* of employees into managerial posts certainly increases the expertise of the total working group, as has been observed in Israeli kibbutzim (Fine 1973; Tabb and Goldfarb 1970) and the United States plywood cooperatives (Berman 1967; chap. 7; Bernstein 1974). In the advanced forms, where a workers' council is superior to the specialized managers (form 7 on dimension 1, fig. 2.2), it may be sufficient that at least these council members have gained an expertise nearly equivalent to the full-time managers. So long as these council members continue to work at regular jobs in the plant (as occurs in the United States plywood cooperatives, for example), or are otherwise held accountable to the interests of the rank and file, the employee group as a whole may be functioning effectively with an expertise nearly matching that of the full-time specialists. A third possibility is for the employee group to engage a staff of experts of its own to advise it on matters where it recognizes that the full-time managers still have greater expertise. Such a system would be analogous to the combination of democracy with expertise practiced in the United States Congress, where elected legislators engage specialized staffs for work on specific issues. United States unions already do this, hiring professional economists to work from the unions' point of view on issues in contention with employers (Derber 1970). The same might be done in worker-participation firms.

Second Additional Component: Guaranteed Individual Rights

Experience shows that it is not enough for participants to possess appropriate information and an ability to use it. They also must be protected against possible reprisals for using that information to criticize existing policies or to oppose proposed policy changes. And they must be free to differ with fellow employees on issues of moment. Without such protection, open dialogue and the important upward flow of suggestions and evaluations would be unlikely to occur effectively or for very long.

A clear case in point is the American Cast Iron Pipe Company: Although worker owned, it lacks real guarantees to the employees against penalties for criticism and is controlled, as a result, by a self-selecting set of managers. If criticism is voiced at all by employees, it is generally outside the company (Zwerdling 1974). Employee participation in this company's decision-making consequently has dropped practically to nil.

Other case histories also demonstrate that, to persist, a participation system must be supported by the rights commonly associated with political democracy: freedom of speech and assembly, petition of grievances, secret balloting, due process and the right to file appeal in cases of discipline, immunity of rank and file representatives from dismissal or transfer while in office, and a written constitution alterable only by a majority or a two-thirds vote of the collective (Gorupić and Paj 1971; Lynd 1974; Flanders et al. 1968; Bernstein 1974).

Apparently the entire set of rights is necessary, not just a few, because each right depends substantially on the others for its successful operation. For example, for effective use, the right to assemble and organize must be accompanied by the right to free speech. Likewise, the right to seek redress of grievances cannot be actualized significantly without the protection of workers' representatives from dismissal or transfer and the guarantee of secret balloting to elect those representatives in the first place.

A second important characteristic of this major component is that, to be effective, such guaranteed protection must be absolute. Scholars of these rights in the traditional societal context have long observed that the power to abridge basic freedoms is the power to destroy them (Brant 1964, p. 41). Experience bears this out in the context of workplace democratization. The reduction of employees' rights led to the emasculation of workers' control in Soviet Russia, Poland, and Algeria (Brinton 1970; Kolaja 1965; Clegg 1971).

This system of rights is not only politically necessary for the employees, but also turns out to be cybernetically valuable for the company as a whole, expanding its possibilities for adaptive self-steering. For example, free speech not only protects individuals; it also furnishes the organization with a wider range of perceptions of its own performance. Criticism, complaints, and specialized information from employees at the bottom and at the far reaches of the organization can improve the accuracy with which decision-making organs at the center assess the state of their organization, its performance, and its environment (Deutsch 1963). Free speech also makes possible an upward flow of positive proposals, actualizing the cybernetic principle of "requisite variety." This refers to the need of self-steering systems to supply themselves with several alternative views and strategies in order to cope adequately with an ever-changing environment (McEwan 1971; Beer 1966).

A major problem that arises in the implementation of this component is the conflict between individual rights and collective rights or needs. For example, the collective need for stable administration could argue that absolute freedom of speech, organization, and so forth, is simply too disruptive, that it causes delay in reaching decisions. The individualist reply would be that to limit this freedom is to risk destroying it altogether, for a limited freedom of speech means the individual may not speak up when he or she sees fit, but only when authorities allow it — which is when they find it in their own interest. The problem is complicated further by the fact that even those democratized enterprises which aim at high individual freedom sometimes produce informal but powerful group pressures against the individual. For example, the supposedly libertarian kibbutzim in Israel admit to aiming for "a complete identification of the individual with society" (Fine 1973, p. 241). "Tyranny of the majority" may indeed become operative in such cases.

Solutions to these conflicts will, perforce, be complex and subtle. Cases of democratization stemming from anarchist movements have perhaps gone the farthest toward preserving the autonomy of the individual. In Republican Spain (1936-1939 period), for example, anarchist unions held individual autonomy to be the inviolable right, and limited their community authority structures by that principle (Dolgoff 1974). A second strategy is to balance carefully the two principles as norms internalized within each participant of the self-managing enterprise. Of particular usefulness here is the balance between individual self-reliance and receptivity to others' needs (see table 2.1, traits 2 and 3). Still another means for satisfying the conflicting rights of the individual and the group is the auxiliary system of adjudication we have identified as an additional, major component of democratization. To that component we now turn.

Third Additional Component: Independent Judiciary

Even though employees may be participating in decisions that affect them, they will not always agree that the rules so democratically arrived at are being applied accurately or fairly. In order to resolve such disputes, an independent judicial procedure within the firm is needed. This system differs from conventional grievance machinery in being broader in scope, more balanced in its power base, and more face-to-face in its implementation.

Specifically, adjudicative systems in democratized firms have the following three functions: (1) settlement of rule infractions in a just manner; (2) upholding the basic rights (those listed as additional component 2); and (3) protecting the bylaws (constitution) of the enterprise from violation by any member, whether manager or managed.

To be able to fulfill these functions, the adjudicative system must be independent of all factions within the enterprise. Various forms have evolved in practice to ensure that independence: use of outside arbitrators or labor ministry professionals to ensure neutrality (Sturmthal 1964; Bloss 1938); a joint tribunal consisting of workers and managers from within the firm to ensure balance (Blum 1968; NICB 1922; Derber 1970); or referring the matter to the entire assembly of enterprise members (or representatives chosen from them by lot) to ensure judgment by one's peers (Berman 1967; Fine 1973; Dolgoff 1974). (For further elaboration, see table 5.2 in Bernstein [1976]).

Whichever form is taken, it is crucial that the impartiality of the adjudicative system be real and be perceived by the managed. Their confidence in the justness of the entire democratization system, not just this component, is at stake. For that reason, the inclusion of peers in the adjudicative system is of special value: Clearly, employees will cling more closely to the participation system if they know that they themselves, not autonomous managers, have the last word on how its rules are applied, how basic rights are upheld, and how the opportunities for participation are guaranteed.[6]

The settlement of disputes and the upholding of rights usually takes place in two stages. First, an act is committed or a person is accused of committing an act that violates one of the organization's rules. This may be handled on the spot by a supervisor's decision which identifies the violation, decides guilt or innocence, and determines punishment or acquittal, or, in the more democratized systems, the matter may be sent to a special tribunal for decision. (Democratization at this stage is still rare.) Second, there may be an appeal, which more commonly involves peers in the judgment process. The employee and accuser each present their view of the incident, and the appeals board or assembly upholds, modifies, or reverses the earlier sentence. Customarily, punishments range from reprimands and warning slips (analogous to traffic citations or demerit points), to temporary suspension of one or more privileges, to explusion. The latter is rarely invoked, least of all in communitarian situations, such as Israeli kibbutzim or Chinese communes. But in Western enterprises (such as plywood coops) it has once or twice been resorted to in a case of repeated drunkenness.

It seems that democratized enterprises have not, in general, developed this adjudicative component as far as they have developed some of the others. In particular, some of the safeguards that evolved in the societal arena to protect the individual from unjust authority are still absent in most democratized firms. Research might beneficially be applied to discover the value such societal principles could bring to the workplace. For example, in the first stage — rule violations — relevant principles that could be added include the following: (1) the accused is presumed innocent until the accuser can prove guilt; (2) the proof of guilt must be established by due process involving judgment by one's peers (fellow workers); and (3) the laws must be equally applied — managers must be as much subject to the process as the managed.

In the second stage, the first two principles are already present, but fairness could be advanced in the appeal process by adding the principle that the review must be speedy, and its sessions must be open to all employees.

Fourth Additional Component:
A Participatory-Democratic Consciousness

In examining prior components, the importance of consciousness has been encountered several times. The various cases of democratization researched for this article indicate particular attitudes and values to be supportive of, and necessary for, effective participation by workers and managers in the joint running of an enterprise. These traits can hardly be possessed in their absolute form, but, the more that each participant exhibits them, the smoother and more effective will the comanaging process tend to be. In other words, each person exhibits each trait to a degree, and, the greater his/her activation of each trait, the more beneficial he/she is to the success of the democratized system and the enterprise.

In addition, each trait has an *opposite* characteristic. The trait and its opposite may be conceived as paired, opposite poles on a single continuum. For example, *self-reliance* is one beneficial trait for democratization (by motivating challenges from the rank and file to managers' mistakes), and its opposite is *dependence*. Any individual can be located somewhere along the continuum that stretches between absolute self-reliance and absolute dependence.

Table 2.2 arrays the major traits (and their opposites) that have emerged so far from the data. Close examination suggests that these traits function together as two overall tendencies, equipping the participants with an ability to create and organize policy and an inclination to resist being manipulated. Table 2.2 therefore lists the major traits in two columns with these respective center column headings. The table also presents the opposite of each specific trait and the two general tendencies which those opposites create (outer columns of the chart).

Data from concrete experiences of democratization alert us to the fact that, while these several traits and tendency systems are adequate for the general membership of the enterprise, an additional set of specific traits is required for those who hold leadership or managing positions in the firm. This is because the exercise of power can, at each moment, change the degree of democratization experienced by the rest of the firm. The crucial people in this regard are the elected leaders of the workers (such as workers' council representatives) and the full-time managers chosen by them or coruling with them. Table 2.3 presents six major pairs of traits crucial to these persons' behavior. The table also shows how the opposites of these six traits tend to diminish the degree of democratization experienced in the firm. One way to summarize the kind of consciousness in power-holders that is positive for democratization is to say that these persons must be not only decision-makers but also educators, not only managers but also democratizers (Mulder 1971; Mao 1963; Adizes 1971). In other words, the power-holder's responsibility in this system is not only to accomplish the economic task of the enterprise but also to develop the participants' ability to be more democratic.[7] This is not done by setting aside special occasions for "democratic exercises" or the like. Rather, it is best accomplished through the day-to-day behavior of the power-holders and through their interaction with the rest of the firm's participants, as much in mundane tasks as in general policy outputs (Fibich 1967).

One important characteristic of the overall participatory consciousness is the internal balancing of contradictory traits. For example, in table 2.2 are both *self-reliance* (trait 2) and *receptivity to others' needs* (trait 3). Without the former, initiative from below would be unlikely to arise, and it is needed in democratization for governing shop-floor tasks and for holding higher management accountable to those below on broader policies. Yet, without receptivity to others' needs, common agreements would be hard to achieve.

If these two traits (and other, similarly contradictory sets) are not successfully combined in the same individual, the organization is likely to experience factionalism as different people condense into groups predisposed to one or the other trait. On the other hand, if the contradictory traits can be combined in the same individual and this combination can be fostered in many individuals, as at least one school of psychology asserts (Maslow 1954; Theobald 1970), then

TABLE 2.2 MAJOR SUBSYSTEMS OF TRAITS ENABLING OR UNDERMINING DEMOCRATIZATION

| | *Relating to Outputs of the Managing Process* | | *Relating to Inputs of the Managing Process* "*Participatory-democratic consciousness*" | |
	More prone to being manipulated	*Less prone to being manipulated*	*Greater ability to create and organize policy*	*Lesser ability to create and organize policy*
1.	Ridigity of thought		Receptivity to the new, flexibility	Overseriousness, dogmatism
2.	Servility, intimidable ⟷		Self-reliance, refusal to transfer responsibility	⟶ Dependence
3.			Facility to compromise, receptivity to others'	⟷ Sectarian
4.	Indifferent, unquestioning ⟷	Inquisitive, interrogative		
5.	Extreme loyalty, deference, credulity ⟷	*Critical thinking:* attempt to avoid distortions and preconceptions self-critical careful differentiation between means and ends acknowledging inevitable limits		⟷ Defensive
6.	Simplistic thinking; black-and-white outlook ⟷	Expects multiple causation		
		Seeks to analyze in depth		⟷ Superficial thinking
7.	Narrow time sense ⟷	Long time sense		⟷ Narrow time sense
Rough (8) summation	Compliance ⟷	Resistance	Activism	⟷ Passivity, abstention

Sources: Paulo Freire, *Education for Critical Consciousness* (New York: Seabury Press. 1974); Theobald (1970); Maslow (1954); Argyris (1954); and Bernstein and White (1973).

TABLE 2.3 ADDITIONAL TRAITS REQUIRED OF POWER-HOLDERS

Discourages or prevents democratization		Fosters or facilitates democratization
1. Desire to maintain exclusive prerogatives		Egalitarian values
2. Paternalism		Reciprocity
3. Belief that leader must set example by appearing infallible (tries to hide all mistakes)		Awareness of own fallibility; admits errors to managed
4. Governing from position of formal power		Governing by merit, explanation, and consent of governed
5. Mistrustful, feels all others need "close watching," hence: intense supervision, limits freedom of subordinates		Confidence in others, hence: willingness to listen and to delegate responsibility
6. Proclivity to secrecy, holding back information		Policy of educating the managed; open access to information

Sources: Blumberg, (1968); Milton Derber, *The American Idea of Industrial Democracy, 1865–1965* (Chicago: Univ. of Illinois Press, 1970); Mauk Mulder, "The Learning of Participation," in *Participation and Self-Management,* vol. 4 (Zagreb: Institute for Social Research, 1973); Pateman (1970); Norton (1974); Tabb and Goldfarb (1970); and Mao Tse-Tung (1963).

democratization will not have to depend on the rare, spontaneous occurrence of such individuals.

A second important contradiction involving the participatory consciousness is that which occurs between the basic tendency toward activism (line 8, col. 3 in table 2.2) and the organization's need for stability and obedience to decisions once made. Some persons have argued that one or the other value should always take precedence, either activism or obedience (Almond and Verba 1963). Others sought to maintain both values, and some of these, such as Mao, regard the tension between activism and obedience to be an inevitable dialectic which can be used for periodic reform of the system. Under their strategy, activism is fomented into an upheaval which is followed by consolidation of the revolutionary values within a new authority structure. In effect, this strategy oscillates between the two values.

Another strategy which holds to both values seeks to harmonize the two within a persistent structure, allowing authority to flow upward from participants when they are choosing their managers or setting long-term policy directly, and letting authority and obedience flow downward when the elected directors make decisions which are to be carried out by the rest of the participants. In this system, activism and obedience are combined within a stable authority structure to give a circular pattern rather than upheavals followed by reorganizations (Bernstein 1973, p. 1; Bernstein 1976, chaps. 2, 3).[8]

Although often difficult to sustain at first without careful, repeated efforts (Rus 1972), the participatory-democratic consciousness appears to have great durability once firmly established in the minds of many members (Dolgoff 1974; Szulc 1972). Space is lacking here for further consideration of the causes of growth and change in this consciousness, but it is discussed elsewhere (Bernstein 1976, chap. 9).

Fifth Additional Component:
Guaranteed Return from the Surplus

Given the assumption that people generally take a job in order to receive an income (aside from having intrinsic interest in the work), it is not surprising to find that usually they demand at least a share in any surplus produced when participation leads to higher productivity, as is often the case (Blumberg 1968, chap. 6). This demand is especially likely to occur if employees regard the time and effort they have put into participation as extra labor on a managerial level, and if they see that their participation has benefited the company by reducing wasteful policies and initiating profitable improvements. Although desire for material gain varies from culture to culture, enterprises in even the least materialistic societies (such as Maoist China or Israeli kibbutzim) make it a practice to feed back a portion of the surplus above the usual wage to their members on a regular basis (Macciochi 1972; Fine 1973). Conversely, systems which fail to provide an automatic return from increases in the surplus, regardless of culture, seem unable to sustain employee participation for very long (Das 1964; Sturmthal 1964).

In practice, the return above wages can come from the annual profits of the enterprise, as in the plywood coops (Berman 1967; chap. 7), or from a periodic calculation of productivity margins comparing present to past performance within each department, as in the Scanlon Plan firms (Lesieur 1958). Some systems choose to avoid an outright monetary payment to participants and instead spend the surplus on a collectively consumable project, such as the construction of a recreation or health center in China (Myrdal 1970) or Yugoslavia (Gorupić and Paj 1971). Yet another form has been devised in some partially democratized firms, where surpluses from increased production have been barred because management anticipates an inelastic market or because union leaders fear the precedent of a speed-up. In such cases, the return from higher productivity has been distributed to employees as time off from work without any accompanying decrease in pay (Maccoby 1975).[9]

Whichever form the return takes, experience shows that it will not be supportive of democratization unless certain guidelines are followed. This is because the return has specific motivating effects on the participants. Unless care is taken to take those effects into account, the economic return will create cybernetically contradictory tendencies within the enterprise and reduce or eliminate participation. Five important guidelines have emerged thus far.

First, the return *must be directly related to what the employees themselves have produced and can control.* For example, in firms where the workers' decisions do not extend beyond the shop to major company decisions such as sales and investments, it would be incorrect to tie return to the whole company's profits. This is because, in a year when the market declines, the return to the employee might be nil, although in his own shop the worker has put forth extra exertion and contributed to several decisions which boosted productivity in that area. If this guideline were not adhered to, the opposite possibility also would create confusion: Company profits might soar in one period because of some fortunate investment or sale of assets totally unconnected to the workers' own efforts. A larger distribution that year would tend to reinforce faulty teams as well as productive ones, and so would wash out the self-corrective potential of this feedback.[10]

Second, the economic return *must belong to the employees by right.* If it does not, and is instead an arbitrary award given by someone outside their control (such as a nonelected manager), then the return becomes merely a discretionary bonus and can be used in a manipulative, paternalistic way. This will tend to damage the participation process, in particular by reducing the values of reciprocity and responsibility found to be crucial for democratization (and detailed within the consciousness component, trait 2, table 2.3, and trait 2, table 2.2, respectively).

Third, the return must be *made to the entire group* of participants, managers included. If only certain individuals receive the return, competition and resentment may be stimulated among the others, especially if they, too, contributed to the overall production process which registered the surplus. That will lead to fragmentation of the group, destroying the cooperative interactions necessary for joint decision-making and production. By the same token, measuring and rewarding the group as a whole fosters and strengthens group solidarity. Workers and managers come to see that they are dependent on one another for future income. It becomes harder then for managers to pretend to themselves that their workers are merely replaceable units, or "just muscle." Status differences between workers and supervisors tend to decline (Brown 1958, p. 81; Jenkins 1973, chap. 12).

Fourth, the return *must be separate from the basic wage.* The necessity for this derives from the fact that the return fluctuates, since it is a feedback from varying productivity or profits. When either might fall below zero, the employee's basic wage would be reduced. Experience has shown that few employees desire to give up their conventional stable income merely for the chance of getting a high return in some periods and risking subnormal wages in others. Most persons have family obligations and other regular expenses which preclude subjecting their income to so much risk. But if the fluctuations fall above a secure, guaranteed level of income, then the return can retain all its reinforcing aspects for democratization.

Fifth, one particularly valuable function the return can serve is that of an *informational* feedback, separate from its monetary reward character. If the return comes frequently, it can usefully inform the participants of the immediate consequences of their efforts. When the surplus declines, participants are alerted to look for problems causing the decline; when it rises, they may take that as one indication that their coendeavor is functioning well. For this reason, some firms like to calculate and distribute the return on a *monthly* basis (Puckett 1958, p. 76); less frequent intervals may also work, but one quarter is probably the limit for retaining the informational value of this component.

The lessons summarized in these five guidelines dispel the confusion sometimes generated when this economic aspect of democratization is compared to conventional profit-sharing or bonus-incentive plans. In profit-sharing, employees receive a return from the surplus, to be sure, but, since they are not in control of company decisions which affect the size of that profit, participation toward enlarging the profit is not directly reinforced. Furthermore, persons who have not put forth any extra contribution are rewarded as much as those who did. The feedback thus becomes a random reinforcer, and, not surprisingly, many firms with profit-sharing schemes consequently report no long-term boost in productivity (Sorey 1975). Employees also are not better informed under profit-sharing about their unit's contribution to the firm, and managers do not receive helpful suggestions from employees when profits decline.

Incentives schemes, a different phenomenon (Fein 1972), also fail to produce the results observable in democratized firms because such schemes usually reward only the individual. This not only tends to produce fragmentation, but also may actually lower productivity below what it was before inception of the scheme, because peer pressure discourages workers from standing out visibly in management's favor. The adversary relationship which places labor on one side and management on the other begins to be transformed in democratization, but it is by and large retained in the bonus-incentive system, and maintains peer pressure among workers against cooperation with management.

WHAT ABOUT OWNERSHIP?

Analysis of empirical cases indicates that transfer of ownership to workers is not absolutely necessary for significant democratization to occur in some firms (see cases in Jenkins 1973, chap. 12; Lesieur 1958). There are also firms which are entirely worker-owned yet lack any degree of democratization (for example, the Chicago-Northwestern Railroad; Kansas City *Star;* Milwaukee *Journal*). Such findings force one to question the common assumption that, to increase workers' power, one must first abolish private ownership.

Close examination reveals ownership to be not a unitary phenomenon, but a package of rights and functions (Dahl 1970, p. 124). This package includes legal title to the property, control over how that property is to be used (that is, its management), the right to dispose of (sell or donate) that property, and first claim on any income accrued through use of that property (such as profits from production). Of the six components so far identified as minimally necessary for democratization, at least two contain rights traditionally reserved to owners. The first component, participation in decision-making, invades the owner's right to *manage* the firm at his sole discretion,[11] and the economic return component invades the owner's right to have *first claim on the profits.* So democratization begins to transfer specific powers of ownership to the employees even before the formal, legal title of ownership may be transferred.

Of course, *complete* worker autonomy and self-management (form 7 of participation, dimension 1) is unlikely to occur without a transfer of the *majority* of rights belonging to the formal owner. Means of achieving this are varied. Perhaps the most common approach has been nationalization, although, in many cases, the workers concerned have not received or retained control but have seen it consolidated within the state (as in the Soviet Union [Brinton 1970]). Another means that evolved more recently is worker purchase of their firm from the original proprietor or from a parent conglomerate (for example, Scott-Bader [Farrow 1965], Vermont Asbestos Group [Achtenberg 1975], or Triumph-Meriden Motorcycle Co-operative [*Economist* 1975]). This can be a very expensive procedure, so occasionally the employees have been aided in their purchase by loans from the state (as in the Vermont and Triumph cases). Still other means have been proposed, but not yet implemented, such as the Swedish trade union economist's suggestion of a gradual distribution of profits to employees in the form of shares until 50 percent of every company is owned by its workers (Seeger 1975).

Given the various difficulties involved in securing complete worker ownership of the workplace, it is useful to keep open a consideration of how much may be achieved short of that transformation. For example, it is possible to envision workers' power expanding in the United States through a gradual narrowing down of stockholders' rights to those of mere bondholders. Outside stockholders would lack any vote (which most do not exercise anyway) but would still be willing to purchase "shares" of the firm because of the "dividend" they would continue to receive. Actually, the payments would no longer be dividends, but interest paid at a fixed rate. Nor would the payments be exploitative, varying as the workers' productivity varied, but they would merely be a "rent" paid by the firm for the money borrowed from these shareholders. Such noncontrolling shares (or, more appropriately, *notes*) have been proposed recently for sale to the United States public by a corporation whose mission would be to raise and lend capital to worker-managed firms (Benello 1975).

Once one considers total transfer of owners' rights, another question arises: to whom? Simply to transfer all rights to the workers may slight the issue of ensuring social responsibility of the firm, and it may lead one to overlook other questions connected with the external, or extraorganizational, dimension of ownership. This external realm actually exceeds the bounds of the present article, whose focus has been the internal rearrangements necessary for a firm to run on a democratized basis. Nevertheless, it is necessary to complete even this brief survey of the ownership component by mentioning a few more issues which arise in its extraorganizational realm. Much more analysis is needed before firm conclusions or recommendations can be made.

First, it is important to recognize that there are more forms that nonprivate ownership can take than are usually imagined. Each has its own advantages and disadvantages which need to be analyzed and carefully considered before preferences are formulated for one form or another. Besides a firm being owned by its workers, it could be owned by their community through the state, as in China (Bettelheim 1974), or through their municipality, as in some United States cities (Brom and Kirschner 1974). Local residents may exercise ownership over an enterprise through direct decision-making in a town assembly, as in Israeli kibbutzim (Fine 1973), or by individually purchasing shares, as in several black community-development organizations in the United States (Hampden-Turner 1975, pp. 241-53). It is even possible to disperse the discrete functions of ownership among several bodies, as is done in Yugoslavia. There, employees make most of the managing decisions, but the local municipality participates in selecting the company manager, and the state retains sole right to sell the company (Hunnius 1973).

Even within the supposedly simple form of full worker self-ownership, there are crucial variants, each having particular consequences for the democratization system. In one form, employees own individual shares of the company, which, on their own, they can sell to new workers whom they find to replace them (as in producer cooperatives [Berman 1967; chap. 7]). This can lead to the irony of successful firms being sold for individual gain to conventional conglomerates (Bernstein 1974, p. 31). In another form of complete worker-ownership, the working group *as a whole* holds title to the firm as in "common-ownership" firms such as Scott-Bader (Blum 1968; Farrow 1965). To join, one is not required to pay a special sum, but to determine disposal of assets one must vote with the others.

Whatever form or forms of nonprivate ownership are arranged, consideration of their effect on the overall economy and well-being of the populace must come into play. The state may be involved in order to assure regulation of the firms in the interest of the overall social good. But too great an accumulation of economic control in the hands of the state can lead to inequities and injustices. The other extreme — little or no state control over worker-owned firms — can create parochialism or enterprise selfishness, as Yugoslavia has noticed (Hunnius 1973, p. 309). Also in a purely market-run economy, development may become severely imbalanced.

These observations point toward the need for worker-managed economies to include some synthesis of central state-planning with local ownership and flexible market-pricing. State planning prevents the irrational and inequitable allocation of goods and resources to which purely market economies are prone, while decentralized ownership and use of market for some prices prevents the tyranny and bureaucratic inefficiency to which command economies are prone. Just such a synthesis was created in Czechoslovakia during the last decade (before it was terminated by the Soviet invasion), and it seems worthy of carefuly study (Šik 1971; Bernstein and White n.d., chaps. 5 and 12). Already social planners seem to be moving in that direction in the United States (Alperovitz and Faux 1975), and one hopes more work will be done to integrate the intrafirm aspects of worker participation in management with the macroeconomic questions of planning, market, and social role of the enterprise.

SUMMARY

Efforts to humanize work have in common the movement away from minute division of labor and extreme specialization of jobs.

Some attempts also introduce participation, enlarging the employees' power vis-a-vis management.

Such participation can extend to many more issues that United States unions currently bargain about. Worker participation has, in some cases, extended up through all levels of the company to worker election of directors and company officers. Moderate forms of worker control, where power is shared on joint boards with management, also exist.

To be successful and self-sustaining, participation needs to be buttressed by at least five other elements: sharing of management level information, guaranteed individual rights, an independent appeals system, a complex participatory-democratic consciousness, and a guaranteed economic return of surplus produced above the employee's regular wage.

Transfer of formal ownership to the employees can, of course, facilitate democratization, but it is not absolutely necessary in the beginning, since a few central rights of ownership are appropriated by the employees within these six components of democratization. Non-private ownership can take several forms, of which worker ownership is merely one. Each form needs to be examined for its consequences not only to worker self-management, but also to the community-service obligations of the firm.

NOTES

1. Consideration of *external* factors necessary for or helpful to democratization is a vast subject all its own. The reader may find discussion of that as theory in Vanek (1970; 1971) and as practice in Hunnius (1973) and Bettelheim (1974).
2. These categories are by nature overlapping, for employee activity is also a means to company ends. The arrangement of issues as though on one continuum is subject to controversy and is meant only as an approximation. Some firms might place choice of product (item 10 in this version) in the category of company goals, not merely a means to the goal of profit. Other companies might regard expansion as a higher goal than profit, as John Kenneth Galbraith and others have argued. The ordering of issues presented here is merely illustrative of the dimension. It was settled upon after consultation with labor union officials and professional business managers who replied to questions concerning how consequential each issue was to the company and its members.
3. Successful performance was defined according to these four criteria: (1) The enterprise had to demonstrate economic viability over a minimum of five years; (2) the system of participatory management had to prove itself self-sustaining and self-reinforcing (in cybernetic terms); (3) the organization's decision-making had to function so that managers were held accountable to (and sometimes were removable by) the managed; and (4) overall effect of working in this organization moved

one toward a more humanizing rather than dehumanizing experience. For elaboration see Bernstein (1976, chap. 1 and pt. 2).

4. These elements, as do the six discussed in the present article, all relate to the internal life of the firm, as mentioned earlier. They are discussed in Bernstein (1976, chap. 1).

5. Several socialist economies have found interfirm competition to be a valuable mechanism for discouraging wasteful use of resources, so it is by no means an automatic assumption that worker control means the complete elimination of a market mechanism. At the same time, these countries' experience also demonstrates the usefulness of the overall planning to tame and supplement interfirm competition in the interest of other needs (Šik 1971).

6. Where the total body of employees is the final tribunal, one might anticipate its decisions being biased consistently in favor of the managed. In practice, this does not appear to be so serious a problem, because the infractions to be decided are often ones that hurt the entire collective, not just management. The collective, from its own perspective, will not automatically side with the individual employee if the facts indicate he has broken one of their important rules (Berman 1967; chap. 7).

7. William Dunn (1973) speaks of the democratized enterprise having *sociocultural* goals in addition to the economic goals expected of conventional enterprises. Related to this is the perspective that employees are not merely a means to the achievement of the organization's economic goals, but that the employees are themselves one goal of the organization's process, namely, the greater humanization or self-realization of the members.

8. Although this may sound no different from Lenin's "democratic centralism," it appears different in practice. The cases cited are producer cooperatives inspected directly by the author as well as a worker-owned firm closely studied in Great Britain. Neither case exhibits the harshness, the intense bureaucratization, or the denial of individual members' rights that characterize democratic centralist organizations founded on the Leninist model, such as the Communist parties of the Soviet Union, Eastern Europe, or France.

9. That way, the surplus is distributed before it accumulates. The company does not increase sales to enlarge profits, nor does it lay off workers to reduce costs (which it could do, now that each worker is more productive). Rather, as soon as workers reach their old baseline of productivity within each time period, they are free to leave work and still be paid for that time. So they experience receiving a surplus, although the company treasury does not pay out any extra currency.

10. This is not to say that the return should never be tied to profits. It can and indeed must be if the sphere of control exercised by the participants is the entire policy of the firm (that is, up through level 16 on dimension 2 and some version of form 7 on dimension 1). In both cases, the principle being followed is that the source of the return is commensurate with the range of control exercised by the participants.

11. Worker appropriation of the management function from the owner is, of course, facilitated by the prior historical divergence of management from ownership first noted and analyzed by Adolf Berle and Gardiner Means in the 1930s.

Part 2

ORGANIZATIONAL DEMOCRACY AND THE INDIVIDUAL

Introduction to Part 2

In his review of the literature on workplace participation more than a decade ago, Blumberg concluded that increases in workers' influence in decision-making led to greater job satisfaction and lessened apathy and alienation. For this reason, expanding the sphere of worker participation is often shown to reduce employee absenteeism, turnover, grievances, strikes, and other indications of worker dissatisfaction (Blumberg 1973; HEW 1973). The contributions in this section confirm this participation hypothesis while offering important qualifications to it.

These chapters explore the relationship between democratic organizations and the individuals in them. Taken together, they indicate that powerful psychological and social rewards accrue to participants in democratic organizations, but they suggest important psychological costs as well.

Schlesinger and Bart, in their study of a feminist abortion collective, show that members gain an increasing sense of autonomy, competence, and personal identity. Russell likewise shows the connection between workplace control and job satisfaction, even in refuse collection, an occupation many consider "dirty."

The major psychological costs of egalitarian workplaces are that they may actually increase interpersonal friction, and they may demand more of a commitment to the job than many members are willing to make. Organizational democracy means that members have to spend time attending meetings, and it involves members in more conflicts with coworkers than does bureaucracy. Mansbridge compares the group process in a democratically managed crisis center and hotline with that in democratic town meetings. Both reveal fears of conflict grounded in their experience. (Similar conflicts can also be seen in some of the collectivist workplaces described in sec. 4).

Traditionally, ownership of organizations has conferred certain control rights. This is the case in conventional business as well as in producer cooperatives. However, ownership and control can be separated.

They are separated in the pure model of self-management, where workers exercise control but not legal ownership. Instead, ownership may be vested in the community, the municipality, a nonprofit corporation, or some other legal entity. It is even possible that nobody would own the self-managed organization, but that it would be held in trust for future generations. The right to participate in organizational decisions can be based on the contribution of one's labor to the work process, rather than on the ownership of shares. Leading examples of this model are provided by the Mondragón cooperatives and by the self-managed network of Breman enterprises in Holland.[1] On the other side of the coin, we can see quite clearly from the piece by Hammer, Stern and Gurdon that worker ownership of stock is not sufficient to guarantee democratic control.

NOTES

1. For a description of the Breman system of self-management, see Joyce Rothschild-Whitt, "There's more than one way to run a democratic enterprise: a case from The Netherlands," *Sociology of Work and Occupations,* 1981.

3

Workers' Ownership and Attitudes Towards Participation

Tove Helland Hammer
Robert N. Stern
Michael A. Gurdon

WORKER CONTROL AND WORKER OWNERSHIP

The philosophy and legal structure of a capitalist economy pro-
ide that the control over a business enterprise and its assets belongs to
its owners. In the traditional organization, this means that the powers
of decision-making rest solely with those who have put up the capital
for the venture or with their representatives, the management. The
workers, of course, are generally not the owners. In principle, they
have put their labor up for hire and signed over the rights of discretionary decision-making to management.

While most workers have no proprietary claim to control over
the production process and its results, they have nevertheless, over
time, gained a certain amount of influence over various aspects of
company management. Through collective bargaining, about one-
quarter of the American work force has gained some say over issues
such as wages, hours of work, fringe benefits, and pensions. In a

Tove Helland Hammer is Assistant Professor of Organizational Behavior, New York
State School of Industrial and Labor Relations, Cornell University. She received her
Ph.D. in Organizational and Social Psychology in 1973 from the Department of
Psychology at the University of Maryland. Dr. Hammer's current research interests
and activities include organizational careers, effects of unions on worker reactions,
and forms of industrial democracy.

Robert N. Stern is Associate Professor of Organizational Behavior, New York State
School of Industrial and Labor Relations, Cornell University. He is currently doing
research on worker representation on corporate boards of directors in the United
States.

Michael A. Gurdon is Assistant Professor, Business School, University of Vermont,
Burlington. He is currently doing research on organizational governance issues,
nontraditional union activities, the impact of regulation on the concentration of
ownership in industry, and the effectiveness of small-scale technology.

number of European countries, the power of the nonowning worker has been extended further by law to include membership on company governing boards, and participation in works councils and shop-floor committees. Since the 1950s, there has been a steady increase in the redistribution of power within organizations as companies have chosen, without legal inducements, to institute different forms of participative management schemes (Dachler and Wilpert 1978; Davis and Cherns 1975).

These forms of labor-management power sharing have some built-in instabilities which make for a certain frailty in any industrial democracy which derives from them. Where worker participation occurs in the absence of legal support, the powers of decision-making granted to the workers can always be retracted at the owner's or management's discretion. Even where a formal legal system of worker participation exists within or outside the collective bargaining process, there are no guarantees that workers will be able to exercise real power or to experience actual joint decision-making. Labor unions vary in strength, which means that they differ in the extent to which they control the outcomes of a bargaining process; worker members on boards of directors also differ in their ability to function effectively as representatives of workers' interests (Brannen et al. 1976).

Worker participation in management has long been promoted by some schools of organizational researchers, and power holders have been warned about the adverse effects of authoritarian organizational systems. The consequences run the gamut from impaired psychological health of individual workers through organizational ineffectiveness and national economic decline to the instability of the political suprasystem. Organizational psychologists from the human relations school up to the quality-of-working-life movement have argued with persistence that self-governance and worker participation in organizational decision-making are crucial ingredients in job satisfaction, motivation, and work performance as well as in the psychological growth and development of the worker (Argyris 1964; Hackman 1975; Herzberg 1966; Maslow 1954; Lawler 1977; Likert 1961). Similarly, worker influence in the production process and in the operations of the immediate work environment continues to be a central feature in sociotechnical theory and job redesign (Herbst 1976; Emery and Thorsrud 1976; Trist 1963; Wild 1976). Worker autonomy and collaborative management at all levels of the organization have been suggested as possible cures for the lack of worker commitment to the organization and its goals, alienation from the work itself, and declining motivational levels which adversely affect organizational effectiveness and national economic growth (HEW 1973; *The Conference Board Report* 1971).

There is considerable debate about the soundness of these propositions, however, and rational as well as empirical doubts about the ability to create a satisfied, committed, nonalienated, and productive work force by focusing solely on the redistribution of control in organizations are often expressed (Bernstein 1976; Locke and Schweiger 1978). The issue of control may be only one factor in a complicated network of conditions necessary to reach a desirable end-state. In Marxian theory, the crucial factor is not who governs, but who owns. Without ownership of the means of production, true control of the production process and its outcomes does not rest with the worker, and it is the objective and subjective experience of ownership itself which returns the worker as an individual to the execution of the work.

Whether worker ownership is a necessary condition for worker control is an empirical question, as is the issue of whether worker ownership leads to a committed, satisfied, productive work force. The research available on worker ownership in the United States, done mostly among producers' cooperatives, has focused primarily on the internal organizational structures and functions, not on the work behavior and the affective responses to the workplace by the owners (Berman 1967; chap. 7; Bernstein 1976). However, a new form of worker ownership has recently emerged in the United States and Canada which has provided the opportunity to empirically examine the effects of ownership on some of the variables which, according to theoretical propositions, should be positively influenced by both ownership and control. In this chapter, we will take a closer look at ownership and its relationship to workers' perceptions of their control in the organization, organizational commitment, alienation from work, and job satisfaction.

THE WORKER-MANAGEMENT-COMMUNITY-OWNED FIRM

As a result of corporate divestitures, several small to medium-size companies have faced complete plant closures in recent years. In some of these instances, unemployment has been avoided through the purchase of the plants including equipment and inventories by employees and members of the surrounding communities (Stern and Hammer 1978). The capital necessary for the successful acquisition of a plant scheduled for shutdown has been raised by a combination of governmental loan assistance, bank loans, and stock sales to workers, managers, and people in the community. Ownership takes the form of stockholding. Since the decision to purchase the firm has been left to the individual employee, these firms generally contain members who buy very different numbers of shares, including some workers who do not buy shares at all. This form of worker ownership differs substantially from that found in producers cooperatives (Berman 1967; chap. 7), where each worker has contributed an equal share towards the capital assets of the firm, and has one vote in the decision-making process. In the current employee-owned firm, few formal procedures have been made for power-sharing among the worker and manager owners, and voting on stockholder issues is based solely on the number of shares held by each person.

Stock Ownership — Does It Affect the Relationship between the Worker and the Work?

A longstanding argument holds that stock ownership in general creates a positive working relationship between employees and the employer (Webb 1912; Williams 1913). Common ownership results in common interests and commitment to the shared goal of organizational success (Lawler 1977) which, as we mentioned earlier, are seen as essential ingredients in worker motivation and effectiveness. If we look at the new employee-owned firm within this framework, we can postulate that some form of psychological partnership should develop between the owners which will lead individuals to act in behalf of the common good. From a Marxian perspective, this form of financial ownership could be seen as one which will remove the alienation from his work experienced by the worker, as well as the alienation felt from the larger political suprasystem.

Whether joint labor-management ownership of conventional stock is a sufficient condition for democratic control over the organization's decision-making process has been doubted by advocates of self-management such as Bernstein (1976), Johnson and Whyte (chap. 8), and Vanek (1975). Stock ownership in itself does not necessarily bring with it power-sharing, and a failure to gain increased influence may detract from the hypothesized benefits of common ownership interests. As a case in point, research by Israel (1971) suggests that, unless workers see themselves as owners in a business venture, the positive effects of ownership on alienation will simply not be realized.

Owners are assumed to benefit from their ownership status. In the traditional capitalist firm, with ownership diffused among a large number of stockholders, the owners benefit financially through returns of their investment. In the producer cooperatives where an equitable distribution of the profits is designed into the original charter of the company, and where owners exercise their control right in a one person-one vote manner, it is clear that each person benefits both financially and in terms of influence over organizational affairs. In the joint labor-management owned firm, the issue of who benefits from ownership is a bit more complex. The initial benefit occurring from the purchase of the firm is continued employment. While there may be additional benefits coming later in the form of direct returns on investments if the company remains successful and grows, the initial benefit has been gained by all employees, regardless of whether they contributed to the purchase. Since everybody benefited independently of his degree of ownership in these firms, it is of interest to examine a possible differential effect of ownership by the actual workers or by the collective. If everybody perceives himself as benefitting from the "indivisible good" (Olson 1968), then the differential effects of ownership predicted on worker behaviors and affective reactions may not be as strong.

In summary, there is theoretical support for the hypothesis that joint labor-management ownership will favorably affect worker commitment to the organization and its goals, and that it will reduce alienation from work if workers feel that they are the true owners of the enterprise. It is not clear whether financial ownership will be accompanied by worker control and influence, however; nor is it clear to what extent the benefits of employee ownership are diffused throughout the collectivity or if they rest only with the actual owners.

OWNERSHIP — THE STATUS AS AN OWNER OR THE AMOUNT OWNED

When workers become owners through the purchase of stock, it seems logical to argue that, the more stock a person owns, the more committed he or she should be to organizational success, and the more responsibility he should feel for the welfare of the company. The worker shareholders should also feel a stronger sense of personal ownership and a stronger feeling of having power in the firm because they have greater capital equity vis-á-vis their financial partners in management.

Ownership, however, is not necessarily reflected only in terms of the amount of capital invested. In the joint effort to purchase a firm, the act of buying stock may be more important than the actual amount purchased. Research by Long (1977) and Gurdon (1978) suggests that the ownership status *per se* is more important in determining worker owners' attitudes towards their company than is the number of shares held. Traditional class analysis has placed owners in a single group without differentiating among degrees of ownership, and Marxian theory would suggest that it is the ownership status itself which creates positive consequences for both the worker and the organization.

Given these theoretical discrepancies in the effects of differentiating among degrees of ownership, it is important to examine both the amount of stock owned by members in these organizations and ownership status *per se.*

EMPLOYEE OWNERSHIP AND OCCUPATIONAL INTEREST GROUPS

Any work organization with a rudimentary division of labor contains different occupational interest groups. The classic division has always been between labor and management, although blue-collar, white-collar, and managerial levels provide a more accurate specification of occupational interests because each group has a different response to its organization and work environment (Finifter 1972; Warner and Low 1947).

In the cases of employee ownership we have studied, the desire to save jobs has been the only motivation, and there has been little, if any, attention paid by the new worker-owners to the larger philosophical issues of ownership and governance (Stern and Hammer 1978). The basic division of labor has remained, the work process has gone unchanged, and the only factor which differentiates these firms from the traditional organization with its competitive and often adversary relationship between the various interest groups is the joint financial partnership. The question of particular concern in these organizations is whether the employee owners in the different occupational groups have managed to translate their joint economic risk into a perception of themselves as a collectivity of owners or whether barriers remain among occupational interest groups.

If ownership overcomes occupational interests of historical standing, then we may expect convergence on the definition of common goals and a strong commitment to attaining these goals, which would equally benefit all owners. If interest-group membership is stronger than the membership in a collective of owners, we can expect some divergence on the definition of organizational actions for the common good. Such a divergence implies internal conflict which can certainly interfere with the progress towards classless, democratically managed organizations. Whenever we examine the effects of joint labor-management ownership in forms which have no ideological foundation except economic success, the occupational-interest-group structure is a variable which may not be ignored.

In the remainder of this chapter, we will examine these issues empirically, drawing on data from two of the employee-owned firms in which we have conducted our research for the past two years.

ORIGINS OF EMPLOYEE OWNERSHIP IN TWO COMPANIES

The Community Furniture Company (CF)[1] opened as a community-employee owned firm in September 1976. It had previously been owned by a conglomerate corporation predominantly involved in high-speed electronic equipment. The conglomerate owned this small furniture factory as a result of a series of acquisitions and mergers which occurred during the hundred-year history of CF, and it was simply the last in a long line of owners. CF was not in the same industry as most of the conglomerate's investments, and returns on investment in furniture manufacture were well below those in electronics. A decision was made at corporate headquarters to close down CF. Rumors of a prospective closing had circulated in the community for some time, and, on 29 March 1976, an announcement of closing was made. The potential impact on a community which already had a higher than average unemployment rate was devastating. Through a series of complex alliances and political pressure, an agreement was reached with the corporate owner to sell to a newly formed local corporation. However, six million dollars needed to be raised for the purchase.

Of this, $2 million were raised through local bank loans which were contingent upon a $2 million loan from the federal government. This loan was, in turn, dependent upon raising $1.9 million in local capital. A community stock sale ensued in which the required funds were raised, despite formidable obstacles, at the last possible moment. The ownership was widely distributed among 3,500 shareholders living within fifty miles of the plant. In a three-town area of 21,000 people, this distribution represented considerable community involvement. Approximately one-third of the stock was held by employees and the rest by other community members.

CF itself employs about 170 people locally and maintains a staff of 50 salesmen around the United States. The plant manufactures high quality, special-order furniture which requires skilled craftsmen and machine operators. Of the local 170 employees, 28 are supervisors or higher level managers. Nonsupervisory employees are represented by two local unions of the same international, one representing the production workers, and the other, office and clerical staff.

The Tricot Knitting Mill (TKM) is a knitting, dyeing, and finishing plant which produces high quality fabric for the lingerie market. It is located in a small community of 25,000 people. It was a highly successful operation when it was bought by a large conglomerate, also in the garment-manufacturing business, in the late 1960s, but the effects of changing business policies brought about by the absentee owner as well as conglomerate mismanagement turned it into a money-losing division for the parent corporation. However, TKM had managed to operate at a profit in every year under the corporate ownership with the exception of 1974 when it had to operate at only half capacity. In the spring of 1975, the conglomerate owner decided to sell the plant. When a buyer had not been found within a few weeks, it was decided to close down the plant entirely.

A short time after the closure was announced, community business leaders, plant employees, and a business entrepreneur with experience in the manufacture of ladies undergarments joined forces to secure $600,000 in bank loans and $150,000 through the sale of stock. At the time of the closure decision, only 70 employees were still with the firm, and the majority bought over two-thirds of the stock. Twenty-six local businessmen contributed to a "save the TKM" campaign, buying 30 percent of the stock, and the company was again an independent operation in June 1975. It very quickly regained its financial footing by developing a small set of clients and returning to its original business practices of producing only high quality merchandise, and it now holds 2 percent of the nylon market in the United States. Returns to higher levels of profitability led to expansion and hiring previously laid-off workers as well as new people.

With 140 employees, this had meant that a majority of those now working in the plant are nonowners. To ensure a wider distribution of stock among the employees, an employee stock ownership plan (ESOP) has been introduced, designed to give pension benefits to all employees, and voting rights to the nonowners after a vesting period. The plant is not unionized.

METHODOLOGY

While the two plants described here are both considered "employee-owned firms" and share a number of common features, there are differences between them in occupational structures (TKM has a negligible white-collar staff), unionization, spread of stock ownership throughout the plants and their respective communities. These differences make it difficult to compare the two plants on all dimensions of empirical interest. We will, therefore, concentrate our data presentation most heavily on the Community Furniture Company, and supplement our findings from this factory with data from the knitting mill.

In both plants, information was collected about the historical background of the firm, interviews were held with employees at different orgranizational levels as well as with community leaders involved in the purchase efforts, and surveys were administered to all managerial and nonmanagerial workers. It is the survey data which will be discussed in relationship to the theoretical issues of ownership, control, commitment, alienation, and job satisfaction.

In May 1977, surveys were administered to the employees at CF, while similar surveys were carried out at TKM in June 1976 and June 1977. In all instances, we administered the surveys on company time. The description of the specific measures used comes from the research done in CF. A more complete discussion of the data collection in CF can be found in Hammer and Stern (1980) while assessment information about TKM is available in Gurdon (1978).

Independent Variables

The theoretical issues concerning ownership and control raised in the introduction of this chapter suggest that we examine the relationships between work-related attitudes and three different independent variables. The first factor is the amount of financial risk or the stake an employee has in the firm. If the financial aspects of ownership, including the voting control which comes to stockholders, are crucial in understanding the meaning of employee ownership, then the actual amount of stock a person owns should be associated with work-related attitudes. As we suggested earlier, Marxian theory would postulate negative relationships between financial ownership and experienced alienation. Commitment to the firm should also follow from ownership, not only because ownership is hypothesized as leading to common goals for organizational welfare, but also because the action taken to purchase stock can be interpreted by the employee as an indication that he or she is indeed committed to the firm and its survival (Salancik 1977). If we follow the traditional psychological model of job satisfaction exemplified in Expectancy theory (Vroom 1964), then the positive outcomes of ownership, such as returns on investments in the job, should allow us to suggest a positive relationship between financial ownership and job satisfaction.

We measured *financial ownership* as the number of shares an employee owned in the company.

There is a second factor which must be considered, however. Ownership itself may be more important than the actual amount of financial investment. Two opposing theoretical concerns lead us to this thought. Ownership may create common or class interests which separate owners from nonowners, and, if this is the case, we would expect these differences to be reflected in the work attitudes. On the other hand, it is possible that employee ownership creates a work place which is viewed as a collective good (Olsen 1968). If nonowners benefit from working in an employee-owned firm without actually becoming owners, then we should find very little difference between the two groups in their reactions to their work place and work situation.

In order to assess the impact of becoming an employee owner, we dichotomized the samples in the two firms into groups consisting of those who owned stock and those who did not.

The third issue of importance when we examine work attitudes is occupational-interest group. It is possible that, despite a change in the pattern of ownership, traditional occupational interests may be sufficiently strong to overcome a sense of common interests and goals. In a great many organizational studies, hierarchical position has been related to the distribution of power and influence, rewards, and work attitudes. Ownership *per se* may not eliminate such differences among occupational groups. We therefore classified employees into the following four groups based on their job titles and descriptions: (1) production or blue-collar workers; (2) office or white-collar workers; (3) middle managers; and (4) top managers.

Work-Related Attitude Measures

Employees' reactions to ownership and to the firm as well as their attitudes towards work were assessed in five conceptual clusters. All measures consisted of items using six-point, verbally anchored scales.

Sense of Ownership. The sense of ownership was measured by two items. One concerned the degree to which each person felt he or she actually owned the firm, and the other asked about the degree of ownership felt by employees as a group. Similar measures were used in both plants.

Sense of Control. The extent to which the employees had a sense of control over what happened in the organization and what happened to its assets was measured in two ways. First, we asked how much each person felt he or she benefited from the ownership of the company, using a one-item scale. Then we used a five-item scale to assess employees' beliefs that they had a right to participate in the company's decision-making process and a right to some say in the plant. Examples of the items included in this scale are: "Employees now participate in major decisions concerning their work," and "Employees have a right to more say in company decisions because they own shares." The reliability of this scale was .79 estimated by the Spearman-Brown formula (Nunnally 1967). Sense of control was also assessed among the workers in TKM in terms of their perceived participation and influence in company decisions.

Job Satisfaction. Job satisfaction was measured by the General Motors Faces Scale (Kunin 1955). This scale consists of six faces ranging from a broadly grinning to a deeply frowning one, and the employee was asked to put an X under the face which best described his or her feeling about the job. In TKM, job satisfaction was measured with a three-item scale consisting of questions about the extent to which people liked their job. Scale reliability here was .84.

Commitment. In CF, we used two measures to assess worker commitment. First, we measured commitment to the organization itself using two items which asked: "How willing would you be to walk the extra mile for the CF these days?" and "If you could get a job elsewhere, how likely would you be to leave?" The estimate of internal consistency for this scale was .79. The second measure concerned more personal responsibility for events in the company. Again, we used a two-item scale whose items were: "I feel personally more concerned with the financial condition of the CF now." The reliability estimate for this scale was .80. Again, the operational definition of commitment was slightly different in the TKM case, where we used a scale developed by Flanders, Pomeranz, and Woodward (1968) that tapped some of the elements used in the CF plant. This scale had high internal consistency reliability as well (.90).

Alienation. To measure alienation from the work itself and alienation from the larger political system, we used two scales developed by Miller (1967) and Olsen (1969). The work alienation scale had five items which dealt with dislike for the work, the lack of pride and accomplishment, and opportunities to do jobs at which one was good. Its reliability was .82. The political alienation scale consisted of four items which all concerned the individual's helplessness and lack of influence vis-á-vis public officials and the government. This scale had a reliability of .77. Only work alienation was assessed in the textile factory, where a seven-item scale similar to the Miller scale was used. Its reliability was .75.

EMPLOYEE OWNERSHIP AND
WORK-RELATED ATTITUDES: RESULTS

Financial Risk

Individuals who hold shares in a company take a financial risk in proportion to the number of shares they hold and the importance of the investment to their overall financial status. Without accurate information concerning personal income, the best available estimate of someone's resources is his or her occupational status. In the present cases, based on information obtained from local union contracts and interviews, wages and salaries apparently correspond to hierarchial level in the organization. Thus, the relationship between financial investment and attitudes toward the employee-owned company were examined for all owners and for owners at each occupational level whenever possible.

When we examine the results from the furniture factory, we find that the number of shares owned by individual employees has only a weak relationship to work-related attitudes. Those who bought more shares of stock do express somewhat greater feelings of ownership ($r = .26$, $p < .001$) and slightly greater perceptions of self benefit ($r = .16$, $p < .03$). They also express greater levels of commitment both to the organization ($r = .25$, $p < .001$) and on a personal level ($r = .14$, $p < .05$), but the amount of stock owned is unrelated to satisfaction,

TABLE 3.1

COMPARISON OF OWNERS AND NONOWNERS ON PERCEPTIONS OF OWNERSHIP, CONTROL, AND ALIENATION FROM WORK

	Community Furniture Company (CF)			Tricot Knitting Mill (TKM)	
	All Owners and Nonowners	*Production* Owners and Nonowners	*Office* Owners and Nonowners	*All* Owners and Nonowners	*Production* Owners and Nonowners
Sense of ownership					
Individual	1977 +[a]	0	+	1977 +	0
Employees as a group	1977 0	0	0		
Sense of Control					
Feelings of control	1977 0	0	0	1976 +, 1977 +	1976 0, 1977 0
Self benefit of ownership	1977 0	0	0		
Commitment					
Organizational	1977 +	+	0	1976 +, 1977 +	1976 0, 1977 0
Personal	1977 +	+	0		
Alienation					
From work	1977 −	−	0	1976 −, 1977 −	1976 −, 1977 −
From the political system	1977 0	0	0		
Job satisfaction	1977 0	0	−	1976 +, 1977 +	1976 +, 1977 0

a. Comparisons are made between the first group (owners) and the second group (nonowners) for each set of data. "+" indicates that the score for the owners is significantly higher than the nonowners using a difference of means t-test. "−" indicates a significantly lower score, and "0" means no difference at $p < .05$.

alienation or feelings of control. The weakness of these relationships is reinforced when we examine them separately for each occupational group, because then the correlations between amount of stock owned and work related attitudes are no longer statistically significant at the .05 level for any dimension.

These results tend to suggest that the effects of becoming an employee owner are not reflected in the amount of financial stake involved. We must look to the idea of ownership itself to find out whether becoming an employee shareholder really differentiates individuals.

Ownership Status

In table 3.1, we present a comparison between owners and non-owners on the five attitude clusters. If we examine the findings from the total samples of employees, we see some differences between the groups. Those who own stock have a greater feeling of ownership as one might expect, and they feel more committed to the organization. They are also less alienated from their work than the nonowners. However, when we look at the issue of the sense or feeling of control and self-benefit from ownership, we find no group differences in the furniture company, but more perception of individual control over the firm among the owners in the textile mill. There is also a different pattern of responses to satisfaction with the job among owners and nonowners in the two plants. These plant differences came about because of a difference in ownership structure in the factories. In TKM, a much higher proportion of owners were managers (40 percent versus 20 percent in CF), and these data reinforce the need to examine reactions to employee ownership among different occupational subgroups in the organization.

In both plants, all managers purchased stock, so occupational-group comparisons were only possible for the nonmanagerial personnel. In CF, this means production workers and office workers, and, since TKM had a very small group of clerical workers, only data from the production workers are presented here. Among production workers in the two plants, only the difference in alienation remains between owners and nonowners, while CF production worker-owners only show more commitment to the organization. An initial difference in job satisfaction among the blue-collar workers in TKM has disappeared a year after ownership. It is worth noting that production worker-owners feel no greater sense of individual ownership than their fellow workers who did not buy stock.

Among the office workers, we see a slightly different pattern of results, in the sense that perceptions of self-ownership are higher among owners, but these same owners express a lower level of job satisfaction than the workers who did not purchase shares. This lower level of job satisfaction seems curious, but, coupled with research on white-collar workers and information about what really happened in the case of CF, it provides a clue to understanding some of the effects of employee ownership. White-collar workers are often described as caught between managerial and production workers. They have identified with management in the past (Blum 1971) as they have similar levels of education and often have aspirations to enter management ranks. In effect, office workers often believe that they should be part of management. This identification may occur despite the general trend toward proletarianization of clerical workers (Braverman 1974; Glenn and Feldberg 1977).

The data show that becoming owners does give white-collar workers a sense of ownership, but does not distinguish them from nonowners in terms of control, benefit, or commitment. They are owners, but they have not benefited from that ownership in accordance with their expectations (Hammer and Stern 1980). As a result, they are relatively deprived compared with other employees and they indicate a low level of job satisfaction. Production workers do not feel similar deprivation because their class position prior to ownership was not ambiguous.

It is more difficult to argue that work alienation is reduced by ownership, however. Employee owners express lower levels of work alienation, but we cannot say whether this is due to their ownership status or whether those with lesser degrees of alienation may have been more interested in the company in the first place and therefore bought stock in it.

Alienation from work is thought to stem from lack of control over the work process and product and from feelings that the work is meaningless (Israel 1971). The commitment and control scales asked about these concepts in connection with employee ownership, and we find that these are correlated with alienation. Among all employees, the correlation between work alienation and feelings of control is .22 ($p < .01$); with organizational commitment, the correlation is .33 ($p < .001$), and, with personal commitment, it is .45 ($p < .001$).[2] All these relationships hold when the sample is split into production and clerical occupational-groups. Among white-collar workers, however, the relationship between alienation and control is much stronger ($r =$

.51, p < .001).

These work attitudes might be related to background character-istics. In order to be sure of the results, the relationships between the scales and tenure and education of workers in the plants were exam-ined. The average plant tenure and education of owners and non-owners are statistically the same, though stock owners tend to have worked for the company a little bit longer. Demographic characteris-tics are not significantly related to attitudes about the organization and work. There are weak negative correlations between work aliena-tion and both tenure and education. Relationships with age follow the same pattern as tenure, and differences between males and females were negligible. In all instances, correlations are low and do not modify the ownership results.

In general, the fact of ownership itself separates owners from nonowners on a number of work-related attitudes, but, on the ques-tions of "Who benefits?" and "Who controls?" as a result of owner-ship, there is no ownership effect. The response suggests that, in the type of employee-owned firm investigated here, some benefits are available regardless of ownership status.

However, there have been few changes in the administration of the plants since the conversion to employee ownership. Without changes toward power equalization, benefits of ownership do not include increased control, and traditional class divisions between labor and management should persist. Differences between individu-als based upon occupational-group membership demonstrate the maintenance of prior occupational interests rather than the creation of common feelings of ownership and control within the firm.

Occupational Interests

If the decision-making structure of the employee-owned firms has not been altered from traditional patterns, then traditional occupational-interest-group conflict between labor and management should still be apparent unless the effects of joint stock ownership are strong enough to overcome these differences. To examine the possi-ble effects of occupational interests, we divided the two ownership samples into groups based on hierarchial position, and compared group averages on each of the organizational and work-related atti-tudes discussed earlier. In the furniture factory, ownership was spread among all employees, and it was possible to divide the sample into four groups: blue-collar production workers, white-collar office workers, middle managers, and top management. In the knitting mill, with a stronger concentration of shares and fewer hierarchial levels, only two occupational groups were used: management and production workers. In table 3.2, we show the group means, while table 3.3 gives the tests of significance between scores for the six possible group comparisons. Again, the signs indicate the direction of the relationship using the first group in each pair for comparison purposes. Because the textile mill had relatively few stock owner employees (fourteen managers and twenty-two production workers), their respective mean scores are presented in parentheses in table 3.2 in the appropriate rows and columns, and only data from 1977 are given. Differences between the TKM group mean scores will be pointed out in the text, rather than in table 3.3, to make this table easier to read.

TABLE 3.2

MEAN SCORES OF OCCUPATIONAL OWNERSHIP GROUPS ON PERCEPTIONS OF OWNERSHIP, CONTROL, AND ALIENATION

	Production Workers (N=79)		Office Workers (N=29)	Middle Managers (N=14)	Top Managers (N=13)	
Sense of ownership						
Self	2.7^a	$(2.4)^b$	2.5	3.4	4.0	$(4.7)^b$
Employees as a group	3.5		3.5	3.9	4.6	
Sense of control						
Self benefit of ownership	3.3		3.6	4.0	4.4	
Feelings of control	2.8	(2.7)	2.6	2.9	3.4	(3.9)
Commitment						
Organizational	4.8	(4.2)	4.5	4.7	5.6	(4.5)
Personal	4.6		4.5	4.3	4.9	
Alienation						
From work	4.3	(4.0)	4.1	4.6	4.3	(5.0)
From political system	4.5		4.0	3.6	3.4	
Job satisfaction	4.7	(4.4)	4.1	4.6	5.2	(5.0)

a. Range on all scales is 1–6 with 1 as a low score on all measures, except work alienation, where lower score means greater alienation.

b. Scores from the textile mill, 1977. N for production workers is 22, for managers, 14.

TABLE 3.3

COMPARISON OF OCCUPATIONAL GROUPS OF OWNERS ON PERCEPTIONS OF OWNERSHIP, CONTROL, AND ALIENATION

	Production— (N=79) Office (N=29)	Production— Top (N=79) Management (N=13)	Production— Middle (N=79) Managers (N=14)	Office— Top (N=29) Managers (N=13)	Office— Middle (N=29) Managers (N=14)	Top Management—Middle (N=13) Managers (N=13)
Sense of ownership						
Self	0[a]	-	0	-	0	0
Employees as a group	0	-	0	-	0	0
Sense of control						
Self benefit of ownership	0	-	0	0	0	0
Feelings of control	0	-	0	-	0	0
Commitment						
Organizational	0	-	0	-	0	+
Personal	0	0	0	0	0	0
Alienation						
From work	0	0	0	0	-	0
From political system	0	+	+	0	0	0
Job satisfaction	+	-	0	-	0	0

a. Comparisons are made between the first group and the second for each set of data. "+" indicates that the score for the first group is significantly higher than for the second group using a difference of means t-test. "-" indicates a significantly lower score, and "0" means no difference.

Combining the data in tables 3.2 and 3.3 suggests that work attitudes in these employee-owned plants display the same patterns which could be expected in a traditional firm. With the exception of job satisfaction, which was discussed earlier, the production and office workers have the same views of the work setting. These groups comprise the traditional labor side of industrial relations. Each of them differs from the top management (those above supervisors) on most of the measures, and the results show that the management feels a greater sense of ownership, control, satisfaction, and organizational commitment (in TKM, the latter two differences are not significant, however). Similarities between the traditional antagonists only occur with regard to personal feelings of responsibility, alienation from work, and sense of self-benefit for the office workers. In addition, the traditional notion that lack of power and low education is related to disaffection with the political system is supported. Production workers express higher degrees of political alienation, are in the lowest hierarchial status in the firm, and have less education than members of the other groups. There are no differences on the work alienation scale among the groups, and their actual scores suggest that employees in these plants are generally not alienated from work (in the subjective sense).

The mean scores also suggest that there are rather high levels of commitment in the plants and relatively little sense of having control among all groups. The feeling that one is an owner in the firm has the widest range of the group means, with the labor side indicating weak sense of ownership compared with management. These weak feelings of control over matters that happen in the company appear consistent with the actual decision-making practices in both plants. The rank and file, be they owners or nonowners, are simply not included in company decision-making on a day-to-day basis, or over major, less frequently occurring issues.

The middle managers represent a group caught in an ambiguous position similar to that of office workers shown in table 3.1. They are often individuals who have been promoted from the rank-and-file labor force, but may aspire to higher status and income. Their major difficulties arise from having to carry out the wishes of top management, but doing so by exercising authority over those with whom they have worked as equals and who probably have class backgrounds similar to their own.

Their scores on the attitude measures are not significantly different from those of any other occupational group except in three rather diverse instances. They show a lower level of organizational commitment than top managers, less political alienation than production workers, but more work alienation than office workers. The means for this group always fall in the middle of the four occupations. The lack of significant patterning of results suggest the ambiguity of their status as part of both labor and management or as part of neither traditional interest.

EMPLOYEE OWNERSHIP AND WORK-RELATED ATTITUDES

The data presented here focus on the relationship between stock ownership in an employee-owned company and work-related attitudes rather than upon traditional variables such as age, job tenure, sex, and education. Both plants became employee-owned less than a year before the studies reported here began, and during that period very little was done to increase employee influence or participation in decision-making or share influence. The results suggest that changing ownership alone has had some effect on organizational commitment and felt ownership of the firm. It may also reduce alienation from work, but it is not associated with higher levels of job satisfaction, feelings of control, or benefit from the ownership itself. Given the nature of the data used in these studies, however, no more than an association between attitudes and ownership can be shown. Those who bought stock may have been different in the first place from those who did not. Among the owners themselves, most traditional labor-management differences continue to exist.

If ownership itself has only a limited ability to break down traditional occupational or class differences, then increased attention must be given to translating the new distribution of benefits from the firm and control over its decisions. Three methods of altering the control and benefit distribution seem plausible in these cases:

1. Management as Benevolent Dictator
Little changed in both CF and TKM over the first period of ownership or the time following the beginning of the studies, and the possibility that management simply does not want to share control unless forced to do so is real. On the other hand, top managers are not explicitly hostile to the idea of shared decision-making but have not really entertained the thought. To some of them, worker participation means a suggestion box.

If management did implement a participation program, it would probably suffer from the same faults as participation schemes in traditionally owned firms. We are thus faced with the bizarre situation of the legal owners of an enterprise, whose ownership provides the underlying source of legitimacy for decision-making powers, being dependent upon management for the introduction of substantive participation. The limits on participation would be carefully circumscribed and controlled. Further, employees in both plants are currently covered by an Employee Stock Ownership Plan which serves as a pension plan for them. The stock in this plan will become the largest block of shares held by a single party and, under the current plan and consistent with current law (Stern and Comstock 1978), management controls this stock. Thus, managers do have the legal apparatus and apparent desire to remain in control of the company.

There is also the possibility that most employees outside of management do not particularly want control. A number of researchers have suggested that workers actually prefer to have others who are technically competent make important decisions (e.g., Pateman 1970; Locke and Schweiger 1978). Of course, workers who have never had the opportunity to make such decisions are unlikely to be comfortable with a responsibility for which they have no practical experience.

2. Worker Education

Pateman (1970) has suggested that the lack of familiarity with participation and equality in decision-making is the reason that workers do not enthusiastically embrace the opportunity to run their own company. Real change in control requires an effort to break this cycle in which lack of control reinforces a disinterest in decision-making. Participation itself has an educative effect, but a certain amount of education is required first. The development of decision skills may occur at the initiation of management (e.g., Scanlon Plan) but seem more likely to emerge at the suggestion of those outside the firm who are interested in participation. Proposals from the union, such as in CF where workers are unionized, are also possible, but again seem unlikely given the current skepticism of labor toward employee ownership and participation. (Zwerdling 1980).

3. Stockholder Pressure

However, in CF, the union has begun to consider learning how to use the stock held by its membership to influence decisions. Under employee ownership, the potential power of voting stock in a block may be the best way to control events. At the Vermont Asbestos Group, another employee-owned firm, dissatisfied worker-owners turned their stock proxies over to a local entrepreneur who used them to overturn the board of directors which had been unresponsive to worker preferences on policy matters.

Use of stock also requires education and outside resources. Employee owners need training in the rights of shareholders and the mechanisms for exercising those rights. A union might be forced to obtain legal counsel to assure influence commensurate with the stock held by members. In addition, stock held in pension funds is a source of power over which workers may want to negotiate.

The difficulty in using stock is that workers may hold only a minority interest. They may find themselves seeking alliances with other shareholders and struggling to maintain unified voting of their members' stock. In this struggle, they may simply buckle under. Between September 1977 and June 1978 alone, for example, 18 percent of the original investors at TKM cashed in their stock, thereby abandoning their property rights, which had not led to control over the company anyway. There is little doubt, however, that the ability to use the resource of stock ownership translates into the ability to alter the orgranization's control structure and to redistribute corporate earnings.

CONCLUSION

A substantial number of employee-owned firms have appeared in the past five years (Stern and Hammer 1978), and they provide a rare opportunity to move productive activity toward a greater degree of shared power. Though ownership of shares seems to have some effect on work-related attitudes in the companies discussed here, the critical issue is clearly the control over the means of production and its product. Stock ownership itself does not provide this control, but it is a resource which may be used to create a greater degree of industrial democracy.

NOTES

1. The names of the companies have been changed to protect the anonymity of respondents.
2. Data from CF only.

4

The Rewards of Participation in the Worker-Owned Firm

Raymond Russell

In recent years, there has been growing interest around the world in various forms of workplace democracy. In the United States, one of the most common manifestations of this upsurge of interest has been a call for the establishment of worker-owned firms (e.g., Rifkin 1977).

Advocates of worker ownership often overlook a number of arguments that have been made against this strategy of workplace democratization. One old tradition, for example, questions the economic viability of worker-owned firms.[1] Another charge is that, even when these firms do succeed as businesses, they are doomed to succumb to various tendencies toward "degeneration." This degeneration takes such forms as an increasing use of a subordinate class of hired laborers and the eventual conversion of a firm by either sale or internal reorganization into a conventional, capitalist enterprise (e.g., Blumberg 1973, pp. 3-4).

A less frequent but logical question is whether these firms are of any material or psychological benefit to their owners in the first place. We know from experiments in conventional organizations that work-group autonomy and participatory management are generally associated with favorable outcomes like higher productivity and increased job satisfaction (Blumberg 1973, chaps. 2-6). But we know

Raymond Russell is Assistant Professor of Sociology, University of California, Riverside. He is currently completing studies of several other democratically organized workplaces, including taxi driver cooperatives and large law partnerships.

The research described in this article was performed while he was at the Center for Community Economic Development and the Institute for New Enterprise Development, both presently located in Cambridge, Massachusetts. Much of this research was supported by Grants MH23900 and MH28053, the Center for Studies of Metropolitan Problems of the National Institute of Mental Health.

very little about what happens when workers own and control an entire workplace. Research on American small businesses, in the meantime, suggests that self-employed workers are not a particularly well-off or happy group. Dov Eden has shown that, although self-employed Americans report somewhat better work attitudes, they score no higher on measures of mental health than do other American workers. Eden suggests that this indicates that the psychological rewards of small-business ownership are too small to justify the greater efforts it requires in the form of longer hours, more responsibility, and the like.[2]

This paper will attempt to shed light on these issues by discussing a unique and long-standing group of worker-owned firms, the scavenger companies of the San Francisco Bay area. From 1973 to 1978, I collaborated with Stewart E. Perry and Arthur Hochner on a NIMH-funded study of these firms. Perry was the first of us to make contact with the scavengers, having begun to observe San Francisco's Sunset Scavenger Company in 1966.[3] Beginning in 1973, our interviews and field observations included four additional scavenger companies that are presently or were formerly worker-owned. In 1977, these data were supplemented by home interviews with 708 Northern California refuse-collectors, of whom 165 were working partners in a total of six worker-owned firms.[4]

THE WORK OF A SCAVENGER WORKER-OWNER

The worker-owned scavenger companies of the San Francisco Bay area were created in and around the 1920s through the merger of many small and independently owned scavenger operations. The *scavengers* were immigrant refuse-collectors from Northern Italy, and took their name from the fact that they recycled a large part of the wastes they collected.

It is significant that the scavenger companies were formed through a pooling of the operations of independent small entrepreneurs, rather than as a worker buy-out of a conventional capitalist firm. For, although they lacked an explicit ideology of workplace democracy, the scavengers were used to being their own bosses, and were determined to work for no one's profit but their own. They therefore stipulated that only working scavengers could own shares in their corporations, and that no stockholder would be permitted to own more shares than any other. In addition, they set the compensation of officers equal to that of all other partners.

The scavengers have retained from their former days of independent operations an unusually direct set of ties to their customers. Each customer is still billed individually for refuse-collection service, and pays a sum proportional to the amount of services received. Many customers contract for such optional extra services as the use of keys, collection from upper floors or from basements, and janitorial services.

Thus, each scavenger partner still functions not only as a refuse collector, but as a business owner as well. Traditionally, a partner has been responsible for maintaining records about each household in his territory and for seeing that each family pays for the services it receives. In practice, this has been a complex undertaking. The records for each household have had to include such information as how much service the family has contracted for (e.g., two cans per week from a second floor apartment, three cans per week collected at streetlevel, etc.), when they go away on vacation, when they receive extra services, and so on. During the day, the partner must remember how much services a household is entitled to, and has to assess and record extra fees for any refuse that exceeds the amount. Until about ten years ago, a scavenger visited each of his customers personally to collect bills. Even today, he may still play a role in disciplining delinquent accounts. Thus, for many a scavenger, the experience of being an owner in his company begins with the sense that "you own your own route."

These proprietary duties of the scavengers appear also to have equipped them well for participation in their companies' collective decision-making apparatus. Shareholders meet monthly or quarterly to decide such matters as the admission of new shareholders, the election of officers, and various major business questions. Fully 87 percent of the partners who responded to our survey reported that they had attended most or all of the shareholders' meetings in their companies over the previous year, and 99 percent (all but two respondents) had voted in the last election of officers. Moreover, 40 percent said that they had served on the board or on some other committee of their company. Perhaps the best demonstration of the political strength of rank-and-file scavengers is the experience of Leonard Stefanelli, who, in 1965, went directly from a job on a garbage truck to the presidency of the Sunset scavengers. This change came as part of a "revolution" in which the company's entire leadership was suddenly voted out of power.[5]

Relations with Coworkers and Customers

One of the first things that strikes anyone who observes the work of the scavenger is that many of them work extremely hard. Here is how Jerry Sanders, another researcher for this project, described his effort to work alongside a scavenger crew in July 1974:[6]

> They warned me that Monday was a tough day, but I wasn't prepared for the next seven hours. . . . By daybreak I was perspiring profusely. The other men were short of breath and nearly as soaked in their sweat as I was. Despite this, they never once stopped their relentless pace. . . not a coffee break, a glass of water, nor even to relieve themselves. We worked straight through from 4:30 to 11:30 without let up! I did get one break of sorts, going to the dump with Eddie at 9, the truck loaded to the hilt with 6 tons of garbage. But even then the other men granted themselves no respite. While the driver takes the load to the dump, the other two continue "pulling out," dragging some sacks full of garbage into the street during the truck's absence. When the driver returns, he follows the trail of burlap sacks, tossing them into the hopper until he catches up with the other men.

It would probably be a mistake, however, to attribute the scavengers' hard work and fast pace simply to the effects of worker-ownership. For one thing, the scavengers, like many refuse collectors around the country, work on a so-called task-incentive system that permits them to go home as soon as their work for the day is done. In addition, the provision of carry-out rather than curbside collection places a premium on the worker's ability to carry as much as possible as quickly as possible. Carry-out collection and task-incentive systems are standard throughout the San Francisco area, and appear to evoke similarly heroic efforts from municipal and private employees as well as from scavenger worker-owners.

Another theme that appears often in field observations of scavengers at work is teamwork and cooperation. Like the level of effort they exert, much of the give-and-take among scavenger crews may be inherent in the design of their jobs. The use of carry-out collection creates built-in advantages for a crew whose members can work independently yet with a high degree of coordination, and who share the driving and loading chores. But one often observes cooperative practices on scavenger trucks that go beyond what would be expected on the basis of these job characteristics alone. For example, when Perry observed one of the last of Sunset's "open trucks" in 1966, he found that the men shared equally the messy task of standing knee-deep in wastes in the back of the truck to redistribute the load and sort out materials that could be recycled.

Another unique practice one hears about at the scavenger companies is that a crew that finishes early may voluntarily offer its help to a crew that is short a man or otherwise overworked. For example, a scavenger named Sal[7] told the following story of a time when he and his men went to the aid of a crew headed by a partner named Joe:

> Joe had requested an extra worker that day because of an unusually heavy work load and had gotten angry when he was refused. After finishing his own work for the day, Sal offered the services of his four-man crew and two trucks (an open truck and a pusher, which is more primitive than a packer), but Joe refused — he was already on his second load by then, and he was still angry.

> Sal told him, "I own your route just as much as I own my own route," and insisted on helping. Joe said OK, he could help, but he had to be sure to close all gates and replace all covers and not cross any lawns. Joe's son, Rick, took Sal to another part of the route and they finished up the work in a big hurry, but Sal laughed about all the lawns they crossed and gates they left open.

Joe's concern about closing gates and replacing garbage can lids is not unusual among scavengers. It is a matter of policy at the scavenger companies that their exclusive franchises in the communities they serve depend on their observing niceties such as these. This lesson was brought home to Sanders when a partner had to remind him twice to be more considerate of customers:

> ...Tony Luccini established himself as one of the most conscientious and fastidious workers I have ever seen anywhere. His first words to me were "Sshh. We have to hold down the talking in these residential areas at this time of day (shortly after 4:30 A.M.)."

> ...He has an obvious pride in the job and identifies fully with the company. At one point, he said to me, "Look, it's Jerry, isn't it? Jerry, if you want to work along with us, that's fine, but watch the spillage in the street when you dump your sack into the hopper." Now, my "spillage" consisted of candy wrappers and peach seeds, not watermelon rinds and beer cans. Tony ended the reprimand with a friendly, "Public relations you know. It means everything for the company. That's what makes us."

The spirit of cooperation and conscientiousness that we observed in the work of the scavengers also showed up in partners' responses to many of the questions asked in the home interview survey in 1977.

For example, scavenger partners were significantly more likely than other respondents to agree with the statement "In my company (or department), if each crew doesn't do their best, we all suffer." They were also more likely to say they make an "extra effort" on their jobs and to describe their relations with coworkers and customers as close and cooperative.[8]

Some independent validation exists for the idea that scavenger partners take unusually good care of their customers. For one thing, their direct fee-for-service relations with customers permit them to offer a range of services that no other metropolitan refuse-collection organization we know of provides. The scavengers' customers show a number of signs of being well-satisfied with this high level of service. For example, one woman who noticed Perry observing a Sunset crew volunteered, "They give such good service." One does hear an occasional story, it is true, about a householder who was treated rudely by one of the scavengers, or who felt intimidated by them. (Some people persist in thinking that, since the scavengers are Italian, they must have a Mafia connection. This is ironic, because, in their old bylaws, the Sunset scavengers cited as one of the virtues of their form of organization the fact that it is an *alternative* to racketeering in the refuse collection industry.) Perhaps the most balanced assessment of complaints against the scavengers was the following, given by a city inspector in San Francisco in 1971:

> The companies make more than 300,000 pickups a week, and we receive about thirty complaints. Of those, maybe twelve are valid. Figure it out. The scavenger companies have a damn good record when you consider that they have more contact with the public than telephone, electricity, or any other public service. Garbage collection is a delicate personal relations job.[9]

It would be helpful to be able to compare the cost efficiency of the scavengers with the performance of more conventional firms. Unfortunately, it is extremely difficult to evaluate the costs of refuse-collection services because they are a function of such highly variable factors as population density, the costs of disposal, and the kinds of service provided. Efforts to achieve some statistical control over all these factors have so far disclosed more complexities than solutions.[10] In 1970, however, the executive director of the National Solid Wastes Management Association estimated that San Francisco's scavengers provide carry-out collection for "probably the lowest charge of any major city in the United States."[11]

The Economic Rewards of Ownership

The scavengers' high productivity, coupled with their ownership of their firms, have helped to place them among the most highly paid refuse-collectors in the country. A partner in a scavenger company derives income from his firm in three different forms — annual dividends, capital gains on the sale of his shares, and wages.

The least significant role in this system of compensation is apparently played by dividends. Among the Sunset scavengers, for example, dividends have rarely amounted to more than 1-2 percent of the current value of a partner's shares. It seems that scavengers' dividends and corporate earnings have deliberately been kept low, both because company profits are regulated by the cities in which they operate and because distributed earnings are double-taxed by the Internal Revenue Service — first as corporate profits, and then as personal income. Thus, partners prefer, as much as they are permitted, to take their income as wages, which are taxed only once, rather than as dividends.

If one turns to the capital gains that partners make on the sale of their shares, Perry's data from the Sunset Scavenger Company indicate that these can be more significant. A block of shares in Sunset that cost $12,000 in 1954 had risen to $21,000 by 1966, and would bring $50,000 in 1976. This averages out as a compound rate of appreciation of 5-6 percent per year. This is a good, but not impressive, performance for a capital investment, especially given the illiquidity of the asset. If one were to evaluate share ownership in a scavenger company on these criteria alone, one could easily conclude that partners would be better off making bank deposits or buying bonds.

The size of dividends and capital gains, however, have never been the most important considerations for a refuse collector who is contemplating the purchase of a block of shares in a scavenger company. When you buy into a scavenger company, one Sunset partner told Perry, "You could say that you're buying a job." This statement is true in at least two senses. A scavenger owns his job, first of all, by virtue of the tenure his shareholding secures for him. It guarantees that he will not be fired or even laid off unless the company can prove gross dereliction on his part. Secondly, in purchasing his shares, the scavenger buys the right to earn much higher wages than he would otherwise earn as a refuse collector. In our home interviews, for example, partners reported mean 1976 incomes from wages and overtime of $22,000, while employees of conventional private firms earned $15,000, and city workers, only $12,000.[12]

Responses to Dirty Work

Another issue addressed in the interviews and field observations for this study was the impact ownership might have on the way refuse collectors feel about their occupation. Other sociologists have occasionally used the term "dirty work" to refer to tasks that a worker is especially likely to find demeaning or objectionable.[13] Refuse collection would appear to be an archetypal instance of dirty work, as it is, both literally and figuratively, "dirty." That is, in addition to being physically dirty, arduous, and often hazardous work, refuse collection is also one of the most stigmatized of American occupations. Earlier studies of American refuse collectors, as well as our own research, have documented the humiliations which are often occasioned by the demeaning stereotypes applied to this work.[14]

There are many reasons for thinking that ownership might be a valuable antidote to unfavorable views of this work. One of the findings of Eden's study of the self-employed, for example, was that self-employment appeared to provide some measure of "immunity to unsavory conditions."[15] In the scavenger companies, the content of the worker-owners' jobs appears also to offer unusual opportunities for taking pride in this work and for evoking respect from the public. The worker-owners' higher incomes may also be of value here, given the often-noted tendency for Americans to judge themselves and others on the basis of the income they can command and the goods they can consume. In addition, it is possible that the very role of owner has the power to counteract the negative connotations of the stereotype of the garbageman both in the worker-owners' and in others' perceptions of their work.[16]

Do scavenger partners, in fact, take pride in owning their companies? We received support for this idea from an unexpected source; the Juarez Scavenger Company, whose partners had recently sold their firm to a nationwide corporation. I asked a few former partners at Juarez what kind of changes had taken place in the company since the sale and how they felt about them. "It all boils down to the loss of one thing," one man immediately responded, "Pride." Another man joined in, "You had *a voice* in running the company [emphasis his]." A third, whom I asked on another occasion, began:

> I miss the meetings. . . . It was a terrific feeling to own a company at 22. . . , I used to walk out of here at night, look back at all the trucks, and say to myself, "This is mine. I own one of these trucks."

It also appears, however, that there are many distasteful aspects of this job that worker-ownership is incapable of doing much to improve. A major problem area in the work of the scavengers is the physical toll it takes. "It gets you in the back. You can't keep it up forever." At one moment, you may hear a scavenger brag about how hard he can work, but, in the next breath, he may start complaining about what it takes out of him:

> Luigi carries out his work with great vigor, obviously enjoying the physical exertion. At one point, he had me feel his biceps and told me that, on this job, "you go home feeling like a bull." Nevertheless, despite his being in good shape, he worried about wearing out, telling me he has slowed considerably from what he once was. Luigi told me that he has had numerous back injuries, but that they have rarely kept him off the job. Giuseppe, in his sign language to me, complained that the work got to his lower back, and Sal said that his back always hurts; the only difference from when he first started and now is that he has become accustomed to the discomfort.

For another scavenger, the worst thing about his job is its monotony. "Imagine doing this every day, " he suggested. "It would get pretty boring, wouldn't it?"

We also saw several indications that worker ownership does not provide immunity to the stigma of dirty work. One former scavenger, for example, told us about how his prospective mother-in-law was quite upset at the thought of her daughter marrying a garbage man. As a result of several rows this man had with customers, he ultimately lost his job as a scavenger. When I last spoke to him, he was studying to be a mortician, which he feels is "a cleaner job than collecting garbage." Another scavenger told Perry he sometimes feels that "People don't want to have anything to do with you. . . . Maybe it is all in my head, but it seems like they go to the other side of the street if they see you coming."

Several aspects of the impact of worker-ownership on job satisfaction and well-being were probed in the interview survey of Northern California refuse collectors conducted in 1977.[17] Scavenger partners did tend to ascribe higher status[18] to their work than did other respondents, and also scored higher on one important indicator of job satisfaction, the likelihood that they would choose this occupation again if they were starting their work life over again. In general, however, partners did not seem to find their work any cleaner or less physically objectionable than did the other respondents.[19] Partners also performed no better than other respondents on measures of self-esteem or on any other aspect of emotional health. In fact, they were *more* likely than other respondents to show symptoms of anxiety and hostility.

It is unclear what should be made of this latter finding. Partners' higher incidence of tension and irritation may be a longstanding by-product of the responsibilities and risks of business ownership. On the other hand, it may be a response to some more recent events that have threatened the futures of these firms. Many of these developments have centered around the role of hired laborers within the worker-owned firms, an issue that will be explored in detail in the following section.

HIRED LABORERS IN THE SCAVENGER COMPANIES

For a generation or more, the scavenger companies showed many signs of being major exceptions to the often-noted tendency for worker-owned corporations to degenerate into conventional capitalist institutions. For example, although the companies have always used some hired laborers (or "helpers" or "extra men," as the scavengers call them), the proportion of nonowners to owners in the companies was relatively stable. As business expanded and the labor force in a scavenger company grew, the number of worker-owners was often correspondingly increased. In the Sunset Scavenger Company, for example, the number of worker-owners swelled from 92 in 1920 to a peak of 320 by 1965.

As was the case in the formation of these firms, the preservation of their worker-owned structures owed little to any explicit ideology. The scavengers had quite practical reasons for increasing the number of worker-owners in their firms. In the first place, since both their profits and their wages fell under the scrutiny of regulatory bodies, the scavengers saw little opportunity to gain by exploiting the labor of other workers. At the same time, the sale of new shares often presented itself as a convenient way to raise new capital, or as a means of coping with the labor shortage brought on by World War II. More generally, the scavengers' unique work methods had been developed by independent scavenger entrepreneurs, and many of them believed that it still required a stake in the ownership of a firm to motivate a worker to discharge his duties conscientiously. According to the 1934 Sunset bylaws, for example, the company founders

> realized that the success of their common undertaking...was impossible unless...each associate or employee was a boss scav-

enger, for it was not to be expected that a hired scavenger would work as well and as willingly as one who is a shareholder. . . .

In these same bylaws, helpers are referred to not as hired hands, but as "apprentices or novices," who have entered the company "not for the salary, but for the opportunity of becoming a boss scavenger after they have become tried and experienced scavengers." Many current partners learned their trade while still in their early teens, working alongside fathers, uncles, brothers, or cousins who already owned shares. A helper who wanted to buy into a scavenger company would normally wait anywhere from six months to a number of years for the shares of a retiring partner to become available. Once he and an outgoing shareholder had agreed on a price for a block of shares, the helper would communicate to the board of directors his desire to purchase them. If the board and a majority of the partners approved, he would be in.

In the 1950s and sixties, a number of changes began to exert a disruptive influence on the scavengers' traditional ways of doing business. Increasing volume, new technology, and disposal problems all called for new infusions of capital into the companies. This, in turn, both made possible and appeared to require a reduction in labor costs. The scavengers accomplished this reduction by centralizing the companies' record-keeping and bill-collecting procedures, which permitted many partners to be transferred off their residential routes. In some cases, these partners' jobs were eliminated entirely; in others, they were replaced with cheaper, hired labor.

For partners, these developments constituted an unsettling but promising set of changes in their companies. On the one hand, the introduction of packer trucks and office billing had reduced the complexity of their work, and made many of their traditional skills superfluous. But many of the tasks that disappeared (like bill collecting and recycling) had not been popular in the first place; partners who transferred off the residential routes often took more interesting jobs in the companies' newer operations, such as driving the automated trucks used to collect commercial and industrial wastes.

In addition, many partners saw that these new developments might make it possible for them to increase their returns on the capital invested in their companies. In some cases, a proliferation of subsidiaries for handling their newer operations presented partners with new and less closely regulated sources of income. At the same time, some aggressive new nationwide *agglomerates* began to turn the entire field of solid waste management into a glamour industry in the eyes of Wall Street. Two smaller scavenger companies quickly sold out to one of these corporations. Other scavenger companies formed agglomerates of their own and began buying up smaller firms in the surrounding areas before the agglomerates beat them to it.

Thus, by the early 1970s, the scavengers had taken several giant steps toward the transformation of their companies into conventional capitalist businesses. A reduction of the skills required on residential routes had made possible an increasing use of hired laborers to do the less desirable work. At the same time, the chance to make bigger profits and capital gains had given many partners an interest in seeing that there would be "fewer ways to cut up the pie." As a result, the scavenger companies now preferred to buy back the shares of partners who retired, rather than permitting them to be sold to helpers.

For the hired laborers in these companies, these changes have constituted a major alteration in their roles. Once thought of as apprentices, helpers are now threatened with becoming a permanent class of second class citizens in a democracy of privileged workers. From their perspective, scavenger institutions now often appear to be a set of mechanisms for assigning the dirtiest jobs to the lowest status members of the organization. Helpers are also paid much less than partners, even though they often do quite similar work (in the 1977 survey, for example, helpers reported mean job incomes of $15,000 versus $22,000 for partners).

It comes as no surprise, therefore, that helpers in these companies have recently shown many signs of discontent. In April 1973, one Italian helper sued his company for not allowing him to buy the shares of his uncle, who was retiring. Later that same year, a group of black and Spanish-surnamed helpers brought a class-action suit against the two San Francisco scavenger companies, charging discrimination in hiring, promotions, and the sale of shares. The traditionally promanagement unions of the scavenger companies have also become more militant in recent years, and, in 1977, for the first time, brought San Francisco's two companies to the verge of a strike.

CONCLUSION

The record of the worker-owned scavenger companies, like that of the plywood cooperatives of the Pacific Northwest, has done much to dispel the notion that worker-managed businesses are less efficient than conventional ones. For a generation or two, these firms sustained high levels of productivity and service quality, not only without sacrificing their democratic structures, but by actively taking advantage of the strengths contained within them. Their decentralized job structures and high motivation enabled them to offer services no other type of organization would have been able to provide. Their productivity and good customer relations, in turn, gave these companies a record that many of their worker-owners could justifiably take pride in.

By 1977, however, many traditional sources of pride in the scavengers' work had begun to disappear, or were severely threatened. Their simplified work methods, for example, were now less different from those employed in other conventional organizations. Moreover, the spirit of cooperation that had formerly characterized the work of scavenger crews had been undermined by new antagonisms within the firms.

The mixed performance of the scavenger companies calls to mind many judgments that were expressed about worker-ownership in the nineteenth century. Marx, for example, while praising the "cooperative factories" for representing "within the old form the first sprouts of the new," warned that they "naturally reproduce, and must re-produce, everywhere in their actual organization all the shortcomings of the prevailing system."[20]

The English cooperator George Holyoake was also critical of many defects of worker-owned firms, but claimed that these faults are not inevitable. The problem, argued Holyoake, is that members of these firms "have no clear idea of the place of capital in them," and therefore allow it "to steal like the serpent of Eden from the outer world into the garden of partnership."[21]

Like Holyoake, the contemporary economists Jaroslav Vanek (1971, p. 10; 1975, p. 34) and David Ellerman advise workplace democrats to exercise great care in the financing of a worker-managed firm. They argue that whenever, as in the corporation, voting rights are tied to the ownership of marketable shares, members have a built-in incentive to maximize their returns on these investments by exploiting hired labor or selling off the firm. Vanek and Ellerman therefore recommend that self-managed workplaces own no assets at all, but, instead, borrow their capital in exchange for interest but no vote from sympathetic lending institutions or from their own individual members.[22]

These suggestions, unfortunately, have come too late to help the scavengers. But other developments, in the meantime, may have tempered the scavengers' enthusiasm for a hasty abandonment of their time-honored practices. The stocks of the nationwide agglomerates, for example, declined dramatically after their early boom, indicating that there are serious limits to what high finance can do for the refuse-collection business. The recent wave of lawsuits and labor disputes, too, has dramatized for many scavengers the danger of too sudden an alteration in their traditional structures. Chances are good that at least some of these firms may retain some semblance of worker-ownership for another generation or two.

NOTES

1. Two early critics of the efficiency of worker-owned firms were Sidney and Beatrice Webb—see their *Constitution for the Socialist Commonwealth* of Great Britain (Longmans, 1920), reprinted in *Worker's Control,* ed. Ken Coates and Tony Topham, rev. ed. (London: Panther Books, 1970), p. 67. The Webbs' criticisms have been effectively answered in recent empirical studies by Derek Jones, "British Producer Co-operatives," in *The New Worker Co-operatives,* ed. Ken Coates (Nottingham: Spokesman Books, 1976) and by Michael Conte and Arnold Tannenbaum, "Employee-owned companies: is the difference measurable?" *Monthly Labor Review,* 101 (July 1978): 23-28.

2. Dov Eden, "Organizational Membership vs. Self-Employment: Another Blow to the American Dream," *Organization Behavior and Human Performance,* 13 (1975), pp. 79-94. See also the Ph.D. dissertation written by the same author under the name of Barry Fine, *Comparison of Organizational Membership and Self-Employment* (University of Michigan, 1970; distributed by the National Technical Information Service, U.S. Department of Commerce).

3. See Perry (1978).

4. The methods and results of this survey are discussed in Art Hochner, "Worker Ownership and the Theory of Participation" (Ph.D. dissertation, Department of Psychology and Social Relations, Harvard University, 1978); and Raymond Russell, "Sharing Ownership in the Workplace" (Ph.D. dissertation, Department of Sociology, Harvard University, 1979).

5. The story of Leonard Stefanelli's "revolution" is told in Perry, *San Francisco Scavengers* and in Raymond Russell, Art Hochner, and Stewart E. Perry, "San Francisco's 'Scavengers' Run Their Own Firm," *Working Papers for a New Society,* 5 (Summer 1977); 30-36. For more on overall levels of participation by rank-and-file scavengers on company decision-making, see Hochner, "Worker Ownership."

6. Jerry Sanders participated in this research project during the summer of 1974. Many of his field observations were incorporated into his report "From Scavengers to Solid Waste Disposal Managers: An Ethnography of Urban Garbage Collectors" (Cambridge, Mass.: Center for Community Economic Development, 1974).

7. This name and most other names of individuals and companies that appear below have been disguised in keeping with pledges of anonymity that were made when these data were collected. The Sunset Scavenger Company and Leonard Stefanelli

have been identified by their correct names in reports of this project by their express authorization.

8. See Russell, "Sharing Ownership," chap. 4.

9. Nick Kazan, "Can Free Enterprise Speed Up Our Garbage Collection?" *New York,* 12 July 1971, p. 43.

10. See the report of the Solid Waste Management Advisory Group to the National Commission on Productivity, *Opportunities for Improving Productivity in Solid Waste Collection* (Washington, D.C.: National Commission on Productivity, 1973), and E.S. Savas, "Evaluating the Organization of Service Delivery: Solid Waste Collection and Disposal," Columbia University, Center for Government Studies, October 1975.

11. Harold Gershowitz, "League of Cities Survey is Unsoundly Drawn," *Solid Wastes Management,* 13 (1970); 48, 91.

12. In a study of the cooperative plywood companies of the Pacific Northwest, Katrina Berman (1967, p. 217; chap. 7) described the practice of paying income to stockholders in the form of wages rather than stock dividends as "crucial" for the preservation of a worker-owned structure. She explained, "Since in most companies no dividends are paid on shares, and in all the major source of income is the wage paid for work actually performed in the plant, shareholders are encouraged to remain at work in the plant. The practice also discourages the accumulation of stock by individuals...as little or no additional income will result from ownership of extra shares."

13. Everett C. Hughes, "Good People and Dirty Work," "Social Role and the Division of Labor," and "Work and the Self," all in *The Sociological Eye* (Chicago: Aldine, 1971); Erving Goffman, *The Presentation of Self in Everyday Life* (Garden City, New York: Anchor, 1959) pp. 44-46; Raymond L. Gold, "In the Basement — The Apartment-Building Janitor," in Peter L. Berger, ed., *The Human Shape of Work* (Regnery: Chicago, 1964); Lee Rainwater, "The Revolt of the Dirty Workers," *Transaction,* 5 (November 1967); 2, 64; Herbert Gans, "The Dirty Work Movement," *Social Policy,* 1 (March/April 1971); 34-35; and Hanna Meara, "Honor in Dirty Work: The Case of American Meat Cutters and Turkish Butchers," *Sociology of Work and Occupations,* 1 (August 1974); 259-283.

14. See Edward Joseph Walsh, "Job Stamina and Self-Esteem" (Ph.D. dissertation, University of Michigan, 1974), and John C. Coleman, *Blue-Collar Journal* (Philadelphia: Lippincott, 1974).

15. Fine, "Comparison," p. 99.

16. In an unpublished survey performed for this project, Joseph Dewhirst made an effort to measure the impact of ownership, income, and several job characteristics on the attributions members of the public might make about a hypothetical refuse collector. Data collected from seventy-two respondents indicated that both pay and cooperative ownership had favorable effects on people's attitudes toward members of this occupation, both independently and in interaction. See Joseph R. Dewhirst, "The Garbageman as a Stigmatized Person: An Empirical Examination of Some Possible Solutions within an Attribution Theory Framework" (1974).

17. See Russell, "Sharing Ownership," chap. 4.

18. See Russell, "Sharing Ownership," chaps. 4 and 5. Respondents' perceptions of the relative status of their occupation were measured with the help of a "job ladder" showing six occupations, ranging from shoe-shiner to physician, and

ordered according to their position on the North-Hatt index of occupational status (Robert M. Hodge, Paul W. Siegel, and Peter H. Rossi, "Occupational Prestige in the United States, 1925-1963," *American Journal of Sociology,* 70 [1964]; 386-402). This procedure was inspired by a similar method used by Edward Walsh, "Job Stigmas."

19. Job stigma was measured by questions that asked how respondents describe their occupations when they are meeting people for the first time, and whether or not they have ever been inclined to conceal their occupation from anyone.

20. Marx, *Capital,* vol. 3, p. 440; quoted in Shlomo Avineri, *The Social and Political Thought of Karl Marx* (London: Cambridge University Press), p. 180.

21. George Jacob Holyoake, *The History of Co-operation,* rev. ed. (New York: Dutton, 1906), vol. 2, p. 338.

22. David Ellerman, chap. 15; and "The 'Ownership of the Firm' is a Myth," *Organizational Democracy: Participation and Self-Management,* ed. G. David Garson and Michael P. Smith (Beverly Hills: Sage Publications, 1976), pp. 31-46.

5

Fears of Conflict in Face-to-Face Democracies

Jane J. Mansbridge

Both in the workplace and in the larger society, small communities tend to avoid conflict. Social scientists have two explanations for this. The most optimistic explanation focuses on mutual understanding. Members of a small community know each other well in many roles and can often make allowance for one potential source of conflict because of a person's or group's contributions in another area. Constant contact in a small community makes friendship easier and deeper, diminishing the incentive for conflict.

A second, less sanguine, explanation is that the very multiple relations that facilitate friendship in a small community also make conflict more threatening. A large community provides protective distance between potentially warring members. In their encounters in a large community, individuals often play only one role — salesperson or customer, Democrat or Republican, policeman or jaywalker. Conflicts in that one role do not carry over to the rest of their lives. The smaller the community, the more facets of one's personality one opens to attack, and the more difficult it is, physically and emotionally, to avoid such attack.[1]

Workplaces are usually rather small communities. Even if the enterprise is huge, an individual's own work group rarely comprises more than a hundred persons. But, in the small community of a workplace, hierarchy can duplicate the protective distance that is provided in a larger community by space, time, and a division into rarely interacting roles. While people on the same level of a hierarchy

Jane J. Mansbridge is Associate Professor of Political Science and Sociology, Northwestern University. She is the author of *Beyond Adversary Democracy* (New York: Basic Books, 1980). She is presently working on a study of the pro-ERA leadership and organization, and a philosophical examination of political equality.

come in relatively close contact in multiple relationships, people on different hierarchical levels normally interact only through one — that of supervisor and supervisee. This social distance between levels of the hierarchy allows conflictual issues, like work evaluation or demands for a raise, to be restricted to relatively brief contact. Hierarchy has a psychological function; it serves to protect individual workers from excessive contact with others on potentially adversary matters.[2]

Egalitarian organizations thus pose a problem for conflict management. Eliminating hierarchy eliminates the institutional buffer zone that otherwise protects workers from one another. Sore spots, like evaluations and the allocation of rewards, become collective crises.

The tensions raised by egalitarian contact are exacerbated when decisions are made, as they often are in alternative workplaces, in face-to-face meetings. Face-to-face assemblies provoke anxieties and tensions that rarely arise when a citizen simply walks into a voting booth and pulls a lever. In a New England community, governed by a face-to-face assembly of all the citizens — the town meeting — a young farmer told me, "I kinda dread going [to the meeting] because I know when I come home I'm going to have the worst headache I ever had, a splitting headache." In alternative organizations that govern themselves through face-to-face assemblies, the workers also get nervous before meetings and develop headaches after them. As a worker in one urban "crisis center" put it, "Yeah, I had a headache after that meeting — I work myself up, and the adrenalin comes pounding out."[3] This chapter will examine the anxieties and fears of conflict that arise in face-to-face democratic assemblies, since such assemblies are typical of the alternative workplace.

Face-to-face assemblies have their advantages. In an assembly of all the members, ideas, emotions, and points of view surface that rarely reach elected or appointed representatives. The rank-and-filers can themselves listen to points in a debate, mull the issues over, ask questions, draw their own conclusions, and make their decisions on how to act. By acting themselves, they make themselves responsible for the collective action. The government becomes *us* not *them.* Moreover, in an assembly, one sees the opposition. Ideas one would normally reject out of hand come from people one knows, people who may have believable reasons for espousing them. Finally, when an assembly struggles through to a satisfactory conclusion on a difficult issue, the very act of congregating produces mutual pride and a feeling of communion.

Partly because of these advantages, and partly because their members distrust any government of less than the whole,[4] alternative institutions often begin their democratic careers with some form of assembly, or town meeting. When they set up such a system, they usually recognize that it will take a great deal of time; they do not usually recognize that it will also generate anxiety. Coming together in a face-to-face assembly creates fears that may not surface consciously and that subtly influence the way decisions are made.

Fears of being made a fool of, fears of personal attack, fears of losing friends and making enemies, and even the subconscious fear of physical violence all emerge when people come together in a face-to-face assembly. To overcome their fears, some people need to build up a head of angry steam before they manage to speak out. A like-minded group will also work itself up emotionally in order to be able to put its performers out on the stage. Because explosions are so close to the surface, participants in the meeting are then likely to downplay conflict. They tend to adopt informal "reassuring" procedures to decide potentially upsetting issues outside of the public area, to suppress the expression of conflict in public, and to press for unanimity in decision-making. These responses then further alienate the newcomers, the partial outsiders, or the potential dissidents in the group.

Fears of conflict, and the patterns of confrontation and avoidance that these fears engender, are not likely to ever be fully eliminated. They reappear in subtle forms even in the most highly trained, sensitive, successful groups. But, once recognized, those fears can be greatly reduced and the patterns of decision-making that emerge to deal with them can be largely brought under conscious control. The purpose of this chapter is to provide enough data, from both a town meeting (the original model for many workplace democracies) and an alternative workplace, to make those fears and those patterns recognizable.

The young man who told me he always came back from town meeting with a headache is not the only casualty of the anxieties that build up in public assembly. In the one small New England town meeting I studied in detail, more than a quarter of the people in a random sample of the town spontaneously suggested that the conflictual character of the meeting in some way disturbed them. An older man claimed he stopped going to the meeting completely because he was afraid for his heart. A man in another town told how his hands shook for hours after the meeting. Others, who stayed away from the meeting altogether, commented, "Well, to me, all's it is is more or less a fight . . . a big argument"; "I just get sick of it. . . [to] sit and listen to 'em argue and wrangle"; or "You get in a lot of hubbub. . . people get quarreling."

In my interviews, months after the town's annual meeting, people told of their fears of ridicule. "If you go there, and you speak up, they make fun of you for speaking up and so on, and I guess people just don't want to go and be made fun of." They had reason for their fears. One older, less-than-prosperous farmer had "spoken his piece" in a rough and ready way in the town meeting before my interview. Townspeople, talking to me of the incident, called him "ignorant," "disagreeable," and "a perfect fool." Other, poorer citizens quietly drew from experiences like his a lesson for themselves. They did not go to town meeting. "I don't care to — well, to tell my part, you know, right agin a whole mess of people. . . I don't know, I don't like to get up in town meeting and say, well, this and that. . . well, everybody's looking, or doing something, and they'll say [whisper], 'She's a fool!' "

The townspeople also told me of their fears that whatever they say will be turned against them personally: "They get so darned *personal* at town meeting." And they told me of their fears of making enemies: "If my neighbor's for it and I'm against it, there'll be trouble."

These fears make some people speak out only when they "get mad." At that point, they find it difficult to listen or to find any resolution other than the one they have settled on. They may also lose some of their self-control, thereby bringing on themselves the very ridicule they had hoped to avoid. In a typical story, one old man told me, "I did speak once, and pretty near got throwed out. Got to speaking too loud. I get to swearing." Groups as well as individuals practice this emotional buildup, with the same loss of ability to hear the other side, although not usually with the same loss of control. In another small town, I attended a pre-town meeting caucus where a small group of citizens rehearsed their tactics over and over, not so much to change them or learn them more thoroughly as to strengthen flagging spirits. They exhorted one another to heroism, vilified the enemy, covered the home team with virtue, and, as this war dance went on, positions hardened. At the town meeting the next day, the group's support gave its members the courage to speak. It also held them to the hard line they had developed the night before.

Because fears are strong, emotions high, and positions hardened, whenever someone takes a controversial stand at town meeting, people at the meeting become "very frightened of what you think. Their anxiety goes SWOOOSH — way up!" To allay this anxiety, the townspeople joke and call each other by their first names. They rarely criticize any misdeed in the meeting. If a road commissioner has "borrowed" one of the town's road machines to do a little illegal work for his own profit, the citizens may actually conspire — consciously and unconsciously — to prevent the matter's coming up at town meeting. If the man has to be punished, or even fired, they would prefer not to have it done publicly. In fact, whenever an official is voted out of office, no matter how ignominiously, someone in the meeting gets up later in the meeting to read a little speech of praise for that person. Active townspeople often solicit nominees before the meeting and then spread the word to prevent anyone running against the would-be official. Even on substantive issues, people at town meeting, like the members of many religious communities, strive for unanimous agreement.

These protective devices have the effect of further excluding those who are not yet full members of the group. The use of jargon, jokes, and familiar forms of address forms a linguistic barrier to the outsiders' participation; the hushing-up of misdeeds deprives them of vital information; the one-candidate election convinces them that everything is "cut-and-dried"; and the pressure for unanimity expressed in the call for a voice vote makes it difficult for people to "have the courage to vote no if they mean no." As a consequence, many others feel that their attendance is pointless: "It's organized their way before the meeting." These patterns also tend to keep problematic issues from arising, to suppress harsh aspects of issues that do arise, and to blur the content of any decision.

The town meeting has a longer history, but is, in its dynamics, no different from any other face-to-face assembly. Exactly the same fears and patterns of avoidance emerge in other organizations that govern themselves this way. Take, for example, an alternative workplace I studied in 1973. This workplace was more successful in meeting its democratic goals than any other participatory organization I had encountered in the late 1960s and early 1970s. A hotline and crisis center, it had been founded in 1967 to provide counselling services to the street people and flower children who surfaced in large numbers that summer. By 1973, it had forty-one paid staff members. They all took the same salary, with standard increases for dependents and special increases for particular cases of need. They divided up routine chores equally; there were no secretaries. They decentralized most decisions to six small work groups, and made decisions for the whole organization by a procedure involving a combination of two ongoing representative committees and a series of regular day-long or weekend meetings called *community days.* All decisions were, in theory, made by unanimous consensus.

Because much of the work in this organization consisted of counselling and therapy, two-thirds of the staff had previous training in group process, focusing on interpersonal relations within groups. This training stood them in good stead in dealing with fear of conflict and its possible consequences. The staff members were young, daring, strong, competent, empathetic, and skilled in therapy. It would have gone against both their training and their natural inclinations to respond to the threat of open conflict by suppressing it or pretending it did not exist. They were likely to tell me that "conflict doesn't bother me, frankly," or "I'm a firm believer in creative conflict." Yet, in the draining work they were doing, they needed even more than the members of the town meeting to feel that they were part of a supportive unitary collective. Conflicts marred that unity. Because resolving conflict required psychological energy when the fact of conflict had already brought energy to a low ebb, even this highly trained, self-conscious group found itself slipping into the same patterns of fear and conflict avoidance as the town meeting.

At the crisis center, community days which had to settle important conflicts raised major tensions: "People would panic and be very tense and anxious." Even the trained, therapeutic staff reported headaches, crying and feeling sick. They told me of their fear of ridicule: "I've just seen people do numbers on people. . . Humiliation is the word." They told me that "people take decisions very personally," and "we find ourselves in meetings into really heavy personal issues." They told me of their fear of making enemies: "I felt really weird standing up there and making a controversial statement at a community day all by myself. Just because I don't like to have people dislike me. And I know this is not going to make me too popular. . . ."

As a consequence, the forty-one person assemblies in the crisis center sometimes seemed almost out of control. "I see it at community days, there are people there with lots of feelings, a lot of combatting feelings, getting them out. . ." "[It's] like World War II in your living room. . .dropping a bomb and hurting people's feelings!"

In spite of their training in how to deal with conflict, the staff at the crisis center fell into many of the same ways of dealing with these fears as did citizens at the town meeting. As in the town meeting, like-minded spirits would meet together the night before, assure one another of the virtue of their cause, and strengthen their collective will against the threat of the next day. In the meeting itself, they would try to help one another overcome anxiety, by sitting together, exchanging glances or touches, and urging each other on. One participant described a crucial meeting to cut the organization's budget as follows:

> I had my eye on Jane [one member of his caucus] and I had Margaret [another] down around my leg and I had somebody beside me and we were all holding each other and we could all feel the weird vibes. I'm looking at Eric [another of his caucus] and my eyes were bloodshot — I mean it was really heavy...we were communicating nonverbally, and we were all really scared, and when Pat [the person chosen to make the group's major statement] stood up, I was looking at her, right at her eyes as hard as I could, to see what was there, and I chanced to look away and I saw that everybody else [on his side] was doing it. Then, when Joe [in his caucus] shifted to look at [the opponents, sitting in another spot in the meeting], so did Tony [in his caucus] and so did Eric and so did Jane and so did Margaret. It was really heavy.

To try to head off heavy conflicts like this, members of the crisis center joked, used nicknames and jargon; they avoided explicit, directed criticism in large meetings; when they had to criticize, they hastened to soften the blow with praise. Caucusing before the meeting often resulted in informal decisions which precluded an open fight, and unanimous "elections" in which only one person declared a willingness to take a job. On substantive issues, the procedural rule of consensus insured at least formal unanimity.

As in the town meeting, these protective devices also had the effect of further alienating newcomers and others not tightly connected to the informal decision-making networks. Jokes and nicknames reassured the older members, but, like any set of family traditions, made the newcomers feel even more out of the picture. The same "participatory" informality which made the older members feel at home also made unlikely any explicit procedure for explaining to a newcomer the cozy abbreviations the staff used or the jargon and rules of the game. Staff members remembered that "it took me about six months just to find out what people were talking about!" "They talked a different language — 'I hear you...' and 'the consensus is...' " Here, too, prior caucusing, or the "groundwork" whereby staff members "cultivate, go around and discuss with people" before the meeting, convinced the relative outsiders that what happened in the meeting itself was relatively ineffective. Moreover, the rule of unanimity made some of them feel that "what consensus means here is that if you disagree with something, with what the majority of people are saying...you keep your mouth shut." Trying to avoid conflict means that "people avoid dealing with things altogether" or "camouflage...the issues." "We waste whole business meetings because things aren't brought up because it would be a heavy issue." When an issue finally made it to a public meeting, many of its more threatening aspects were never mentioned. Those least connected to informal decision networks sometimes concluded that, by the time they go to a meeting, the decision "had already been sort of set up."

Face-to-face democracy does have these effects. Conflict becomes potentially "more exposed and more out in the open." participants get "super hepped up to everyone's vibes." Representative democracy seems, therefore, to have the latent function of protecting the average citizen against the problems engendered by conflict. When conflict is unavoidable, many of us would rather hire someone else to fight our battles for us.

This said, however, it does not follow that an organization committed to making decisions in full assembly can do nothing about these problems. Neither the fears nor the avoidance patterns that derive from them can be eliminated, but both can be drastically reduced. In the alternative crisis center I studied, I saw much less fear and avoidance of conflict than in the town meeting. Consciousness of the problems, training in group process, and the invariable division of each large meeting into smaller groups had reduced most people's fears and had inhibited conflict-avoidance.

Consciousness goes a long way toward reducing paranoia. Knowing that face-to-face democracy creates special problems at least makes participants less likely to blame both each other and themselves. Members of the crisis center were not conscious of all of the effects of fear of conflict, but had identified and removed some of them from the sphere of blame. One participant felt all right about saying, for instance, "Conflict is a difficult thing...what people fear [is that] if they express their opinions about a certain matter, other people will be alienated — which is a legitimate thing to worry about. I don't like people not liking me." Prior caucusing, in-group language, muted issues, and pressures to go along with the crowd are big enough problems in themselves without the participants blaming the existence of those problems on moral flaws in their own or each other's characters.

Consciousness, not surprisingly, also makes it possible to watch for and try to prevent emerging problems. Many of the more organizational-minded members of the center did this with some success. After the crucial budget-cutting meeting, for instance, one participant reflected in relief that, "We didn't avoid issues, we didn't camouflage as we sometimes do with positions that are in conflict ...That's always been my initial fear, that we won't come out with the issues."

The habits of thinking and reacting that one learns in counselling or in group process training also stand face-to-face democracies in good stead. The rules of encounter provide guides to expressing oneself and understanding others that minimize misinterpretation: saying "I feel..." instead of "You are...," repeating the other's intellectual or emotional meaning where there might be misunderstanding ("I hear you saying..."), and paying attention to the moment. Encounter training provides experience in conflict itself; other forms of training provide a vocabulary for talking about the dynamics of the group: "I think we've just been scapegoating Tom." Most of the members of the crisis center had such training and worked at counselling all day long. As a consequence, whenever one or two of them disagreed, those not immediately involved in the conflict were likely to take, consciously or unconsciously, the role of therapist. They would try to ensure, for example, that each side in the conflict understood what the other was saying, and that each brought out all the issues it felt important. Relying on the support of such a group gives the participants in a face-to-face assembly more courage. Moreover, confidence in dealing with conflict develops with experience. As one of the members of the crisis center told me after a conflict-torn meeting, "I think we somehow know where the danger line is intuitively, and somehow, in spite of the fears that we'll get over that [line] into a very destructive process, we somehow know enough to keep short of that." He had developed some confidence in the group, although his continual repetition of "somehow" revealed that he could not believe the process was certain.

Structuring some of the conflict so that it takes place in small groups can also help reduce both the fears and the avoidance patterns that the fears engender. The crisis center, for example, divided every large community-day meeting into groups of five to ten members for part of the discussion. Those small groups were explicitly structured so that advocates of each major side in the impending conflict appeared in each group. Because the pressure for "air time" is not so great in small groups, each participant legitimately feels more in control of the group. In a small group it is easier to break in and say one's piece at an intellectually and emotionally appropriate time. Extended dialogue between two participants can take place without the other participants becoming as irritated as they might in a large group about the loss of their own potential speaking-time. Participants have an opportunity for explaining themselves at more understandable lengths. The grace of more time thus has two beneficial consequences for the resolution of conflict. First, it lets information emerge more fully, with clearer emotional and intellectual connotations and with issues clarified that can only be clarified when others have a chance to pursue detailed questions. Second, the reduced time-pressure allows participants to relax and to listen more carefully and openly to what the others have to say.

As well as providing more time per person, the small group reduces the strain of presenting oneself in "public." Participants can voice personal grievances, which often lie at the root of larger conflicts, in a relatively intimate setting. One fairly shy woman reported, after the budget-cutting community day in the crisis center, "I got angry at _____ in my small group, but I felt really good about the process, that there was a way to release that anger." Another woman who had been criticized the same day had a similar experience: "I liked my small group. I felt that at least there people were trying to listen to one another."

In a large group, however, any negative statement must be made before a large number of people. The intense emotional buildup that often seems required to bring up major conflicts in a large assembly is not conducive to listening to others or to working these conflicts out. Moreover, the presence of so many others can tranform the assembly into a stage, where one's posture or image is more important than achieving the satisfactory resolution of conflict. After this same large meeting, which one participant described as being so "heavy" that his group had to give each other maximum emotional and physical support, another participant concluded:

> In my small group, things were much more friendly and supportive. People were much more antagonistic in the large group, and things seemed more out of hand. I really didn't like to see _____ get slashed like that, although I got my digs in, too. I didn't feel good

about what I said; I said it in a very nasty way. I felt like I was
attacking _____, and I didn't want to do that.

Dividing into small groups to discuss the major points of conflict
allows participants to see that their opponents are human.

If one has decided that the conflict in which one is engaged is
irreconcilable, that the outcome is zero-sum, and that, whatever one
side wins, the other side must lose, the techniques suggested above
will not always prove productive. Training in group process and
dividing a large meeting into small groups facilitate perceiving a
conflict from another's point of view. Although the insight so gained
can be used by one group to fight the other, it more often reduces
one's own will to fight. If conflict is indeed irreconcilable, it is often
tactically better not to weaken oneself by beginning to care about
what happens to the enemy.

The techniques of conflict resolution via empathy may also be
biased in favor of certain individuals. People with verbal skills and
people who are accustomed to getting results through emotional
manipulation may gain an advantage when an organization tries to
resolve its conflicts by applying the techniques of group process.[5]
Breaking a large meeting down into small groups, for example, may
not increase the proportional participation of a minority,[6] but will
divide up the minority's members, depriving them of the support of
others who share their feelings.

Alternative organizations will generally be composed of people
who see many of their interests as similar and most of their conflicts
as reconcilable. Such organizations can therefore use group training,
small groups, and other such techniques to reduce the fears that arise
from conflict and the patterns of confrontation and avoidance that
stem from fear. Without conscious attention, these patterns can
seriously distort the making of decisions. Even with conscious attention, such patterns are never likely to be eliminated. The purpose of
this chapter, therefore, is to warn those least frightened of conflict —
those who may be the most active, the most militant, or the original
founders of the organization — that not everyone is as fearless as
they. Indeed, they themselves may have fears, and may be indulging
in patterns of avoidance and confrontation that, on reflection, they
would prefer to avoid. Its purpose is also to reassure those most
frightened of conflict that these problems are universal, endemic to
the making of decisions in public assembly, and susceptible to ameli-
oration. Finally, this chapter will have succeeded in its purpose if
members of organizations which make decisions in face-to-face

assembly come to realize that the patterns of avoidance and confrontation that they perceive are not just the result of the evil, conspiratorial, and power-hungry or the apathetic, lazy, and stupid characters of their fellow participants, but are to some degree inherent in the process of making decisions face-to-face.

NOTES

1. For explanations of the greater avoidance of conflict in small communities by the greater vulnerability of their citizens to collective sanction, see Robert A. Dahl and Edward J. Tufte, *Size and Democracy* (Stanford: Stanford University Press, 1973), pp. 92-94; James Barber, *The Lawmakers* (New Haven: Yale University Press, 1965), pp. 123-149; F.G. Bailey, "Decisions by Consensus in Councils and Community," in *Political Systems and the Distribution of Power,* ed. Michael Banton (London: Tavistock, 1965); and Ronald Frankenberg, *Village on the Border* (London: Cohen & West, 1957), p. 18. See also George Simmel, "Conflict" [1908/1923] trans. Kurt H. Wolff, in Kurt H. Wolff and Reinhard Bendix, *Conflict and The Web of Group Affiliation,* (New York: Free Press, 1955), pp. 43-44; and Lewis Coser, *The Functions of Social Conflict* (New York: Free Press, 1956), pp. 67-85.

2. At least in France, informal norms seem to extend this pattern one step further. In an extreme aversion to face-to-face conflict, the French worker often criticizes not his or her immediate supervisor, but rather an individual one level up the hierarchy, while the immediate supervisor reacts in kind by refusing involvement in conflict and only passing down decisions that originate one level up (Crozier 1964, pp. 40-56, 54-55, 220-229).

3. The two cases reported here comprise part of a larger study of radical democracies published as *Beyond Adversary Democracy* by Basic Books in 1980. For more on the town meeting, see my "Conflict in a New England Town Meeting," *The Massachusetts Review* 17 (1976): 631-663. For more on the crisis center, see my "Acceptable Inequalities," *British Journal of Political Science* 7 (1977): 321-336, and my "The Agony of Inequality" in John Case and Rosemary C.R. Taylor, eds., *Coops, Communes and Collectives* (New York: Pantheon, 1979). In both the town meeting and the crisis center, the data are derived from observation of meetings, open-ended interviews with participants, and responses to a structured questionnaire. I have also studied in detail a women's center organized along generally anarchist lines, and have observed or been a member of sixteen other participatory democracies.

4. Murray Bookchin, in his 1968 essay "The Forms of Freedom," (*Post-Scarcity Anarchism* [Berkeley: Ramparts, 1971, p. 169]), exemplifies the self-protective use of face-to-face assemblies:

> The factory committees, which will almost certainly be the forms that will take over the industry, must be managed directly by workers' assemblies in the factories. By the same token, neighborhood committees, councils and boards must be rooted completely in the neighborhood assembly....The specific gravity of society, in short, must be shifted to its base — the armed people in permanent assembly.

In another example, a Chicago high school student of the late 1960s wants democracy by face-to-face assembly because "No one can represent me. I'm the only one who knows what I'm thinking and no one else can present my views." Center for New Schools, "Strengthening Alternative High Schools," *Harvard Educational Review* 3 (1972): 319. For more on the desire for face-to-face democracy, see my "The Limits of Friendship," in J. Roland Pennock and John Chapman, eds., *Participation in Politics: NOMOS XVI* (New York: Lieber-Atherton, 1975), pp. 259-262.

5. Sue Katz and the Anarchist Amazons, who tried to bring a working-class perspective to the radical women's movement in Boston in 1969 and 1970, made this point against the then largely middle-class "consciousness-raising groups" in the women's movement.

6. The limited data I have from one community day in the crisis center suggest that, at least during that one day in that organization, the relation between advantaged status and speaking was as great in the small groups as in the large public assembly.

6

Collective Work and Self-Identity: Working in a Feminist Illegal Abortion Collective

Melinda Bart Schlesinger
Pauline B. Bart

This paper is an attempt to illustrate some of the ways in which people change when they participate in a democratically structured group that performs a vitally needed service.

In 1969, abortion was still illegal, although the need to terminate unwanted pregnancies was great. The right to abortion on demand was one of the key principles of the emergent Women's Liberation Movement, a demand later expanded to the right of women to control their bodies. There were semiformal and informal referral systems where women were given names of abortionists. One of these volunteer, informal, referral services was operated by a University of Chicago student from her dormitory, and she wanted a group to take it over. A group of women living in the Hyde Park community near

Melinda Bart Schlesinger is a community-living-service social worker, Vance County Mental Health Services, Henderson, North Carolina, and Adjunct Professor of Social Work, East Carolina State University, Greenville. She works with retarded children and adults and their families.

Pauline B. Bart is Associate Professor of Sociology, Department of Psychiatry, Abraham Lincoln School of Medicine, University of Illinois, Chicago, and also has an appointment to the Chicago Circle Campus of the University of Illinois. She has written, with Linda Frankel, *The Student Sociologist's Handbook* (Scott Foresman, 3rd ed., 1980). She is currently writing a study (Free Press, forthcoming) of women who were attacked and who avoided being raped.

This paper was presented at the Meetings of the Society for the Study of Social Problems, August 1979. A more general discussion of the illegal abortion collective was presented at the Meetings of the American Sociological Association, Chicago, 1977, "Seizing the Means of Reproduction: A Feminist Illegal Abortion Collective: How and Why It Worked." The authors gratefully acknowledge the support of the Boston Women's Health Book Collective for the content analysis for this study, several members of Jane (the abortion service), and Joyce Rothschild-Whitt for critically reading this paper.

the University of Chicago had begun to develop feminist consciousness. Many of these women had been in the peace and civil rights movements, and, when the Chicago Women's Liberation Union was organized, it seemed logical to them to counsel women and help them to obtain illegal abortions. Thus, they took over the task as well as the pseudonym Jane from the student. At that time, no one thought that eventually they would be performing abortions. Moreover, they made the assumption, which was later dispelled, that the abortionists to whom they were referring the women were M.D.'s.

Because the group could provide a steady supply of customers, they were in a better bargaining position than were individual women who needed abortions. Thus, they were able to negotiate with the abortionists, who had to lower their rates and to agree to perform some free abortions. The Jane women also lent the clients up to fifty dollars to help them pay the fees, funds which were taken from the fees of women who paid the full amount.

Once the women in Jane learned that the abortionists were not M.D.'s, they realized that lay persons could perform competent abortions; they knew the abortions were competent because of the feedback from the clients. Thus, when one abortionist taught one of the women how to perform the procedures, she taught the rest, and they fired the professional abortionists. The hierarchy of the group flattened because the abortionist could no longer choose which women would assist at the procedures, and any woman, at any stage of her pregnancy, with or without money, could obtain a humane, demystified abortion from this group of women whose safety record for the first trimester abortions equalled that of New York state when that state legalized abortions. At first, because of the relatively high fees paid to the illegal abortionists, the clients were more likely to be students, since they could afford those fees. However, in the winter of 1971, when the women took over and made it possible to lower or eliminate fees so that any woman at any stage of her pregnancy could obtain an abortion, the abortions were done primarily *with* [their word] poor black women from the "projects." The clients did not constitute a homogeneous group, however. They ranged in age from eleven to fifty, and in occupation from policewoman to Weatherwoman.

During its four years of operation, from 1969 to 1973, Jane proved that abortions could be performed safely, humanely, and very inexpensively by nonprofessional paramedics working in apartments.

The following roles existed in Jane when the women assumed control:

First-trimester abortionist

Long-term abortionist	Sometimes called *midwife*. (Long terms were for abortions that took place after the first three months of conception.)
Big Jane	The administrator.
Call-back Jane	Also an administrator, who returned the calls left on the answering tape by the women wanting abortions.
Driver	Transported the women from *the Front* to the place where the procedures were done and back to the Front, the place from which the women and their significant others left.
Worker at the Front	One woman described the responsibilities of this position (called *working the Front*) as those of a stewardess with radical feminist consciousness.
Assistants	Gave shots, inserted speculums, dilated cervixes.
Counsellor	Everyone was supposed to counsel. The process consisted primarily of demystifying the abortion procedure. It was done either with individuals or with groups.

Ideally, all women were expected to try to perform every task. While everyone had to counsel, not all women wanted to assist with abortions, and fewer wanted to do them, either because of lack of time, commitment, interest, or skill. The ideology was that everyone *could* do everything, rather than an ideology supporting a division of labor and specialization. It was thought that the women with whom they were doing the procedures would benefit by seeing the Jane women change jobs, since it demonstrated that the skills were easily transferrable and not mystical. Rothschild-Whitt (chap. 1) seeks "to identify some of the structural commonalities which link these new collective organizations and to develop a theoretical framework for understanding them," and lists nine principles which contrast such organizations with bureaucratic organizations. The principles relevant to the role-chart, and which the informants agreed were applicable to Jane, are that equality of status was attempted through task-sharing, that differentiation was minimized to "eliminate bureaucratic division of labor," and that role rotation, teamwork and task-sharing resulted in the above as well as in "demystification of specialized knowledge." Women in Jane learned through the apprenticeship system, and work roles were holistic. Because everyone counselled, grounding her work in the experience of women needing abortions, understanding why that woman chose not to have that child at that time, no one experienced the alienation that medical personnel sometimes report when involved in abortions (e.g., Denes 1976).

While in the nineteenth century, before physicians attained hegemony, women did perform abortions for other women (Mohr 1978), there is no current sociological literature on lay abortions. Standard sociological organization-theory does not accurately predict the behavior of collectives, as Rothschild-Whitt notes (1976a), since these "movement organizations" (Zald and Ash 1964) neither transform means into ends in the quest for survival, nor do they bureaucratize charisma. Radical alternative and self-help health clinics have been studied, however. Peterson (1976) found that a feminist health clinic did not achieve its goal of providing real alternatives because "by remaining within the model of delivering medical services, the clinic's structure . . . [was an] extension of the regular delivery system" making "paramedical workers out of nonprofessionals" in spite of their countervailing ideology. Moreover, inequality between client and practitioner remained, since the practitioners controlled the definitions of services because of their greater knowledge and access to scarce resources. Taylor (1976) gives another example of an alternative health service which did not meet its goals. However, Kleiber and Light (1978) describe a successful alternative structure for women's health care, and Marieskind (1976) found that a self-help clinic "was a potential resource of value, particularly for dealing with shortages of health personnel and changing sexist medical practices" (1976). Marieskind notes that the value of a self-help model, whether it be Parents Without Partners or AA, "lies in the fact that it efficiently utilizes an untapped medical resource — the cooperation and participation of the patient." However, none of these studies have addressed the social psychological issues which this paper focuses on: the effect on the participants of participating in such organizations.

METHOD

Obtaining the women's permission to be interviewed about the service, or Jane, was difficult. They considered it ironic for a group that was antiprofessional and antiacademic to be studied by an academic, although they were not concerned (with one exception) about their illegal activites becoming known. Seven of them had been arrested, but, after the Supreme Court decision legalizing abortion, the charges were dismissed.

But some of the key women decided to trust Bart because she had been active in the women's movement, her self-presentation was not "professional," and she did not have a grant, which was considered proof of her not having been co-opted. These women told the other members that Bart could be trusted, and, for the most part, there was no difficulty obtaining interviews. Some women even called asking to be interviewed. Everyone contacted, including women who were originally reluctant, ultimately agreed to be interviewed. They were promised input into the study, and, indeed, this and other papers have benefited from their cooperation.

Kleiber and Light, who studied the Vancouver Women's Health Collective, also received feedback from the collective members (1978, p. 17), but, unlike Kleiber and Light, Bart could not observe the collective at work. However, she has observed and received health-care services from other feminist clinics, one of which was partially staffed by former Jane members.

The interviews were unstructured at first, and became semistructured when the important issues emerged. Sometimes this resulted in interviewing members more than once. The interviews were then coded, and this paper deals with answers coded in the following areas: career goals, personal task competency, personal growth, political growth, increase in feminist orientation, and demystification of the medical profession (N=34). Thus, the various aspects of personal change could be recorded (table 6-1). Such changes will be discussed including the negative experiences some women experienced (table 6-2).

TABLE 6-1

ASPECTS OF PERSONAL CHANGE EXPERIENCED BY WOMEN IN JANE

Number	Kind of Change
17	personal "growth" and increased sense of competence
16	political "growth" and increased feminist orientation
5	changed career goals
8	changed attitudes toward doctors
46*	

*The sum is more than 27 because some women changed in more than one way.

TABLE 6-2

EFFECT OF THE SERVICE ON THE MEMBERS OF JANE

Number	Change	Direction of Change
22	yes	positive
3	yes	both positive and negative
2	yes	negative
7*	no	———
34		

*Many of these seven women already were politicized and/or considered themselves competent. Twenty-seven of the thirty-four women experienced a personal change.

FINDINGS

Personal Growth and Increased Competency

The categories of personal competency and personal growth were collapsed because they overlapped. Seventeen women reported changes in categories, with some women reporting change in both categories. Frequenty, personal growth was perceived as a result of their increased sense of competency. For example, one woman said, "I entered the group as a real quiet, shy person, hardly able to articulate anything at all. By the time I left, I was the strong person in the group. I had learned all the skills that were available to me. I developed a great deal. Now I am a functional, happy, normal person." The second reported, "I would make dumb jokes and try to put them [the women coming for abortions] at ease. Before that, I was real shy and would never talk to anybody. It made me come out of my shell." (table 6-1)

Fifteen of the women expressly mentioned competency and its effect on their self-concept. The following quotes illustrate two examples of this change:

> I could learn and I could pick up skills. It made a whole lot of sense the way people learned through the service. . . . There was a whole thing of responsibility and respect that I don't think I've really had a whole experience with before. What it did was give me a whole different sense of myself and what I was capable of doing.

> I had a real good feeling about myself and I was real confident. I was able to do a lot of things at one time, and I knew that I was doing them well. That felt good, and I was real happy with myself.

The service made it possible for these women to experience a new sense of competency. It has been found that women perceive themselves as less competent than men in achievement-related areas (Frieze et al. 1978, p. 59). Moreover, the literature, both popular and empirical, suggests that housewives are particularly vulnerable in this area (which is expressed in the phrase "I'm just a housewife.") These women are, in fact, not married to their houses, but Parsons has called a housewife a "pseudo occupation" (1942), and Ferree has found that working-class housewives have lower self-esteem and feelings of competence than a comparison group of women who were employed either part- or full-time (1976). Several of the key members who started Jane were housewives.

This increased sense of competence had political overtones for several of the women, one of whom maintained in a statement which is the essence of the Jane philosophy, and, indeed, of the self-help philosophy:

> I had achieved something. . . I can do things that I never felt I could do. I think the important thing about the service is that people really learn that, if it's necessary, you can take the tools of the world in your own hands. All that crap about how you have to be an expert. . .it's just a ruse to make you feel incompetent in your own life. One thing we all learned is that, if you want to do something, you can learn how to do it.

Specifically with regard to the tasks in the service, she remarked:

> You think you could never stick your hand into a toilet bowl full of blood and vomit and pull out a placenta and look at it. You think you could never put a needle into somebody's ass. But if you have to do it and you're the only person who can do it — you do it. And once you've done it, you say, my God, I can do this. It's not terrible. You wouldn't want to do it every day, but you can do it. You're not going to be weak. You can be responsible for yourselves and your brothers and sisters.

Another woman whose comment had political overtones maintained, "I could take a taboo apart and learn the skill involved. This reduced the power things had over me and increased my own sense of self as a person who could do this." Thus, we see that these women's experience in a democratically structured organization gave them the feeling of regaining control of their lives.

Finally, there were some changes with regard to personal growth that did not involve feelings of increased competency per se. One woman maintained, "my participation in the service grew me into the person I was meant to be." A second woman remarked, "I can't remember a time in my life when I felt so good about doing something. It was such an incredible experience when it came to helping people." The second statement supports the work of Reissman (1965) and Braeger (1965) on the beneficial effects of helping on the helper.

Political Growth and Feminist Orientation

Originally, the categories of political growth and feminist orientation were to be analyzed separately. Upon examining the data, it appears that almost everyone who recognized political growth connected it to or also recognized feminist growth. Some of the women did not mention feminist growth explicitly, but implied it from their discussion of issues such as health care. Sixteen women felt some type of change in the feminist/political arena as a result of participation in the service. While all of them recognized that at least some aspect of their feminist politics had developed, six of these also mentioned more general types of political growth. Some of these six felt that their politics became more anarchist. One woman maintained, "We found that working without a set of rules is a very efficient thing to do. If we had to label ourselves, we would call ourselves anarchists." Evidently, for some of the women, working in a democratically structured group caused them to reject any type of authoritarianism. Another group of women maintained that the service caused them to become more radical. One woman remarked, "By the time I was finished with the service, I was more and more frustrated and convinced that I didn't want to be part of the political, economic, or medical systems...I felt that we had to do it ourselves. I was more a radical than a reformist."

One type of increasing feminism resulting from participation in Jane was that many women felt a change in their relationships to other women. Some examples of this change are illustrated by the following quotes: "I am constantly amazed at the process and relationships I had with women [in the service]. These became a source of power with me. I then describe that as feminism."

> I may be more friendly towards women...I think before I would have some women friends but not many. Suddenly, I had almost exclusively women friends. I guess it [the service] changed my attitude about women...I do know them better.

> ...being involved in Jane, especially in the counselling part where one has to talk to many women and being up at the Front, I found that under the skin it didn't matter if you were big or black or white or green or small or fat or rich or poor. Women had to deal with the same problems, and it radicalized me in that respect. I feel that tremendous kinship to women and I find that I seek out women...

Such increased positive feelings — indeed, one might call it female bonding — were probably most effected by the female world in which they participated (see Smith-Rosenberg 1975 for a description of this world in the nineteenth century), for both the women's coworkers and the clients were women.

The second type of feminist growth involves a more general type of orientation toward women's issues. The following are examples of this type of change:

> I wanted to be a person who did things, but I wasn't. The service was the first thing I ever did, and I've been active ever since in feminist things.

> I didn't really have a direction that I was going in — I didn't know what I wanted to do with myself. What Jane did for me was radicalize me and get me involved in women's issues.

> [Before the service] abortion interested me as an issue particularly. Feminism didn't interest me at all...I discovered I could get them an abortion but there were all these other things wrong with their lives...I got more into thinking that what's wrong with a woman's situation is that she is a woman...Then there was a way of looking

at what was going on in their lives and that made sense to me. There
was an instrument they could use to make their lives better. The
service was a very politicizing thing.

Career Goals

Working in the service influenced the career goals of five women.
All of them are in health-related areas. Two are in nursing school (one
is a nurse midwife), two are giving women's self-help courses and
making speaking engagements, and one is in medical school. All of
them maintain that the service had a major impact on what they are
doing now. (It should be noted that the number of women who fit this
category is very small, because it was often unclear if Jane had been
the primary influence on their career goals.) The student in nurse
midwifery, noting that some people find it contradictory that a
woman who was involved in "killing babies" should be helping
women to have them, remarked, "It's all part of the same thing. It's all
part of letting women do what they want to do."

Demystification of Medicine

The *medical mystique* refers to the deification of physicians and
things associated with them. It involves a perception of physicians as
superpeople with a quasimystical power which may not be questioned by lay people who could not possibly know as much. Eight
women recognized change in their attitudes toward the medical
profession. All of the women in this category realized the absurdity of
the medical mystique and questioned what doctors could do and did.
With the exception of one woman, all of those who fell into this
category also recognized an increase in their task-related competency. Furthermore, change in this area was also highly associated
with feminist/political growth (five out of seven). The following
quotes are examples of this type of change:

> I guess before the service I was locked up into thinking about how I
> should act, especially with doctors. If they said something to me, it
> was like law. If a doctor said something to me, then of course I
> would do it. The service made me question, and, the more I found
> out about what they tell people, the more skeptical of them I got. At
> this point, I wouldn't like to go to a doctor for anything.

> As a result of Jane I know that people who have an intelligence of
> ninety or above can learn to do anything that the doctor does.

> I think that the doctor was cut down to size . . . He's just about as big
> as I am, no more no less. He's a technician who learned a trade. He's

not some fantastic creature. He's as fallible as I am.

Another woman told how her experience as an abortionist in Jane resulted in better treatment for her child when he was seriously cut and had to be taken to the emergency room. The staff refused her entry, claiming she would become upset or faint at the procedure. Needless to say, she knew she would not, and she was able to successfully insist that she be in the room holding her child's hand. When she was told that she would have to bring him in several times a week for the dressings to be changed, she insisted that she could do it herself, persuaded them to teach her how, and saved herself time, particularly important because she was employed. Her son was saved the additional alienating experience of hospital care. One could note the irony of a woman's training in abortion helping her be a more competent mother, saving her son from the exacerbation of distress that is a frequent response to hospital treatment because of separation from parents. Thus, by learning the skills involved (or seeing others learn the skills), the women realized that almost anyone has the ability to do some of the things that doctors maintain only they can do.

Negative Cases

There were five people whose experiences in the service were less than positive. Two of the women were in Jane for a relatively short time, and one admits that, had she been in it longer, she may have had a more positive experience. One saw the service as being very hierarchical and resistant to change. She felt she cared more about women than other women in the service. She maintained, "It was probably the first experience that made me cynical...for the sake of the good that people see they really do ignore some of the other crap that goes on." This was at a time when males were running the service. Thus, it was more hierarchical.

As Rothschild-Whitt (chap. 1) notes, participation in collective organizations is time-consuming because of the democratic process which attempted to achieve consensus. The Jane informants agreed that this was the case in Jane. One woman especially resented giving her time. Other women could not meet this and other demands of the organization, and, for them, the experience became a negative one.

Three of the women did not perform medical procedures. Performing such tasks often led to a positive experience. One of these women wanted to but was not allowed. Another was considered too slow. The third one thought it "icky." The fourth person wouldn't counsel, and the fifth was seen as an incompetent abortionist. Thus, none had good experiences doing procedures, and such good experiences were associated with an overall positive experience in the service.

Rothschild-Whitt (chap. 1) notes that, because of the emotional intensity of collective organizations, an intensity which is both threatening and satisfying, criticism is concealed or softened. This observation is true for Jane since the issue of how to deal with incompetence caused interpersonal conflicts. It was difficult to fire incompetent workers. Frequently, they were isolated socially in the hope that they would get the message that they were not wanted. One abortionist was fired, and the woman firing her reported that it was the hardest thing she ever did in the service. Dealing with incompetency was particularly difficult for another reason. When mistakes are made in clinics or hospitals, not only is there backup equipment and personnel, but an informal system is available to cover up such errors. Because Jane was illegal, their resources for dealing with mistakes were limited. They did have arrangements with sympathetic physicians so that seriously ill patients could be cared for at some hospitals. In addition, they had the necessary self-presentation skills to see to it that women with serious problems would be admitted to hospitals in any event. Moreover, they coached women on how to manage such experiences. However, women told me that, even though competence was extremely important, they felt that, if any one person could be fired, they themselves were at risk.

General Changes

One section of this paper was going to deal with general types of change (those who mainly changed politically, those who changed personally and those who changed in both respects). Political/feminist and medical-profession attitudes were to be seen as political, while personal growth/competency and career goals would be viewed as personal. Upon review of the data however, it appears that all categories are so closely entwined that to distinguish among them in such a manner would be arbitrary. For example, often personal competency is related to self-help and the "we can do it ourselves" attitude, which is very political. This finding is also consistent with the tenet of the women's movement, that "the personal is the political." The following quote illustrates this:

> The whole aspect of self-help and self-determination was important. Having breached this by learning medical skills, I began to

really feel that I had power...It was such a good feeling of overcoming some of my own taboos that I began to see that as a real important thing for all women.

Only four of the women who mentioned more than one category of change stayed exclusively within either the personal or political category. Perhaps the only trend to be found is that all those who expressed positive change in any category were very involved in the service. That is, they were in it for at least a year, learned some of the medical skills involved, or had strong social ties to the women in the service. It should be mentioned at this point that perhaps the number of women who changed was no larger because some of the women came into the service with some of the ideas discussed. Thus, while their attitudes may have been reinforced, they were not changed by participation in the service.

Although there was no party line on most issues, the basis for belonging to Jane was a commitment to the ideal of women maintaining control of their bodies. In fact, some members claimed that the lack of such a line was one factor accounting for Jane's success. Because large segments of the membership were relatively homogenous (Bart 1977), social control could, for the most part, be based on "personalistic and moralistic appeals rather than direct supervision" (Rothschild-Whitt 1979). But the informants disagreed that the members were selected because of their sharing of "basic values and world view"; such sharing, they claimed, was true only on the issue of abortion. However, we would conjecture that a vocal proponent of the war in Vietnam would have had difficulty participating no matter how much she was committed to a woman's right to abortion. The diversity was among various liberal and left positions, with feminist anarchism becoming the major emergent philosophy.

Zald and Ash (1964) note that movement organizations differ from full-blown bureaucratic organizations since they want to change society rather than provide it with a regular service. This position is supported by Jane's disbanding after the Supreme Court decision legalizing abortion.

Since the organization was committed to the ideal of women maintaining control over their bodies, this control was more fully realized when the women learned they could gain control by learning the procedures and becoming independent of the male abortionists. The democratic structure that the women introduced appears to be much more conducive to the ideal of controlling their lives, and was, in fact, an example of it. As the women gained control, the hierarchy flattened, and more women could do more things. Thus, more members of the organization had the opportunity to experience the feeling of self-determination. The virtues of a democratically structured organization can be clearly seen in terms of the numbers of women who were able to become fully involved and committed. As King-Janus (1956) and Pearl (1964) maintain, commitment to an ideal is an important aspect in determining to what extent the "helping person" will change.

It should be pointed out that the democratic structure was not the only aspect of the service that was conducive to growth. The fact that the problem was so immediate and the results so concrete caused many women to feel their experience with Jane was especially meaningful. One might think that the illegality aspect would be detrimental to some women's self-concept. It is interesting to note that this did not occur. Rather, the illegality added to the immediacy of the problem and caused the women to really feel that they were providing an essential service. The fact that they were providing an essential service was one of the reasons the women gave for the success of the service (Bart 1977). As Rothschild-Whitt (1976a) notes, "it is unlikely that members of a collectivist-democratic organization would be able to maintain their self-conscious resistance to more cost-efficient models of organization if they were in the business of producing goods or services which were similar to and competing with those produced by bureaucratic organizations."

Through their direct involvement with a medical procedure, the women learned more about their bodies. The importance of learning skills and gaining information about certain medical procedures cannot be overstressed in terms of the beneficial effects it appears to have. This educational and informational aspect would seem to be quite essential for any group. Again, a democratic organization, which allows more members to receive more information, would certainly be more conducive to this outcome.

Thus, any organization which desires its members to grow in positive ways would probably be most effective if it allows as many members as possible to become actively involved in learning skills, gaining information and participating in decision-making activities. It should be mentioned, however, that if this organization demands the level of competency and commitment that characterized the service, some members may have negative experiences because of their inability to meet these high standards.

CONCLUSION

This paper described the changes in women participating in an illegal feminist abortion collective. Their sense of competence and autonomy increased, they became more radicalized and feminist, notably increasing their identification and bonding with other women. In addition, their experience in providing health care led to a demystification of medicine generally.

This study not only demonstrates that the belief that only physicians can perform safe abortions is incorrect, but it also shows the limits of the current ideology promoted by the "human potential movement" that people grow by taking care of themselves, by being their own best friends — in short, by focusing on their own needs rather than on other people and their needs.

One of us (Bart) calls this ideology "the growthspaceautonomy approach" and has pointed out that it can function as a legitimization of psychopathy. After all, cancer is also growth. The dichotomy between taking care of oneself and taking care of others is demonstrably false. It was, indeed, by taking care of *others* that the Jane women fulfilled their own potential.

We will close with a statement from one of the women exemplifying this process:

> You can do some of them [medical skills] right and you can do them well. It makes you feel like you can do anything in the world.

Part 3

LARGE-SCALE WORKERS' COOPERATIVES: CASE STUDIES

Introduction to Part 3

Part 3 describes some of the most successful examples of democratic management in large-scale organizations, as well as some failures. With the exception of IGP, all the enterprises discussed in the articles are producers' cooperatives.

Dating from the 1920s, the plywood industry provides a long-standing example of workers' cooperation in the United States. Today there are some fifteen plywood plants in the Pacific Northwest owned by their workers on a one person, one vote basis. The plants average 100-300 workers in size. As Berman points out, overall take-home pay compares favorably with union wages in conventional plywood firms.

Productivity in the cooperative plywood factories is high, with estimates ranging from 25 to 60 percent productivity gains vis-á-vis conventional plywood firms. It is not hard to imagine how workers' ownership interest in the firms coupled with their right to run the firms on a democratic basis would contribute to the impressive quality of work and productivity witnessed in these coops. The plywood coops do have managers, chosen by elected directors, but the cooperative structure has eliminated the need for numerous management positions. The workers themselves carry out many supervisory, executive, maintenance and plant improvement functions, and they are versatile, able and willing to do a variety of production jobs. The plywood firms teach us that a cooperative job design may dramatically reduce the management to worker ratio, therefore lowering the administrative overhead needed to run a firm.

The second example in this section comes from abroad — Johnson and Whyte's analysis of the remarkable network of worker-managed industries that has been established in the Basque country near Mondragón, Spain. Over the last twenty years, this cooperative network has grown to include over 18,500 member-workers in over eighty firms. Member enterprises include the largest producer of refrigerators and stoves in Spain. The Basque model is important because it shows the effectiveness of an interconnected system of cooperatives aided by key supporting institutions. These include a technical college, a credit union (the Caja Laboral Popular, with over 200,000 members) that has helped to finance the cooperatives, and the Caja's interpreneurial division which develops detailed feasibility studies before launching new ventures.

Common elements exist in both the plywood factories and the Mondragón firms. In both cases, workers put up a portion of the capital needed for the business (originally about \$1,000/person in the plywood companies, and \$1,800/person in the Mondragón Cooperatives) and have contributed additional capital through withheld wages. In both the American and the Spanish workers' cooperatives, pay differentials are strictly limited by the collectivity of members. In practice, this means that the average worker receives more pay than in comparable jobs in private industry, though top executives receive less. This trend toward a reduction in income inequality is evident wherever workers have become significantly involved in company decision-making.

Such cooperatives have their limitations, as can be seen from the British examples discussed by Edelstein. His account of cooperatives in England indicates the aggressive response of workers in Europe to plant closings. Three of the firms he describes, the *Scottish Daily News,* the Triumph motorcycle company, and Kirkby, were taken over by their employees when the companies announced they were closing. In the first two cases, workers who were being laid off sat in and occupied the productive facilities in an effort to keep them going. As plant closings continue in this country, such militance may spread. Direct actions such as these, coupled with new legislation that may be introduced in Congress, may effectively begin to redefine the "right" of a company to deprive hundreds or thousands of persons of their livelihood.

The British cases show that decisions to reopen shut-down plants are political as well as economic in nature, and that they are not always successful. The *Scottish Daily News* was reopened with the aid of a government loan of only 1 million pounds, and Triumph-Meriden, a combined government grant and loan of 5 million pounds. Even with the government loan, the *Scottish Daily News* folded once more. For several years Triumph-Meriden was doing better. But the fate of this company was similar. Competition from Japanese models was intense, and caused the plant to close. Kirkby Engineering, which refused a new government-backed loan, died in 1979.

The final example in this section is Zwerdling's account of IGP, a Washington, D.C., based insurance firm specializing in group policies. Its 340 workers own half the corporation's stock, elect half the board of directors, and have a considerable input into all aspects of organization policy.

IGP is a modern company using advanced computer technology to sell insurance. In 1976, its sales were $60 million and its profits about $1 million. James P. Gibbons, the company's president, started IGP in 1964. Several years later, he placed half the stock in a trust that is voted by the employees, one person, one vote. He still owns the other half.

Democratic management works relatively well at IGP, but it must grapple with some structural problems: much of the clerical work is tedious, new employees are not selected on the basis of agreement with the philosophy of democratic management, and employees have not had to risk any of their own funds to capitalize the company. Nevertheless, this company may prove more the exception than the rule. There are probably few entrepreneurs like Jim Gibbons, who of their own volition would turn over ownership and considerable control of a flourishing multimillion dollar enterprise to its workers. However, there are abundant opportunities in this country for workers, trade unions, and members of local communities to prevent the layoffs that accompany plant closings and to revitalize local economies and communities by establishing cooperatives. This will be discussed further in part 5.

7

The Worker-Owned Plywood Cooperatives

Katrina V. Berman

Worker self-management, in the form of worker-owned cooperatives, has been important in one manufacturing industry in the United States for over half a century.[1] In eighteen plants in the Pacific Northwest producing softwood plywood, workers in the plant as individuals are owners of the enterprise with direct management control.[2] Each member has an equal voice in operating and investment decisions and in the selection of a board of directors to supervise operations. The worker-members have residual claim to all earnings over nonlabor costs, and bear any losses incurred.

There have always been a few known worker-cooperatives in other industries as well,[3] and undoubtedly there are others that have gone unrecorded.

Worker cooperatives have been a significant part of the plywood industry since its beginning.[4] The pioneer plywood cooperative, established in 1921, was one of the first eight plants producing plywood and contributed extensively to the development of the industry's manufacturing technology. By 1942, five additional cooperative plants had raised the worker-owned share of industry output to 20 percent, and it is estimated that these and additional coopera-

Katrina V. Berman is an economist specializing in Industrial Organization, with experience in government and university teaching. She is currently Research Associate, University of Idaho, and a member of Hylarion Associates, a research and consulting firm. Her publications include *Worker-Owned Plywood Companies* (1968), and "Long-Run Theory of the Labor-Managed Firm: Comment" (*American Economic Review*, Sept. 1978). She is a consultant and expert witness for plywood cooperatives in tax litigation. Her current research includes the econometric study of comparative productivity of worker-owned and nonworker-owned plywood plants.

This chapter is the English text of her article, *"Les Coopératives Ouvrieres dans l'Industrie du Contreplaque,"* **Autogestion** vol. 32 (November 1975): pp. 47-64.

tive plants accounted for 20 percent to 25 percent of total industry capacity for the next fifteen years, until 1957, despite the industry's growth. The number of worker-owned plants has decreased since, however, with no new cooperatives organized, and continued expansion of the industry has diminished the cooperative share. Cooperative plants still accounted for 14 percent of industry capacity in 1964 and about 12 percent of the total in 1974. Of the eighteen plants in 1974, all had been operating for at least twenty years, and one for thirty-four.

FORMATION AND HISTORY OF THE WORKER-OWNED COMPANIES

The first worker-owned plywood enterprise, the Olympia Veneer Company, was organized in 1921 with 125 workmen skilled at various trades, as shareholders. The members contributed $1,000 each from their savings, built the plant (with the aid of a bank loan), installed equipment themselves, and worked without pay, except for absolute necessities, for the first year. Pay and bonuses to worker-owners, however, soon rose as much as 150 percent above the pay of employees in conventional plywood plants, although early bonuses were paid in additional shares of stock (two for each worker-owner) rather than in cash, because of the company's need for additional capital. The subsequent financial success of this company was an inspiration for later plywood cooperatives, and its operating methods set a number of precedents followed by later companies.[5]

The next three worker-owned companies to be organized, in 1939-1942, were also started and almost entirely financed by groups of working men (including, for two plants, former members of Olympia Veneer) who built their own plants. All three were quickly successful (aided by the wartime demand for plywood) and have been considered among the most efficient and prosperous companies in the entire industry. One of these firms is still operating as a cooperative. The other two, as well as Olympia Veneer, after more than thirty years of operation, sold out to conventional firms for substantial gains to the shareholders.

Like the early cooperatives, some later ones set up new producing organizations on the initiative of groups of workers (sometimes with a nucleus from an existing worker-owned company) or, occasionally, of a local citizen group. In other cases, however, worker-owned organizations took over existing, operating plants. The plants thus converted to worker ownership had been unprofitable for previous owners and often were scheduled to close down because of lack of available economical raw material or age and obsolescence of the plant. (Five plants were twenty-five to forty years old, and some were among the first built in the industry; efficient plant design has been substantially altered by technological change.) Some selling owners in these cases were interested in helping the workers achieve successful operation. More, however, appear to have used sale to a worker-group as a way to obtain a price above the plant's true value, or to obtain a lucrative exclusive sales (or, less frequently, log-supply) contract for the cooperative's output. Although a sales-agency agreement could be initially helpful (and this is a sales method satisfactorily used by several worker-owned companies), the exclusive sales contracts forced on cooperatives by former owners proved detrimental in several cases, and disastrous for the cooperative's survival in at least one instance.[6]

One important method of organization for new plants, and for some conversions, was through the efforts of outside promoters seeking financial gain from fees, commissions or profits on sale of stock, continuing payments for "management" services, or selling rights to the cooperative's output. Some of these promotional arrangements imposed a lasting operating or financial handicap on the cooperative. Promoters were particularly active in the early 1950s, and avid speculation developed in plywood cooperative shares. Against this background, fraudulent promotions were possible. Criminal charges resulting in convictions of two groups of promoters in the mid 1950s revealed elaborate fraudulent schemes which sold over 600 shares at $1,000 each and had additional membership applications pending. The widely publicized fraud trials cast suspicion on all worker-ownership projects and are probably partly responsible for the lack of subsequent additions to the cooperative group.

Over thirty plywood cooperatives were organized in total, although not all operated at the same time. The fate of all the cooperatives that are not now operating as such is not known. It appears that some never reached full operation, several sold out to conventional corporations at substantial gains to the worker-owners, and the rest went bankrupt, closed, or sold out for other reasons.

The operating cooperatives, varying in size, have, in terms of capacity and sales, averaged close to the average size of plant in the industry, and not far from the average size of company in an industry in which there have been only a few very large firms. The plywood worker cooperatives are diverse in products and in other respects. Most cooperatives have from 100 to 300 workers, although they have ranged from 60 to 450. Nonowner workers have been employed at most plants, varying from one or two to around 50 percent of the plant work force, with an average of probably 10 percent to 25 percent at different times. Some plants are organized to operate permanently with a large nonmember labor force. In some relatively unsuccessful plants, the nonmember percentage fluctuates. Members leave when outside pay is higher than the return available in the cooperative plant and return when the cooperative hourly return improves. Some firms also have subsidiary veneer plants close to log supplies which are staffed by nonmember employees. Where nonmember employment is substantial, the hired workers are covered by union contracts similar to those at conventional plants.

The financial record of the plywood worker-cooperatives has varied among companies (as the varied circumstances of their founding might suggest) and over time. However, it can be said that the return to members per hour of work has been above the union average rate most of the time in most of the cooperatives, and at some time in all of them. In a few plants, the hourly return has been, nearly continuously, 50 percent or more above the union average.[7] (Even in high-return plants, however, the hourly return — equal for all members — has not always been above the highest union rate set for a few of the most skilled workers.) Because of more continuous operation in the cooperative plants, annual incomes have compared even more favorably, and even in cooperative plants with low hourly rates they have been above those of union workers.

METHODS OF OPERATION

The membership and operating methods established by Olympia Veneer were followed by later cooperatives in the industry. Members purchased stock in equal amounts entitling each holder of *working shares* to a preferential right to employment and to one vote in membership meetings and in selection of the board of directors. The members own their shares individually and may resell them, but a share resold by a member must first be offered to the company; if the company does not buy, its approval of the private purchaser is required. (Shares have been resold privately and through newspaper classified advertisements under "Business Opportunities.") Dividends are ordinarily not paid on shares or, at most, are authorized in small and limited amounts. Therefore, the value of a share derives from the right to employment and to any higher income obtainable from work in the cooperative. Initial prices of shares were low, but most companies have required shareholders to contribute additional capital usually through withholding earnings. Resale prices of shares have varied widely, from near zero to a current selling price for one company of $55,000. High-priced shares are sold on time-payment contracts that may provide for suspension of payments if the purchaser's income from the company falls below a certain figure.

Net earnings of the cooperative after payment of other costs, even those paid as bonuses at the end of the year, have always been distributed to members in proportion to hours worked. Thus, shareholders not working in the plant — because of illness or otherwise — receive no income. The cooperatives have received favorable treatment under the federal corporation income tax laws. Following an early Olympia Veneer ruling, cooperatives have been allowed to treat high hourly payments to worker-owners as deductible business costs rather than as distributions of profits subject to tax. The ruling was based on demonstrated higher value of owner-workers in production, and required proof of this superior productivity in each case whenever challenged by the tax authorities. These tax problems may have been beneficial in continuously focusing attention on productivity. In 1964, another court decision held that worker-owned plywood companies could qualify for special tax treatment as cooperatives under certain conditions. The companies, most originally organized as ordinary corporations, thereupon reorganized under cooperative statutes and began using in their operations the methods and terminology developed by retail and agricultural marketing cooperatives.[8]

Bylaws of the companies usually set forth at length the rights and obligations of members, including methods of job assignment, handling of grievances, procedures for optional equalization of working hours, and disciplinary procedures. As an example of the latter, a member may be explicitly required to take a job assignment and to follow the directions of the man in charge of that department, at the end of a specified chain of command reaching down from the board of directors through the manager, plant superintendent, and shift foreman. Refusal to follow orders subjects a member to penalties, from a warning to suspension for a year or more for the fourth offense. For drunkenness or smoking on the job, no initial warning is provided. A member refusing to do his work or found unfit may be discharged by unanimous vote of a quorum of the board of directors, subject to appeal to a membership meeting where a majority vote is final. This type of procedure for achieving labor discipline was not provided in all companies at the outset, but has been developed as the necessity was recognized.

General shareholders' meetings elect officers and directors and make major decisions, such as decisions on investment, borrowing, sales contracts, or major expenditures. Quarterly or often monthly operating and financial reports, and reports of the frequent board-of-directors' meetings, are posted in the plant and may also be sent to members' homes to assist informed participation.[9]

CONCLUSIONS

What conclusions and lessons for self-management can be drawn from the experience of the worker-owned plywood companies? There are nine.

First, the most obvious, and the most important, conclusion to be drawn is the demonstration that a worker or producer cooperative is a viable form of manufacturing enterprise. This conclusion contravenes the beliefs of some early socialist writers. A workers' cooperative can compete successfuly in a private enterprise economy and yield high incomes and income security for its members. The variety of operating methods and circumstances in the worker-owned plywood companies shows flexibility of this organizational form, and their continued ability to survive and prosper despite considerable change in the industry shows adaptability. Little or no resistance to technological change has been evident.

Is the viability of worker cooperation demonstrated only for the plywood industry? Is the plywood industry especially favorable to cooperation, to account for the unusual concentration of cooperative plants in that industry?

Some characteristics appear to be favorable. Rapid growth in product use and a variety of product distribution methods and outlets have facilitated marketing of the cooperatives' output. Marketing has also been aided by the product quality standards and certification established by the industry trade association, which also engages in research and promotional activities benefiting cooperative as well as other members; the cooperatives, however, as strong supporters of the association, are partially responsible for the effectiveness of its programs. Industry characteristics favorable to cooperation — but not unusual in United States manufacturing as a whole — include a relatively modest size of plant in terms of both capital requirements and number of workers needed, and a relatively simple manufacturing process using semiskilled labor, with labor costs a significant share of total costs. Conversion of logs of varying qualities into plywood panels of different grades offers opportunity for the higher value productivity of labor which is the basis of cooperative success, but similar opportunities appear to exist in other industries.

On the negative side must be listed instability of the product market and uncertainty of raw material supply. As plywood is used chiefly in construction, demand is highly seasonal and also subject to strong cyclical variation, with consequent price fluctuations. The raw material — logs suitable for peeling into veneer — is variable and somewhat unpredictable in quality, unevenly distributed, and subject to depletion geographically. It is not available from any regular source, and procurement involves a variety of methods, including bidding on standing timber which must then be logged by an outside contractor. Raw material prices are not uniform or predictable, and there is persuasive evidence that nontimber-owning companies suffer substantial price disadvantages. Difficulties for cooperatives have increased in the last two decades. Quality of raw material and availability to independent firms have increasingly declined and prices have risen sharply. Technological change in manufacturing has accelerated, with rapid adoption of new methods assured by the continued building of new plants. And the expansion of industry capacity and by-product character of some timber companies' plywood operations have resulted in a downward price trend despite the increased raw material costs.

On balance, it appears that the plywood industry was moderately favorable to cooperative operation in the formative years of the cooperatives' organization, but not sufficiently so to account for the unusual clustering of cooperative plants. The impetus to worker ownership in the industry was probably the example of the successful early companies. Certainly, in the past twenty years, the plywood industry does not appear to have been especially favorable. There is no reason to limit the conclusion of the viability of worker cooperation to the plywood industry.

A second conclusion is that the basis for cooperative success is the superior productivity of member-workers shown repeatedly in a number of measures, such as physical volume of output per man-hour of work, quality (grade and value) of product, and economy of material and equipment use. Superiority in these three directions has resulted in value added per labor hour in some cooperatives more than twice that in conventional plants. Members not only work harder and more carefully, but eliminate need for many positions by performing supervisory, executive, maintenance, and plant improvement functions, as well as becoming able and being willing to do a variety of production jobs as needed. Superior labor productivity has yielded high incomes to members of some cooperatives, and has enabled other enterprises to survive and return adequate incomes by offsetting high nonlabor costs. Continuous high-level operation is another characteristic that lowers costs and bolsters incomes. The superior productivity of member-workers in plywood cooperatives is due to their superior motivation and is in line with other productivity findings under conditions of participation and direct financial gain. In the plywood companies, participation has been shown to be statistically correlated with financial success.[10]

Third, the plywood worker cooperatives have shown particular ability to survive under adversity. The companies operate on a continuous basis when low prices force conventional firms to shut down production. Many of the plants taken over from conventional firms have survived and prospered under handicaps found intolerable by the previous capitalist owners. The superior productivity of cooperative labor, as noted, offsets handicaps such as an obsolete plant. Continuous operation, due to member willingness to work longer hours, also helps these plants to return adequate incomes. A final survival tactic is provided by member willingness to accept lower hourly return if necessary. Most firms at some time, and some for prolonged periods, have reduced hourly rates, sometimes below union levels, to cope with adverse conditions, while continuous high-level operation has maintained incomes.

Fourth, cooperative operation is not an automatic guarantee of success. Worker enterprises, like other businesses, must have adequate capital and equipment, sales outlets, raw material sources, and management. Members must recognize that their incomes are produced by their own work. They must be willing to accept labor discipline within the plant, to delegate adequate management authority, and to defer immediate income payout when the longer run financial needs of the enterprise require retention of earnings. These requirements and defining the role of the hired managers have caused problems, particularly at the beginning (managers have tended to be fired frequently), but the problems have not been so insuperable as early theoretical writers feared. The most persistent difficulty of cooperatives operating in a private enterprise economy has been in obtaining adequate capital from private capital markets, since only limited return and no management control can be offered to capital suppliers. This is a difficulty that could be remedied by governments, and the plywood companies have, in fact, obtained some financing from the Federal Small Business Administration.

Fifth, unlike previous United States worker cooperatives, the plywood companies since Olympia Veneer have not lost their cooperative character gradually over time,[11] though some employ substantial numbers of nonmembers. Members sometimes indicate awareness that decreasing the number of members would increase the size of each remaining slice of the earnings pie. The persistence of the cooperative form nevertheless may be due to several factors. Limitation of share ownership, voting rights based on membership rather than capital, and the practice of paying out earnings on the basis of hours of work leave no advantage in multiple-share or nonworking share-ownership. Many companies have not had adequate capital to buy up shares. The tendency of many members to think as workers rather than as owners, which has handicapped cooperative long-run planning, may have helped avoid concentration of share ownership by company purchases. The continuous emphasis in the federal tax controversies on the superior productivity of member labor and the importance of this productivity in the generation of earnings may have supplied constant reinforcement for a desire to remain cooperative.

Sixth, the record of the plywood worker-cooperatives for permanent or long-run survival in cooperative form is more dubious. Reasons for the disappearance of over one-third of the cooperatives organized should be investigated. (Many noncooperative plywood plants also closed in this period, however.) The sale to conventional ownership, despite prosperity, of two of the three prewar cooperatives suggests that the cooperative form may be vulnerable to success as well as to failure.[12] However, special characteristics, particularly valuable timber holdings bringing a speculative price, may make these two companies unrepresentative. Approaching retirement age for the shareholder majority has been a contributing factor in the sellouts as well as the more common closings, which some companies seek to avoid by conscious staggering of shareholder ages.

Cooperative-share transfers present problems in a private enterprise economy. Financing of share transfers is usually not available from capital supply institutions. If a cooperative is successful, shares will have a high value. A prospective worker buyer can usually pay for his share only out of future earnings over a long period of time, and the seller must accept such terms. This creates pressure for a retiring worker to sell to a conventional corporation that can pay the full purchase price immediately. New members may also be receptive to a capitalist takeover bid because of the pressure to complete payment of their shares. Share transfer is another area where government supplements to private capital markets could aid worker cooperation.

Seventh, employment of nonmember workers appears to have been so universal in the plywood worker cooperatives as to suggest it is a necessity, although, in some enterprises, nonmember labor has been minimal. Nonmember workers may be necessary to supply a required skill, training, or certification (such as that of licensed electrician) which is not available and cannot be recruited on a membership basis. Office help may be largely in this category, although some firms have women members and some have men working in the office. (A few women members also work in production.) Employment of a nonmember plant manager or superintendent has been practically universal, probably because managerial qualifications command a higher remuneration than members receive, although another reason is the view that greater detachment vis-a-vis the members is desirable. Certain necessary trades may also command a higher pay scale.

Temporary replacement for members who are ill or on vacation (often by young relatives of members) frequently accounts for many of the nonmember work hours. Further, short-run variations in labor needs due to business fluctuations cannot easily be met by adding and dropping members (membership usually carries a right to employment). Finally, some plants have used nonmembers continuously for high-level operation. When the initial number of shares is insufficient to man the plant adequately, issuance of additional shares would presumably be a remedy. But, since assurance of continuous employment is important in attracting and retaining members, a cooperative group may wish to limit memberships to the number that can reasonably be assured of employment under all market conditions. Even sustained periods of high-level operation will then require additional workers. Some less successful cooperatives, as noted, have been dependent on hired workers because some members leave the plant for higher-paid jobs elsewhere, retaining their shares pending improvement in the plant's fortunes, or for job insurance.

Nonmember workers are usually paid above the union scale, which is sometimes higher than the member hourly return. Nonmembers, who contribute no capital and do not share the risks and responsibilities of members, benefit from the continous employment provided by cooperative plants, fringe benefits given all workers, and the usually high plant morale.

Eighth, although a few plywood cooperatives have given extra compensation to members performing a few more difficult jobs, most — and the most successful — provide uniform hourly remuneration to all members regardless of job assignment. They consider equal pay rates to be an essential feature of cooperative operation, to minimize friction. Equal pay is important economically also in facilitating the flexibility of job assignment that is a major basis of superior cooperative productivity. Procedures have also been established to equalize yearly incomes by giving first choice on overtime work to members with fewer work hours credited.

The plywood companies have shown that higher compensation is not necessary to induce workers to train themselves for and take difficult and responsible jobs. In fact, members compete for these jobs. Lead jobs in each department, when vacant, are awarded automatically among those who bid for them, on the basis of seniority, time since last successful bid, and qualifications, except that, where qualifications are particularly important, the award is made by the board of directors.

Finally, members of the plywood worker cooperatives are in direct control of the entire range of enterprise decisions. The degree of participation varies among enterprises and among individuals, and some members are interested only in their pay. Most worker owners, however, make full use of their self-management opportunities. Even where authority is delegated to the board of directors, general members are actively involved in attempting to influence the board. Members receive the regular hourly rate for attending membership and committee meetings and delinquents are pressured to attend. Because of the intimate daily involvement of members with the company and each other, the practice of self-management tends to be more intense in worker cooperatives than in other types of cooperatives. This is probably true of democratic institutions generally. The worker cooperatives are also subject to the drawbacks of democracy. Decision-making is cumbersome and time-consuming. Restrictions placed on the board of directors to preserve general-member authority sometimes prevent response to advantageous opportunity. Internal plant political activity can distract attention from the production job and develop into factionalism that hinders decision-making, and has occasionally even led to violence.

Problems of this type, as much as more conventional business difficulties, may be behind the demise of some plywood worker-cooperatives. Development of group solidarity and shared commitment to joint effort are important to cooperative success. This may require individuals with an unusual ability to work together closely in a group. Another necessary characteristic which is also not universal, but which is perhaps subject to development or improvement with education, is the ability to look ahead and plan for the future, to resist the pressure for immediate earnings payout in order to reinvest in the plant to maintain its technological capability.

Members of the plywood cooperatives have been primarily interested in opportunities for steady employment and higher incomes, and have not seen themselves or the company as pioneers in a self-management movement. This relatively practical orientation (as contrasted with the missionary spirit of the nineteenth century Knights of Labor cooperatives for example) may be a factor in the relative success of the plywood cooperatives. Nevertheless, being one's own boss in one's own firm has been an important motivating force and source of satisfaction. Studies suggest that ownership may be important, and self-management without ownership might not produce the same gratification.

Instances of cooperation among the worker plywood companies give evidence of some sense of solidarity. Some of the firms have a joint sales agency, although they also sell independently. Most belonged for a few years to a separate Worker-Owned Plywood Association. Companies in the same area exchange operating and financial statements and occasionally advice. Some members have been influential in organizing new cooperatives.

The members of the worker-owned plywood companies in the United States have developed structures and procedures establishing a significant industrial organizational alternative, and have proved its viability for the modern industrial economy, not merely for their own industry. They have shown that persons in their capacity as producers can establish industrial self-governance and democracy, maximize participation, humanize work on a factory production line, improve income equality, and release the forces of productive energy, craftsmanship, and pride in achievement. This has been accomplished without benefit of revolutionary theory, trade union ideology, or a political movement, and without assistance from organs of government,[13] the capitalist economic society, or organized labor.[14,15]

NOTES

1. The following are the principal references on the worker-owned plywood cooperatives: Berman (1967) discusses the history and experience of the companies through 1964 and summarizes the earlier fragmentary studies of them; this book includes a study of the industry and a brief summary of earlier producer cooperative history. Bellas (1972) focuses primarily on the companies' managers but includes statistical correlations of company financial performance 1963-67 with other company variables. Paul Bernstein (1974) reports primarily on plant visits in 1973, stressing worker attitudes.

2. As of 1974, the worker-owned companies were: (1) in the state of Washington, Buffelen Woodworking Company, Tacoma; Elma Plywood Corporation, Elma; Everett Plywood Corporation, Everett; Fort Vancouver Plywood Company, Vancouver; Hardell Mutual Plywood Corporation, Olympia; Hoquiam Plywood Company, Hoquiam; Lacey Plywood Company, Lacey; Mt. Baker Plywood Inc., Bellingham; North Pacific Plywood Inc., Tacoma; Stevenson Co-Ply Inc., Stevenson; Puget Sound Plywood Inc., Tacoma; (2) in the state of Oregon, Astoria Plywood Corporation, Brookings; Linnton Plywood Association, Portland; Medford Veneer and Plywood Corporation, Medford; Milwaukie Plywood Corporation, Milwaukie; Multnomah Plywood Corporation, Portland; Western States Plywood Cooperative, Port Orford.

3. Worker cooperatives were probably most numerous in the twenty years following the Civil War when over 130 were sponsored by an early national labor organization, the Knights of Labor, and many others were formed independently. Most of these late nineteenth century cooperatives were short-lived, however. They were victims of business incompetence, unscrupulous suppression efforts by competing capitalist manufacturers (cooperatives of those days had little legal protection), and lack of lasting trade union support. Worker cooperatives in the twentieth century were few and scattered, and those financially successful tended to lose cooperative character by extensive hiring of outside labor and decline in numbers of working owners until only a few remained; those few resembled a partnership.

4. Production of plywood from softwood (principally Douglas fir, but not including other western softwoods, and recently southern pine as well) is considered a separate industry from hardwood plywood-production in the United States. While finished, sanded, softwood plywood (such as the cooperative plants produce) competes in some uses with hardwood plywood, the major part of the demand for softwood plywood, and the spectacular growth in demand, have been for construction purposes, based on the structural properties of Douglas fir. Although some low-grade construction plywood is now made in the southeastern states, for the first forty years, the industry was confined to the north Pacific area of North America — in the United States, western Washington and Oregon and northwestern California — the home of coast-type Douglas fir. The manufacturing process is a production line operation composed of several steps using different equipment and processes, requiring considerable strength and dexterity and (preferably) attentiveness and some judgment.

5. The later history of Olympia Veneer, however, has not been followed by the other plywood cooperatives. Like the producer cooperatives in other industries, Olympia Veneer gradually lost its cooperative character. The number of working shareholders began to decrease early in the company's operation, apparently by the purchase of shares by the company, and increasing proportions of nonowner workers were employed, especially after acquisition of two additional plants. When the company sold out in 1954 (it had changed its name to Associated Plywood Mills Inc. after sale of the original Olympia plant), working shareholders were a small minority of the work force. The $15-million sale price represented $120,000 for each of the original 125 shares.

6. One cooperative successfully sued the sales agent (former owner) for breach of contract in failing to maintain a national sales organization for the cooperative's products as agreed at time of sale, but the award of $1.5 million damages for lost earnings was too late, and insufficient after costs of several years' litigation, to stave off bankruptcy.

7. For example, in 1964, for thirteen of the reporting sample of sixteen companies, the hourly rate of return to shareholders (including bonuses) was above the union average rate; for one, equal to it; and for two, below; the average for the sixteen was over 20 percent above the union rate. Berman (1967) and Bellas (1972) divided the companies into two equal groups according to five-year financial performance; the average hourly rate reported for the "high" group was substantially above the union rate for the entire period 1963-67, although the average for the "low" group did not quite keep up with the rise in union rates 1965-67.

8. Thus, worker-owner members are *patrons*, hours worked are *patronage credits*, payments made to members are *patronage dividends*, with interim payments not wages but *advances*, etc.

9. Effectiveness of communication between management and the general membership varies in different plants, and is a factor in cooperative success. See note 10, infra.

10. The study by Bellas (1972) calculated correlations of plywood cooperatives' financial success with various company measures. The only company statistic found significantly correlated with financial performance (besides total capital) was the percentage of workers who were members, and a high statistical correlation (significant at the .005 level) was found between performance and a measure of "participation" developed from frequency of membership and directors' meetings, member participation in management, and communication between directors and the membership.

11. See footnotes 3 and 5, supra.

12. Bellas (1972) holds that cooperatives are vulnerable to success because a successful enterprise will expand through acquisition of other producing units and use of increasing amounts and proportions of nonmember labor, and will so lose the participatory features that make it successful. This view, however, equates success with expansion. There is little support for this contention in the record of the worker plywood-companies since Olympia Veneer.

13. The favorable tax treatment accorded plywood cooperatives by the courts (and continuously and vigorously disputed by the executive branch) has affected only the companies which have already achieved substantial prosperity.

14. Although in one case the industry trade union unsuccessfully challenged conversion of a plant to worker ownership as an illegal abrogation of the union contract,

the labor union attitude has, in general, been one of uneasy neutrality. Union leaders fear that successful cooperatives could make union members dissatisifed, and that unsuccessful ones threaten labor standards.

15. 1978 note: Since this article was written, the number of plywood cooperatives has been further reduced, to fourteen or fifteen. The firms that have ceased cooperative operation, even the two which sold out to noncooperative interests (one of which has since failed and been shut down by the capitalist purchaser), succumbed to financial difficulties aggravated by unusual and accelerating pressures in the western plywood industry: environmental demands requiring large capital expenditures, locally depleted timber supplies, and raw material prices increasing 400 percent over a seven-year period and as much as 90 percent in a single year. Their demise, after over twenty years of cooperative operation, in the face of such unusual stresses does not support Bellas's thesis that the cooperative form is "basically unstable" (see note 12, supra) which hinges on predictions for financially successful cooperatives.

8

The Mondragón System of Worker Production Cooperatives

Ana Gutiérrez Johnson
William Foote Whyte

This is a success story in a field where failure has been the general rule — a rule well summarized in the following statement by Paul Blumberg:

> ...Producers' cooperatives, which do involve workers significantly in management, have repeatedly been proved both economically and socially an inappropriate vehicle for workers' management. Economically, they have always been plagued with chronic shortages of capital, stemming from their inadequate initial resources, and the hostile milieu in which they operate makes borrowing from the private capital market quite difficult. In the Western world, they are economically inconsequential, especially when compared to the flourishing consumers' cooperative movement.
>
> Socially, producer's cooperatives have a tendency to "degenerate" as the Webbs and others observed long ago, due in part to the lack of outside public control of their activities. This "degeneration"

Ana Gutiérrez Johnson is currently a Research Associate at the Center for International Studies, Cornell University. She has collaborated with William Foote Whyte on a book about the Mondragón cooperatives, and has worked on a second documentary film, *Auzo Lagun: A Women's Cooperative.*

William Foote Whyte is Professor, Department of Organizational Behavior, New York State School of Industrial and Labor Relations, Cornell University. He has also served as President of the American Sociological Association (1980). Since 1976, he has been directing Cornell University's New Systems of Work and Participation Program (with funding from the Center for the Study of Metropolitan Problems of the National Institute of Mental Health), and continuing into late 1981. He has been involved in a study of the Jamestown Area Labor-Management Committee as well as in the employee-ownership and worker-cooperative studies.

Reprinted with permission from the *Industrial and Labor Relations Review*, Vol. 31, No. 1 (October 1977). © 1977 by Cornell University. All rights reserved.

takes some of the following forms: transforming the cooperative into a simple profit-making, profit-seeking business, indistinguishable from a private enterprise; exploiting a monopoly situation, often to public disadvantage (as has happened in Israel); closing off of cooperative membership; raising the cost of membership to a prohibitively high level; and resorting to the anti-cooperative device of taking on hired labor. (Blumberg 1973, pp. 3-4).

The Blumberg statement applies very well to the general scene, but there is one important exception: the system of production cooperatives centered in the small Basque city of Mondragón in Spain. If we can come to understand the conditions that have enabled this system to overcome the well-documented general rule, we shall advance our knowledge regarding the human potential for extending worker ownership and management in production organizations.

The system is so complex that we can present here only a preliminary interpretation based upon 1975 field work (seven weeks by Johnson, two weeks by Whyte) and extensive documentary records. Johnson has continued the study with field work beginning in 1977, but this report is based upon the 1975 field project and subsequent analysis.

COMPONENTS OF THE SYSTEM

The first firm of the cooperative system of Mondragón was founded in 1956 by five men supported by a larger group of friends; by the end of 1976 the system had grown to sixty-five firms with 14,665 members. The firms' production ranges widely, from the labor-intensive process of furniture-making to the manufacture of sophisticated machine tools and heavy equipment. All those working in the coop become members after a brief probationary period, with the exception of a few specialists brought in by contract to perform jobs for which there is not sufficient talent within the system.

The industrial cooperative complex was built upon three institutional bases. The first was an educational system that grew out of a two-year technical school originally founded to provide training for the young people so that they could qualify as skilled workers upon entering employment. In succeeding years, the school's program was expanded to include instruction up through the college level, leading to engineering degrees, and the student body was expanded from twenty-four in the first year to over a thousand today. While the curriculum concentrates on technical subjects, the school itself is operated in the form of a cooperative.

In the years following the formation of the first industrial firms, the educational system developed two additional supporting institutions. One was Alecoop, a cooperative factory that serves a dual purpose. Students work in the firm five hours a day to earn tuition and living expenses so that they can devote another five hours to their educational program. Alecoop produces components used by the other production cooperatives and also takes on jobs in the open market.

Recently, the system set up another support — a two-million-dollar building containing offices, research laboratories, and shops, and designed to undertake projects of long-term importance that cannot be expected to yield short-run benefits to particular firms. Although the older firms of the system have maintained their own research and development units to provide technical innovations for the near future, this new complex will enable a larger scope of planning.

The second institutional base upon which the coop of Mondragón was built was the League for Education and Culture, a broad association of parents, teachers, students, and supporters from the community. The league has played the important role of linking the educational system to the cooperative firms and to the community in general. Members of the league have helped to work out legal and political problems with municipalities and with the national government.

The third institution was a credit union, the Caja Laboral Popular, which was founded in 1958 to support the expansion of the industrial cooperatives. The Caja has been growing at an accelerating rate: in the eight years up through 1974, membership multiplied twenty-two times and assets thirty-five times. By the end of 1976, membership had reached 206,841.

INDIVIDUAL LEADERSHIP FOR
COLLECTIVE ACHIEVEMENT

Although this system has been built upon the integrated efforts of many people, its origins and main line of development can be traced to Father José María Arizmendi, a veteran of the Spanish Civil War (on the Republican side) who settled in Mondragón in 1941 and began working to revive two moribund church associations, one including parents, the other including blue-collar youth. Don José

María prided himself on never having made decisions for others. Nevertheless, it was his concern for combining practical and technical development with a social mission that led to the founding of the school, Escuela Politécnica Profesional. He also wrote the first draft of the constitution and bylaws for the first production cooperative, and the document that finally emerged for that firm has provided the framework for every firm founded since then.

It was not Don José María who first proposed the rule that the ratio between top and bottom pay in a cooperative should not be greater than three to one (the then prevailing relationship between workers and supervisors in private firms), but he was influential in maintaining this exceptionally low differential. The first forty members of the original firm, Ulgor, voted for the three-to-one ratio with little debate or recognition that the members were establishing a policy that would bind thousands of future members in scores of firms yet to be created. Since the policy makers aim to equate the weighted average of all rates of pay in the cooperative firm with the weighted average prevailing in comparable firms in private industry, where the ratio may be as high as fifteen to one, the Mondragón formula means that workers entering at the bottom of the scale earn substantially more and that executives toward the top of the scale earn substantially less than their counterparts in private firms. (The pegging of average wage and salary rates with private industry was designed to assure the members that the profits or surplus of the cooperative firm would be based upon superior productivity and not upon a lower wage bill.)

While others worked out the technical formulas, it was Don José María who particularly shaped the decision to distribute each member's share in profits or surplus to the accounts members held with the firm, rather than paying out these shares in cash. As we shall see, this was a critical decision for organizational growth.

It was also Father Arizmendi who first urged the members to found the Caja Laboral Popular. As one of the founders of Ulgor commented, the idea seemed absurd to them at first.

> We told him, yesterday we were craftsmen, foremen, and engineers.
> Today we are trying to learn how to be managers and executives.
> Tomorrow you want us to become bankers. That is impossible.

Father Arizmendi continued to argue that cooperative production organizations could not develop to their full potential without capital, that credit would not be available to them under acceptable conditions through private banks, and that therefore they must build their own banking system. Within two years after the founding of Ulgor in 1956, the Caja came into being.

The cooperative educational system was first supported by community contributions and small tuition fees paid by students. As the cooperative production firms grew in numbers and in financial strength, they provided increasing support for education. Nevertheless, as the educational system expanded in numbers of students and especially in the more costly programs at the college level, it seemed that substantial tuition increases would be required. Don José María argued that it would be a violation of cooperative principles to exclude intellectually qualified students too poor to pay such tuition. Instead, he proposed an organizational solution: Alecoop, the cooperative student-operated factory.

Was José María Arizmendi a charismatic leader? The term suggests one who speaks eloquently, stirs deep emotions, and builds a personal following. According to the founders of Ulgor, Don José María was never an eloquent speaker; in fact, especially in the early years of the movement, he often had trouble finding the words to express his ideas. It was not always easy to understand what he was getting at, yet the members listened patiently and reflectively, for they sensed that he was following a vision of a better world that they could help create. Clearly he did stir emotions, but they did not come to center upon himself. He stirred people to *think* and *act*. An apt description of the essence of his leadership comes from the present Director of the Escuela Politécnica, Javier Retegui: "[Arizmendi] sees the future — and makes us face it."

Although Don José María never held an executive position, he had influence as a trusted and revered advisor at every stage in the development of the system. He was the chief actor in linking Mondragón to the surrounding social, political, and economic institutions. Through the League for Education and Culture, he was in continuous contact with authorities and local citizens. He did research on social security and health care systems to help the cooperative organizations develop needed programs that were not supported by the state. His legal research helped the cooperatives take advantage of laws enacted to help other organizations and to support other purposes.

Few individuals in history have been as socially creative as Don José María, and yet his creations never depended upon him for survival, development, and expansion. Well before his death in 1976, the leader had achieved the institutionalization of the social system he inspired and guided.

THE ECONOMIC AND CULTURAL BASE

When the outsider first hears of the Mondragón system, he is likely to ask himself, as we did, "How could such a thing happen in Spain?" The fact is that the Basque country, while politically part of Spain, differs considerably from Castile and other southern provinces that have created the image of Spain projected to the outside world. The differences are linguistic, economic, and cultural. Although the Basques also speak Spanish, they have their own language, which is not related to Spanish or to any other Indo-European language.

When the Mondragón cooperatives began, the Basque country was one of the few parts of Spain that had a well-developed industrial tradition. There were a number of small and medium-size metallurgic and manufacturing firms in the area, based in part on natural resources such as iron ore. Population growth and the scarcity of agricultural land had shaped a system of inheritance that displaced many young adult males from the land and into industrial towns. Spain's relative isolation from the rest of the world gave the Basques a comparative advantage in reaching the general Spanish market, which began to grow rapidly in the 1950s.

The Basques also had a comparative advantage for industrial growth in their attitudes toward manual labor. In Castile and Andalucia, for example, to be considered *hidalgo* (meaning "illustrious," derived from *hijo de algo,* literally "son of something" or of somebody special), one must be above working with his hands. In the Mondragón area, on the other hand, according to native writers:

> ...in order to be considered "hidalgo" it was enough to demonstrate that one was descended from ancestors native to the province, and to dedicate oneself to manual work was not an obstacle, as in other parts of the country, to being hidalgo.[1]

In addition to the enterprising spirit and dedication to industrial work on which the Basques pride themselves, there is another very important cultural characteristic, called by the Basques the "associative spirit." We see this spirit in the after-work promenade in Mondragón (as in other Basque cities). Groups of three to six or eight men or women walk together from bar to bar, taking a few sips of wine at each stop and then moving on. Such groups come together directly from factory or office, and, in the same group, we may see men in rough work-clothes and others with white collars, ties, and business suits. If we watched day after day, we would see the same men together again and again. Basque social groups last for years.

This associative spirit, which cuts across class lines, is supported by their high evaluation of social equality. Greenwood points out that the Basques (especially those of Guipúzcoa) have traditionally held the concept of "collective nobility."[2] Regardless of social class differences, all native-born Guipúzcoans are of pure Christian blood and thus considered noble (and therefore equal) by definition. Caro Baroja has made a similar observation regarding social class differentiation in the Basque country, which he calls a matter of "private right" (*derecho privado*) as opposed to "public rights" (*derecho público*), meaning that inequality has not been accepted beyond the level of personal interactions of people involved in exchange processes.[3] In a study of conceptions of equitable payment for work, Johnson found that the students in the cooperative school-factory in Mondragón manifested an overwhelming preference for egalitarian choices.[4]

The prevalence of traditional gustatory societies tells us not only that Basque males love to cook and eat their justly famous cuisine, but also that *they trust each other*. Díaz-Plaja estimates that there are in the Basque country about 2,500 of these societies with some 35,000 members, an average membership of 14.[5] Each society owns or rents a meeting place, which consists primarily of kitchen and dining room. Here the members eat and drink together at regular intervals. Beyond that, each member has a key and is free to come in at any time to eat and drink anything in the house. On the wall is a pad on which the member records what he has consumed and signs his name. At the end of each month, he receives a bill from the treasurer. Basques tell us that cheating is unheard of. If a member fails to record something he has taken, it is only because he forgot it; when in doubt, he errs on the side of recording more than he consumed.[6]

The cultural base is obviously important, but it should also be noted that Alecoop, the Caja, the school, and the firms are all designed to reinforce sentiments of mutual trust and social solidarity.

THE MANAGEMENT OF GROWTH

The expansion of the production cooperatives has been managed in two ways: through the fission of existing firms and through the creation of new firms by the Caja Laboral Popular. The growth and fission of firms have been made possible by the reinvestment policy of the system. According to the original program, which has been maintained with little variation, at the end of each fiscal year the surplus (profit) of the cooperatives is divided into three parts. A total of 30 percent is set aside for two purposes. Ten to 15 percent goes for social benefit to the community (including support of the educational system), and the remaining 15 to 20 percent is set aside as a reserve fund to be maintained by the cooperative firm. The remaining 70 percent is distributed to the members in proportion to hours worked during the year and rate of pay received. This bonus is not paid in cash to members, however; it is deposited to the account each member holds with the firm. This fund is treated by the firm as debt to members or bonds on which interest is paid annually. The minimum interest paid is 6 percent, supplemented by (a) an allowance for increases in the cost of living, and (b) an additional variable interest up to 3 percent depending on the size of the surplus. In recent years, members have been receiving about 13 percent on their accounts. A member in good standing who leaves the firm with proper notice is allowed to take out 80 percent or more of the money deposited in his account, the rest being retained as a reserve fund for the firm. If a member is discharged for disciplinary reasons or leaves without notice, the firm may retain up to 30 percent of his account. When the member reaches retirement age, he may withdraw 100 percent of the money in his account. With a very young system, there have been few retirements so far. So as to avoid serious drains on capital in future years when many members are retiring, the Caja Laboral Popular, the credit union in which the accounts are deposited, may try to persuade members to accept annuities rather than lump sum payments. It is also considering joining Spain's social security system.

The prevailing policies regarding distribution of surplus were written into the constitution and bylaws of Ulgor, the first firm. Within the first two years, when Ulgor had only forty members, two of them proposed that the members' 70 percent be paid out in cash. This proposal was vigorously debated and rejected, primarily in response to the perceived need to strengthen the firm. In effect, the members voted to uphold a policy of deferred personal gratification and accelerated organizational growth. This policy has not been seriously challenged in recent years.

The founders of the system believed that it would be easier to maintain a true cooperative with small organizations than with large ones. Therefore, as a firm reached the point where it developed a new line of production that could provide a basis for a new firm, that new firm was spun off the original firm. Thus Ulgor has given birth to six other firms. To avoid prejudicing the interests of members who shift to the new firm, which cannot be expected to be highly profitable at once, and to maintain economies of scale, the six firms growing out of Ulgor have combined with the original firm to establish a cooperative conglomerate called Ularco. Finance, legal services, market research, and personnel functions are centralized within Ularco. The earnings of all the Ularco firms are pooled, and the members' 70 percent is paid out according to the same formula regardless of firm membership. The centralization of personnel administration also makes it possible to shift members from one firm to another within Ularco, so as to avoid situations where one firm is laying off members while another firm is expanding.

The creation of new firms is the responsibility of the entrepreneurial department of the Caja Laboral Popular. Up until about 1973, the Caja simply responded to proposals brought to it by prospective founding members, but the savings deposited have risen so rapidly that it has become necessary for the Caja to develop an active promotional program.

The entrepreneurial department now has approximately 70 employee-members and a program of social and economic research and technical assistance in the development of new firms. While the first firms were established in or around Mondragón, the Province of Guipúzcoa (in which Mondragón is located) has the highest density of population of any comparable area in Europe, and, in recent years, has had close to full employment. Thus, new firms launched there would have to attract migrants, further compounding the population problem. The Caja, therefore, now concentrates its entrepreneurial efforts outside of Guipúzcoa — but still within the four provinces making up the Basque country. Also, in response to the increasing level of education and technical training within the Basque country, the Caja is now favoring the creation of more capital-intensive enterprises, which also provide opportunities for high levels of skill and training. These points indicate that the Caja is becoming increasingly important in the social and economic planning for this region of Spain.

In its entrepreneurial program, the Caja puts as much stress upon finding a group of people prepared to band themselves together to form a cooperative as it does upon the technical and economic feasibility of the enterprise. When the Caja finds such a group, its representative begins exploratory discussions regarding the type of enterprise to be created. When the discussions become serious, the Caja representative raises the financial question: is each member of the founding group ready to put some of his resources into the new enterprise? For groups that are not prepared to back their rhetoric with money, the project goes no farther. The commitment of money by the surviving groups is taken as evidence of seriousness of purpose, and the plans move on to the next stage.

The Caja does not finance any new enterprise without a feasibility study. The group is asked to nominate a person qualified to make such a study. If the group cannot recommend anyone with the required qualifications, the Caja proposes two or three individuals and asks the group to choose one of them. The feasibility specialist then works for one to two years within the Caja, his salary being paid by the Caja but being charged as a debt to the enterprise that is still to be borne.

Once a project is approved, 20 percent of the capital of the new enterprise is put up by the founding group, another 20 percent by the Spanish government through a program that makes loans to any new firm in terms of the number of jobs created, and 60 percent by the Caja. Many private firms fail for lack of working capital. The Caja meets this need for its new firm by covering the deficits during the first two years of its operation. However, the system is built upon the principle of not giving anything away; in addition to the salary of the person making the feasibility study, the 60 percent of the capital provided by the Caja and the sum of the losses incurred during the first two years all are charged as debts of the new firm to the Caja.

In the recent past, members of new firms have been required to contribute approximately $1,800 each. Anyone who does not have $1,800 can borrow from relatives, from a bank, or even from the Caja Laboral Popular. The resources required of the founders of a collective firm are much less than what the launching of a private enterprise would cost its entrepreneurs, who would not have 60 percent of the support provided by the Caja nor any arrangement to support the losses through the first two years.

The Caja also provides management-consulting services, especially to the new firms, helping them to set up the organization, determine the qualifications for the various positions, establish the system of accounting and cost control, and so on.

The Mondragón system is exceedingly dynamic, both economically and technologically. Not only has it become the largest producer of refrigerators and stoves in Spain, but it has also been selling approximately 20 percent of its output in international markets. Furthermore, Mondragón has been able to outbid private firms in industrialized nations for contracts to build turn-key industrial plants in developing nations. Also, while no set of firms can be completely independent of its economic environment, the record of Mondragón in the recession year 1974 provides evidence of its remarkable strength. During 1974, the Mondragón record shows membership (employment) up 7.5 percent, surplus (profits) up 26 percent, and exports up 56 percent.

SOCIAL GAINS AND SOCIAL PROBLEMS

Up to this point, we have demonstrated that Mondragón is exceptional among production cooperatives for its economic and technological dynamism. Has the system produced comparable social satisfactions?

That question cannot be answered in an introductory statement such as ours. Mondragón personnel people have carried out some employee surveys that indicate a good deal less than complete job satisfaction and yet show practically no one indicating any likelihood of leaving his firm.

The meaning of the survey responses can only be evaluated, for our purposes, when we have opportunites to compare them with responses of workers in comparable private industry employment. The expressed commitment to stay with the firm is supported by the exceedingly low turnover figure of 3 percent per year — and some of the 3 percent is accounted for by young wives dropping out to have children. This low figure is even more impressive if we place it in the context of a labor market in the Basque country that is becoming increasingly tight in recent years, so that members have not lacked alternative opportunities. It may be argued that many more members would drop out if it were not for the 20 percent of their original contribution and profits credited to their account that they would have to leave behind them. On the other hand, in many firms in the United States, employees accumulate substantial equity in an eventual pension that they lose entirely upon quitting, and yet turnover rates tend to be far higher.

We do not want to give the impression that we have discovered utopia. Especially in recent years, the system has encountered increasingly pressing problems that are requiring its leaders to reexamine the structure of the firms and the social processes involved in instituting change and in conflict resolution. Here is a brief interpretation of the problems on which Mondragón organizational leaders are now working.

The founding members believed in democracy and cooperation, but they were also dedicated to hard work. They believed further that, in order to compete with private enterprise, they would have to adopt the established methods of modern private management and industrial engineering. Thus, although top management is selected by the members, members of middle and lower management are appointed from the top down, and the immediate supervisor may direct his work force just as autocratically and inflexibly as his counterpart in the private firm. Furthermore, the organizational planners unquestioningly followed the pattern of *scientific management* in breaking jobs down into simple, routine operations and in structuring the work flow with assembly lines. Only one major principle of scientific management was rejected by the system: individual or group piece rates. Everyone is paid for the time worked, with the rate determined by the observations and estimates of industrial engineers — an aspect of procedures that became a point of controversy in recent conflicts.

It is clearly no coincidence that the most serious labor conflicts and the only strikes experienced by the system have occurred within Ulgor, the giant of the system. Even though Ulgor has spun off six new firms to make up Ularco, its success in becoming the largest producer of refrigerators and stoves in Spain brought with it steady expansion in numbers of members until, at the time of a brief strike in 1974, Ulgor had over 3,500 members in two plants. Size and growth together had made it impossible to maintain the informal, face-to-face relations that can prevail in small organizations.

As in the other firms, the members of Ulgor get together once a year to elect the Management Board, which in turn selects the general manager and other key members of management. This is the only direct influence the members have through formal channels in choosing members of management and guiding their policy.

There is another organ — the Social Council — designed to provide the members with channels for influencing management decisions on matters affecting member welfare. Intended to provide a more direct form of representation, the council is supposedly made up of one representative for every ten members, with constituencies being set up in rough correspondence to departments and work units. The maximum size of any Social Council is limited, however, to sixty members. This has the practical advantage of avoiding creation of a body so large as to be unwieldy, but, in the case of Ulgor, it results in a ratio of one representative to more than fifty members, compared to one-to-ten in nearly all of the other firms.

There appear to be more deep-seated problems with the Social Council than this question of ratios between representatives and members. According to the constitution of the cooperatives, the chairman of the Management Board is also chairman of the Social Council, and the Social Council has no direct power; it functions only in an advisory capacity to management.

There has apparently been a growing belief among members of Ulgor that the Social Council serves mainly as a one-way channel of communication from management to workers and does not provide channels through which workers can influence management. Since the Management Board has both the power and, apparently, the more interesting and challenging jobs to do, socially and politically active members are naturally inclined to run for positions on the Management Board, and Ulgor has found it increasingly difficult to recruit candidates for the Social Council.

The problem came to a head in the course of a program of comprehensive reevaluation of jobs throughout Ulgor. Management had come to the conclusion that the existing rates of pay no longer reflected the responsibilities or the skill and knowledge requirements of positions, and worker-members had also been complaining about some aspects of the rate structure. Thus the reevaluation was initiated. The studies were carried out in a fairly traditional industrial-engineering manner. Although members were interviewed to get a detailed account of their activities and responsibilities and were periodically informed, the job-evaluation committees made all decisions as to how the evaluations should be weighted. One of the general conclusions of the job evaluation was that managerial positions had grown in responsibilities over the years without corresponding increases in pay, and therefore an upward revision of the point score for many of these positions was recommended.

At the same time, the evaluators found that the work of many lower-level positions had been simplified, so that some reduction in point score for those positions was in order. With the new rate structure, the committee also introduced a supervisory evaluation of individual workers, with a possible range from zero to plus .03. That is, the individual whose job was classified at 1.3 could be paid at the rate of 1.30, 1.31, 1.32, or 1.33 — the small but symbolically significant differential being determined entirely by the judgment of the worker's immediate supervisor.

Even though the job evaluation program retained the three-to-one range between top and bottom jobs and, on the average for all jobs, the new rates were slightly higher than the old ones, the release of the committee's final report provoked a storm of protest. There was widespread protest against the supervisory evaluation, coupled with a demand to eliminate it and simply add .03 to the rating of all jobs. In an attempt to cushion the blow to those whose job point-scores had been reduced, the committee ruled that no one would have his pay reduced in his present job and any reduction would take effect only as vacant jobs were filled. This did not pacify the critics, some of whom claimed to be especially offended that management would decide that their jobs were not worth their current pay rates but would simply give them the difference between the old and new rate.

The job-evaluation committees had established a grievance procedure through which point scores on *individual* jobs could be changed, and many were, in fact, changed. However, no provision had been made for changing the bases of the job evaluation, which had been established through a two-year study and discussion process among commmittee members.

The leaders of the protest movement sought to place their grievances before the Management Board. The board ruled that, as specified in the constitution, such matters must be taken up first with the Social Council. Some of the protesters were members of the Social Council, but they had come to the conclusion that this organ was useless as a channel for redress, and they insisted upon meeting with the Management Board. When the Management Board stood firm in its refusal to meet with them, the protesters turned to direct action and organized a strike. The strike was very brief and not effective in shutting down production altogether. (It involved both Ulgor plants and 414 members and began 27 June; all were back at work by 4 July.) The constitution of Ularco distinguishes between sympathy strikes in support of general political positions and strikes in response to internal problems of the firm. The Management Board is free to impose mild, if any, penalties in the case of a sympathy strike, but expulsion from membership is supposed to be automatic for those provoking a strike in response to internal problems. Accordingly, 17 of the strike leaders were expelled, and 397 received lesser penalties.

They, in turn, followed the constitution and got the required one-third of the membership to sign a petition calling for a general membership meeting to consider the revocation of penalties. After several tense and stormy meetings, the membership voted to sustain management's position, and the dismissals were upheld by a vote of about 60 percent of those attending.

While the job evaluation results were sustained by the membership, the strike was obviously a traumatic experience for leaders and followers alike. This experience precipitated a period of reexamination of the structures and processes of governance of the cooperative. The Social Council undertook a self-study aimed to determine how it could become a more effective organ for representing worker problems to management. This self-study process was still going on at the time of our field trip, some months after the strike.

RESTRUCTURING WORK

As a result of the job evaluation process itself and the aftermath of the conflict, leaders of the system set out to inform themselves about what was being done in other parts of Europe (especially Sweden) regarding the restructuring of the work place. The first innovations along this line in Mondragón were begun in 1974 in Copreci, a member firm of Ularco, with a work force of 832, at that time devoted to manufacturing components for domestic appliances. A large part of the work here had been organized and based on assembly lines. With the strong support of the Workers Council of Ularco and Copreci, the personnel staff — working closely with Copreci management and engineers — began exploring ways in which the quality of working life might be improved without sacrificing productivity.

Although management officials were concerned about worker discontent, they were not responding to any direct demand for work restructuring. The crisis had made management painfully aware of the inherent contradiction between the typical job-evaluation system, which attaches monetary value to factors such as responsibility and initiative, and Tayloristic systems of work organization, which do not permit any scope for such factors among low-level jobs. The planners therefore recognized that, if they were going to act rationally, they would have to change either the job-evaluation system or the jobs to which that system would be applied. Staff people and managers then began exploring ways of restructuring jobs to offer greater opportunities for such characteristics as personal responsibility and initiative, which were so highly valued in their social philosophy.

Innovations were introduced first into those departments in which workers and supervisors seemed particularly receptive and interested. Each potential change was discussed thoroughly with the group and the supervisor. Management made it clear that the changes would be voluntary: those who wished to continue to work in the traditional assembly line would be allowed to do so. By the time of our visit (April 1975), assembly lines had been eliminated in several departments. Members did their work around tables and had taken over most of the traditional supervisory functions of organizing, directing, and inspecting their own work. The personnel staff also worked with these semiautonomous groups to help them manage their relations with other work units, such as those supplying them with parts, maintenance, and shipping. Although each group agreed to meet a minimum standard of output for a time period, as specified by management, the members were free to go at their own pace, working faster and slower in different time periods, instead of at the constant pace dictated by the assembly line. Such changes were accompanied by a new pattern of consultation and discussion with worker-members, so that — in Copreci at least — the democracy that had prevailed in community government was steadily extending itself into the work places.

Although it is too early to present detailed results of these changes at Copreci, the indications of the first few months were highly encouraging. Worker surveys indicated favorable reactions to the changes and increased job satisfaction. Management reported that, on the simpler assembly jobs, productivity had increased. On more complex jobs, the previous output standards had been maintained but with an appreciable reduction in rejects and reworking of units, which meant an increase in overall productivity on these jobs also.

At the time of our field study, management had not yet taken any steps to change the structure of work in Ulgor, where the most critical needs exist. The problem there was not lack of awareness of needs but existence of technological constraints. For the small assembly operations of Copreci, the work tables could be substituted for assembly lines with small cost to the cooperative. In Ulgor, the situation is completely different. There the conveyor lines are built to move large and heavy refrigerators and stoves through the plant. Abandoning this imposing assembly line system would require major new investments. At the time of our visit, engineers were working on plans for the restructuring of Ulgor, but, because the existing technology could not be changed piece by piece, as at Copreci, the Workers Council naturally required more extensive studies and cost estimates before agreeing to support such a major change.

CONCLUSIONS

When first hearing of Mondragón, those who long ago concluded that producers' cooperatives have no future in the industrialized world find it difficult to take the system seriously. They tend to reject its significance in the following terms:

1. No general conclusions can be drawn from a single case.

2. Mondragón's success is dependent upon the unique Basque culture.

3. Mondragón's success is dependent upon a unique human being, Don José María Arizmendi.

Therefore, they conclude, the saga of Mondragón is a human interest story of no general significance.

Let us assess these criticisms. In the first place, it is misleading to dismiss Mondragón as if it were a single case, comparable with individual firms that have appeared and disappeared in the course of United States and European history. Mondragón includes a growing number of industrial firms, an extensive network of institutions for savings and industrial investment, an educational system, a student-operated industrial cooperative, a research and development center, and a number of consumer cooperatives — all linked together in mutually supporting relationships. Nothing remotely like the Mondragón system has ever appeared before anywhere in the world.

In the second place, Mondragón clearly runs counter to two of the key generalizations applied by Paul Blumberg to industrial producers' cooperatives and noted at the outset of this article. Mondragón is not "plagued with chronic shortages of capital." Capital accumulation has been so rapid that the Caja Laboral Popular has had to develop an extensive entrepreneurial campaign creating new firms to utilize the available capital. Also, barring a complete financial collapse of the whole industrial and banking system, there is no possible way in which a Mondragón firm can "degenerate...into a simple profit-making, profit-seeking business."

What should a scientist do when he encounters phenomena that appear to violate previously well-established generalizations? If he immediately seeks reasons to disregard the new evidence, he is unlikely to contribute to the advance of knowledge. Some skepticism is, of course, justified, but the scientist should at least consider the possibility that the new findings may have some general significance.

Third, Mondragón is not robbed of general significance because of the role of either the Basque culture or Don José María Arizmendi, although clearly neither of those factors is transferable to other settings. It may indeed take a great man or woman to create and further develop a social invention of the magnitude of Mondragón, yet lesser human beings can examine that invention and seek to apply what they can learn from the structure and social process of Mondragón to organizations and organizational systems they themselves seek to build within their own cultures.

The general significance of Mondragón appears to us to be in the following structural and policy elements:

1. Mondragón has solved the capital accumulation problem in two principal ways. Since 70 percent of the profits are distributed to the members only by being credited to their accounts, the firm has 85 to 90 percent of profits to reinvest, instead of 15 to 20 percent (the reserve fund). In addition, drawing on the *private* savings of its rapidly growing membership, the Caja Laboral Popular has financed roughly half the growth of the industrial firms.

This experience suggests that, if the founders of an industrial cooperative firm want that firm to survive and maintain its cooperative character, they should establish a policy of retaining member shares of profits in the accounts of the firm rather than paying them out in cash. Such a policy must be established at the outset or not at all, since the members can hardly be persuaded later to give up what they have been receiving as current income.

Since in the United States credit unions would be barred by law from investing in risky new firms, the Caja model may not be immediately transferable. However, the bill to establish a consumers' cooperative bank extends such support to producers' cooperatives.

2. The Caja has developed an entrepreneurial and planning organization that has become a major influence in the social and economic development of the Basque region. Instead of being guided by principles of *profit maximization,* the Caja looks upon profits as a *limiting factor.* The firm to be created must be judged to be economically viable, but, beyond that threshold, investment decisions are based upon judgments of the social and economic needs and interests of the people directly involved and in terms of long-range plans for the development of the region.

In other countries, industrial producers' cooperatives have arisen and disappeared as isolated cases, having little or no relation to each other. Such firms have not had a supporting organization like the Caja, constantly creating new cooperative organizations. Nor have they had policies and procedures allowing them, as they grow, to spin off new cooperative firms, such as the six firms born out of Ulgor.

3. Mondragón has established a form of ownership that makes it practically impossible for the industrial firms to revert to private ownership. In the United States, employee-owned firms have generally been based upon individual stock ownership. Under that form of ownership, the firm can disappear or lose its cooperative character either because it fails or because it is too successful. Success calls for expansion, but the original employee-owners are not anxious to dilute their equity by having the firm issue stock to newly hired workers. In addition, when the firm has been successful over a number of years, retiring employee-owners will hold stock valued so high that incoming workers will not be able to buy into the firm (Berman 1967; Bellas 1972). Or, as recently happened in the case of the *Kansas City Star,* a private investor may make an offer that the employee-owners feel they cannot afford to refuse.

There are ways of organizing firms on a one-worker-one-vote basis and protecting the continuation of this form even under current United States laws.[7] But, unless founders of new employee-owned firms have something like the Mondragón model in mind, they are likely to establish ownership in the traditional United States style, with potential power directly linked to the number of shares owned. They will thereby be practically guaranteeing the eventual disappearance of the firm as an employee-owned enterprise.

4. The integration of mutually supporting organizations — from education to banking to research and development to manufacturing — has clearly been important to the success of the Mondragón firms. We cannot expect such a fully integrated organizational system to develop in the United States, and yet past research and experience suggest that the cooperative industrial firm existing as an island in a sea of private industry and commerce has poor prospects for long-run success. Therefore, those who seek to apply Mondragón lessons to the development of industrial producers' cooperatives in the United States would be wise to examine the possibility of building some of the supporting and collaborating organizations that may be essential to the long-run success of the industrial cooperative.

Yet other important lessons can be drawn from the difficulties and partial failures encountered by Mondragón. First, for self-managed organizations, "Small is beautiful," to extend the doctrine propounded by Schumacher (1973) for technology. The founders of Mondragón saw expansion in terms of the spinning off of parts of existing firms or the creation of new ones rather than in the building of giant enterprises. In fact, six new firms have been spun off of Ulgor, although, for reasons beyond the scope of this paper, Ulgor continued to grow, reaching over 3,500 members at the time of its most severe labor troubles. In fact, by the end of 1974, more than a quarter of the total membership of all the industrial firms was within Ulgor.

When a firm has only 100 to 200 members — as is the case in most of the firms — everyone knows everyone else, and considerable worker participation in decision-making may take place informally. A firm as large as Ulgor, however, has long since passed the limit where informal social processes can offer workers a sense that they are participating in decision-making. Leaders of the Mondragón system are currently still struggling with the task of creating a formal system for promoting large-scale participatory democracy.

Second, there is an inherent contradiction between Taylorism (or scientific management) in the organization of industrial work and one-worker-one-vote governance of the industrial firm. This contradiction was not recognized in the early years of the Mondragón system. The founders of Ulgor believed that, in order to compete, they had to adopt "modern" methods of management, a theory that led them to design organizations with assembly lines, work simplification based upon specialization and routinization, close supervision, and so on.

It is only in recent years that the inherent contradiction has become recognized. Now, while they continue to regard the one-worker-one-vote principle as a necessary feature of their system, the policy makers have recognized that a single annual election of the board of directors does not give the members a sense of participatory democracy nor does it by itself permit the full development and utilization of human talents and efforts within the work place. As they are now consciously working through the contradictions of Taylorism versus participatory democracy, the policy makers are vigorously experimenting with new forms of work organization, eliminating assembly lines, developing autonomous work groups, and setting up processes of worker participation in decision-making at the shop level.

This process of resolving contradictions was still in its early stages at the time of our field work in 1975, but already one of the firms had made changes in work organization comparable in magnitude and significance with the most advanced work along this line taking place in Scandinavia and elsewhere. The speed of change is impressive testimony to the fact that the leaders of Mondragón are not simply following a doctrine laid down for them years ago by a remarkable founder but are building a learning system that facilitates their adaptation to new problems and new conditions.

NOTES

1. Jose Letona Arrieta and Juan Leibar Gurich, *Mondragón* (San Sebastián: Graficos Izarra, 1970), p. 101.

2. Davydd Greenwood, *Unrewarding Wealth* (New York: Cambridge University Press, 1976), pp. 10-12.

3. Julio Caro Baroja, *Los Vascos* (Madrid: Ediciones Istmo, 1971).

4. Ana Gutiérrez Johnson, "Cooperativism and Justice: A Study and Cross-Cultural Comparison of Preferences for Forms of Equity Among Basque Students of a Cooperative School-Factory" (M.S. thesis, Cornell University, 1976).

5. Fernando Diáz-Plaja, *El Español y los Siete Pecados Capitales* (Madrid: Alianza Editorial, 1966).

6. For studies of Basque culture, see particularly Caro Baroja, *Los Vascos* and *Estudios Vascos* (San Sebastian, Editorial Txertoa, 1973). For additional general information on Mondragón, see F. Aldabaldetrecu, and J. Gray, "De L'Artisanat Industriel au Complexe Coopératif: L'Experience de Mondragón." *Archives Internationales de Sociologie de la Cooperation* (July-Dec. 1967) Paris; Robert Oakeshott, "Mondragón: Spain's Oasis of Democracy," in Jaraslov Vanek (1975); and Pablo Trivelli, "Algunas Consideraciones sobre las Coopérativas Industriales de Mondragón," *Revista Eure* (no. 7) Santiago, Chile.

7. See George Benello and David Ellerman, "The Funding of Self-Managed Enterprises," *News From the Federation for Economic Democracy*, 1 (1977).

9

The Origin, Structure, and Problems of Four British Producers' Cooperatives

J. David Edelstein

Although many dozens of British producers' coops were established under the inspiration of the Guild Socialists in the early 1920s, most of these were fairly small and were wiped out within a few years by an economic depression. Currently, the only older producers' coop with well over a hundred workers is the little-known Equity Shoes Ltd., which dates from 1886 (see Editors' note on page following). Of six moderately large producers' cooperatives in Great Britain in 1975, three were formed with financial assistance from the Labor Government under the Conservatives' 1973 Industry Act. Two of the six larger coops, Scott Bader and Bewley Cafes, were converted from privately owned companies in 1952 and 1973 respectively.[1] Not much interest has been shown in producers' coops by British consumer coop societies, which have retail sales of over $3,500,000,000 a year (*London Times*, 28 May 1975), or — until recently — by the trade unions.

THE *SCOTTISH DAILY NEWS*

The immediate impetus to the struggle which resulted in the formation of the *Scottish Daily News (SDN)* coop was the imminent

J. David Edelstein is Professor of Sociology, Syracuse University. The basic research for this chapter was conducted while he was a Visiting Professorial Fellow, Centre for Contemporary European Studies, University of Sussex. He is currently writing on workers' control in large organizations as related to the political process in society.

This chapter is a revision of a paper presented at the 71st Annual Meeting of the American Sociological Association, New York City, 1976. Some of this material appeared in J. David Edelstein, "Trade Unions in British Producers' Cooperatives," *Industrial Relations*, 18 (Fall 1979): 358-63.

closure, on twelve days' notice, of the Glasgow plant of the *Scottish Daily Express (SDN*'s predecessor) and the *Scottish Sunday Express* in March 1974, and the transfer of publication to Manchester, England. Another newspaper of the Beaverbrook chain published in the same building, the *Evening Citizen,* was bought by the rival *Evening Times* and discontinued at the same time. The loss of 1,850 jobs was considered a disaster in Scotland, and Lord Beaverbrook's[2] Glasgow workers received a great deal of sympathy inside and outside the labor movement. However, it was not until April 1975 that the *SDN* coop was formed, and publication began on 5 May — after a year involving an occupation of the plant, lobbying, and fund-raising.[3] The staffing level was 500 workers of all kinds for the publication of five regional editions in Scotland, with an anticipated circulation stabilized at about 250,000. The Sunday edition was discontinued.

A turning point in British industrial relations and politics occurred with the worker sit-in at the Upper Clyde Shipbuilders (UCS) in 1971. This unsuccessful attempt to prevent the liquidation of the shipyards by the Conservative government received national attention because of the occupation itself and the demands for nationalization under workers' control. The sit-in was studied and emulated elsewhere with improvements in the strategy for setting up committees for security, finance, and food; dealing with the legal aspects of the occupation; and utilizing the mass media.

The Secretary of State for Industry during the period of the *SDN* coop's formation was Anthony Wedgwood Benn, a left-labor member of the cabinet who had become the most prominent (and controversial) proponent of workers' control in Britain. He advocated government support for moves toward workers' control initiated from below. Benn was shifted to the less sensitive cabinet post of Secretary for Energy in June 1975, under great pressure from industry and the Labor Party's right wing.

Even the presence of a sympathetic secretary for industry did not prevent excruciating delays in the formation of producers' coops, not only at *SDN*, but elsewhere as well. The workers who founded the Triumph-Meriden coop, which manufactures high-priced motorcy-

---

Editors' note: Of the four British producers' cooperatives discussed by Edelstein, one, Equity Shoes, is an older established firm. Three, the *Scottish Daily News,* Triumph-Meriden Motorcycle Company, and Kirkby Manufacturing and Engineering, were formed in 1975 as a reaction to plant closings. Kirkby, though mentioned, is not discussed in detail.

cles primarily for the American market, struggled for eighteen months — those workers who lasted. There have been a number of complications in forming a coop under duress: finding financial backing, assuring investors or the government of a stable market for the product, finding lawyers with producers' coop experience, negotiating as favorable a price as possible with the former owners, and obtaining credit from suppliers. It seems clear that much more money and practical assistance will have to be provided or facilitated by government if many more large or moderate-sized producers' coops are to be established in Britain.

The Board of Directors

Complete control over the management of *SDN* was vested in a worker-dominated board of management known as the Executive Council, subject only to the veto of an Investors' Council (to be described) on borrowing money, issuing or allotting shares of the company, involving the company to a material extent outside the publishing business, or reducing dividends to shareholders below 40 percent of the previous year's profits. However, the availability of such profits was to be decided by the Executive Council.

The Executive Council consisted of six "shop-floor representatives," to use the language of an early Discussion Document, two councillors elected by a majority vote of the Investors' Council from among its own members, and the general manager and editor *ex officio* with vote. Occupations or trade unions were not represented on the Executive Council as such; elections were by secret ballot of workers (holders of "employee shares") at a general meeting. However, election by or from subgroups at the general meeting was possible if it were so decided. The general manager and the editor were elected by the majority vote of the Executive Council, and it picked its own chairperson, who had to be a shop-floor representative.

Investors

The Investors' Council consisted of eight members: five elected at a meeting of holders of ordinary shares, with *SDN* employees ineligible as candidates; two elected by the Executive Council from among its own number; and the general manager *ex officio*. Employees of *SDN* could vote if they had invested in ordinary shares. The general secretary of the Scottish Trades Union Congress, James Jack, was one of the two initial representatives of the Investors' Council to the

Executive Council. The other was the millionaire publisher and former Labor Member of Parliament, Robert Maxwell.

Financing

Maxwell invested £114,000 in ordinary shares in the initial financing of the coop. The government was prepared to lend the coop 50 percent of the capital cost of £1,200,000, provided £475,000 was "irrevocably received" from elsewhere (in effect, from the sale of shares). Maxwell had agreed to buy one share for every two bought by the workers themselves.

The workers bought £200,000 of stock from their unemployment pay, all but £30,000 of this for ordinary shares which would permit voting in elections to the Investors' Council. The final £175,000 was raised from stock sales at large, with the Scottish Graphical Association (£5,000) and sympathetic workers among the purchasers. Finally, Beaverbrook accepted £725,000 in secured and unsecured notes toward the purchase of his plant and equipment.

One common problem in the formation of new producers' coops under threat of plant closures is negotiating a reasonable financial arrangement with the owner. This may involve not only a purchase price, but also interest charges, as in the case of *SDN*. In the case of the Triumph-Meriden motorcycle coop, there was also the question of marketing arrangements, and, specifically, the question of the price of each cycle to the former parent company which was to handle the sales for the first two years. The pressure on the workers arises from deadlines imposed by government, from the obvious pressures built up during a long period of unemployment (over a year in the case of both *SDN* and Triumph-Meriden), and from a fear of being left with nothing at all.

There are also pressures on the private owner to reach agreement with the workers, including the cost of plant maintenance and the tie-up of capital during a sit-in, adverse publicity, and the fear of antagonizing government (subsidies may be wanted for other operations). Workers on strike may also stop the shipment of goods at an owner's operations elsewhere.

Organizational Structure and Philosophy

The prospectus states: "The Executive Council has complete control over the management of the Company subject only to the express powers reserved in the Investors' Council. . . ." The Discussion Document states that the "Council's role will be to decide on general and long-term policy," and that general meetings of workers "will be held quarterly or more often as required to keep everyone informed and everyone involved." Thus, strictly speaking, the membership meeting had only advisory powers. However, *SDN* had no detailed constitution or bylaws, although I was told that the need for these was recognized, as was the need to remedy some defects in existing rules or practices.[4]

There was little unusual about the departmental structure of the *SDN* coop. The general manager was the senior executive officer, but he did not interfere in editorial matters. The managers of the production, circulation, advertising, and finance divisions reported directly to the general manager. There were from three to eight departments within each of these divisions, with a foreman (overseer) and one or two assistant or working foremen (working deputies) in each department of the production division, the largest. I was told that the number of foremen had been reduced by somewhat more than the amount required by the reduction in work force, and the workers had taken on more responsibility.

Under the editor were assistant, managing, and production editors, with a night editor reporting to the assistant editor, and then news, features, sports, pictures, and other departments. The general manager was recruited from a management consulting firm, from which he took a year's leave of absence.

On the face of it, the operating philosophy of *SDN* was to elect the editor and general manager and to let them get on with it: to let the manager manage under general policy set by the Executive Council, and, most significantly, to allow both to appoint their underlings. Such seeming common sense, often expressed in almost this way, is the conventional wisdom of British (and American) society, although it does not have universal acceptance. (The Workers' Action Committee chose all of the initial supervisors because there was no one else to do so at the time).

The concepts and ideology of the semiautonomous work group, job enrichment, and creativity in work had apparently made little headway as such in three of the four producers' coops I visited in June 1975, the exception being Triumph-Meriden. However, all claimed, implicitly or explicitly, a more relaxed and participative style of supervisory leadership, and solidarity and loyalty to the coop as important motivators of their workers. The question of survival of the three new coops no doubt made personal gratification through work appear a secondary consideration for the time being.

The strong unions in the printing trades continued to function at

SDN and provided vehicles for some degree of participation in decision-making. The shop-floor chairperson of the Executive Council, Allister Mackie (Maxwell was cochairperson) told me, "I, as a workers' council member, ignore trade union problems so as not to usurp their function." As a trade unionist, he also felt strongly that unions should not be represented as such in management. In contrast, the top management at the Kirkby coop, both originally and eventually as embodied in its constituion, was under the control of the shop stewards committee and especially of its two conveners, who were legally responsible for the coop's activities (Eccles 1976, p. 163). Day-to-day power rested with the two conveners, the general manager, and the financial controller.

The Role of the Unions

In each of the larger departments, at least, including those with white-collar workers, there was a Father of the Chapel (called an FoC; a woman would have been called an MoC), elected annually; a Clerk of the Chapel, elected for two or three years; and a Committee of the Chapel, all functioning as union members. There were fourteen chapels at *SDN*. Presumably, some departments (which may have had as few as eight members) consisted entirely of members of a single union, but this was not necessarily the case. At plant level, there was a Fathers of the Chapels Committee, usually called the FoC's Committee, with a convener. This interunion, joint shop-stewards committee had the functions, in American terms, of both a grievance committee and a negotiations committee. Many aspects of the union-management agreement could be changed at any time, as is common in Britain.

There was the equivalent of a closed shop for most of the production unions, as is the rule in the printing industry. The union stewards were supposed to keep their unions informed of significant developments in the plant.

The key role of the Fathers of the Chapels Committee in the printing industry was to be maintained or strengthened under the *SDN* coop, according to the Discussion Document, as follows:

1. The FoC's Committee was to discuss "production improvements (subject to union co-operation)," which seems to imply positive suggestions rather than simply reactions to those from management.

2. The FoC's Committee was to serve as "liaison between Works Council (the Executive Council) and work force," which could be analagous to a role in a private industry but which sounds uncharacteristically positive here.

The liaison role of the FoC's Committee was to be strengthened in two ways. First, "Chapels making approaches to the Works Council *on any issue* [emphasis added] will do so through the FoC's Committee. The approach eventually will be a joint one between the chapel concerned and the FoC's Committee and, if required, the appropriate union official [from outside the plant]."

Second, "A member of the Works Council will be available to be in attendance, if requested, at all meetings of the FoCs, to report to the FoCs on Council decisions."

According to Jimmy Roy, the production manager, "The FoC's Committee meets to discuss the departments' problems, and possibly to discuss them with me. There could be a manning problem; or a matter of sick pay...."

And, on innovations in production, Roy said, "In quite a few instances, suggestions have come through the FoC's Committee. We are in a transition period. I can see the FoC's Committee falling into a definite pattern."

The unions were also expected to contribute to the success of the enterprise by allowing a greater flexibility with respect to work practices. However, on being asked whether trade lines might be crossed eventually, Roy replied, "You couldn't, from a union point of view, and a fair amount of retraining would be involved. Jobs are interlinked, but only by the flow of the work. There are only a few areas where the union set-up allows for retraining."

A detailed disputes procedure provided, in the event of a failure of a chapel (represented by a union official if the chapel desired) and the Executive Council to resolve a dispute, "that the case will then be referred to an Advisory Council comprising union branch secretaries," after which the union member or chapel may "process the matter through normal trade union machinery." The Advisory Council was unique to this disputes procedure.

The legitimacy of a stoppage seemed to be recognized only when it was called by a national union, in which event the disputes procedure would not apply. Workers are warned, in a somewhat ominous conclusion: "Acceptance of this procedure will be a condition of employment on all employees."

Industrial relations under the coop improved greatly over the normally abrasive relations in the printing industry, and one is entitled to wonder whether the unions' conventional role in a coop might eventually have become less significant, especially in a plant with only several hundred workers.

The Wage Structure

All three of the new coops I visited started out with new and much simplified wage-structures which moved in the direction of equalization, and which substantially raised the relative and absolute pay of the least skilled manual workers. At *SDN,* there were only two grades of manual workers, the skilled tradesmen, who received £60 per week on night shift, and all others, mostly members of Natsopa, who received £52.50. Foremen received 15 percent more. When asked about possible alienation among low-status workers, Roy said that most of the now more numerous suggestions he was receiving were coming from such workers.

Journalists received 15 percent more than skilled tradesmen on night shift, or £69 per week, apparently without respect to day or shift work (*SDN* is a morning newspaper). There was also a specialist rate — for political news, for example — which was 18 percent higher. The editor received £150 per week, with the same salary anticipated for the general manager after a permanent manager was employed. Clerical workers were relatively underpaid; "experienced workers" on shift work received only £33 per week. There were no women manual workers (and only five or six women journalists), so low clerical pay was sex-related.

The simplification of the pay structure contributed toward better industrial relations, and possibly toward greater productivity. Roy stated, "From a production view, virtually all snags are ironed out before I even hear of them." Interdepartmental relationships were also much improved. There was a feeling of tolerance when things went wrong, where "they would be up in arms" previously.

At Triumph-Meriden, there is substantial savings in the payroll department, due to the precise equality of all but two managers' paychecks. There is no overtime in a normal week, and people are not docked for sickness.

The First Executive Council Election

The established principle at *SDN* was one person, one vote. There were, of course, only six worker-representatives on the ten-person Executive Council, but the *ex officio* editor and general manager were elected by the council itself. Shop-floor representatives were to be elected for three-year terms, with two retiring annually to assure continuity of operation.

The results of the first regular election, after six weeks of operation, were surprising and disturbing to many. There were thirteen nominations for the six posts. Four of the six original worker-representatives were reelected, including three craftsmen. The only Communist on the council was defeated. One craftsman was replaced by the assistant editor, who had been prominent on the Workers' Action Committee. However, the other "shop-floor representative" was the millionaire publisher and major *SDN* stockholder, Robert Maxwell, who had been on the original Executive Council as a representative of the Investors' Council and cochairperson. The two replaced councillors had been among the most outspoken of Maxwell's critics.

Leadership Crisis and Demise of *SDN*

Whether it was cause or symptom, Robert Maxwell's election to the Executive Council of the *SDN* coincided with the beginning of the end. About two months later, in early August, with circulation below the break-even point, the Executive Council voted to hand over executive authority for the paper's circulation and advertising to Maxwell. The general manager resigned a week later, and Maxwell then described himself as the chief executive officer. Allister Mackie, who had led the Workers' Action Committee, resigned from the Executive Council on 15 September, stating that "the democratic structure of management had been replaced by autocracy." Maxwell claimed that *SDN* was still a cooperative as long as he could be sacked as executive officer. On 21 September, the *Sunday Times* ran a one and one-half page exposé, "How Maxwell Sabotaged the Workers' Dream," charging him with authoritarian rule and implying that he wanted to take over the newspaper for his own ends. Maxwell resigned as chief officer on 1 October, citing the adverse effects of the *Sunday Times* article. The *SDN* had been losing over £15,000 each week.

The government refused to provide or facilitate the obtaining of £250,000 requested to keep going until spring, with publication planned on a "twenty-four-hour basis" rather than a morning-paper basis only. A meeting with Prime Minister Harold Wilson produced no results. Maxwell bid to buy the building and facilities, but the liquidator (nominated by the Executive Council) rejected this bid as too low. The paper shut down on 8 November 1975, with the workers threatening to occupy the building again to prevent the removal of machinery.

The main problems of the coop clearly lay with the market, or its adaptation to it. But it was the depressed state of the newspaper industry which led to its formation. The coop could have been saved, at least for a while, but for the political timidity of the government. The workers claimed that it would cost the government £1,250,000 a year to keep them on the dole. In addition, the coop never really had the active support of the Trades Union Council, or even of most of the printing trades unions.

There have been other reasons suggested for *SDN*'s demise, and these seem to have played contributory but nevertheless important roles. Mackie regarded a dependence on Maxwell as "the basic weakness" of the coop, and wrote in great detail about Maxwell's attempt, from the very beginning, to gain control by highly unprincipled means (Mackie 1976). A weakness in editorial direction, resulting in a flabby stylistic and editorial identity, has also been claimed. *SDN* drew back from a somewhat more radical political stance shortly after its formation, but remained left-of-center by British standards.

It is ironic that, on the day before closure, the press reported Labor Party proposals (as distinct from those of the Labor government) for aid to new, independent, smaller periodicals, and for industrial democracy in the press ranging from workers on boards to full cooperative ownership.

EQUITY SHOES LIMITED

The Equity Shoes Limited coop, in Leicester, is an economic but not a participative success, after ninety years in production. Its well-documented history povides some clues for the avoidance of a similar decline in participatory democracy. The original rules were based on those of a French cooperative stove factory, with very few changes (Kirkham 1973, pp. 47–8).

Committee of Management

The president and the eight other members of the Committee of Management are elected for two-year (formerly one-year) terms by a general meeting, with half of the ordinary committee posts subject to election each year. The rules do not require secret ballot, but one must be taken on any matter if demanded by any ten members present at a membership meeting. The general manager and the secretary are not *ex officio* members of the committee. Any member of the committee "may be removed from office at any time by two-thirds of the votes cast at a special meeting of the society" (rule 55). Committee members currently receive extra compensation of £35 per year.

The committee has the power to appoint a general manager, a secretary (who is in charge of all books and records), and at least technically "commercial travellers," although the former two can be removed only by a two-thirds vote. The committee has "full power to conduct the business of the society and to exercise. . . all the powers of the society" except a few prescribed "or otherwise required to be exercised by the society in meeting" (rule 64). However, there are exceedingly few matters which the ordinary membership meeting may not be "required" to take up, since, in addition to its usual business, it may act on "any other matter of which at least 28 days' written notice" has been given "by any member" (rule 38iii). A special meeting must be called at the request of any twenty members. Thus, constitutionally, the membership can exercise far greater potential power than was the case at *SDN*.

Organizational Structure

Nonemployees of Equity Shoes, either individuals or organizations, may purchase up to 1,000 one-pound shares, with the permission of the Committee of Management, and, if five or more shares are held, may cast not more than one vote at a membership meeting. Mr. S. W. Pepper, the secretary, told me, on my visit in June 1975, that only two or three of 1,120 nonemployee shareholders attended the last membership meeting (technically a shareholders' meeting), and that, as far as he knows, nonemployee attendance has always been very low. One hundred retail cooperative societies are shareholders.

The current situation with respect to participation was summarized by the secretary:

> The board [Committee of Management] used to meet weekly and there were quarterly [monthly until the 1940s] membership meetings in addition. In time, there was no one at membership meetings but the board members. Now we only have annual general meetings [plus a meeting for nominations]. Thirty-one people attended the next-to-the-last general meeting, and fifty-two were at the last one. . . . Four of the board members work in offices. Of the other five, three work in the lasting department. Until this last year, three people out of the clicking department were on the board. . . .

Question: Are there any sub-committees, under the board or

otherwise?

> There is only one these days, the social and welfare sub-committee; we used to have more. We found it was time-consuming — matters only went to the board, anyhow. Also, our superannuation fund has trustees. (He added that private companies in the shoe industry haven't usually had retirement funds.)

Question: How are supervisors chosen?

> At one time, they were entirely chosen by the board, and presently by the manager; and it is better now. For example, we may have no repesentative from the clicking room, so how could the board decide...? The managing board could take back the decision....

> At one time, the board would appoint a manager and promptly tell him how to do the job. Now, the general manager runs the factory day-to-day.... There was board interference in technical and working matters. A supervisor could seldom be right. There was a period of change — gradually over the past twenty years. The very beginning of the war saw a change....

Question: Isn't the ideal situation supposed to be for board "interference"?

> It is the ideal, but...all the board members work every day. It is extremely difficult, under those circumstances, to get the whole picture. So many things are happening....

> The board meets monthly, but...we could call a meeting sometimes on half an hour's notice.

Question: Are there many emergencies?

> Only when things happen outside our control; inside the organization, no. We have a very good working arrangement. People don't interfere with the workings of other people.

Question: How about industrial relations?

> The shoe industry is a trouble-free industry anyhow, so we have never been put to the test. I don't think we have had a strike in the industry in this century....

> All board members are members of unions. Now we don't have stewards on the board [at the moment], but for a long time we did have. But no one *regards* themselves [*sic*] as shop stewards.... [They are]...regarded as people who collect subscriptions [dues]. This may be a matter of the shoe industry....

Wages are paid according to the national agreements of the respective unions in the shoe industry. Sixty percent of the work force are on piecework. Most of those on the sewing operations are women. The secretary commented, "Almost 100 percent of the piecework rates are standard in the industry. . . . Perhaps we refer to the union on such matters three times a year."

There are no problems of lines of demarcation between unions in the shoe industry. Nevertheless, people tend to stay within their own departments.

Question: Is there any ideal of people knowing many jobs?

> At one time, we would employ a school-leaver, and he would do a little of everything. . .[during]. . .a probationary period of six or seven years. Now, a school-leaver wants to do piecework immediately. Outside forces intervene.

The major technical and business decisions appear to involve annual style changes in women's shoes (men's shoes are not made), which are resolved primarily between the five designers and the sales people, and the occasional introduction of new machinery for specific operations. The secretary commented, "We could go through a normal year without any major investment decisions. We may lease a machine for a temporary style. The last major thing was when the warehouse had to be rebuilt, in 1964."

Workers' suggestions on improvements in production seem not to reach the level of the Committee of Management, and, according to the secretary, the current committee makes few suggestions on its own; but he emphasized that the *current* committee "are a very placid lot." However, the manager "goes around the factory all day, and is known to most since he was a lad," so suggestions may be made informally.

Analysis: The Equity Coop

After my visit to Equity Shoes, I tentatively concluded that the general decline in membership participation was due primarily to economic stability and success — the absence of important problems — and, secondarily, to the weakness of unionism in the shoe industry. There had indeed been economic success, with good profits since 1968 and a dividend of 13 percent of annual salary to workers in the most recent year. A source in the cooperative movement, outside of Equity, told me that Equity was thought to have had for many years the best general manager in the British shoe industry.

However, a somewhat different explanation of democracy's decline emerges from a historical study of Equity by Mavis Kirkham (1973). The effective power of the individual craftsmen, work groups, and the membership was lost only after numerous struggles over perhaps fifty or more years. Initially, the workers in the departments lost power to the elected Committee of Management, which argued that it ruled in the name of all the workers, not just a segment of them; later, the committee lost power to the manager and his supervisory hierarchy. The latter did not take place simply because of the greater size and complexity of the organization and its technology, although an understandable failure to anticipate these developments undoubtedly played a role. More important in the transfer of power was a frequent failure of the committee to reach substantial agreement on important questions, and the referral of these problems to the manager for resolution. The managers then became accountable for lack of economic success, and, more often than not, became the scapegoats. For a protracted period, each manager was eventually fired, the victim of a downturn in business. This tendency could conceivably surface again in hard times. It is not uncommon in other producers' coops.

But the managers under pressure pointed to "bad workmanship, carelessness, indiscipline...as the source of the troubles. The reactions of its officials were deliberately based on the same premises as these of management elsewhere" (Kirkham 1973, p. 89).

Therefore, business crises were usually met by management-directed steps towards greater efficiency and lower costs of production, which sometimes threatened the job security of sections of the workers and perhaps cowed them into accepting a more passive role. Now that most "managerial" problems appear to have been resolved, promotion is again from within, as in the early days, and this in turn may add to the passivity of those seeking supervisory posts. Merit increases are also outside the control of workers in the departments.

But perhaps most fundamental in the decline of democracy was the failure to provide an ideology and channels for workers' control over the daily life of the coop. Kirkham writes of the early Equity cooperators that their ideas on sharing in management were sketchy and without foundation in basic principles. This was compatible with democratic organization so long as the coop was small and consisted of craftsmen with control over their individual work processes. But there was no provision for joint control with increased size, and the existence of a workers' board made a concentration of power in the top officials appear safer.

Many of the advantages of the cooperative remain. There are no outside directors or capitalists to absorb any considerable share of the profits. The supervisors and white-collar workers apparently work harder and longer without extra pay. No nonprobationary workers have been fired for a long time. There is little turnover, and most of the older workers know the coop's history and are loyal to the cooperative concept. The meetings to fill the infrequent vacancies in the elected board may be attended by half the workers. Interpersonal relationships at the work-group level appear to be good, according to an outside survey made in 1968. But Mavis Kirkham chose to sum up by damning with faint praise: "Although for most of its employees Equity is not now basically different from any other shoe firm, it is considered to be a good firm to work for" (Kirkham 1973, p. 98).

If there is a lesson, it would appear to be that power should be devolved to work groups, departments, and departmental committees, and these should assume routine administrative as well as watchdog functions to the extent compatible with efficiency, which a great deal of previous research shows would be considerable. This devolution, together with a supporting ideology and a general membership constitutionally more powerful than the Executive Council, would seem to be necessary for a stable workers' democracy.

There is also obviously a contradiction between cooperative ideals and the requirements for rank-and-file participation, on the one hand, and considerable disparities in income on the other. Economic success and the recruitment of workers committed to cooperative ideals would permit a movement towards a greater equality.

THE TRIUMPH-MERIDEN MODEL

The Triumph-Meriden motorcycle coop near Coventry began with 160 workers in March 1975, soon increased to over 300, and, in February 1977, had 700 workers. It has an unusual work force: "Families have served apprenticeships at 'The Triumph' man and boy. Those who have hung on [while trying to establish the coop] have worked there for 10, 20, and even 40 years. They 'live, breathe and dream motorcycles' " (Huckfield 1974, p. 29). Perhaps these factors contributed to the workers' willingness to accept equal pay for all except the two officials, as already described. At any rate, the equal pay certainly removed some of the problems which unions ordinarily deal with, and facilitated a different role for the unions in the coop.

Each of the eight unions in the plant elects one member of the board of directors, which is a policy-making body. When I asked a board member why the smaller unions should have equal representation, he replied, "We are all in this together, aren't we?"

Bill Lapworth, the regional official of the Transport and General Workers, who played a key role in setting up the coop (together with a local Member of Parliament), holds one of the three outside directorships. One of these, not yet filled at the time of my visit, was reserved for a representative of the government (see *Platform*, the paper of the Cooperative Party, July 1975).

The shares of the company are held jointly by three trustees, solely to meet the requirements for the corporation form which the coop adopted. There was no capital raised by the sale of stock, and even the workers individually own no shares; the nearly £5,000,000 in capital came primarily from a grant and a long-term loan from the government. The original trustees included the Labor Member of Parliament from Meriden.

The trustees *must* vote as instructed by the "beneficiaries," meaning the workers. The workers elect a "beneficiary committee" of eleven from their ranks to assist in breaking a deadlock, should the beneficiaries not register a 75 percent majority on any matter at a meeting which must be attended by at least half the workers (Carnoy and Levin 1976, p. 49).

There are no supervisors or foremen, but rather *organizers* and *coordinators* appointed by the elected board of directors. I was told that the organizers "ask people to do things rather than order them." And, of course, the organizers receive the same pay as other workers.

There is a five-person elected *grievance committee* which, as the final court of appeal for workers, can overrule even the preceding level consisting of the chairperson and two other directors (Fleet 1976, p. 106).

The equalitarianism and the supposedly semivoluntary nature of supervisory relationships at Triumph-Meriden seem to make this coop similar to the Israeli kibbutz and to other communitarian coops. Triumph-Meriden's organizational form and *SDN*'s seemed somewhat suited, at least, to their respective situations.

But the equalitarianism and even the existence of Triumph-Meriden are far from secure. In February 1977, it borrowed £1,500,000 from private enterprise, with government backing, and it may soon require more capital to update its high-priced Bonneville motorcycle (sold mostly in the United States).[5] It has become dependent upon private enterprise for its marketing arrangements, and for jobbing contracts for assembly work, which now account for more than half of its capacity. Finally, management consultants that the coop has needed to sort out its production problems have been provided by big business, and some of these have suggested the need for more professional (and conventional) managers and foremen, and for engineers (*London Times,* 9 February 1977). The nature of Triumph-Meriden's products and its need for capital make it highly dependent on outside support.

Thus far, it has survived without compromise of its ideals, although in 1978 there was external pressure (ultimately unsuccessful) to introduce a bonus of £4 per week for the 250 skilled workers in the work force of 650, "related to the achievement of output targets" (Smith 1978).[6]

CONCLUSION

There are certain *similarities* in how the three new coops were established. They had no direct connection with, and little if any assistance from, the established consumer coop movement. Rather, they were born in industrial strife, to "save jobs," involving sit-ins and work-ins, with little previous thought on the part of most workers about the possibility of a workers' cooperative. In each case, the structure of the new coop was improvised, and was highly dependent upon the ideas of the leaders, who knew of no adequate precedents elsewhere.

In each case, also, there was a movement toward more equal pay, although there were major differences in how far this went. Finally, relationships with management became more informal and less hierarchical. This applies to both the production manager and to lower-level supervisors, and, of course, to the workers' representatives on the boards of directors or executive councils.

Some important *differences* among the four coops in organizational structure and relationships are the following:

1. Subgroup representation on the managing board (or the absence thereof).

2. The formal pattern of ownership, with respect to outside shareholders especially. One coop has no outside shareholders, while another permitted shareholders to vote (on certain restricted matters) in proportion to their holdings of stock.

3. Relationships with government, with respect to the provision of initial capital and — potentially more important — the right of government to a seat on the managing board.

4. The extent of wage inequality.

5. The role of the trade unions within the plant, especially with respect to traditional trade union functions (collective bargaining). This ranged from a full shop-steward system and quite formal relationships with management over working conditions through a union role in representation on the managing boards (and a neglect of traditional functions). However, even in the former instance, the union became much more of a medium of communication than formerly between workers and management.

6. The *formal* powers of the workers collectively, as distinct from their representatives on the managing boards. The range was from virtually full power to advisory powers only (at *SDN*).

7. The nature of first-line supervision, from conventional powers to advisory only (at Triumph-Meriden).

8. Ideology, especially concerning equality of pay, and the powers of work-groups as related to supervision, although in no case has a formulation been provided.

It is obvious that some of the above are interrelated. It is *as though* the connecting thread was an equalitarian or inequalitarian ideology: equal pay and purely advisory first-line supervisors go hand in hand. And, where these have occurred, the trade unions have ceased to play a conventional, collective-bargaining role.

However, ideology can't have been the sole origin of these differences: the pre- and post-cooperative occupational structures must have helped determine them. The journalists at *SDN* would hardly have accepted equal pay with office clerks and semiskilled manual workers. On the other hand, one could hardly have predicted the precisely equal pay at Triumph-Meriden from its occupational structure. The solidarity of the workers, due to long tenure and an identification with the product, seems to have played a role. Even here, I suspect that a different leadership would have opted for a relatively equalitarian, but still differentiated, pay structure, so ideology was probably a factor.

All of the producers' coops seem to have been quite efficient; production has not been much of a problem. In the oldest coop, and thus far in one of the newer, Kirkby, income has been above that in capitalist-owned firms; working conditions are probably superior in all of them. The new coops have also been quite democratic in practice, perhaps barring the Maxwell interlude during *SDN*'s emergency. Even at Equity Shoes, the formal powers of the membership remain, and could be reasserted without a constitutional revolution, although it would probably take a crisis for this to occur. There is not enough evidence, as yet, concerning how much or how well workers or their representatives might determine the overall directions of their firms, but there is little reason to doubt that they could make a contribution.

The future of producers' cooperatives lies in the realm of politics. A viable cooperative sector could exist in Britain, given the support of the Labor movement and considerable (perhaps massive) aid from the government. This may require a social revolution, but, before one states this definitely, one should look at France, and especially Italy, where the producers' coop movement is much larger and stronger. And the ideology of the most vocal advocates of producers' coops in Britain is certainly far from that of the early artisans, or from "every person a capitalist." In Britain today, producers' cooperation is put forward as an alternative to unemployment on the one hand, and to nationalization (where it seems such could be avoided) on the other. Some liberals may advance the idea as a cure for featherbedding, inefficiency in general, and alienation, but most of its vocal advocates are democratic socialists. Many of them call for the application of "cooperative principles" — that is, democratic management — to nationalized industry. The movement for producers' cooperatives has become part of the larger movement for workers' control. But the failure of the Labor government to carry out its own program means that any *substantial* progress towards workers' control must await a broader acceptance of the idea among working people as a *practical* proposal, accompanied no doubt by an upsurge of industrial militancy and a general leftward movement in the country.

EPILOGUE

The October 1978 *Labour Leader* reported that the Kirkby coop "faces collapse because the Government (then still Labor) is refusing them £2.9 million over the next three years"; this in spite of the fact that the government had recently set up a Co-operative Development Agency. And *The Economist* of 14 April 1979 reported that the Kirkby coop was in the hands of a liquidator who was still trying to find new capital to keep the plant in operation. The two largest

British trade unions had refused to provide financial assistance.

The Triumph-Meriden coop was in serious trouble before the Tories won the 1979 election: it had applied for a waiver of interest payments due in June 1979, due, as it turned out, two months after the Tory government took over. With a declared Tory policy against saving unprofitable enterprises, the survival of Triumph-Meriden seems very much in doubt (*The Economist,* 14 April 1979). Thus, by this time, all three of the producers' coops formed in struggle in 1975 may very well be out of existence; at any rate, the future for the two longest survivors seems bleak indeed.

It is obvious that new coops which take over failed enterprises must usually be in a financially unstable state for some time, especially where they must operate as isolated firms. Certainly all three of the new coops experienced shortages of capital, but, in addition, they had their own specific problems. The Kirkby coop operated in a building which was much larger than needed for its reduced work-force and level of production, thus requiring a relatively heavy cost of heating and other expenses for maintenance.[7] The Triumph-Meriden coop lacked control over its marketing arrangements for export, was apparently hampered for a while by government red tape, and had to compete against foreign companies which could sell motorcycles at lower cost. The *Scottish Daily News,* as a new newspaper, had to create its readership, and very quickly withdrew from its original intention to reflect "a radical point of view, providing a real challenge to the right-wing monopoly of the Press" (*Scottish Daily News,* Discussion Document). It was argued later that *SDN* suffered seriously from a lack of editorial direction, with a blurred "philosophical" and stylistic identity (e.g., Mackie 1976, p. 132). But, basically, the newspaper had an uncertain market.

It seems both sectarian and foolish to argue that industrial producers' coops cannot play a useful role within a socialist movement, but, nevertheless, cooperatives do not seem to be *the* road to democratic socialism in Britain or elsewhere.

NOTES

1. Scott Bader does not claim to be a coop, although it is affiliated with the Industrial Common Ownership Movement. The scope of the term is currently under dispute in the British producers' coop movement.
2. Sir Max Aitken, briefly Lord Beaverbrook after the death of his father in 1964 until he renounced his barony. He headed what was called the Beaverbrook Newspapers Ltd. chain until 1977 (currently Express Newspapers Ltd.) and was referred to as

"Beaverbrook" by workers at the cooperative.

3. Allister Mackie wrote me later that, initially, he and another member of the Action Committee regarded the likelihood of actually achieving a coop as remote; they were primarily protesting "so that employers and governments in the future would hesitate before embarking on a policy of unemployment." I was also told at another new coop that, initially, the demand for a coop was primarily a negotiating ploy.

4. The 700-worker Kirkby Manufacturing and Engineering Cooperative, near Liverpool, was still discussing a proposed set of rules at the time I visited them, and, at Triumph-Meriden, I was told that there has been no time to really work out a structure for the organization; the pressure of production had been too great.

5. For some months, the Treasury held up the release of £2,000,000 of the £6,000,000 arranged for the Triumph-Meriden motorcycles through the Export Credit Guarantee Department, causing an accumulation of 1,000 machines in stock. The Treasury "insisted on documentation for every sale in every country and State " (*Financial Times,* 25 October 1975). This of course caused great financial and storage problems for the coop. The formalities were finally cleared.

6. Some on the British left have argued that producers' coops would inevitably lead to the payment of sub-standard "wages" — that is, in effect, to exploitation by the capitalist system. Thus far, Triumph-Meriden workers have received lower pay than comparable workers in their region, but, as mentioned above, two of the four coops have provided above-average incomes. In addition, the lowest paid workers are likely to benefit most from cooperatives. What might be called self-exploitation is a danger, but it is far from inevitable.

7. Based on a conversation with Derek Jones.

10

At IGP, It's Not Business as Usual

Daniel Zwerdling

Consumers United — usually called International Group Plans, or IGP — is the $60 million, worker-managed insurance corporation just ten blocks from the White House in the financial heart of Washington, D.C.[1] Its 340 secretaries, accountants, file clerks, salespeople, and other employees own half the corporation and elect half the board of directors. In just five years, this insurance corporation has developed the most important experiment in worker self-management in North America. It's an ongoing experiment, not a finished model; the democratic decision-making structure changes so often, as workers grapple for the "best" system, that, by now, some of this information may well be obsolete.

Self-management advocates in the United States have never before had a good home-grown example to learn from. While collective groceries sell plenty of brown rice, and democratically, too, they're too small for most people to take seriously. The plywood cooperatives in the Northwest have held on for twenty years, but now many are selling out to conglomerates. The Vermont Asbestos Group, Rath Packing Company, and other firms prove that workers can take over their company and run it profitably, while keeping the decision-making as traditional and autocratic as ever.

IGP, by contrast, is a modern, white-collar company using advanced computer technologies in a competitive market. It's a

Daniel Zwerdling is a free-lance journalist based in Washington, D.C., who has written numerous articles on the food industry and workplace democracy. He is also a national correspondent for the National Public Radio network.

Based on an article by Daniel Zwerdling in *Working Papers for a New Society,* Spring 1977, reprinted with changes by permission of the publisher.

successful corporation that earned about $1 million in profits last year. Workers at IGP aren't leftist college graduates like workers at so many collectives. Instead, they are a typical assortment of middle- and lower-income office workers — 46 percent white, 43 percent black, two-thirds female, and only one-third with college degrees.

Most important, IGP is a firm where rank-and-file employees really do exert fundamental powers. For example, 85 percent of the workers turned out for the 1977 board of directors election, an enviable turnout in any political campaign.

"Look, just say we are completely in charge of our own jobs from day to day," a claims clerk told me. "I mean that individuals like myself, making close to [IGP's] minimum wage, make decisions on our own that could affect a whole insurance plan, such as whether certain people are eligible to receive claims or not — decisions which only a manager could make at any traditional insurance company."

The board of directors election was sheer political drama, for the incumbent board was staging a coup of sorts, trying to impose more traditional corporate work styles. Board members were proposing widespread layoffs in a company that forbids laying workers off. The workers' policy would be to institute across-the-board pay cuts, rather than layoffs, with the highest percentage cuts for those with the highest salaries. The cuts would be considered loans, to be repaid by the company at 6 percent interest. The board wanted to bring back worker-attendance records in a company where keeping track of attendance is forbidden. And the board wanted to give management the power to fire workers in a company where firings are controlled by a worker court.

But the entire board was ousted, and the workers elected a new board with "democratic" views. "It was a major showdown, a turning point," one insurance clerk told me. "The people — and democracy — won."

The lessons IGP offers are not all about success. It faces some serious problems and has made some tactical mistakes from which self-management activists can also learn. The experience at IGP suggests that the road to self-management will be a difficult and painful process — but then, so is any social change.

The self-management system remains wobbly and sometimes embattled, plagued by managers who resist giving up their traditional powers and by production clerks who don't know how to assert their newfound powers. And despite the dreams of some advocates of worker self-management to the contrary, there are employees at IGP who say they could not care less about making important decisions about their work lives.

"I would love to go back to a traditional company, punching time clocks and being told exactly what to do, when and how to do it," one clerical worker told me. "I just can't stand the confusion anymore."

James P. Gibbons, the current president, founded IGP in 1964 with three partners and an IBM 1401 computer. Gibbons had earned a reputation in New York as a spectacular insurance salesman, and now he wanted to try a new marketing concept. Instead of using a sales network to sell insurance door to door, IGP would sell group health insurance by computerized mass mailings to members of groups — from the Air Force Sergeants Association to the staff of *Family Health* magazine. The idea took off, and, in five years, Gibbons had 100 employees handling $10 million in premiums.

Gibbons says he considered business just a way to make a living while he pursued more cosmic visions of social and political change. He marched — and was twice arrested — in antiwar, antipoverty, and civil rights protests, and says, "I was marching for the power of people to control their own lives.

"I had always thought I'd sell the business and use the money to set up some sort of foundation, like the Stern Fund or something, and give money to political causes," Gibbons says. He's sitting at his desk, which is one among many in a large room; there are no executive offices at IGP. "But then I started thinking, 'What's the point? Set up another foundation that is trying to change the very people and system that gives us all our money?' It occurred to me what we really had to do was create an economic institution that was self-sufficient. And that," Gibbons says, "is when I became consciously committed to making this company a self-sustaining, living model of social change.

"What I've done," he says, "is to create the first corporate power structure in this country which the employees have the power to change as they want. I'm not talking anything short of a total revolution."

The birth of democracy at IGP was a paradox. Gibbons imposed self-management on the workers as the enlightened monarch of a tiny nation might liberate the masses by beneficent dictate. One day in spring 1972, he announced he was transferring half the company ownership to the employees in a nonsalable, profit-sharing trust.

He discovered it wasn't all that easy. Worker ownership and control are so rare in this country that there aren't any legal structures set up to achieve them. Gibbons couldn't just give away his stock, as it turned out, without paying astronomical gift taxes.

"It took us almost two damn years just to work out the arrangement," recalls George Allen, a veteran member of the board of directors. "There just weren't any models to follow." What finally emerged: Gibbons doubled the shares of IGP stock from 250 to 500. Then he — technically, the company — "sold" half the stock, or 250 shares, to a special employee trust. Any employee who works at IGP more than six months is automatically a member of the trust until he or she leaves.

The trust didn't give the company any cash for the stock; instead, it gave the company an IOU to pay back the value of the stock, plus 6 percent interest, over approximately a decade. The value of the stock was fixed at around $1.7 million, based on an independent appraisal of the company's book value.

Now, each year, the board of directors votes to distribute a certain amount of the corporate profits to the workers, by transferring it to the trust. Under IRS regulations, the company can give the trust a maximum amount of profits each year equal to 15 percent of the corporate payroll. In 1976, for instance, the corporation made about $1 million profit, and the board voted to transfer half a million to the employee trust, which was somewhat less than 15 percent of the payroll.

But since the employee trust is still paying off its IOU for the stock, it immediately pays back fifty cents of every dollar of profits that the board transfers to it. The company doesn't pay taxes on the profits that it gives to the trust, nor on the money it gets paid back.

Each employee gets credited with an equal share of the profits each year; a manager earning $30,000 a year gets the same dollar amount as a mail clerk earning a third as much. Employees don't actually get to take their profits home, although they may borrow up to 25 percent of the profits they've accumulated at merciful interest rates — 8 percent, compared to the more than 11 percent they'd pay at a bank. When employees leave IGP, they will get their share of the profits in one of three ways: all at once, spread over five to ten years, or in the form of an annuity purchased from a life insurance company. They'll also get a portion of the current book value of IGP's stock, based on how long they've worked there.

Six months after Gibbons decided to set up the employee trust, he announced that employees would begin electing half the board of directors (Gibbons appoints the other half). And then he began creating a network of employee committees which, he decreed, would gradually make the corporate decisions traditionally reserved for executives.

To understand the evolution of self-management at IGP, you have to appreciate one point: Gibbons never pursued self-management for self-management's sake. "Hell no, self-management isn't the end objective, the end objective is maximizing humanness," Gibbons says, "creating an environment of justice, equity, equality, beauty, truth — an environment where each member of the community has the opportunity to grow and develop in his or her own unique way, to self-actualize."

The whole reason for self-management, Gibbons says, "is to give workers the power to protect themselves against arbitrary uses of power by management. But if we achieve self-management without achieving these other goals, I'll consider the experiment a failure."

Most companies around the country that have instituted some form of worker participation have used it as a tool for making the business more successful. The worker participation scheme at Procter & Gamble is so profitable that management considers it a trade secret, like the method for manufacturing Pringles. But, in Gibbons's revolution, the business itself has become the tool, the tool for creating a radical society, "a utopian community," as he puts it. He has proclaimed his goals in a credo, emblazoned on a silver poster and taught to new employees on their first day on the job:

> Goal I: To build a lasting economic institution which helps satisfy the real needs of our client organizations. . .and to provide quality service. . .[while] making enough profit to keep the corporation in existence. . . .

> Goal II: To build this institution on a foundation which maximizes the humanness of everyone involved, and which creates a new ethic for economic institutions — an alternative model for business.

"The very idea of creating a humane society within a business institution," Gibbons acknowledges cheerfully, "is an enormous paradox."

WHO DECIDES

Gibbons and IGP employees have spent five years groping for a sensible decision-making structure. There have been so many committees created, modified, abolished, then resurrected again, that even veteran employees can't remember them all. Today, the basic structure at IGP is this:

The *worker teams* are autonomous work groups throughout the company, each with about six to a dozen employees who perform the same job. Clerks who pay claims to military clients, for instance, work on the military claims team. Although team power has never been defined on paper, in practice, the teams are responsible for organizing and managing the company's day-to-day work, and for handling staff hiring and firing.

Each *department* is composed of several teams. Department-level decisions, such as staffing levels and budgets, long-range objectives, and coordinating the work of the teams, are made democratically by a *department operating committee.* The committee includes the *team leaders* (a worker representative elected from each team) and a *department coordinator* whom the team leaders help select. A department coordinator doesn't have the powers of a traditional corporate department head, but he or she is supposed to guide the staff and carry out the decisions of the operating committee.

Each *division* includes several departments. Division-level policies are made by the *division operating committee,* which includes the department coordinators, a representative elected by the workers, and a *division coordinator* elected by the department coordinators. The division coordinator — called a center forward in IGP's lingo — is supposed to carry out the decisions of the committee, not give orders like a boss.

The *corporate operating committee* is made up of the handful of top managers who run the corporate business from week to week. It's the least representative committee of all. Except for one member directly elected by the workers, the members are hired by the board. The corporate operating committee reviews all major policies and corporate operating strategies devised by the lower committees before sending them for approval to the board.

The *board of directors* is half chosen by Gibbons and half elected. The board is supposed to be the ultimate decision-making body, the final vote on major policies from investments to sick leave to wage scales.

I've left two of the most important committees until last, because they operate outside this chain of responsibility. The first is the *personal justice committee,* the worker-elected court. "All decisions of the Personal Justice Committee shall be final," company policy says, on disputes over pay, promotions, leave policy, job transfers, anything. The only exception is firings, which employees can appeal beyond the court to a special committee of three worker representatives and three managers.[2]

The committee that created the court is the *community relations assembly* (CRA), the worker congress. Its twenty representatives are elected by popular vote. At least one CRA representative sits and votes on virtually every committee in IGP, which ensures that at least one direct representative of "the people" votes on every decision.

But the guts of the CRA's job is to formulate all the workplace policies that directly affect employees, from vacation rights to production standards, from hiring guidelines to wages. The CRA doesn't have final say, according to corporate policy, but sends its recommendations for "review" by the corporate operating committee and "approval" by the board.

When I first visited IGP in 1974, I began asking the employees, "But does it *really* work?" It was a simplistic question that reduced the complex power relationships to an absurd yes or no. For instance, how much power can employees exert over their day-to-day work life? How much power over corporate finances and business? How much power can employees exert over financial questions that directly affect them, such as wages and benefits? And, just as important: no matter how much or how little power the employees have available through formal voting, how much power do they actually assert?

When it comes to the day-to-day life in the "economic community," as Gibbons calls it, the rank-and-file employees have enormous power available — and they use it. File clerks making under $10,000 a year hold an impromptu meeting one morning and vote to revamp the entire central files system, the heart of the corporation. Clerks churning out new insurance policies take a break to decide who should answer the telephone; they vote to rotate the hated task. A team of researchers, who answer clients' questions about their insurance policies, vote to hire a job applicant they interviewed the day before. The department coordinator hasn't even met her. "A department head," one researcher says, "shouldn't stick his nose into team business."

The worker teams also wield effect control over firing fellow employees, although the power is slightly ambiguous since team leaders and department coordinators also have the power to fire; the company has never firmly resolved just whose power should take precedent. In practice, though, the rank-and-file employees have made firing a rare event in this company. A small drama flared one day in the life insurance department, when the team leader tried to fire a worker he said "wasn't producing." He backed down when her teammate marched angrily to his desk and declared he had no right to dismiss a teammate without consulting the team first.

Some employees at IGP complain that it's becoming *too* hard to get rid of troublesome and unproductive employees — "it's kind of scary to stand up to someone you've been friends with and say, 'sorry, you're not working out, you've got to go,'" one claims clerk says. But workers do it. "We fired a dude last week," a mailroom clerk says. "When he didn't carry his load, we had to do the extra work. We warned him, had meetings with him, put him on probation — he wouldn't listen." He appealed to the personal justice committee, but the court upheld the team's decision.

The clerks paying insurance claims and peering in the microfilm machines don't exert direct power over department and division-level policies, since they don't have a direct vote on the operating committees. But most employees I talked with say they aren't interested in worrying about long-term planning and budgeting.

They can, however, exert considerable informal power over department and division decisions when they feel the issues touch them directly. For one thing, there's a company commandment called the "IGP Decision-Making Model": it declares that no decisions may be made until all the workers directly affected have been consulted first. But, more important, the workers exert power because there is an assumption at IGP that leaders are supposed to act on behalf of the employees and to watch out for the employees' interests.

"We don't assert ourselves very often by taking initiative," says one claims examiner, "but people resist because they know they have the right to resist." When one department announced it was installing a new computer system to keep track of claims, for instance, the claims team announced they didn't like the system and would refuse to use it. "The computer people were forced to sit down with us and design it the way we liked," one team member said.

Managers who don't respond to the rank and file don't survive in their positions very long. "We called our department head before a meeting of the entire department to air a lot of grievances," one researcher says, "and one of the big issues was, do the people have confidence in the top man? We were terribly, painfully honest with him. We gave him a vote of confidence only to give him another chance."

IGP employees also wield considerable power over the broad policies that govern their work life through their community relations assembly. On paper, the CRA seems like a glorified employee sounding board — one that has the empty "power" to *recommend* policies — since all CRA policies must be submitted for review and approval to the corporate operating committee and the board. Many employees at IGP have never taken the CRA seriously for precisely that reason. Since Gibbons created the committee four years ago, CRA representatives have suffered occasional periods of inertia, paralyzed by self-doubt as they ponder whether they really have any power.

"We've had a problem trying to figure out what our role is and what our limits are," one representative told me. "Look, none of us have really believed we could ever have the power to do anything important," another says. "I mean, how many of us have ever been on a company committee like this before and been asked to make corporate policies?"

But, however powerless these representatives may feel, last year's CRA, which workers say was the strongest they can remember, revised all the major workplace policies and got the disciplinary system working. Gibbons and several board members have consistently prodded the CRA to assert itself more. "The CRA acts like it's asking permission from the [corporate] operating committee," says board member George Allen, a professor in the school of business at the American University. "But I'd like to see the CRA become equal in power to the operating committee."

Viewing IGP through descriptions of the CRA, the teams, and other committees misses the spirit of employee power and freedom there, a spirit that contrasts dramatically with employee feelings at traditional white-collar firms. A claims examiner at Geico, a major insurance company with headquarters in Washington, tells what it's like at her office:

> A bell rings at 8:30 and if you're five minutes late they reprimand you. (She is speaking at home because "I'd get fired if I talked to you at the office.") Clerks aren't supposed to drink coffee at their desks and they're not supposed to talk, unless it's about business. Supervisors assign us our work each day, and if we ask questions they tell us "It's not yours to wonder why, just do as you're told." I ask questions anyway, and they've classified me in my personnel file as an "insubordinate."

At IGP, clumps of workers sit on their desks, drinking coffee and chatting about a recent CRA vote to reimburse workers for meals, transportation, and even babysitting fees if they work after hours or on weekends. Work in one department comes to a noisy halt when the research team throws a baby shower for one of the teammates; the department coordinator doesn't scowl; he takes some wine and a piece of cake. There's no morning bell at IGP. "I've been coming to work at noon lately because I'm training some horses every morning at a stable," a reseacher in the life insurance department says. "I stay and work until eight o'clock."

My Geico acquaintance has "never even met the company president" — but Gibbons and three top managers take forty-five minutes one morning simply to meet with an angry IGP employee who has questions about disciplinary procedures "which just can't wait." And workers at Geico are afraid to speak out. I dropped by the IGP board of directors campaign assembly last year and heard one candidate, a twenty-four-year-old claims clerk, declare that "Gibbons has been feeding us a lot of bullshit and it's about time the people bring it to a halt." He received some healthy applause; then everyone adjourned to a conference room for a wine and cheese party and the vote.

UPS AND DOWNS

There's a sharp dichotomy at IGP between the daily world of work and the world of business. When it comes to making decisions about what insurance packages to market, what strategies to use, and what investments to make, the rank-and-file employees have little voice.

The theory behind the structure at IGP has been that "employees don't have any business making decisions about finances if they don't have financial expertise," one researcher explains. Instead, representatives accountable to the rank and file are supposed to make such decisions. Until a couple of years ago, financial decisions were handled by a finance committee, most of whose members were elected from each department. But it didn't work. For one thing, in the effort to be as democratic as possible, membership was rotated so often that individual representatives couldn't build up enough knowledge of the committee to play a meaningful part. To make matters worse, many of the representatives had little financial background, and the company made no effort to provide training.

"Frankly, the meetings were terribly frustrating," one elected representative told me. "Half the time I didn't know what they were talking about." Both these factors increased the tendency of the chief financial officer, the chairman of the committee, to "play the cards close to his chest," as one finance committee member recalls. "He controls the books, he controls the figures — so he'd make a recommendation and we had little choice but to nod our heads. We should have been more forceful, I know," the representative says, "but we were intimidated."

Since then, the finance committee has faded away. Now most of the power to make financial and marketing decisions rests with the corporate operating committee, far from the rank and file, although there are still a few possibilities for direct worker involvement. The chairperson of the CRA votes on the committee, but so far none of the chairpersons have learned enough about the business to take an active part. And the board of directors, which is half elected by the employees, does have the power to reject operating committee decisions. A few years ago, the directors acted like a rubber stamp. "One year the board hardly even met," recalls board member George Allen. Recently, the board has been asserting itself more and more as the voice of "the people." When managers on the operating committee insisted that they should control wage scales, for example, the board insisted that *it* would make the final decisions. "The operating committee is mostly managers," one board member explained, "when the people should have a large say in deciding wages."

Workers at IGP do exert substantial power over financial issues that touch them directly. The CRA drafted the last major wage-scale revision after consulting with "the people"; it was changed little by the board. CRA representatives also selected the company-paid health insurance plan, one of the most generous packages at any company in Washington.

And, when really crucial financial policies come up, the board turns over the decision to the entire work force for a vote. It was the rank and file who voted to establish the $9,450 minimum annual wage, and it was the workers who decided how to divvy the profits. Most managers, not surprisingly, wanted to apportion profits as a percentage of salaries. But the rank and file, the two-thirds earning under $11,000 a year, voted to split the profits equally, to president and mailroom clerk alike.

Now the caveat: despite the successes at IGP, the self-management system does not work as well as it might. For every team that asserts its autonomy and power, employees point to a team that shrinks from responsibility. For every decision that a committee reaches by democratic vote, workers point to a committee that waffles and submits to the decision of a self-styled boss. "There isn't one department in this community where the philosophy is even half working," Gibbons says with frustration. "This place," says Larry Bonner, a former member of the top operating committee, "is a mass of contradictions."

And the contradictions are nourishing worker discontent. The corporation preaches trust, maximizing humanness, and a new quality of work, yet the absentee rate is increasing, turnover is high (up to 15 percent during the last few years), and some departments are mired in chronic backlogs and sloppy work. You can read the discontent in managerial memos that float around, talking about "tremendous tensions, anxieties, character assassination, and balkanization." And you can read the mood in the only graffiti scrawled on the men's room stalls: "IGP employees need to organize a union to protect and increase their working conditions," a dissident wrote in bold blue. "Self-management is a clever farce to keep wages low." About 25 percent of the work force apparently agrees and told a company-wide survey in 1975 that IGP needs a union.

Workers at most companies, the social surveys tell us, are discontent with the status quo — their lack of power, their isolation, their alienating role as a cog in a vast corporate machine. But, at IGP, the workers' discontent stems from change; normal corporate power relationships have been turned upside down. Self-management at IGP has put power and responsibility up for grabs; and neither the managers nor the rank and file have ever been trained by this society to handle it.

What training and skills are needed for a self-managed enterprise to fulfill its potential? Advocates who have worked with democratic decision-making institutions emphasize some characteristics that make a self-managed enterprise strong. To begin with, workers need a sense of personal confidence, responsibility, and autonomy to manage their work and to make decisions on their own. An IGP employee, formerly a telephone operator, explains her plight: "At Bell Telephone, we had to raise our hands just to ask permission to go to the bathroom. But, at IGP, we're supposed to do everything on our own. No one tells us anything." "The fact is," says a file clerk who used to work at the post office, "a lot of people need a boss standing over them, telling them exactly what to do."

While workers in a self-managed firm need independence, they also need to feel responsible to the collective. "I thought self-management meant you can get your work done whenever you want," one policy issue clerk told me. She was angry that her team reprimanded her for taking three days off during a hectic week. "That's not self-management," Gibbons writes in one of the two-page philosophical treatises he occasionally passes among the employees, "that's anarchy!"

And, if committees are made the cornerstone of decision-making, employees must master the art of listening to others, sharing opinions openly, and hammering out a consensus acceptable to the whole group. In some of the countless IGP committees, members talk at once and can't hear what the others are saying, or they shrink from saying anything at all and let one or two members dominate. I attended CRA meetings that accomplished nothing because representatives straggled in forty-five minutes late, and team meetings that wasted time because workers felt too nervous to say what they really felt. No wonder two-thirds of the workers told the 1975 survey they think most committees are a waste of time. "God so loved the world," reads the sign on one worker's desk, "that he didn't send a committee."

Yet, "The problem is not in having committees," George Allen writes in the company newspaper, "but in how they operate." Committees of top managers aren't much better off. I watched managers on the corporate operating committee spend an hour trying to figure out why they tended to ramble instead of focusing on specific topics. They finally realized they had never prepared an agenda.

Many employees do plunge into the democratic decision-making process. Over 40 percent of the workers at IGP have served on at least one committee. But, as in any organization, from the PTA to SDS, when a minority of the participants take on most of the burden, they get exhausted before long. "After six months here, you just burn yourself out," says Jane Suppan, a researcher who has belonged to the CRA and many other committees. "And you still have your normal work to put out."

I met one young claims clerk who serves on so many committees that she occasionally does her insurance work over night, and gets no sleep. She's an extreme case, but reflects the dilemma. "Even if we wanted to participate in decison-making," says a woman with two children, "we can't afford the time. We've got to get home and put supper on the table."

While many employees feel overwhelmed and confused by their sudden rise to power, managers at IGP feel uncertain about their fall from it. Consider the qualities that mark a good manager in a self-managed enterprise. "Damn it, don't think of yourselves as managers, think of yourselves as leaders," Gibbons fumes at an operating committee meeting. "*Manager* implies control; *leader* implies government with equal rights." As self-management advocates emphasize, a good leader shares information with the rank-and-file employees, delegates power as much as possible, inspires and motivates workers rather than giving orders, and, most important, sees his or her role as working on behalf of the workers, not over them.

"Now you tell me," Gibbons says with a sigh one day, "where you can find leaders who have administrative and insurance experience who also believe in these democratic values? Right — nowhere."

"Managers are afraid and confused here because they lose the power of being the boss," says Del Clark, a former member of the corporate operating committee. More than a dozen top managers — *leaders* — have come and gone since I first visited IGP in 1974, largely because they couldn't handle democratic-style leadership. "At my last job, if a secretary so much as talked back to me, I could have said, 'Shazam, you're fired, finished,' " one department coordinator says. "But now, at IGP, if I try to boss someone around, *I* could be fired, or least deposed. After twenty years in the cutthroat business world, it's hard suddenly having to accept a secretary or mailroom clerk as equals."

And most leaders at IGP complain that group decision-making takes too much time in a business that demands quick action; and unless all the members of a committee are doing their required part, they're right. Some leaders have become so afraid of crossing the line between providing leadership and imposing dictatorship that they shrink from exercising any initiative at all. "And then," one division center forward says, "inertia sets in."

"I'm telling you, it's absolutely impossible to make every decision democratically," says Del Clark, who used to be center forward of the largest division in the corporation, with 200 employees. "Our committee would take three weeks trying to solve a problem I could have solved like that" — he snaps his fingers — "in a couple days, and we'd get ninety-nine problems a week. The department heads on the committee would all agree to do certain jobs during the week, and then at the next meeting they'd say they didn't have time. So if I took action on my own, I'd be accused of being a boss. If I didn't, the work wouldn't get done and, as division head, I'd be blamed for it. I got so frustrated and confused," Clark says, "I just had to resign." Now

Clark works in a nonleadership position, doing what he calls busywork.

Put employees together with managers who are equally unprepared for self-management, and you have a vicious circle. Teams, the CRA, and other committees don't meet their responsibilities, and the work falls behind. Tensions rise as people sense the system isn't working; instead of asking themselves how to solve it, they blame their leaders for failing them. The leaders blame the rank and file for dragging their feet and withdraw in defensiveness and secrecy. The workers become more hostile, "and then we all ramble along in no real direction," one researcher says.

The stalemate inevitably ends when a strong leader, usually Gibbons, impatient and furious at the breakdown, frantic for the system to work, plunges into the power vacuum and imposes his own solutions. I watched Gibbons undercut his own carefully nurtured democratic structure many times, pleading, "This is a business, we've got to go on." He solves the immediate crisis but contributes to a more profound crisis in the long run: cynicism.

"We have no power to do anything, really," a team leader scoffs after Gibbons has intervened in her department to solve a work backlog. "Uncle Jimmy tells us we have the freedom to do what we want, but then he just goes ahead and does what he wants anyway."

"I feel like I'm really suffocating here, we've got no influence over anything," a claims clerk told me. Then she paused. "Well, I guess it depends on a person's initiative. I'm the type of person who doesn't ever do anything. I mean, they *say* you can do things here, but I don't believe they really feel you can do it."

One employee wrote in the company newspaper:

> Lots of us come from such uptight work or school environments that it's hard to eye a less structured situation without suspicion. Knowing only gross manipulation by employers or instructors, we expect it.... We look for the fine print, sure that we're being had.... At least the old system clearly defines the enemy. Are we strong enough to risk a system where there may not be an enemy, other than our own cynicism?

Many employees do acknowledge that, when the system doesn't work as it should, they are at least partly to blame. "The mechanisms are all here, the freedom and power are all here for us to really take control and run this company the way we want," a young claims examiner named Kurt Carr told me before he became elected department coordinator. "Why don't we? I don't want to call it ignorance. Let's call it lack of education — lack of education in democracy."

LEARNING SELF-MANAGEMENT

Education in democracy is one area where IGP has failed the employees. The transition to self-management is expected to be difficult, but Gibbons neglected to make it smoother by creating long-term training programs to teach employees self-management values and skills. True, IGP has made some attempts at education: new employees take orientation courses in the philosophy and finances of the business, and, at one time, the board of directors held seminars with workers to teach them how the employee trust works. Over the years, the company has hired various consultants to help committees work more effectively, and now the company has its own in-house team of troubleshooters who float from crisis to crisis, attempting to teach employees how to tackle problems and solve them on their own.

But these sporadic attempts to spread a little democratic or financial knowledge among the work force have failed, as Gibbons acknowledges: "I'm tired of these ad hoc, hit or miss, part-time efforts to solve problems. We need a long-term training program, and I want someone to get to work on it full time." But he adds in the same conversation: "People don't understand that we don't have the luxury of time for all this training. We're not an educational institution, we're a business, and we have economic problems that have to be solved." But that may be a deception. The time the workers would divert to self-management training, say a couple of hours each week, may be vastly outweighed by the time they now waste in ineffective committees and in complaining.

What kinds of training programs could IGP develop?

1. Regular seminars for all employees on the history, philosophy, and experiences of self-management. If workers at IGP learned there were historical roots to Gibbons's visions — if they knew that workers in Yugoslavia as well as plywood cooperatives in the Northwest were grappling with the same sorts of problems — they might feel more grounded in a movement, rather than alone and adrift.

2. Regular seminars on how the business operates, from marketing insurance packages to investment finance.

3. Regular forums, perhaps once a month, where top leaders could discuss the current financial status of the business, key issues up for debate in the corporate operating committee or the board, and could answer questions from the employees.

4. Weekly meetings between CRA representatives and their "constituents," to share more immediate information about possible grievances or problems, policies pending in the CRA, and new policies that employees would like to propose.

5. Methodical training in the art of group decision-making, for every committee from the work teams to the board. The training should be handled by full-time employees skilled in group dynamics.

6. Special training for every leader, teaching techniques from the art of chairing a meeting to demystifying technical information so the rank and file can understand it.

What are the prospects for long-term education and training at IGP? The question is synonymous with a more fundamental one: What are the long-term prospects for self-management at IGP? For, although the tensions are healthy — they indicate the corporation doesn't squelch people but nourishes intellectual and emotional ferment — they are reaching a stage where they will move people in one of two directions: toward a more stable and smoothly working self-management structure, or back to a more traditional corporate hierarchy.

"We're at a critical turning point in this community," Gibbons acknowledges, "where the experiment is up for grabs. The people here have the power to throw me out, throw out all the values I stand for, even piss on me if they want."

For a time last year, it seemed as if Gibbons's values would be thrown out. The company, like the nation, is constantly swinging through varying political moods, and last year was the year of the conservatives. To begin with, IGP faced considerable financial pressures: after ten years of spectacular growth, the company's income began leveling off, partly because of the national economy and partly because, after years of dominating the mail-order health-insurance market, IGP began to face some stiff competition.

Although the corporation was making a profit, some employees felt it wasn't enough, especially at a time when some long-term debts were coming due. And employees were tiring of the constant changes in Gibbons's experiment. "People tend to be a lot more conservative when things keep changing," one researcher says. "They need something secure and stable to hold on to. And here," he laughs, "what you write about us today will be totally different six months from now."

The rank-and-file employees voted their mood in the 1976 board elections: they defeated the "liberal" candidates and elected a Washington bank president and an IGP manager known for his traditional, straight-line approach to business. Gibbons, who in the past had appointed such people as a Marxist economics professor and a civil liberties lawyer, picked three top managers with conservative fiscal reputations. "I figured it was time to put some financial knowledge on the board," he recalls.

To a point, most employees seemed to approve of the new climate. The CRA and the board revamped the election process so rank-and-file employees had far less power in selecting top leaders; and workers started putting more pressure on fellow employees who took too much advantage of liberal leave. Kurt Carr said at the time:

> The place has the feel of a Republican administration. The company is really cracking down now and become more conservative, and putting emphasis on the bottom line. But I think it's a healthy thing for democracy here in the long run. Things were getting too chaotic. We just have to be careful that it doesn't swing too far in a conservative direction.

But the climate did swing too far, as top managers began to argue that IGP's obsession with democratic values and workplace freedoms was damaging the corporate profits. When a board resolution called for the end of some of IGP's basic workplace freedoms, however, the political mood swung back. In 1977 the managers were ousted from the board, and a new group of directors known for their "liberal" and democratic outlook sat in control of the corporation. Gibbons's new appointees were especially important. One was Dr. Michael Maccoby, a self-management specialist who helped design the joint United Auto Workers and Harman International Industries shopfloor democracy project. The other two were rank-and-file workers. "I'm saying, 'let's put people on the board again who will implement people policies, and not just think about profits,' " Gibbons said.

The events at IGP — the widespread conservatism, culminating in the effort by top managers to toss out fundamental worker powers and freedoms — suggest that the firm confronts a difficult paradox: As the workplace democracy grows stronger and employees feel more assertive, workplace democracy itself may come under increasing attack. For, until last year most employees, including top managers, went along with Gibbons's visions even if they grumbled under their breath. "Nobody in this company comes right out and says to Jim's face, 'democracy sucks,' " a former board member told me. But as more and more employees feel assertive, those who oppose Gibbons's goals are boldly speaking out. And the strongest opposition is among the leaders, who feel they have the most to lose.

A former member of the corporate operating committee told me:

> I came to IGP hoping to make vast sums of money but I've finally accepted the truth. This is not a company where any of us will get rich. Do you know that Jim could make $1 million a year if he wanted, yet, when the board tried to raise his salary from $50,000 to $100,000, he threatened to quit? There are no stock options for us; a guy making $25,000 a year will leave with the same money after twenty years as a mailroom clerk making less than half as much. We don't get power here, or prestige — most of us don't even have a private office. Demoracy is nice but I'm not sure I want it at my business.

A few months after we talked, he quit.

Ironically, one of the major obstacles to full self-management at IGP will continue to be its most dynamic force, Jim Gibbons himself. The employees at IGP never asked for self-management. Most probably never even dreamed of it. Gibbons alone dreamed the self-management vision, imposed it on the employees, and, with his charisma, made it work. But now Gibbons's role is starting to stunt self-management's growth, for the employees can't quite shake the notion of Gibbons as the beneficent monarch, themselves as grateful subjects.

"I know I've got to go," Gibbons says, "because this experiment won't really have worked until it can function without me." He talks about giving his half of the stock and his board of director seats to a trust, which would be controlled by IGP's clients, making the corporation jointly controlled by the workers and the "community" of clients. So far, the plan is little more than a dream, primarily because the clients have shown little interest.

IGP faces questions that every self-managed enterprise must ask and answer. Can a workplace democracy survive if some of the employees don't care to participate? According to the extensive but unscientific 1975 survey, less than half the employees who responded wanted "a lot of say" over selecting management, and not even one-third said they wanted "a lot of say" over hiring and firing fellow workers and deciding how corporate funds should be spent. The company confronts serious problems because not enough workers take an active part, yet some employees argue that demanding worker participation is itself an anti-democratic rule. "Participation does not mean that everyone *must* participate," writes George Allen. "It only means that each person is given the *opportunity* to do so."

Can a workplace democracy survive if some employees, including its leaders, actively oppose it? Should the company hire only job applicants who swear they're committed to Gibbons's goals? Must every employee share the same values for the structure to survive? Some employees suggest careful screening of job applicants: "We certainly don't want to hire people here who are opposed to the whole idea," says one veteran IGP employee. But others argue that rejecting workers who don't embrace the democratic and humanitarian vision in effect *sabotages* those visions.

Fran Heaps, an administrator, says:

> What some people are demanding is that we all have to share the same goals, and I say horseshit. As a citizen of this country, I don't have to have the same values as my next door neighbor, do I? We have systems and safeguards in this country which give me the right to be who I am. We have systems and safeguards at IGP too. Yes, some managers tried to toss out the system, but the people stopped them — which shows the system works.

The system does work — better than any other self-managed enterprise in the country, and, I would argue, better than any other corporate system in America. Despite the problems and tensions at IGP, 340 rank-and-file workers and managers are operating a $60 million corporation — and making a profit — with a degree of freedom, democracy, and equality never before achieved by a major corporation in the United States. If they're facing problems, every corporation faces problems. The difference is that workers at IGP can shout their complaints and problems if they want, without fear of getting fired. More important, they've got the power to change the corporation.

NOTES

1. Consumers United Group, Inc., is the official name for a holding corporation with three subsidiaries: Consumers United Insurance Company, which underwrites the insurance; International Group Plans, which sells the insurance; and International Group Plans Administrators, which services the insurance clients. In practice, they operate as one company, and employees refer to the whole operation as IGP.
2. Official IGP policy also guarantees "full protection of your individual rights as a citizen of these United States, in particular freedoms articulated in the Constitution and known as the Bill of Rights."

Part 4

SELF-MANAGED COLLECTIVES: CASE STUDIES

Introduction to Part 4

Part 4 is about alternative service organizations and collectively-run retail businesses. These case studies illustrate the positive satisfaction workers derive from control over their workplaces and the connection between control and collectives' support of humanistic values. The members of the legal collective, for instance, feel their form of organization permits them "to be more human," "to face the world a bit more joyfully," and to struggle successfully against sexism. The Seattle collective members are "proud of the products we make/sell, proud that they are healthy and of good quality."

Whatever the comradery and personal satisfaction of working in a collective, money remains a persistent problem for many. Many coops and collectives can afford to pay their members only substandard wages. For example, pay in the law collective, the free school and the Seattle Workers' Brigade averaged only $300 a month (during 1972-74). Other collectives have been able to pay their worker-owners salaries that are more or less comparable to those paid in mainstream work organizations. The members of a collective auto repair shop, for instance, paid themselves $750-$900 monthly (in 1976-77) depending upon need.[1] The same is true for some of the well-established food coops. Many of the long-standing cooperatives in America, such as the scavenger coops in San Francisco (chap. 4) and the plywood coops in the Pacific Northwest (chap. 7) have managed to pay their worker-owners incomes considerably higher than those paid in the same industry.

One reason some collectives can pay their members salaries that are comparable to those paid in conventional firms is that they charge customers somewhere near the going rate for the goods or services they provide. A problem for many collectives is that, if they raised their prices to market levels, they would price out many of those they aim to help with their services. The availability of government-backed loans from the National Cooperative Bank or other sources, access to management and technical consulting, the existence of third-party funds to reimburse providers of services, and member-training in business skills and in democratic management may enable collectives to become more successful as businesses and to pay their worker-members more. This is part of the purpose of the New School for Democratic Management's community enterprise program: making business skills more readily available to members of democratically managed enterprises.

In addition to this issue of pay and of generating a surplus, the papers in this section address the issue of power. Collectives are dedicated to minimizing differences in knowledge and skill, as noted by Rothschild-Whitt in chapter 1, because these so often lead to inequalities in power even within organizations that are committed to democracy. Knowledge sharing, job rotation, team work, and apprenticeships are devices that are used to minimize such inequalities.

Lindenfeld, too, discusses problems of power in alternative organizations, particularly delegating authority, obtaining consensus, and conflicts between workers and clients or consumers. The latter arise out of differences in interest between staff and clients (e.g., teachers vs. parents and students in a free school) or between worker-owners and hired workers in some cooperatives (chap. 4). Workers may use their control of an organization to further their own interests as against those of consumers or the community. This has been a continuing problem in the self-managed industries in Yugoslavia. In worker cooperatives, partners may use their power to obtain higher income for themselves, while not allowing newly hired workers to join the coop. This permits the worker-owners to resist diluting their equity, but it leaves the coop with a two-class system of worker-owners and ordinary hired workers.

If this challenge to balance worker interests against client or customer interests is not met, consumer coops are especially vulnerable to a shift from customer/community control and high member-involvement to a gradual concentration of power in the hands of paid staff. This has happened in a number of food coops as they have grown from volunteer buying clubs to larger and larger storefronts with paid staff members, and it was also the path taken by Briarpatch, the auto repair cooperative described by Jackall.[2] In another selection, Newton describes an attempt to resolve the problem of balancing worker interests with member/consumer interests adopted by the Wheatsville Food Co-op in Austin, Texas.

Wheatsville owes part of its success as a food cooperative to the Austin Community Project, a federation that has flourished in Austin for several years. A similar federation existed for some time in Seattle, Washington; Pearson and King describe some of the difficulties that led to the dissolution of the Seattle Workers' Brigade.

More successful examples of cooperatives and collectives that have formed federations exist elsewhere. A cooperative federation serves numerous member organizations in the Twin Cities area of

11

Is Anybody There?
Notes on Collective Practice
Santa Barbara Legal Collective

Law communes and collective law practices have been labeled interesting and exciting experiments. They are experiments in the delivery of legal services to people whose lack of money and power severely limit their access to any form of legal assistance. As a law collective, however, we are something far different from a poverty-oriented, socially-conscious law firm. We are, instead, an association of lawyers and legal workers whose primary goal is social and political reform, both within the contemporary legal system and within a legal system we envision for the future. Because of the nature and goals of our practice, we have faced unique financial, organizational, and attitudinal problems. This article explores many of these problems and describes our solutions to them.

Writing an article such as this is not easy. Reaching out to so many unknown people to explain who we are and what we do presents serious problems. We do not want to emphasize the trivial or uninteresting, but issues of real concern to a collective practice include many mundane details. It is with these trepidations that we embark on a discussion of how our office actually functions and how we hope to implement our plans for political, social, and legal reform.

At the time of this writing, the members of the collective included Warren Adler, attorney; Karen Blasingame, attorney; Emily DeFall, legal worker; Richard Eiden, attorney; Jo Anne Frankfurt, legal worker; Norman Roberts, legal worker; Jeannie Rucci, legal worker; and Richard Solomon, attorney. Most of the collective's members first met during the arson trial stemming from the burning of the Isla Vista branch of the Bank of America. At that trial, some were defense attorneys and some were defendants.

STARTING OUR PRACTICE: THE PROBLEM OF ATTITUDE

During the first two years of the Santa Barbara Legal Collective's existence, we struggled much, learned a great deal, and drastically altered our modes of thinking and methods of practice. Throughout the process, we maintained and refined our perceptions of the goals and principles which originally brought us together.

Our decision to practice law collectively was not made overnight. Meeting for several months prior to opening our doors, we decided upon common goals and the methods for attaining them. Time and experience have greatly improved our practice. We have found it possible, with our structure, to operate an office efficiently, to perform competent legal work, and to combine legal with political work in an environment which is nonalienating for ourselves and our clients. Our practice provides us with an income without charging high fees, and permits us to grow steadily toward becoming the kinds of people we envision building and populating a new society.

Politics and social change are our motivating forces. Essential to our politics is the concept that possessing legal skills makes us no better and no different from all other people. We are not entitled to take their hard-earned money in the name of professionalism. That is not to say that we do not charge fees. But our fees are set as low as possible, yet high enough to pay our overhead expenses, and salaries of from $210 to $275 per month. Additionally, we view our clients as our brothers and sisters. We attempt to demystify the law so that, when they come to us for help, they not only have their specific problems resolved, but they also learn something about the operation of the "system" and what they might do the next time a problem arises. This occurs not only in our one-to-one encounters with people in the office, but also in our lectures and other outreach programs in the community. This fall we are organizing a people's law school.

In order to accomplish our ideals, it was first necessary to change our own attitudes. It was essential for us to discuss and agree that money does not play as large a role in happiness as we had been taught. We must continually discuss the professional attitude that is developed in law school, as it separates legal people from other people and fosters an unhealthy and overlarge ego in lawyers. Self-confidence and the knowledge that we provide competent legal assistance, coupled with the support and criticism of comrades in and out of the office, take the place of the traditional "lawyer's ego," and provide us with the security and aggressiveness necessary to effective lawyering.

Attitude changes do not come from a mere theoretical or intellectual understanding of what might be a more desirable attitude. Collective practice means supporting each other in our individual struggles to overcome personal ties to elitism, sexism, and professionalism. Various other faults, like personal insecurity and occasional obnoxiousness, are often dealt with as group problems. We meet often in *criticism meetings* to formulate policies and programs to correct these faults. We feel criticism should be carefully considered and thought out before it is voiced. We try to be gentle and objective, rather than abrasive, and we attempt to avoid personal attacks. When receiving criticism, we strive to consider each statement carefully, regardless of its nature or source. We find it better to make criticisms when the situation warrants, rather than to allow problems to go unresolved while resentments build. By using these guidelines, we have improved both our practice and our ways of relating to other people.

DAY-TO-DAY OPERATIONS

Our office is open from 9:00 A.M. until 5:00 P.M., five days a week. The week is divided into ten half-day reception shifts. Since there are presently eight collective members, five of us do two shifts each week for one month, while three members have a month free from reception duty. We change the schedule at the first business meeting of each month. The receptionist answers phones, greets people when they come in, and is also responsible for such tasks as keeping the reception area neat.

We have a regular business meeting every Monday in the late afternoon. Cases which have come into the office the previous week are discussed, and an attorney and a legal worker are assigned to each case. A person may be assigned to a case because she or he is familiar with that area of law, or for the opposite reason — so that the member may learn that subject area. Working in pairs affords an opportunity for members to educate each other in specific areas of law. General business takes up the remainder of the agenda. This includes such items as vacation schedules, new membership applications, office purchases, and seminars that members might attend. By utilizing self-discipline, we have learned to cover an amazing amount of material in a brief and relatively painless meeting once each week.

Every Tuesday evening, we hold a *study meeting*. The format is loosely structured around topical units lasting six to ten weeks. Every other week, we discuss a reading chosen to illuminate a particular point or area of interest, and, generally, for each meeting, one person is assigned to select and provide the reading and lead the discussion. On alternate Tuesdays, we discuss whatever seems important. At one meeting, we discussed this article. Sometimes it is a local political issue; at other times our Tuesday meeting is a *criticism meeting*. We have just completed a unit on introductory economic theory and are about to begin a unit on women's issues — sexism, feminism, working women, and other experiences of women in a sexist society.

Perhaps a few more details would help clarify the way the collective supports us as members. As mentioned earlier, our salaries are all below $300, with the exception of one member who has a family and receives additional money when needed. While we all have a commitment to live on low salaries, our general policy is to allocate money according to needs. And, since it is hard to exist for long periods on such low incomes, we have arranged to provide some necessities at collective expense. Gas is charged at a local station, and the collective pays for all repairs on cars. In return, cars are treated as quasi-collective, which means that, while one or two individuals may have primary access to and responsibility for a vehicle, all cars are subject to appropriation by a transportation-needy individual at an ad hoc "car conference." We are building up a supply of automobiles so that soon there will be one for each member; however, in the past we have had access to only one or two vehicles. Consideration was given first to those whose needs were greatest, and the sharing worked relatively well. Medical bills are sometimes paid, and loans or special grants are given when the need arises. Everyone decides whether extra money should be appropriated. Food is purchased and kept in the office refrigerator, eliminating the need to go out for lunches which might otherwise be a drain upon our scarce time and money.

DIVISION OF LABOR

One aspect of our practice which is necessary to an understanding of the collective's operation is the concept of *legal workers*. These are people who have had little or no formal training in law, and who became interested in doing this type of work for political or practical reasons. After short periods of time in our office, all legal workers are able to fulfill most of the functions of practicing attorneys (with the notable exceptions of those functions legally prohibited, such as appearing in court, giving legal advice, and visiting individuals in prison). An example of this is a woman in our office who, after having done legal work for less than a month, prepared a writ of mandate to the California Supreme Court which overturned Santa Barbara's residency requirement for city council candidates.

Admittedly, our biggest fear of an office without traditional divisions of labor was that the work would not be done as quickly or as well as necessary. Since attorneys do their own typing, some individual pleadings take twice as long to prepare. But having non-attorneys in the office who also prepare pleadings helps to offset this time loss. The overall effect, we feel, is that everyone develops his or her legal skills, and, as a group, we become more effective and efficient than if the more menial jobs were left to the nonlawyers, as occurs in the traditional mode of practice. Working together and learning from each other has proven that an equitable allocation and sharing of the work produces a much more successful collective effort.

Often the legal workers are asked questions such as : "Why are you not in law school?" or "Do you plan to attend law school?" There are obvious advantages to a bar card; however, since the legal workers are already doing productive work without one, it is difficult for them to stop for three years to attend law school. But we do have an arrangement that promises to solve the dilemma. There is a program in California whereby students can qualify for the bar by studying under any attorney who has actively practiced in the state for the past five years. This program includes in-office work, the reading of law, discussions, examinations, and reports. Luckily, one of our attorneys qualifies as such a mentor, and he can assume the responsibility of training and supervising the study of those members of the collective who want to participate in this program. Thus, a legal worker may obtain a bar card without leaving the collective.

POLITICS AND LEGAL PRACTICE

Since all collective members share a strong belief in the necessity for restructuring society, we devote all of our abilities and legal skills to that end. Specifically, this means we support the liberation stuggles of Third World people, of insurgent unionists and farm workers, of women, children, prisoners, student radicals, and antiwar protestors. In short, we support all people who are oppressed because they were not born with money and power. This support manifests itself in many ways, and we often represent clients in political cases for reduced fees or totally without compensation.

Relating our politics to our legal practice is a constant concern. Like every other decision made in the office, questions of legal tactics in specific cases are examined in light of our commitment to advance the causes of justice and social change. This commitment requires, among other things, that we devote considerable energy not only to decision-making but also to refining our political goals, and to working toward their fulfillment.

Besides our own study meetings, we maintain extensive correspondence with other like-minded collectives and law offices, in part through our active membership in the National Lawyers Guild, an association of leftist legal workers, law students and lawyers. If our structure has developed largely from internal, organic needs and intuitions, our substantive practice has thrived on advice and support from, and the exchange of experiences with, our comrades in other parts of the country. Additionally, we depend on friendly local attorneys for answers to questions that occasionally arise, and their experience and support have been invaluable.

Finally, our roots and contacts in the community are crucial to the effective integration of our politics and our legal practices. It is fundamental to our notion of serving the people that we keep the needs of the people foremost in our work. There seems to be little need, at least in our practice, to define *the people* with analytical precision. We maintain a relationship of trust and cooperation with those elements in the community which we believe to be vital and progressive. Many of our decisions are made with their input, and our relationship with them has been generally productive.

Although our political consciousness is the distinguishing characteristic of our legal practice, we must still fulfill the obligation to advance the best interests of our clients. This is implicit in any law office subject to the economic and ethical constraints of our present legal system. We have eliminated some of the areas where these obligations conflict by categorically refusing to accept certain types of cases. For example, since a prime defense tactic in rape cases is to attack the integrity of the prosecutrix, we will not represent accused rapists. No matter how persuasive the defendant might be in protesting his innocence, we refuse to assume his defense since it might require harassment of a woman and implicitly contribute our support to a system which often punishes the victim before the rapist.

More difficult problems arise in the areas where the legal system forces us to advise clients to compromise their own interests. The most common instances involve the criminal defendant who must be told that taking a case to trial may cost three times more in legal fees than will pleading guilty to a lesser charge. We are taught in school that the defendant is offered more protections in the criminal justice system of America than in that of any other country. Not until entering legal practice did we learn that these paper protections often exist only to the extent that the defendant can afford to buy them.

Equally significant, and perhaps more interesting than the strictures placed upon the criminal defendant, are those imposed upon the insurgent unionist. Our labor practice is by no means extensive enough to qualify us as experts in the field. We do, however, have some experience in representing wildcat strikers. Emotionally and politically, wildcatters are close to our hearts, as working people with real and immediate grievances and as rebels with powerful feelings of solidarity and class loyalty. In two recent instances, we have faced irreconcilable contradictions between the short-term interests of our clients in accepting tentative concessions and returning to work, and their long-term interest in controlling their own lives. Ethical dilemmas compounded themselves like figures in an accountant's nightmare. The decisions, of course, were left to our clients, but, as their legal advisors, we could not ignore the fact that wildcatters have no place in the rigid structure of labor law. In its application, federal labor law has its main effect in encouraging the petrification of major labor unions, all in the name of promoting "industrial peace." Its ritualistic formulas of fair and unfair labor practices, its penalties against unions that step out of line, and the power given to established unions all serve to retard the development of truly independent and representative labor organizations. However, as our practice in this area expands, we hope to develop a fuller understanding of this area of law to meet the needs of our clients and, at the same time, to contribute to an ultimate political solution of their plight.

PERSONAL AND SOCIAL PROBLEMS IN THE COLLECTIVE

A pervasive factor of our experience in the collective is intensity. Trying to improve our legal work, our politics, and ourselves, as well as assuming the responsibilities of operating an efficient law office, are not tasks undertaken lightly. Perhaps at first we underestimated the amount of work required by these tasks, but our desire and optimism gave us the courage to begin, and our successes, the energy to continue.

Although it may seem incongruous with what has been said about the amount and intensity of our work, we feel the need to do even more. As mentioned earlier, we have followed a program of relating to individuals and groups in the community that we feel are progressive and whose politics we support. We do legal work for these people, and we also support them in other ways. In essence we see our goal and theirs as one and the same.

Long hours are not uncommon. Weekly evening meetings and occasional weekend meetings mean that we see each other a great deal under the pressure conditions of our work. Often, we are unable to spend as much time with each other socially as we wish. This loss is felt strongly. We have found that setting aside time to meet socially is necessary if we are to work together comfortably.

Were we to single out the largest problem we have encountered, perhaps it would be the enormous amount of responsibility required to keep the office running smoothly. Many times, a problem will be resolved with a decision that begins with, "Well then, everybody will do the following," and the success of that solution depends on everyone doing just that. With no management and no supervising bureaucracy, we must depend on our own self-discipline to assure that each and every thing gets done properly. After so many years of mother and father, teacher, professor, boss, or sergeant telling us exactly what to do every hour of the day and night, it takes time and effort to learn to work for ourselves as individuals and as a group.

One of the most critical personal and social problems we face in the collective is combating sexism. Sexism is as oppressive in a law office as it is in any other setting. In our case, outsiders generally assume that all the women in the office are clerical help, and all the men are professionals. Regularly, people who call when one of the women is on phone duty ask, upon hearing a female voice, "Is anybody there?" Originally, some of the nonprofessional men seemed to enjoy this, but discussions resulted in an understanding that this confusion was misleading our clients and perpetuating unwarranted stereotypes.

At present, there are a number of ways we combat sexism internally. First, of course, there is our method of practice. Everyone in the office is equal in all matters; no one person does more typing or answering of phones. We are all conscious of the gaps between us in some fields of expertise, and strive, by learning and teaching, to close them. We also meet regularly in groups to study, criticize, and support each other in overcoming deep-seated personal biases. All of us are aware of the differences in the socialization processes that men and women undergo. Overcoming the effects of differing socialization requires our unending attention. These problems and others have confronted us and continue to confront us. We deal with each one individually, but we have learned that a principled discussion which formulates guidelines for dealing with a problem helps reduce its adverse effects.

CONCLUSION

One of our concerns in writing this article is frankly propagandistic: we want to persuade at least some lawyers to try the collective form of practice. We think the American legal profession would benefit from more practitioners working in egalitarian, nonsexist environments.

What does a collective offer the card-carrying lawyer? Admittedly, most lawyers find it difficult to sacrifice those peripheral privileges earned by hard work and pain in law school. Even the most sympathetic young lawyers are sometimes put off by the prospect of spending time typing and sweeping an office floor at the cost of producing more cerebral legal work.

When all is said and done, collectives have only one advantage over traditional forms of practice: in many ways, they permit practitioners to be more *human.* One of the most dread afflictions of the legal trade — lawyers' ego — cannot survive in a collective atmosphere. The constant struggle against sexism has served to improve our feelings toward members of the opposite sex — a benefit which pervades our entire lives. Finally, the feelings of comradeship cultivated through hard work are of incalculable value. And, most importantly, the opportunity to take only those cases which our consciences can tolerate enables us to face the world a bit more joyfully than is too often true among our brothers and sisters working their ways to partnerships.

Untimately, though, the benefits to lawyers are only byproducts of the main purpose of collective practice. Without a commitment to thoroughgoing social change in America, sooner or later more lawyers will find the sacrifices of collective practice too great to bear, and the opportunities elsewhere in the profession too tempting to resist. We have found that our political perspective — which has been developing continuously over the years — has played a major role in shaping our success. We only hope that others will share our concerns for justice and change within the legal system, and that they, too, will consider collective practice.

12

Problems of Power
in a Free School

Frank Lindenfeld

This is an account of some problems of power encountered at Summerhill West, a free school in California. The school was one of many begun in this country during the 1960s and 1970s. Like the new wave food coops, free clinics, or antiprofit restaurants, it was an alternative organization organized in opposition to and as a replacement for established institutions.

My narrative is based on reflections as a participant-observer during 1966-70. As a parent and one of its founders, I was actively involved in the original school and its successor. I served initially as the president of its Board of Directors, and later as the school's director.

Summerhill West grew out of meetings of interested parents, students, and teachers which I helped organize in 1966. Our school opened that fall with about twenty students ranging in age from 6-14 and three or four staff members. The flavor was decidedly informal, with the students often barefoot and dressed in ragged, patched jeans. The boys and girls called teachers by their first names.

Emotional expression was encouraged, and students greeted each other and the teachers with generous hugs. Their speech was often interlarded with various swear words.

Our teachers were mostly in their twenties; they were recruited on the basis of ability and enthusiasm, rather than the possession of formal teaching credentials. Students were not required to attend classes. There were few examinations and no grades. Regularly scheduled classes were often held outdoors. In addition, teachers and volunteers provided individual tutoring and counseling sessions for each student.

Revised version of a paper presented at 72nd annual Meeting of the American Sociological Association, Chicago, September 1977.

The main goal of the school was to provide an alternative to public school, where students could learn and develop at their own pace. Summerhill West's commitment to an antiauthoritarian, participatory-democratic ethos and its emphasis on the emotional development of students was made clear in its brochures. It attracted parents in sympathy with the ideas expressed by A.S. Neill in *Summerhill* (1960). The problems of power at our school did not stem from disagreement with its central goals, but rather with differences about how to implement them in practice and how to resolve the conflicts that developed between parents, students, teachers, and administrator.

There were four overlapping channels through which school policy was decided: by the staff, by school meetings of students and teachers, by the Board of Directors, and by the school's administrator. The balance of power shifted among these during the years described here, with the greatest weight held sometimes by the administrator, the staff, or the governing board. The students' say was circumscribed by the interests of the parents and the teachers, so that school meetings resolved such issues as student discipline but not hiring and firing staff. Nevertheless, students did have a potent veto over teachers they did not like: they would simply refuse to attend classes or activities organized by such a staff member, who would eventually get the message and leave.

The school was embroiled in a number of internal conflicts, leading twice to crises so severe that it fractured into two or more parts. The first came only a few months after school began. The youngest teacher, about twenty, was accused of bringing marijuana to the campus in disregard of school rules; for this alleged infraction, the headmaster dismissed him.

The teachers sided with their colleague, who appealed his case to the Board of Directors. At a hearing, the board split four to three in favor of the teacher, and was critical of the headmaster. The latter refused to reinstate the teacher. Subsequently, the board relieved the headmaster of his administrative duties. As he was the school's landlord, however, he, in turn, evicted the school corporation from the property. For the rest of that year, he only recognized the authority of one faction of the parents who organized an interim administration. Out of concern for the students, the teachers did not go on strike, though they were eager to quit and form a new school. It was difficult to find another site on short notice, however, and so the school continued in a state of uneasy truce between headmaster and staff until the end of the school year, when the two factions parted company. The headmaster subsequently organized his own school, in which the parents loyal to him enrolled their children. The other parents and the teachers continued with the school in a new location. The governing board decided to dispense with a headmaster and turned the administration of the school over to the collectivity of the teachers.

Our second year began smoothly. The teachers were in full charge of the school. A couple of the parents on the board, including myself, usually attended staff meetings and participated in the discussion and resolution of any school business. The staff ran the school as a collective. Decisions were arrived at by consensus of the eight or nine full- and part-time teachers meeting weekly as a group. The meetings took place in the evenings, and students did not attend. There was no administrative specialization among the staff, and many of the tasks were rotated. The period of staff control of the school was successful in almost every respect, but led to conflict over pay which split the school once again.

A crisis occurred when the teachers voted themselves a one-third salary increase during the middle of the semester, funds for which were to come from tuition paid in advance. This level of expense threatened to bankrupt the school well before the end of the year. The new salaries, $500 per month for full time and $300 per month for three days per week, were *not* high in comparison with industry or public schools. They were higher than typical "movement" pay at that time, however. As Rothschild-Whitt (1976b) has pointed out, low pay-scales in alternative organizations keep them democratic because there are no high-salary jobs to give participants a vested interest.

The financial problems of the school were linked to the fact that it was supported entirely by private tuition. The tuition was $100 per month, but parents who could not afford this paid less. As taxpayers, the parents were already paying the bill for public schools. Tuition for our school was felt by some as an additional tax they were barely able to afford. One way private schools can attain a sound financial base is not to offer tuition scholarships, effectively limiting their pupils to the chldren of the well-to-do. A preferable alternative would be the adoption of some variant of the voucher system, allowing parents to purchase schooling with vouchers redeemable at either public or private schools.

After the salary increase, some of the parents decided to reactivate the governing board. At a special joint meeting of the board and staff convened to deal with the issue, the divisions between the two sides became very apparent. Board members suggested reducing salaries to meet income, and tying the number of paid teachers and their level of remuneration to school income. The teachers rejected this in favor of a fixed number of positions at fixed salaries. They proposed a continuation of deficit spending but were unwilling to assume responsibility for raising additional funds. Following a heated discussion, the board dismissed two teachers in an economy move and appointed me unpaid business manager. This was done over the strong protest of the staff, who were dismayed that the board reclaimed its delegated powers. Feeling betrayed, most of the teachers resigned and took a majority of the students with them.[1] The former staff members did not work together, but formed several separate, small schools, the most successful of which was the Los Angeles Free School.

That spring, I reorganized Summerhill West and became the school's director. Our financial problems made it imperative to admit new students, and we began to accept boarders as well as day students. We kept the school open that summer to help pay the rent. By fall, enrollment had grown to about fifty students with several full- and part-time teachers. There were so many boarders (almost half the student body) that we rented three houses in town to accommodate them and hired several houseparents. The full-time teachers were co-opted as board members, and we added a student representative as well, but there were few board meetings. Decisions were made in meetings of the staff or in general school meetings of students and staff.

The only conflict that year started when one of the houseparents wanted a friend of his to work at the school. He invited his friend to live in a boarding house without consulting others on the staff. Though some of the students liked the new man, few of the teachers wanted him to stay. The houseparent insisted his friend remain, and soon the school members chose sides. We were faced with a controversy between the houseparent and the students on one side, and the teaching staff on the other. The situation developed into a major dispute because of the lack of unanimity among the staff. It was enough to have one dissatisfied houseparent to rally many of the teenagers to his point of view. In most such arguments, the teenagers almost automatically opposed whatever an "authority figure" such as myself seemed to favor.

By spring of 1969, we learned our lease would not be renewed and began looking for another site. At about the same time, we received an inquiry from a Hayward parents' group which wanted to set up a free school there. A representative of the group visited us, and, after some negotiation, we decided to merge our efforts. The Hayward parents invited me to be the director of the new school, and to take along the staff and the boarding students.

The new school was called Pegasus. It began with an enrollment of approximately thirty-five students, half of whom were teenage boarders. There were four or five teachers, but no houseparents; the boarding students were by now managing their own affairs, doing the shopping, cooking, etc. We reorganized the Board of Directors so that it included four parents, three staff members, and two students. A Hayward parent and pediatrician was elected president.

At the Hayward school, there were several disputes over the issue of choosing permanent staff members. The problem was not so much with hiring as firing a staff member. The usual procedure was for prospective staff members to work at the school for a probationary period of two months, after which their status would be reconsidered, and the regular staff would decide whether to retain the new person permanently.

For example, during 1969-70, the school's secretary wanted to become a teacher. The secretarial job was one of the most frustrating in the school, because the secretary was the only one pinned down to the office; students and staff were free to go on field trips, and students were not compelled to attend classes. The secretary had been hired at the beginning of that year to help raise funds, to take care of the office routine, and to answer mail and phone. After a couple of months, she dropped the fund-raising activities, and began spending part of the day with the teenage students, counseling and giving driving lessons. These were much more satisfying to her than the office activities. It soon became apparent she did not want to do the secretarial work at all; she asked to be a teacher, and we agreed to let her try.

By the end of the probationary period, some of the staff felt she was not responsible enough, though most had no objections. The teenagers unanimously urged us to keep her. After several meetings, the staff finally agreed to a compromise in which she would be a part-time teacher, but, as she had her heart set on full-time (and full salary), she left.

The final division of the school into elementary and secondary halves was made smoothly and without acrimony. During the first year in Hayward, we began to plan permanent housing for the boarding students, in place of such makeshift arrangements as converted lofts and garages on the property. One of the parents was an architect; in partial exhange for tuition, he drew plans for a dormitory that could be built by the older students themselves. We persuaded a bank to extend $10,000 credit for materials and made preliminary surveys for the dormitory.

At this point, some of the parents of the younger students voiced doubts about continuing to mix day and boarding students. One of their major concerns was that the "hippie" values of the older students might somehow corrupt the younger ones. They were also reluctant to cosign for another mortgage. The objectors carried the argument; instead of degenerating into a factional conflict, as might have happened previously, the school arrived at a consensus that the teenagers would move to another site. The building plans were shelved, a new site for the teenage boarding campus was found, and the school divorced peaceably into an elementary day school in Hayward and a secondary boarding school-commune in Mendocino. The Medocino school continued for several years; one reason it broke up is that there was no attempt to replace graduates with new younger students. Pegasus continued as a day school through 1977, when financial difficulties forced it to close.

DISCUSSION

Alternative organizations, including the free school described here, are generally committed to working in an egalitarian, nonbureaucratic, participatory-democratic manner. The locus of authority resides in the entire collectivity, rather than in a particular executive position at the top. There are few written rules, agreed-upon procedures, or standards and criteria for job performance. Most problems that arise are considered on a case-by-case basis. This is a strength of such organizations, in that decisions are not based upon abstract rules but rather on the concrete circumstances of individual cases. The very informality and ad hoc consideration of issues as they arise by the collectivity is also a major weakness, however. To the extent that rules and procedures are vague, disputes may be more vehement because there is legitimately room for greater latitude in interpretation and differences in opinion than in bureaucracies where most procedures are spelled out.

Moreover, like any other organization, alternative organizations face various dilemmas of power (Kinkade 1974). Three of these problems are explored in more detail below: delegation of authority vs. decision-making by the entire organization; consensus vs. major- ity voting; and worker (teacher) control vs. community and client (parent and student) control.

Delegation of Authority vs. Decision-Making by the Entire Organization

The delegation of authority is an issue that must be faced even by small alternative organizations. Although the school was a collective in which the membership as a whole was the ultimate authority, in practice it was not feasible to gather all the parents, teachers, and students together more than a few times a year. Thus, the authority to make policy decisions was delegated to the Board of Directors. The board also met infrequently, and so entrusted day-to-day administra- tion of the school to the staff and the director, when there was one.

The organizational structure of the school was, in fact, formally similar to that of public schools. There was a governing board, elected by the parents, teachers, and students, and (except during the second year) an administrator. Our experience that year shows that, if an organization is small and members participate in frequent meetings, a director or headmaster might not be necessary. The school worked well without a formal division of labor, although many coordination functions were in fact performed informally by one of the teachers. The school's ideal was to make major decisions in weekly school meetings where each student and teacher had one vote. This ideal was often violated for several reasons. First, some deci- sions had to be made on the spot by staff members between meetings. Second, even when decisions were arrived at in democratic meetings of students and staff, practical implementation was usually left in the hands of a staff member. The way a teacher interpreted a decision affected how it was done and even whether it would ever be carried out. But, most importantly, the adults involved did not want to give up their power on issues of money or personnel. The staff, including the teachers and the director, felt they had more at stake than either students or parents, because their livelihood depended on the school.

Further, our school attracted many teachers, older students, and even parents who held strong antiauthoritarian attitudes and values and who were ambivalent about the exercise of authority, even by officers or delegates elected by and responsible to themselves. This was partly a product of the "do your own thing" philosophy that many school members believed in. The members' ambivalence about power and authority and distrust of managers was reflected both in a lack of clear delegation of powers and in constant criticisms of the headmaster or director. Students and teachers did not want to be bothered with taking care of minor administrative problems; the students, especially, resented too much time spent in meetings. Nevertheless, teachers and students often griped about any decisions that were made without them. As Hawley (1974) has pointed out, managers in nonbureaucratic organizations are subject to far more criticism by members than those in bureaucracies. Managers in nonbureaucratic organizations are criticized for their actions and also criticized when they do *not* take action.

The delegation of tasks, sometimes to the director, sometimes to a staff member or committee, enabled the school to function well. Effective delegation of responsibility and trust in managers or committees chosen by the membership is essential for the smooth operation of a democratic organization. Otherwise, members become swamped with constant meetings about trivia and lose interest in participating. The students and teachers did not want to decide all the issues; they wanted only the power to change those decisions made by delegates that they did not approve of.

Consensus vs. Majority Voting

Like many other alternative organizations, the free school often used consensus decision-making in place of majority voting. An advantage of consensus is that organizations proceed only along lines acceptable to all of the members, who become committed to decisions by taking part in formulating them. Moreover, the majority is not always right and the consensus process insures that minority voices of conscience are listened to. A disadvantage is that such decision-making may be slow and tedious and that the objections of one person or a tiny minority can keep the entire organization from necessary action. The larger the number of persons in a group meeting, the more difficult consensus procedure becomes, because even one "no" may constitute a veto.

At the all-school and staff meetings, we strove for consensus when possible, though this sometimes meant lengthy arguments and discussions. There was never any clear demarcation between decisions to be arrived at by consensus and those that could be made by majority vote. This distinction only grew out of our practice. Because there was general agreement among teachers, students, and parents on such basic values as noncoercive education, the consensus process was usually not too cumbersome.

Power conflicts erupted especially over hiring and firing staff. Usually, a new teacher would be evaluated by the other staff members at the end of the probationary period and retained or dismissed. At first we used majority voting for making this decision. In a couple of instances, however, strong reservations were expressed by a minority of the staff about keeping a probationary teacher. Several teachers insisted they did not want to work with the new person. This led to the position that there had to be consensus on retention decisions. If there was even one strong objection, we did not retain the probationary staff member.

Before we settled on consensus for hiring and retaining teachers, we resolved some disputes with the more traditional majority vote. This meant that a teacher or teachers dissatisfied with a retention decision of their colleagues could take the issue to the students, who became strongly attached to new teachers and almost always favored their retention. This did not change the outcome of the decision, but the majority-vote system meant that staff disagreements sometimes polarized the school into contending camps.

With less important issues, the consensus process meant that minority opinions were voiced, but the dissenters would not stand in the way of majority action. On the two occasions discussed above, when minorities felt there was an important issue at stake and would not back down, the school split into separate organizations. These splits would probably have occurred no matter what the school's voting procedures.

Workers' Control vs. Community/Client Control

The greatest influence on decisions at the school was exercised by the staff, including myself when I was the school administrator. The role of parents and of the students was secondary. In part, this was a reflection of the greater emotional involvement of the teaching staff with the school: in many ways, the staff *was* the school organization. Even those parents on the Board of Directors were only peripherally involved with the school; they had their own work and other interests that occupied much of their time and attention.

The issue of how much say teachers would have and over what vs. how much say the parents would have plagued the school throughout its history. The two major splits in the school were, in part, reflections of struggles for control between staff and parents. The school's ultimate authority was vested in the membership, primarily parents, acting through the Board of Directors. During the beginning of the first year, the dominant faction on the board was allied with the teachers, against the headmaster and a faction of "newer" parents that sided with him. Later that year, the second group gained power, primarily because the headmaster controlled the school site. During the second year, the board turned over its authority to the teaching staff, so that the teachers were running the organization in every respect. The board retained its powers, perhaps a serious deficiency in that the teachers' control may not have seemed real enough for them to accept full responsibility for the consequences of the decision to raise their own pay.

The main dispute between parents and teachers centered around money. Funds to pay for the school came primarily from tuition paid by the parents. The major expense of the school was for teachers' salaries. The parents wanted to keep the tuition relatively low; the teachers wanted a living wage. In the absence of government or foundation subsidies or major fund-raising activities, the only source available to pay for salary increases was an increase in tuition, and such an increase was resisted by the parents. There was no way to make this issue vanish.

A major defect of our school was that it gave lip service to democratic participation by the students, but many of the important issues were not brought up for resolution in school meetings where the students had the controlling voice. Neither the parents nor the teachers were prepared to take the risk of genuine student participation.

Some of our early difficulties might have been avoided if there had been either no board of directors, or a board even more representative of parents, students and staff. Actually, the Mendocino offshoot of the original school had no governing board, but conflicts among staff members and between staff and students continued (the parents were far away). The question is not how to avoid conflict; it would be hopelessly utopian to imagine we could construct an organization that engaged in vital activities, yet was devoid of conflict. It is rather how to find some mechanisms whereby conflicts can be peaceably worked out and where the legitimate interest of all parties involved in the organization can find expression.[3]

Alternative organizations need a structure that allows for *both* workers' and community membership influence on organizational policies. This can take one of several forms:

1. Worker-controlled organizations, where those who work in the organization are the ultimate authority, one person, one vote, or where they elect a majority of the governing board.

2. Member-controlled organizations, where consumer-members are the ultimate authority, one person, one vote, or where they elect a majority of the governing board.

3. Pluralistically controlled organizations, where both workers and consumers elect half of the governing board or where there is recognition of the interests of three or more parties, no one of which has a majority on the governing board. When organizations are small enough, as in many coops and free schools, it may be preferable for all the full-time staff to be on the governing board, and, in fact, to constitute half its members. This may help insure against a division of the organization into workers vs. management.

The pluralist approach was the one the free school eventually adopted. At the school, the composition of the governing board was changed several times in the direction of more balanced representation. The first board was self-elected; it consisted of parents and community members co-opted to it, with an *ex officio* membership of the director. Then the board was elected by the parents, with one representative of the staff. Still later, the organization shifted to a more equal representation of staff, students, and parents, so that no one of the three interest groups had a majority on the board.

The question of how best to balance interests of workers, clients, and community has no clear answers. Formulas for alternative organizations that place power in the hands of a management board with only minority representation of its workers may safeguard the interests of clients and the community at large, but at the expense of continuing the split between labor and management. Those that place power in the hands of the workers must recognize that worker-controlled firms, like other organizations, may sometimes further their own interest at the expense of clients or consumers.

The comanagement structure eventually adopted by the free school is one of many possible answers to the dilemmas of power, where there are several important constituencies in an organization. The existence of these constituencies — parents, teachers and students — was recognized by giving each some representation on the school's governing board. The greater involvement of the staff was recognized by delegating primary responsibility for day-to-day operation of the school to them, working through a consensus process, and to the school administrator when there was one. Students were involved in many decisions through the one person, one vote system of school meetings.

Although issues of structure are important, democratic functioning of alternative organizations also depends on the existence of a cooperative attitude among the members. This includes trust and confidence in delegates and managers and committees chosen by the membership, so that minor decisions do not have to be taken to the entire body. Conflicts of interest between workers and clients, managers and members, are inevitable even in alternative organizations, and cannot necessarily be eliminated. It helps to institutionalize mechanisms whereby such conflicts can be resolved. Beyond that, it is important to have workers and members who understand that conflict is normal and who are prepared to deal with each other on the basis of mutual concern and respect.

NOTES

1. Several teachers later sued the school for wages they would have received under the salary scale they had voted themselves.

2. The bureaucratic nature of the public schools forced on our organization a greater degree of record-keeping than we would have liked. To facilitate student transfers, the public schools requested transcripts and records. Since we did not keep records the same way as the public schools did, these had to be specially created. Likewise, a continuous stream of calls and letters from building inspectors, health officials, etc. led us to develop a special position to keep up with their visits and correspondence.

3. The issue of workers' vs. member control also arises in food coops, another variety of alternative organization. Some coops are dominated by the membership, which elects a Board of Directors that sets policy, hires managers, etc. Other coops are run by their workers as worker-managed organizations, with only minimal input from customers or members (Newton, chap. 13). Even in coops controlled by the membership, the active participation and interest of most members (even including board members) is not as strong as that of the managers and workers, for whom the coop is a source of livelihood. Thus, there is a tendency for the workers, and especially the store managers, to give precedence to their own interests when there is a conflict between lower prices vs. higher pay.

   For example, the self-managed food coops in Washington, D.C., federated into Strongforce, have been criticized for being too insulated from commuity influence. The main decisions about the stores are made by the several persons that work there; those who shop there don't have much more say than they do in the operation of any chain supermarket. As Zwerdling (1975) points out:

   > The stores are still operated and controlled by small private groups. Stone Soup and Fields have their suggestion sheets where shoppers can write comments about the store, and the collectives have open meetings where outsiders can participate. But in the end, when decisions are actually made, do these necessarily give shoppers much more power than Safeway's suggestion box?

In 1976, the workers in one of the stores concluded that coops were a dead end, and decided unilaterally to sell out to a private business. This decision was narrowly averted by other members of Strongforce.

13

On Structure and Decision-Making

Gary H. Newton

When someone talks about governance or government, I always think of someone telling me what to do. Therefore, I won't discuss governments or governance. What I want to talk about is *self-management*.

FORMAL VS. INFORMAL STRUCTURES

The sixties saw a rejection of the establishment. Structure was confused with hierarchy and bureaucracy and thrown out with all the bad points of the status quo. Remember the SDS meetings with no chair, an open mike, and endless discussion? The open meetings seldom made any detailed decisions about activities or demonstrations. Usually, smaller groups organized the activities and made the detailed decisions. These smaller groups usually were not formally chosen, but emerged. In fact, most people at the demonstrations didn't even know who organized them. What the movement of the sixties threw out was formalized structure. Contrary to what we might like to think, there is no such thing as a structureless group. Any group that comes together will eventually structure itself. If formal, consciously chosen structures are rejected, then informal structures will emerge.

Informal stuctures are the basis for elitism. The existence of informal structures means that the rules of how decisions are made are known only by a few, and only these few will make most of the decisions. The few who make the decisions under this informal

Gary H. Newton is a Research Associate with Community Consulting Group, Austin, Texas, a firm providing technical assistance to nonprofit organizations and cooperatives. He is also active in the Community Gardening Movement.

Reprinted with permission from *Communities*, March-April 1976.

structure are seldom accountable — they are many times not even visible as the ones who make the decisions. For everyone to have access to input into decisions, structure must be explicit, not implicit. This is not to say that formalization of structure eliminates informal structures. But it does interfere with giving informal structures predominant control by providing a legitimate (recognized and accepted) structure for decision-making. With the formalization of structure should come clear definitions of responsibility. Who is responsible for what should be clear to all. If it isn't then there can't be accountability.[1]

WHO SHOULD MAKE WHAT DECISION?

An answer to the question who should make what decision is important to defining structure. Austin Community Project, a federation of consumer coops, producer collectives, and organic farmers, has answered this question, at least on a theoretical level. In their proposed goals statement, the members state, "decisions should be made by those affected by the decisions, and people should have input in proportion to how much they are affected by them."[2] Turning the theory into practice is where the struggle begins. Ultimately, everyone is affected by millions of decisions. Because of the complexities of our world, we can never be involved in all of the decisions which affect us. So what structure will allow us to make the decisions on which decisions we would like to delegate?

COLLECTIVES VS. COOPS

Two different models of alternative organizations are emerging in the new food coops.[3] The authors of *The Food Co-op Handbook* describe the differences:

> Some co-ops are highly participatory and others lean toward community service. In participatory co-ops...the work is done by the members, who are also expected to make the decisions for the co-op. Community service co-ops are run by small groups of committed activists...concerned with bringing inexpensive, high quality food to as many of their neighbors as possible and creating a source of alternative employment at the same time.
>
> In practice there are few purely participatory or purely community service co-ops. Paid coordinators or management collectives often run participatory co-ops, and most community service co-ops expect some degree of input from their members.[4]

The West Coast has provided some of the most vocal proponents of community service coops (they call them *worker collectives*). They have some very valid criticisms of participatory coops (member coops). An Ananda Marga coop group in Seattle criticizes member coops:

> ...experience has demonstrated that member cooperatives eventually either become much like conventional retail stores, reducing individual participation to a token level, or where there is a strong reliance on membership participation, the co-op is weakened by a lack of consistent, competent help. These more participatory cooperatives frequently lack strong leadership or the capacity for dynamic growth over extended periods of time. Monthly or quarterly membership meetings are poor forums for conducting business and making operational decisions. Such matters are better handled by active members and paid workers, who generally have the greater capacity for formulating viable policy than the fee-paying members who lack time for, or interest in, active participation. In fact, it is workers who usually show up for meetings and dominate the decision making process.[5]

A West Coast trucking collective criticizes participatory coops as being non-political:

> ...they are compelled to solicit and respond to community demands regardless of how narrow-minded and selfish that community may be. This robs them of any initiative, and restrains them from actively raising community consciousness around issues having political overtones, for fear of alienating their community and losing its support.
>
> This is not to say that cooperatives' only interests are economic, but sooner or later it comes down to that. . . . Cooperatives do not challenge the basic structure of the old system, and they do not challenge any preconceived notions we have of ourselves and of our beliefs. Since the old system remains unchanged, the cooperatives begin to take on its values and weaknesses, and result in the situation we have today: cooperatives succeed in business but fail in spirit.[6]

David Morris and Karl Hess, writer-activists, encourage community control of economic and political institutions. They note, "The primary problem with worker collectives is how to stop them from becoming extended 'mom and pop' stores, that is self-serving except with ten owners rather than one."[7] But probably the most significant criticism of worker collectives is that they fail to empower powerless people. They are good as far as they go, but they don't go far enough. They don't give people the right to have a control over part of their life. David McReynolds, a long-time nonviolent social activist, describes the feeling many people have:

> We now have a whole category of Americans who are broken people.... A radical black leader lamented to me that even in the office of his organization in Harlem they couldn't keep typewriters unless they were locked up and nailed down — the people stole each other blind. These are people who are taught that they are without worth.... But when these people are empowered — the word *empowered* is crucial here, for we are not talking about *our* making decisions *for* them, but creating a situation where the powerless have power and take responsibility.... The revolutionist should not romanticize people but neither should we underestimate the power of people, given responsibility, to function responsibly.[8]

Even the so-called empowered people have very little to say about how things are decided or who decides them. Worker collectives don't solve this powerlessness.

A NEW HYBRID

What is evolving in the food coop movement is a new hybrid coop which is trying to answer the criticisms of both the participatory coops and the community service coops (worker collectives). Wheatsville Food Co-op, a new coop store in Austin, Texas, is one such hybrid. All power in this coop flows from the community as defined by the membership of the coop. There are general membership meetings as often as necessary, with at least one per semester (the neighborhood served has a large percentage of students). At these meetings, the membership sets the goals and directions of the coop; selects representatives to the coordinating committee; approves financial and labor budgets (there is an extensive labor exchange system in Austin Community Project between the coop stores, producer collectives, and organic farmers). The general membership has the right to call meetings, initiate policy changes, and recall workers and committee members. The coordinating committee (all members serve on working committees besides their coordinating role) prepares financial and labor budgets as well as other information for the general membership; hires collective workers who are nominated by other workers on the collective; reviews the worker collective periodically; and makes emergency decisions which are automatically reviewed by the general membership. The coordinating committee has the right to fire collective workers. The worker collective is responsible for management of the coop store (they oversee finances, inventory, cashiering, and maintenance). They make day-to-day operational decisions. They are responsible for all work which needs to be done to operate the store. Working with them are working committees with specific tasks (i.e. recycling, child care, delivering food to the elderly, bookkeeping). Wheatsville's structure is a combination of a worker collective and a participatory coop. The workers maintain control over their work situation. This coop is worker self-managed and community controlled. It meets the description of collectives which the West Coast truckers use:

> Fundamental to the collective organization is the elimination of any graduated scale of authority (hierarchy), and decisions are made by those directly affected by them (direct democratic process). In a collective:
>
> An individual is no longer working for a manager, nor a manager working for an owner, rather each of us becomes an integral part of a common work effort necessary to meet human needs, sharing work and decision-making alike.
>
> There are no bosses, and no leaders. Each of us takes responsibility of being our own boss; our own leader. Job functions are equitably distributed. We share those that are hard or tedious, and we share those that are easy and fun, restoring dignity to work because we work for ourselves and decide for ourselves when and how our energy is to be contributed.
>
> Those of us with skills and experience, share with those lacking in them. Those of us without skills learn them, and become accustomed to the responsibility that goes with them.
>
> We engage in vigorous struggle to rid ourselves of negative influences of the past. The selfishness of individualism, the arrogance of elitism, the terror of racism, the insecurity of sexism, and the mistrust in jealousy.[9]

At the same time, the general membership controls the direction of the coop, providing community control. This relationship between the membership and the workers creates a new solidarity. Social capital is also created with formalized community input. *The Food Co-op Handbook* explains why:

> Participation creates social capital. That is, working cooperatively creates positive feelings toward the co-op, which are as necessary to its operations as financial capital is. These good feelings motivate co-op members to relate better to each other and to support the food co-op in bad times as well as good.

When a retired man on a fixed income gives $50 of his savings to the Boston Food Co-op after it has just been robbed, we can see social capital converting itself to financial capital. When people shopping at the different co-op stores in Minneapolis drop what they're doing to stand in the cold to help unload the delivery truck from the ———— Warehouse, social capital is again at work.[10]

Wheatsville's division of decision-making and labor is also beginning to answer the objections to both models presented. The neighborhood orientation of the store preserves a limit to the size of the store. When it grows too large, it will split in two. The worker collective provides competence and continuity. The working committees and the worker collective provide the dynamic leadership for the coop. As long as the worker collective is political and constantly going through a process of criticism and self-criticism, the members will catalyze the coop as a whole to become more political by starting dialogue on different issues. Because the collective cannot act on directional decisions without dialogue with the community, the collective cannot become isolated from the community. This new hybrid coop is a basic change in the way workers relate. It is also a new way in which workers relate to consumers. With the general membership having decision-making power, each is empowered with control over his coop. With this relationship with the coop and the worker collective, members are more likely to question their own work situation. The worker collective provides a model for the members of the coop to emulate in their own work situations.

There will be many more evolutions and revolutions in the structures of institutions around us. As long as broad input is allowed and considered, I don't think bad decisions can be made. As Mao says, correct ideas come from social experience. We are entering a new era in organizations because we are learning from our social experience.

NOTES

1. I have relied heavily on Jo Freeman's "The Tyranny of Structurelessness," *MS.* 2 (no. 1, July 1973): 76-78, 86-89, which has a more thorough discussion of this subject.
2. "Austin Community Project Statement of Goals," Dec. 16, 1974. Mimeographed. Available from Austin Community Project, 1602 W. 12, Austin, TX 78703. Send $.10 and a self-addressed stamped envelope.
3. I have drawn heavily from a letter by Bhudeva (Bill Meacham) to Sectorial Social Security Board Members of Ananda Marga, 15 December 1975.

4. The Co-op Handbook Collective, *The Food Co-op Handbook* (Boston: Hough-ton Mifflin Co., 1975), p. 32.

5. Seattle Collective of the Universal PROUTist Youth Federation, "Progressive Cooperatives" (Pamphlet), Sept. 1975, pp. 2-3. Available from UPYF, PO Box 12233, Seattle, WA 98112.

6. Los Truckaderos, "Beyond Isolation: The West Coast Collective Food System As We See It," Sept. 1975, pp. 9-10. Available from Los Truckaderos, 1600 Woolsey St., Berkeley, CA 94703. Send some money and a self-addressed stamped en-velope.

7. David Morris and Karl Hess, *Neighborhood Power: The New Localism* (Boston: Beacon Press, 1975), p. 57.

8. David McReynolds, "Building Our Movement," *WIN* magazine 9 (no. 40, Nov. 27, 1975): 8, 11.

9. Los Truckaderos, p. 11.

10. The Co-op Handbook Collective, p. 114.

14

Seattle Workers' Brigade: History of a Collective

Peg Pearson
Jake Baker

This is a formal notification that C.C. Grains no longer wishes to be a part of the Seattle Workers' Brigade. We feel that our priorities and needs are no longer the same as those of the other businesses. We want to become a more efficiently run business — one that is capable of offering our customers and community better service, and that is less frustrating to us as workers. We want to work in a more stable collective, and to have more control over the decisions made that affect our workspace. We want to become a much more positive example of worker self-management. We feel, because of its complexity and lack of a solid base of unity, that trying to attain these goals as part of the Seattle Workers' Brigade is, at least for the present, counterproductive. To learn how to effectively manage ourselves (a new experience for most of us) is a difficult thing to do even in a place where we work together every day, and we feel that trying to learn to manage other workspaces at the same time is well beyond our current capabilities.

— from a statement written by
C.C. Grains, February 1977

The Seattle Workers' Brigade was a large collective, a business owned and managed by those who worked in it. In its last year of operation, it was made up of four *teams* or member businesses: Little

---

Alan King, then known as Jake Baker, left the Little Bread Company in July 1977. He joined with the Oroweat Baking Company as a baker, and helped to negotiate the first Works-Management Committee at its Vancouver, British Columbia, plant. He is now pursuing a degree in Mathematics and Economics at the University of Washington.

Sarah Yarrow, then known as Peg Pearson, was active in the Seattle Workers' Brigade. She is now living in California.

Reprinted from Puget Consumers' Co-op *Newsletter*, No. 54, June 1977, by permission of Puget Consumers' Co-op.

Bread Co., a whole-grain bakery; Corner Green Grocery, a retail natural-foods store in the Pike Place Market; Cooperating Community Grains, a warehousing operation which supplies Washington, Alaska, and parts of Idaho, Montana, and British Columbia with organic grains, nuts, beans, cheese, and other products; and a central bookkeeping team. In May 1977, after two and a half years together, these businesses dissolved their legal and financial ties and began to operate independently of one another. This is a history of the Seattle Workers' Brigade, explaining why it was formed and why it split up.

The roots of the Seattle Workers' Brigade lie in the Cooperating Community, an informal association of about fifteen Seattle area workers' collectives and consumer coops that met regularly through 1972, '73, and '74 "to discuss actions related to the politics of food, the search for alternative sources of food, and the goal of unifying city and country within an interdependent self-sufficient organization." The Cooperating Community was quite active in its early years. City people were organized to help nearby collective farms with planting and harvesting; three service collectives, Child Care, Alternative Finance, and Black Duck Motors were set up for the use of the community; and a General Fund was started (largely with money from Puget Consumers Coop) to capitalize member businesses. Several new collectives, including C.C. Grains and Community Produce, were formed and grew rapidly.

In 1974, the energy of the earlier Cooperating Community was beginning to wane. The organization had grown and become more complex. It became harder to decide what priorities would determine the use of community resources (what few were left unspoken for). For that matter, since decisions had to be approved by consensus, it was more difficult to make every decision. Many groups, combating inexperience and inefficiency in an uphill climb to develop their own businesses, became frustrated with the often unproductive CC meetings and activities. Several groups left the CC, and others went out of business.

In the summer of 1974, a group of people concerned by the growing autonomy of the Cooperating Community businesses, met together and wrote an analysis of what they felt were the problems that held the CC back from meeting its potential as a viable force for revolutionary social change. They decided that "the bulk of our problems in CC stem from our lack of unity on the goals and purposes of CC," specifically that "Cooperating Community has, as yet made no definite commitment to socialism, to radical social change, and to mass political action." This lack of commitment to socialism was reflected in several ways:

1. Wages varied from business to business.

2. In a socialist society, use of socially created resources should be determined socially, but, in the Cooperating Community, use of socially created resources was determined predominantly by the individual businesses.

3. Collective and coop members usually put their groups' needs first and were sometimes suspicious of the other businesses.

4. The CC activities, for various reasons, appealed, for the most part, only to people of middle-class background, which was in contradiction to the goal of using the CC as a base for mass political action.

The failure of Cooperating Community to actively pursue radical social change led various CC members to propose a new community structure. They recommended that the local alternative businesses join together into one legal and financial entity, sharing capital, tools, machinery, planning, bookkeeping, and personal skills. This structure would remove some of the conditions existing in CC which were in contradiction to socialist ideals. It was felt that combining alternative businesses into a "collective community" would provide the left with a valuable political experiment. Additionally, the combined structure was seen as being a more efficient use of resources. It was hoped that the businesses would be financially stronger together than they were apart, enabling the community to expand and grow.

EARLY DAYS

In October 1974, the Seattle Workers' Brigade was formed in response to the needs and criticisms of parts of the Cooperating Community. However, only four businesses, Alternative Finance, Black Duck Motors, Little Bread Co., and C.C. Grains agreed to be a part of the brigade. The other CC businesses, for personal, practical, or political reasons, decided to maintain their autonomy. This created hard feelings between some CC groups and the brigade businesses, which lasted for months. The smallness of the brigade was disappointing when compared to the vision its founders had of a large, unified, socialist organization with a potential mass-political function.

The first months of the Seattle Workers' Brigade were filled with projects and problems. The businesses joining the brigade were restructured into teams based on the types of work that needed to be done; baking, warehousing, processing (milling and making cereals), transportation and maintenance, bookkeeping, and central planning. Wages were set at $350 a month for full-time work, plus additional money for workers with children. It was hoped that, by paying $350 a month (people had made less before), the brigade would attract members who were not young, white, and downwardly mobile. This dream soon proved to be unrealistic however — the wages people paid themselves did not reflect the earning capabilities of the brigade, and it lost money rapidly. Still, hopes of attracting working-class members were strong, so, instead of dropping wages to a workable level, people were asked to leave as much of their money in the business as they could and not to withdraw it until business was booming. However, though most people took very little money for a while, many soon developed such financial problems that it was decided that people could withdraw their back wages on request. The money left in the business — the Boom Fund — eventually amounted to about twenty thousand dollars before wages were finally lowered to $232 a month, a level which reflected the actual productivity of the business, in July 1975. This debt was a drain on the brigade's finances throughout its existence, and is still not totally paid off.

Meanwhile, as the brigade struggled to organize itself, the Cooperating Community was becoming increasingly shaky. In part because of intergroup resentments stemming from the formation of the brigade, and in part because the brigade was so involved in its consuming internal problems that it had little energy for anything else, the CC decided, in the winter of 1975, to stop meeting for a while. "A while" has turned out to be a long time indeed — to this day the impetus has not existed to resume formal communications between Seattle area alternative businesses.

The next series of crises in the brigade centered around the issue of decision-making. Proposals were initiated by individuals, refined in a representative liaison group, then returned to the teams, who attempted to reach a consensus agreement. If consensus was not reached, the proposal went back to the liaison committee, and so forth, for three weeks. If consensus was not reached in three weeks, the proposal could be passed if two-thirds of the brigade members agreed to it. In addition, there was a Planning Coordinating Team which handled such matters as meeting labor needs, dealing with insurance and lawyers, public relations, budgeting, and other financial planning.

These processes turned out to be very time-consuming and frustrating, and almost everyone agreed that a new approach to decision-making was in order. But some people felt more centralized planning was needed and wanted to greatly extend the powers of the Planning Coordinating Team, while others felt that decentralization was what was needed and wanted everybody to get together and make major decisions as a large group in one place. The decentralists were in the majority, so the liaison committee and the Planning Coordinating Team were disbanded. Responsibility for most financial planning and budgeting was given to the bookkeeping team and a representative budget committee. The main decision-making body became the brigade meeting, held monthly. At this meeting, interbrigade matters such as budgets and financial affairs, new trucking schedules, and major capital expenditures were reviewed and approved. Each separate team had weekly meetings to conduct its affairs, and, in addition, each team assigned some management responsibilities to individuals. Decision-making by consensus was dropped, and everything was agreed upon by simple majority.

In the summer of 1975, the brigade found that being part of the same big business did not necessarily mean that all the teams were going to work well with each other. Some members of the trucking and maintenance team were becoming increasingly alienated from the other teams. They saw their work in the brigade as being just a job, and did not want to put a whole lot of time into developing efficient work practices, improving communication, or *criticism self-criticism*. Members of the other teams felt that these T & M workers were using the loose work-structure to do as they pleased. Tension grew, and, after months of struggle, it was decided to disband the team. Trucking and maintenance functions were taken over by the warehouse and bakery teams, and several of the truckers were eventually asked to leave the brigade. There were also problems of supply and coordination between the warehouse and the processing teams, who shared the same building. Again, tension was high, and communication was low. This issue was resolved by integrating the teams into one warehouse team.

In the fall of 1975, the brigade was given the opportunity to open a store in the Pike Place Market. Most people were excited about the idea of expanding into retailing, and felt that the relocation was excellent. The store would expose many shoppers to collective self-management, and would, hopefully, generate some much-needed profit without requiring too large a capital investment. So, in January 1976, the Corner Green Grocery and Natural Food Store opened for business.

This completed the first year of the Seattle Workers' Brigade. The net worth of the brigade was a negative $19,500, a loss of $27,212 over one year of operation (Oct. 1974 to Oct. 1975). The outlook was not bright; the brigade was committed to making massive Boom Fund payments, to supporting a fledgling business (Corner Green Grocery) which would eventually cost $20,000. Brigade meetings were tedious and unproductive, the business was rife with structural inefficiencies, and high turnover of workers was the norm. Though people were becoming more aware of a need for greater work efficiency and better financial planning, decisions such as the one to start the Corner Green Grocery showed that the brigade was still acting more on what "sounded good" than on realistic financial planning.

TENSIONS OF THE LATER YEARS

In 1976, the financial consequences of the current commitments and past errors of the brigade were partially borne by the community in the form of higher prices, but were mostly carried by the workers. Wages remained at $232 a month for most of the year, rising to $265 in December. Work hours were still long. Still, the situation definitely improved as the year went on. The bakery, though losing large amounts of money in the first part of the year ($5,000 in May alone) was able to tighten up its operation, and, by the end of the year, had added $3,000 to the net worth of the brigade. The Corner Green Grocery learned a great deal amidst the complicated and competitive produce market at Pike Place, and was beginning to show a profit in the last months of the year. The warehouse expanded its product line, and, in April, moved to a larger warehouse in Ballard. It bought a forklift, which increased its warehousing efficiency greatly. It made $3,000 to $6,000 monthly, which was applied toward reducing past debts. The bookkeeping team and budget committee gained new skills and guided the brigade into a stronger financial position.

In 1976, the political direction of the brigade also underwent some changes. Though the brigade had never really developed a unified political stand — in spite of all the rhetoric that marked its early history — there was a definite change in emphasis from socialism and joining mass movements to feminism, becoming a positive example of worker self-management, and just plain staying in business. Sexist attitudes were confronted more openly than in the past, and an effort was made in most teams to hire more women than men in order to maintain a balance in power. People were still very committed to the concept of worker self-management, but realized that, if wages remained so low, work habits remained so spaced-out and inefficient, and the group processes necessary to keep the business going remained so draining, no one would take the concept seriously. Economic expediency was accompanied by a certain amount of political righteousness as the brigade strove to become a more efficient and professional business.

In May, the milling operation, again a separate team, became an all-women workspace and changed its name to Rubyfruit Mills. Though there was some fear that the millers would become isolated and not want to interact with the brigade members who were men, and talk of how men and women should struggle together to conquer sexism, the idea of a women's space was generally accepted. Most brigade members were supportive of the needs of women to work with each other, gaining skills, strength, and confidence in a space where dealing with sexism was not an immediate necessity. In the summer, unfortunately, it was found that the mills needed extensive ventilation improvements, and, since the brigade simply did not have the financial resources to apply to them, they were sold to Fairhaven Mills, a collective in Bellingham. Since many brigade members still felt that having an all-women space was very important, it was voted to have C.C. Grains become woman-run in August. Though some people felt uncomfortable having such a large portion of brigade jobs closed to men, again the idea of having the warehouse run by women was generally supported.

In January 1977, C.C. Grains decided that it no longer wished to be a part of the Seattle Workers' Brigade. The warehouse members were tired of high worker turnover, frustrated by the amount of energy it took to keep the brigade running at just a minimally acceptable level, and worried about what they felt was an increasingly complacent attitude toward financial management. They felt that the other teams were not seriously confronting major problems facing the brigade. It seemed as if you could struggle and struggle to make the brigade a better, more productive place to work, but the results of most of your actions were lost in the complexity of day-to-day business. The warehousers felt a strong need to see the results of their efforts more concretely, and felt that this would be more likely to happen if they were concentrating on running one business with ten people than if they were trying to keep track of three businesses and forty people.

The idea of C.C. Grains leaving the brigade greatly concerned the other teams. There was an atmosphere of apprehension and anxiety; rumors were abundant. The main fear was that the bakery and the corner grocery would not be able to survive on their own — the warehouse generated most of the brigade's net return, and, at times, had been relied on to offset losses in other parts of the business. Many people were also upset about the political implications of splitting up the brigade. They felt that collectives are most effective politically if they work together, using principled *criticism self-criticism* to work out mutual problems. It was felt that isolation could lead easily to becoming just a few more hip capitalist businesses.

The first brigade meeting at which this issue was discussed was very tense. The bakery, grocery, and bookkeeping teams were frustrated by the inflexibility of the warehousers, who had decided that they definitely wanted out of the brigade and were not willing to compromise themselves by considering any structure short of total split. The warehousers were frustrated by what they felt was an inability of the other brigade members to see the obvious — that the brigade's structure was too complex and its workers too inexperienced to expect collective, efficient, and cooperative management.

After the first meeting, things got easier. Some informal discussions were held between teams and these helped to clear the air. The bakery, grocery, and bookkeeping teams felt better about the idea as they found that the warehouse's motives for leaving the brigade were, for the most part, principled. C.C. Grains workers relaxed and became less defensive as they realized that the other teams were not going to force them to remain in a situation they found frustrating and futile. As the idea became familiar, and as the arguments pro and con became more pragmatic, most members of the bakery and the grocery teams found the concept of autonomy to their liking. The brigade had been a fairly constant source of frustraton to all, and its deficiencies outweighed its positive aspects. The teams felt that, by doing their own bookkeeping and financial planning, a greater level of business integrity could be maintained, and costly mistakes like those of the bakery in the spring of 1976 could be avoided. People also realized that the businesses could continue to interact socially and politically whether they were a brigade or not. Little Bread Co. and Corner Green Grocery decided not to remain together in the event of a brigade split.

In March 1977, a vote was taken and it was agreed to dissolve the Seattle Workers' Brigade, pending development of a suitable settlement. A representative task force was appointed to work out the details of the dissolution.

Now that the brigade had decided to divide into three businesses, it remained to be decided how to divide up the assets and liabilities of the corporation. It was no problem to decide where the assets were to go. Each business kept the machinery, tools, and supplies that it used, and shared assets such as office supplies, desks, and such, were divided according to need. Deciding who would assume the debts was more difficult. Most people wanted to take into account that C.C. Grains had a higher earning potential than the other businesses. It was generally accepted that the warehouse would assume the bulk of the brigade debts, but some felt that this was not enough, that the warehouse should also pay a cash sum to the bakery and grocery. There was a lot of confusion as to how much net worth each business needed in order to remain reasonably financially solid, and it was this, rather than a desire to penalize one team or another, that made it so difficult to decide what a fair financial settlement would be. Eventually, it was decided that it would cripple the warehouse's cash flow to pay the other teams a cash sum, but that it would assume responsibility for all loans, all of its own accounts payable, and most 1976 taxes. In addition, C.C. Grains agreed to sell to the Little Bread Co. and the Corner Green Grocery at a discount. Every team was fairly satisfied with these arrangements, so the legal papers were signed, and the businesses ended their formal relationship.

CONCLUSIONS

The Seattle Workers' Brigade was an experimental collective community. It plainly failed to meet the expectation of its founding members (which is not surprising when one considers their expectations). When the problems and disappointments encountered by coops and collectives in the years of Cooperating Community are compared to those encountered by the collectives that made up the Seattle Workers' Brigade, one finds few differences. The workers are still predominantly young, white, middle-class, unskilled, and upsettingly transient. Mistrust and inadequate communication between groups and individuals is still common, though many people do seem to be learning more about how to deal constructively with negative feelings once they arise. And we never did develop any but the most flimsy political unities, let alone a mass movement. We can predict that these conditions will continue to exist in the future as well. The

Seattle Workers' Brigade has taught us that a change in legal structure is not enough to overcome decades of social conditioning.

Perhaps we have not, and are not, trying hard enough. But then we must consider the form of political expression we have chosen to use. Small businesses are by their very nature absorbing and exhausting. Worker self-managed businesses are especially so — the way the work is organized is unfamiliar and, for the most part, untried. Collective members are left with little spare time and creativity to devote to outside social and political activities.

Still, much of value cames from working in a collective such as the Seattle Workers' Brigade. The hard work and responsibility wears people out, but those who do stay learn some valuable, if sobering, lessons as they struggle to apply the spirit of collectivism to real work conditions. We are constantly reminded of the contradiction of running a collective in a capitalist society — constantly asking ourselves whether we are compromising our politics too much for the economic good of the business or vice versa. This juggling act we do between visionary politics and the realities of economic survival in this society makes us more aware of how the capitalist system works, how it affects our lives. This awareness is not earth-shattering, but it is an important step in developing our personal and collective ideologies.

Different people have derived different morals from their experiences in the brigade, but, in general, the idealism of the earlier collective took on a more pragmatic hue as the years passed. Most of us no longer expect our work in the collectives to directly shake the foundations of capitalism — we are too much a part of the *real* system no matter how much we call ourselves *alternative*. But we do expect our collective experiences to shake our personal foundation of greed, competition, and insecurity; we expect to learn cooperation. Working in a collective gives us the chance to experiment with noncoercive working relationships. We can learn to recognize and confront oppressive forms of power and authority in our workspace, such as sexism, class chauvinism (based on economic or educational advantages), and power maintained through unwillingness to share skills or information. We develop the ability to organize our work democratically. We learn to initiate ideas and actions, to accept responsibility, to give and receive constructive criticism, and to compromise.

There is a last, but very significant, reason why working in a collective can be a beneficial experience. We are proud of the products we make and/or sell, proud that they are healthy and of good quality, and proud that we do our best to avoid buying our food from greedy capitalists. We are able to support small farmers and encourage them to grow organically by providing them with a market. We are doing work which we feel is truly valuable, and we are learning a lot about our society and ourselves as we do it. This, if nothing else, is worth a great deal.

Part 5

WORKPLACE DEMOCRACY AND SOCIAL CHANGE

Introduction to Part 5

This concluding section of the anthology focuses on the relevance of organizational democracy for broad-scale societal change. Democratic workplaces, whether large or small, help create jobs and build community economic strength at the same time that they provide models of how a new society could be organized. Insofar as they are successful, they demonstrate that democracy in the workplace can be effective, efficient, and satisfying for its personnel. At the same time, they help to spread the idea of cooperation in the workplace, and participatory-democratic ideas may eventually find their application in other business, government, or community organizations.

A long-range goal of the movement for workplace democracy is nothing less than the establishment and spread of a democratic economic sector in various regions of this country. This ambitious goal could be aided by regional federations providing democratic workplaces with mutual aid, by the establishment of supporting institutions for education, technical services, and financial assistance, and by the growth of a parallel political movement. As the history of social change in America reveals, alternative institutions have played a crucial role in transforming our society, beginning with the pivotal contribution they made to the American Revolution. Without a broader political movement with which to align themselves, however, they have been insufficient as agents of social change.[1]

The potential impact of the worker-owned and worker-managed enterprises discussed in this volume will be diminished if there does not also develop a nonsectarian political movement dedicated to breaking up economic concentration and vesting a greater degree of control over productive facilities and service organizations in communities, municipalities, workers, and consumers.

As Gorz reminds us, even if the current struggle for workers' control does not win more than a few immediate demands, it is part of a broader process of education and "conscientization" that may lead to a more participatory, democratic economy.

The demand for democratic control over organizations, whether they are corporations, nonprofit organizations, or government agencies, is becoming the focus of considerable political debate in this country. One poll shows clearly that the American public is already ahead of its so-called leaders on the issue of economic democracy. When presented with the option of working for a government-owned company, an employee-owned and -controlled company, or a stock-holder corporation, two out of three respondents in a 1977 Hart poll said they would prefer to work where employees own and control the firm. Tom Hayden, running for the Senate on a platform of economic democracy, attracted a significant minority of California voters in 1976. By 1980, a new national coop bank had been established, with 10 percent of its funds earmarked for producers' cooperatives. And in 1979 and 1980, several bills promoting employee ownership were introduced in Congress, with numerous cosponsors. Economic democracy seems destined to become a major issue on the political agenda for the 1980s.

Where multinational corporations have closed factories and thrown employees out of jobs, workplace democracy provides a real alternative. Reopening such shut-down plants under some form of worker and community ownership has proven very appealing to the involved parties, especially where the closed plant is one that vitally affects the economic health of a whole town or region. This was the case with the Campbell steel works in Youngstown, Ohio. Alperovitz and Faux discuss the feasibility of reopening the Youngstown plant with worker and community ownership; their plan received wide-spread community and religious support in the Mahoning Valley of Ohio.

The Youngstown proposal to reopen the Campbell works, though ambitious and innovative, was never implemented because it did not receive the necessary federal financing. Had it been implemented, a project of this magnitude (the factory had employed 5,000 workers) could have publicized widely the use of worker and community ownership as one solution to the problem of plant closings. In our judgment, however, the Youngstown proposal contained some serious shortcomings: First, it was never made clear how a plant of this scale could be democratically managed. Further thought needed to be given to the design of jobs and of a new management structure. Second, because steel is an ailing industry, beset by foreign competition, aging machinery, and the need for the infusion of tremendous capital investments, the Youngstown proposal was requesting federal assistance of over $500 million. This investment averages out to well over $100,000 per job saved, which, by almost any standard, appears excessive. Had the plant been reopened and failed once again, it may well have been taken as a showcase of the failure of worker and community ownership, rather than a result of preexisting conditions that have affected the entire industry. (This is more than a theoretical possibility, as the demise of several large recently established workers' cooperatives in England shows [chap. 9]).

Lindenfeld discusses the relevance of workers' ownership and control to the problem of unemployment caused by plant closings. Where parent companies wish to divest themselves of a plant, it may be possible to combine worker-community ownership with democratic management. Workers' cooperatives can succeed, Lindenfeld argues, where corporations fail because the cooperatives do away with need for excessive managerial personnel.

Taking a different tack, Kanter, Stein, and Brinkerhoff discuss an alternative route to developing democratic workplaces: building participatory-democracy *within* conventional bureaucratic organizations. They have met with considerable success in their efforts to develop a "parallel organization," one which allows for greater individual opportunity, participation and power, within an otherwise bureaucratic structure. This model for introducing change may be applicable in many corporate bureaucracies.

The Ellerman paper tries to develop a legal framework for workers' cooperatives that can incorporate stock ownership at the same time that it guarantees control to those doing the work. In order to protect the right of workers to have a say in management and to receive the fruits of their labor, Ellerman argues, it is necessary for cooperatives to avoid the traditional legal model of stock ownership.[2]

Of course, setting up a cooperative, even with the best legal form, is no guarantee that it will continue to operate in a democratic manner. Paula Giese's piece tracing the history of food cooperatives shows how some of the larger, more successful coops became co-opted, institutionalized, and diverted from their original social change purposes. This reminds us that democratic organizations must continue to be sensitive to the perennial problems of institutionalization and oligarchization and must pay attention to the factors that would help them resist these processes.

Where, in the struggle for workers' control, are the labor unions? The Benello article argues that the American labor movement has not been particularly favorable towards workers' ownership or control. With some notable exceptions, American union leaders have rarely challenged the so-called prerogatives of management and much of their leadership has had an almost instinctive distrust of workers' control, because greater rank-and-file democracy could diminish their own power. Nevertheless, the need to cope with plant closings and corporate divestitures is leading many unions to support worker ownership and workplace democracy if only as a means of saving jobs and retaining their membership.

Promoting collectivist and cooperative enterprises, encouraging the reopening of closed plants as worker-community owned and controlled companies, and working to develop participatory-democratic forms within bureaucratic organizations are promising avenues for social change in America. Admittedly, there are many obstacles in the way, including the widespread public acceptance of the idea of hierarchy as the only legitimate form of work organization, the lack of capital available to democratic workplaces, and the opposition of those who hold power in our society today. Nevertheless, the faint outlines of a movement for economic democracy are on the horizon. Fueled by urgent economic difficulties (of which the United States decline in productivity vis-à-vis other advanced industrial nations plays no small part) and by the public's declining confidence in almost every major institution in our society, a very broad spectrum of the American public is beginning to ask for greater participation rights in the institutions that affect their lives. In communities all around this country, people have for years been protesting policies taken by local institutions (the schools, medical delivery systems, etc.) that are adverse to community interests. As a result, we have begun to see the development of greater community control over community institutions. Now this insistence on self-governance is spreading to the economic sphere. It has become painfully clear that business decisions vitally affect community life. At the extreme, a plant shutdown can decimate a community, leaving several jobs lost in the town for every job lost in the plant; a bank's decision to redline a certain section of a community can lead to its rapid decay; a firm's decision to release toxins into the local environment can produce significant medical problems in the area, and so forth. It will be no surprise if those most directly affected by a company's decisions — community members, consumers, and most especially, its workers — come to demand a greater share of control over its policies. This book has tried to provide some examples and some conceptualization of what democratic control over economic enterprises might look like and how it might be encouraged.

NOTES

1. On the historical relationship between alternative institutions and social change, see Roberta Ash, *Social Movements in America* (Chicago: Markham Publ., 1972); and the concluding chapter of Joyce Rothschild-Whitt, *Alternatives to Bureaucracy: Conditions and Dilemmas of Organizational Democracy*, forthcoming.

2. An important example of self-managed enterprises that have succeeded in separating ownership from control in the way Ellerman suggests are the Breman enterprises in Holland. Here the enterprises are not "owned" by anyone. The capital to run them is "rented out" to the workers, for which the capital investors receive a fixed return (like interest), but the workers, through their elected workers' councils, retain rights to control the firms by virtue of their input of labor. For an examination of the Breman system, see J. Rothschild-Whitt, "There's more than one way to run a democratic enterprise: self-management from the Netherlands," (Beverly Hills: Sage Publications, 1981, vol. 8, no. 2), in *Sociology of Work & Occupations*.

15

On the Legal Structure of Workers' Cooperatives
David Ellerman

PROPERTY RIGHTS AND PERSONAL RIGHTS

A corporation is an artificial legal person that has certain natural (or artificial) persons as its legal *members*. These legal members are commonly called the *owners* of the corporation. These persons hold the *membership rights* which consist of (a) the voting rights to approve and amend the bylaws and to elect the Board of Directors, which appoints the management, and (b) the rights to the pure or *economic* profits of the company. These membership rights are attached to the shares of stock of the corporation. The shares of stock also carry the net book value or net worth of the company's assets. In a conventional corporation, the shares of stock are pieces of property that may be bought and sold. Hence the legal rights attached to the shares — namely, the membership rights and the net book-value rights — are both *property rights.* The distinguishing and defining characteristic of a conventional corporation, usually called a *capitalist corporation,* is that the membership rights are legally treated as property rights, which are interpersonally transferable.

Property rights are juxtaposed to *personal rights,* which are assigned directly to natural persons, usually because the people play certain functional roles. Hence, the personal rights may not be bought, sold, or otherwise transferred between persons. For example, suppose a person votes as a member of a union, votes as a citizen,

David Ellerman is Assistant Professor of Economics, University of Massachusetts at Boston, and is the staff economist of the Industrial Cooperative Association. His research focuses on the theory and practice of worker-managed firms.

votes as a board member in a nonprofit corporation, and votes as a shareholder in a conventional corporation. Which of the voting rights are personal rights and which are property rights? One way to answer the question would be to consider which of the rights could be sold to other people. The same answer would be obtained by supposing that the person died (thereby extinguishing his or her personal rights) and then considering which rights survive to be exercised by the person's estate or heirs. In either case, the answer is that shareholders' rights are property rights whereas the other voting rights are personal rights.

WORKERS' COOPERATIVE CORPORATIONS

The shares in a conventional corporation could be owned by absentee investors, employees, consumers, suppliers, or the government at the local, state, or national level. These different patterns of private or public ownership do not change the basic structural characteristic of the conventional capitalist corporation — namely, that the membership rights are property rights to be owned by various legal parties. An entirely different type of corporation would be obtained if the membership rights were not legally treated as property rights at all, but rather as personal rights assigned to those people having a certain functional role.

The concept of a self-managed firm, worker-managed firm, industrial cooperative, or workers' cooperative is arrived at by defining the functional role as that of working in the firm. In a conventional corporation, there already is one legal right assigned to the functional role of working in the firm, namely the right to receive wages (including salaries). If the wages are lumped together with the pure economic profits, then the result is the revenues net of the nonlabor costs. The result is obtained by starting with the equation defining the economic profits: Economic Profits = Revenues – Nonlabor Costs – Wages, and then moving the labor costs or wages to the other side of the equation. Hence, in a workers' cooperative corporation, the people who work in the firm would hold, by virtue of having that functional role, the usual membership rights (voting and pure profit rights) plus the wage rights. This can be restated as a definition: *A self-managed, worker-managed, industrial cooperative or workers' cooperative corporation* is a corporation where the voting rights to approve and amend the bylaws and to elect the board which appoints management, and the rights to the revenues net of nonlabor costs are both personal rights assigned to the functional role of working in the company.

This definition specifies a workers' cooperative as a generic concept, or ideal type. The legal statutes in the various states for so-called workers' cooperative corporations may or may not realize this generic structure. In fact, they do not (see below). The generic definition can be used to criticize the "cooperative" statutes and to serve as a guide to the internal restructuring of a corporation so that it will function as a genuine workers' cooperative. It is also possible to consider corporate structures where the membership rights are also treated as personal rights but are assigned to some other functional role such as that of being a consumer of the firm's output, a supplier of some raw material or agricultural product, or even a local resident. That would yield generic definitions of the concept of a consumers' cooperative, a marketing cooperative, and a community-managed corporation respectively. However, normative principles will now be presented which entail the assignment of the membership rights to the functional role of working in the company.

NORMATIVE BASIS FOR WORKERS' COOPERATIVES

The first normative principle is the *democratic theory of government* applied to the workplace. The democratic principle states that all and only the people who are to be governed by a government should have the vote in electing that government. The application of the principle of democracy or self-government to the workplace means that the voting rights to elect the workplace management should be assigned to the functional role of being managed by that management. Who has that functional role? Who are the people who are managed by (i.e., who take orders from) the management of the corporation? The absentee investors, the consumers, the suppliers of materials, and the local residents are not managed by and do not take orders from the management of a corporation. Only the people who work in the company have that functional role. Hence, the application of the democratic principle of self-government to the corporation entails that the voting rights should be assigned to the functional role of working in the corporation.

The second normative principle is the *labor theory of property* applied to the production process. The labor principle states that people should have the rights to the (positive and negative) fruits of their labor. The products or outputs of a firm are the positive fruits of the labor jointly performed by all the people (blue- and white-collar) who work in the firm. The used-up nonlabor inputs, such as the consumed raw materials and intermediate goods and the expended services of the machines, buildings, and land, represent the negative fruits of the labor of the firm's workers. The market value of the produced outputs is the revenues and the market value of the used-up nonlabor inputs is the nonlabor costs. Hence, the net value of the positive and negative fruits of the labor jointly performed by the workers of the firm is: revenues – nonlabor costs = wages + economic profits. From the legal viewpoint, it is the corporation itself as a legal person that owns the produced outputs and that is liable for the used-up nonlabor inputs. Since the labor theory of property states that the workers should jointly appropriate the positive fruits (the produced outputs) and be jointly liable for the negative fruits (the used-up nonlabor inputs) of their combined labor, the labor theory implies that the workers should "be" the corporation from the legal viewpoint, i.e., that the workers should be the legal members of the corporation. In terms of value, the labor theory of property implies that the workers should have the rights to the net value of their positive and negative fruits, namely the residual: revenues – nonlabor costs = wages + economic profits.

Hence, the democratic principle of self-government and the labor theory of property imply that, in a corporation, the voting rights and the rights to the revenues net of nonlabor costs should be assigned to the functional role of working in the firm — which is precisely the definition of a workers' cooperative corporation. Since the wage rights are already assigned to that functional role in a conventional corporation, a corporation can be transformed into a workers' cooperative corporation by changing the membership rights (the voting rights and economic profit rights) from marketable property rights into personal rights attached to the worker's functional role.

WORKERS' CONTROL AND COMMUNITY CONTROL

The democratic and labor principles entail workers' cooperative corporations as opposed to both the traditional capitalist corporations and the community-owned or government-owned enterprises of the traditional socialist view. While workers' management is inconsistent with community or government ownership, it is not inconsistent with an appropriate type of *community control*. Much of the debate about community control vs. workers' control is based on a failure to distinguish between different types of control. The community control argument is usually based on a loose formulation of the *affected interests principle* — e.g., anyone whose legitimate interests would be affected by the decisions or actions of another party should have a right of control over that party. But there are two quite different kinds of control. There is *indirect control,* wherein one party may exert a negative influence on another party by vetoing or otherwise constraining certain decisions or actions of the second party. And there is *direct control,* wherein one party makes the decision of the other party. For example, if person A's legitimate interests (e.g., personal or property rights) would be affected by certain proposed actions of person B, then A could exert indirect control over B by not consenting to the proposed effects on A's person or property. This indirect control is quite different from the direct control of making B's decision, since it leaves B free to choose another option that affects A agreeably or that doesn't affect A at all.

The affected interests principle can only be valid when *control* is interpreted as indirect control: a party whose legitimate interests would be affected by the activities of another party should have the right of indirect control over the second party by vetoing or otherwise constraining the activities to protect those interests. For example, it is often argued quite plausibly that, after an industrial plant has been located in a community for many years, then it becomes interwoven into the fabric of the community in such a myriad of ways that the community should have the indirect control right to veto or otherwise constrain the shutdown of the plant so long as it is economically viable. That sort of indirect community control is quite consistent with the direct workers' control embodied in a workers' cooperative corporation. Even if all the workers would decide to pack up and move the business elsewhere, the local community should be empowered to veto or otherwise constrain that decision. However, many traditional socialists tend to transform the case for indirect community control of businesses into an invalid argument for the direct community or governmental ownership of companies by the implicit semantic shift from one sense of control to the other.

THE OWNERSHIP OF A CORPORATION

The analysis of corporate structure given above is useful in understanding the somewhat peculiar notion of *ownership* of a capitalist corporation. It is not the concept of the corporation owning assets, buildings, or land that is peculiar — only the notion of owning the corporation itself. Conventional corporations, labor unions, non-profit organizations, and even townships and municipalities are all organizations legally controlled by their voting members. The concept of *membership* applies to all of these organizational entities. Certainly a labor union, a nonprofit corporation, or a community may own property, but the members of a union or a nonprofit corporation do not own the organization itself, and the citizens of a community do not own the township or municipality. In other words, these legal entities may own property, but they are not themselves property. In contrast, a conventional corporation not only owns property but is a piece of property itself. Its members are its owners, and it can be bought and sold. Why the difference?

The reason why the one legal entity is property while the others are not is the basic fact that the membership rights in a conventional corporation are property rights, whereas the membership rights in the other organizations are personal rights attached to the persons of the members. It is only when the membership rights are property rights that the members become owners and the legal entity itself becomes a piece of property. Another basic difference between a conventional corporation and the other organizations considered above is that only the corporation violates the one person, one vote rule. Again, this is due to the basic difference in the treatment of the membership rights. When the membership rights are property rights, then one person can buy many of them and thus vote many times as a *multiple member*. When the membership rights are personal rights attached to a certain functional role, then a given person either has the functional role or doesn't, and thus either has the vote or doesn't. The possibility of multiple voting does not arise.

In a workers' cooperative corporation, the membership rights are personal rights attached to the functional role of working in the firm. Since the membership rights are not property rights, the worker-members are not owners. While a cooperative owns property, it is not itself property that may be bought or sold. Here again, a workers' cooperative corporation should be sharply differentiated from a privately owned capitalist firm and a publicly owned socialist firm. The traditional capitalism vs. socialism debate revolves around the question of whether business enterprises should be privately or publicly owned. "Labor" governments in Great Britain have bought (i.e., nationalized with compensation) private firms which subsequent Tory governments have sold back to private interests. Workers' cooperatives embody a third way, wherein the firm is not a piece of property at all to be privately owned, publicly owned, or even "socially owned" (whatever that means). It isn't owned at all. A workers' cooperative is a democratic work-community which assigns the membership rights to the people who work in it just as a democratic living-community assigns the citizenship rights to the people who live or reside in it. A workers' cooperative could no more be sold to a group of investors than Cleveland could be sold to a group of oil sheiks.

EMPLOYEE-OWNED CORPORATIONS

This analysis of corporate structure can also be used to differentiate a workers' cooperative corporation from a capitalist corporation where the employees are the owners, i.e., an *employee-owned corporation*. This distinction is especially challenging if it is assumed that each employee of the conventional corporation owns exactly one share (so the one person, one vote rule is followed), and that there are no absentee owners. Such an equalitarian, employee-owned corporation would superficially seem to be indistinguishable from a workers' cooperative corporation. The example is designed so that the workers would have the same legal rights in each case. The difference is that the workers have those rights for entirely different structural reasons in the two cases. In the workers' cooperative, the membership rights are assigned to the workers as personal rights because they work in the firm. In the employee-owned corporation, the workers happen to also own certain property rights which are the membership rights in the corporation where they work. In the absence of any special constraints in the employee-owned corporation, the wealthier employees or even absentee investors could buy numerous shares. Employees could sell their membership rights while remaining workers, and new employees would have to buy in to become members. In an employee-owned corporation, the membership rights are not structurally attached to the functional role of working in the firm so that, in the course of normal events, there will soon be nonowner employees and nonemployee owners. Hence, such a corporation will typically not remain employee-owned for very long.

THE EMPLOYER-EMPLOYEE RELATION

In contrast to the employee-owners of an employee-owned corporation, the worker-members of a workers' cooperative corporation are not owners since their membership rights are not held as property rights. Similarly, the worker-members of a workers' cooperative corporation are not employees. The employer-employee relation is the legal relationship wherein the employer buys from the employee certain labor services as a market commodity in return for their price, the wage or salary. The hiring or renting of an entity, such as a car, truck, apartment, or parcel of land, for certain purposes and a given time period can be equivalently described as the purchase of certain services of the entity such as car-days, apartment-months, or acre-years. Thus, the purchase of certain man-hours of services of a person could be equivalently described as the hiring or renting of the person for the given purposes and time period. In the employer-employee relationship, the employees do not legally own the positive fruits of the labor (the produced outputs) and the employees are not legally liable for the negative fruits of their labor (the used-up nonlabor inputs). Instead, the employer legally owns the produced outputs and is legally liable for the used-up nonlabor inputs. In addition, the employer is legally liable for "using-up" or "employing" the "inputs" of the "commodity" labor services, and the wages or salaries are paid to satisfy that legal liability.

In a workers' cooperative corporation, the worker-members *are* the corporation; it is their legal embodiment. The workers, in their corporate embodiment, own the positive fruits of their labor (the produced outputs) and are liable for the negative fruits of their labor (the used-up nonlabor inputs). Instead of selling their labor for a wage, the worker-members are selling their outputs in return for the sales revenues and paying the costs of the nonlabor inputs. The income of the worker-members is not the market value of their labor as a commodity but the net market value of the positive and negative fruits of their labor, i.e., the revenues – the nonlabor costs. Since the labor of the worker-members is not sold as a commodity (i.e., the workers are not hired or rented), the employer-employee relation does not apply to a workers' cooperative corporation. The worker-members are not working for anyone else; they are working together on a cooperative basis.

The inapplicability of the legal categories of *employees* and *owners* to the worker-members implies the inapplicability of the economic and accounting categories of *wages* (= income of employees) and *profits* (= income of owners or employers) to the labor income (= revenues – nonlabor costs) in a workers' cooperative corporation. Part of the annual labor income would be advanced to the worker-members on a weekly or monthly basis, but it would not be wages in the sense of the price of labor services. The remainder of the annual labor income would be left at the end of the fiscal year, but it would not be profits in the sense of the residual left from revenues after buying the labor and nonlabor inputs. The words *wages* and *profits* might, out of sheer linguistic inertia, still be applied to the advanced and unadvanced portions of the labor income, but these words would not have their traditional connotations.

RESTRUCTURING A CONVENTIONAL CORPORATION

In America today, there are no statutes, cooperative or otherwise, which are designed to implement the conceptual definition given above of a workers' cooperative corporation. The only means of realizing such a cooperative is to start with the outer shell of a conventional business corporation or a statutory cooperative corporation, and then rework the articles of incorporation and bylaws to restructure the company so that it will function as a genuine workers' cooperative corporation. The focus here will be on restructuring a conventional business corporation, since virtually the same internal surgery is required in the case of a statutory cooperative corporation.

Taxes will be ignored in this discussion of corporate financial structure and accounting, since they only complicate the matter without changing the conceptual relationships. In a conventional corporation, the legal rights attached to the shares are: (1) the membership rights, which consist of the voting rights and the economic profit rights, and (2) the right to the net book value of the corporate assets. Economic profits should not be confused with the accounting profits or corporate net income. The interest on net book value is not counted as an expense by accountants, but it is counted as a cost by economists. Hence, corporate net income = accounting profits = economic profits + interest on net book value. The shares are held as property, and there is no cut-off date on the economic profit rights, so the rights to all the future economic profits are attached to the shares. Hence, the economic value of the shares = the present value of the future economic profits + the net book value of the corporate assets.[1] The value of the shares can be presented very simply as the net book value or net worth, which is the sum of the past capital subscriptions for new shares and the accumulated past retained earnings, plus the present value of the future economic profits, which is the discounted sum of all the future increments in value accruing to the shareholders.

The bundle of rights attached to the shares in a conventional corporation must be split apart in a workers' cooperative corporation. The membership rights must be partitioned off from the net book-value rights, since a new worker will earn the right of membership simply by working in the company. But, if the shares are conventionally valued, then giving each newly accepted member a share carrying the right of membership would be to make an unwarranted gift of a proportionate part of the net book value to each new member. If, on the other hand, each new member is required to buy the share at book value, that is an unnecessary and probably prohibitive restriction, since the worker should by right receive membership by working in the firm. The only solution is to split off the net book value from the shares by creating another corporate mechanism to carry that value — namely, *internal capital accounts.*

The present value of the present and future economic profits remains attached to the shares after the net book value has been partitioned off by the creation of the internal capital accounts. The economic profits plus the wages in each time period equals the net value of the positive and negative fruits of the labor of the firm's workers during that time period. Since the future workers will earn that value, including the future economic profits, those profits cannot remain attached to the shares held by the current workers. The future workers should not have to buy the right to the fruits of their labor from the present workers. The bundle of rights to the present and future economic profits must be split up so that the right to the economic profits of each time period can be assigned only to the workers of that time period. Similarly, the bundle of present and future voting rights must be split up so that the voting rights in each time period can also be assigned only to the workers of that time period.

This temporal segmentation of the bundle of profit and voting rights is accomplished by treating the shares of stock as *membership certificates* assigned to the functional role of working in the company. Each new worker is issued one membership share, i.e., a share of common stock functioning as a membership certificate, after being accepted as a member. For practical purposes, there should be a fixed trial or probationary period, after which the new worker must be either accepted as a member or let go. Also, for practical as well as legalistic reasons, there should be a membership investment required of each new member that could be fixed in amount (e.g., $500) or fixed relative to pay (e.g., two weeks' pay). Part of the standard members' investment could be considered as the "legal price" or consideration "paid" for the share. When a worker terminates work in the cooperative company, the member's internal account is closed, and the membership share is automatically forfeited back to the company in return for its legal price (unless all of the member's investment has been eaten away by losses). In this manner, a corporation can be appropriately restructured so that the current membership rights (current voting and economic profit rights) are assigned as personal rights to those people currently having the functional role of working in the firm (i.e., current workers).

Each member has an interest-bearing, internal capital account which keeps track of the portion of the net book value which is imputed to that person. The initial balance in each member's account is the membership investment. At the end of each fiscal year, the retained net income, which could be positive or negative, is split among the members' accounts in whatever is considered an equitable fashion, e.g., equally per dollar paid, or equally per hour worked. The membership investment plays the role of a "security deposit" against which retained losses may be debited. Theoretically, there are several methods that could be used to pay off the member's accounts. At any time, part of the balance in a member's account could be evidenced by negotiable notes so long as a sufficient security deposit or "cushion" remained in the account. If not before, the payoff would begin whenever a person terminates membership by leaving the firm.

From the company's viewpoint, the best payout would be in the form of interest-bearing perpetual debentures or notes, which pay interest but no principal, and which could be sold by the worker in the debt capital market. But, in present circumstances, these notes would sell at such a prohibitive discount that another payoff mode must be found. A more practical procedure, which does not presuppose a suitable external market, is to have the company itself pay off both the principal and interest of the notes over a period of years. In any case, these notes representing the worker's portion of the net book value would be property rights that could be sold or passed on to the worker's heirs. As positive net earnings are retained, all current internal accounts are increased, and then some of the earnings could be used to pay off the older or retired members. The internal account system would then function as a revolving "loan" fund between generations of members as the older members would slowly pass the internal debt on to the younger members.

There are a few complications which are encountered in practice and which will not be discussed in detail here. For example, in an uncertain world, the likelihood of eventually paying out each member's account is increased by maintaining part of the net book value in an unindividuated collective account that never needs to be paid out. The collective account would function as a permanent capital base that isn't "turned over" as the membership turns over. Corporate tax breaks also complicate the structure. Some corporate income tax can be avoided by construing part of the retained net earnings as wage bonuses that are paid out and then loaned back to the company. Since the money is loaned back to the company as debt capital, it cannot be recorded in the usual equity internal accounts. Hence, there is a new debt account for each member which records the retained earnings that are interpreted as loaned back wage bonuses.[2]

The internal restructuring described above consisted of two main parts: (1) the creation of the *internal accounts* to split the net book value away from the shares, and (2) the use of the shares as *membership certificates* assigned to the workers' functional role. With this internal structure, the workers will *function* as the worker-members of a workers' cooperative corporation. But this internal restructuring does not change the external law, which presently does not have any such statutory legal form as a "workers' cooperative corporation" as defined above. Hence, from the external legalistic viewpoint, the worker-member is an "employee" of a corporation with a prearranged stock purchase system. Then the external law also views the worker-member as an "owner" of a share in the corporation with a certain mandatory repurchase arrangement for the share keyed to the worker's employment in the firm.

AN EVALUATION OF ALTERNATIVE STRUCTURE

The model of a workers' cooperative corporation and the theory behind it can now be used to critically evaluate several alternative structures. The legal statutes for cooperative corporations differ somewhat from state to state. The model of a statutory cooperative corporation considered here is a composite of characteristics common to most statutes. In a statutory cooperative, the distinctive characteristic is that each shareholder gets only one vote regardless of the number of shares held. Moreover, some "dividends" may be distributed in proportion to "patronage" instead of shares owned.

Sometimes the bylaws require that each shareholder own the same number of shares — a standard *ownership block*. There usually are requirements that each shareholder should have a certain functional role depending on the type of cooperative (e.g., marketing, consumers', housing, or workers' cooperative). There are no internal capital accounts, so the only way for a shareholder-member to recoup the value of retained earnings is by ultimately selling the shares at a higher price.

The fundamental flaw in this statutory cooperative structure is the failure to separate the net book-value rights from shares, which carry the membership rights, by creating the system of internal capital accounts. Like the shares in a conventional corporation, the shares in a statutory cooperative carry *both* the net book value or net worth (membership fees plus retained earnings) and the membership rights — with the differences of one vote per member and dividends distributed according to patronage. Hence, a new worker must pay in a proportionate part of the net worth (which could be $20,000 or more in the plywood-workers' cooperatives) in order to get membership rights. Since few workers can be found to buy such prohibitively expensive shares, new workers will tend to be hired as nonmembers. The lack of any serious market for such shares among new workers creates considerable pressure for the retiring workers to sell to outsiders interested in the investment. The bundling together of the membership rights and the net worth creates tendencies towards nonmember workers and nonworker members. Hence, the unpartitioned structure of the statutory workers' cooperative corporations causes them to exhibit suicidal tendencies like those of the employee-owned corporations. If these statutory cooperatives succeed economically, then they will tend — by their structure — to fail as workers' cooperatives. The workers will tend to be progressively differentiated from the members, and, eventually, the retiring members will probably sell out to a conventional corporation in order to recoup their share of the net worth.

Professor Jaroslav Vanek was the first modern cooperative theorist to realize that so many of the traditional workers' cooperatives had failed not simply because of the hostile environment, but because of an inherent structural flaw in the cooperatives themselves. Professor Vanek's initial analysis[3] of the structural flaw was incomplete and needs to be somewhat recast. According to Professor Vanek, the culprit is self-financing or internal financing (i.e., financing through the retention of net earnings) as opposed to external financing. The solution, according to this theory, is to have 100 percent external financing. Since traditional financing sources are unlikely to provide such debt capital, Professor Vanek argues for the creation of special financial institutions devoted to workers' cooperatives.

While special financial supporting institutions for workers' cooperatives would, of course, be desirable, the point is that such banks and 100 percent external financing are *not necessary* for workers' cooperatives to be properly structured. In order for a workers' cooperative to be properly structured, the net book value must be partitioned off from the membership rights. Self-financing through retained earnings increases net book value whereas external financing does not. In the theoretical limiting case of 100 percent external financing, the net book value would be zero, so the point of separating it from the membership rights would be moot. But, in general, the net book value or net worth must be partitioned off from the membership rights, not driven to zero. This can be accomplished by the creation of the system of internal capital accounts. Moreover, Professor Vanek explicitly recognizes the appropriateness of internal financing in the form of "redeemable savings deposits of members."[4] This recognition implies that the analysis must be recast in terms of criteria other than internal vs. external financing. It is useless to redefine *external* financing to include some forms of internal financing (e.g., via internal accounts), since the new criteria will still be needed to distinguish the external from the nonexternal forms of internal financing.

The real point is to separate the net book value from the membership rights so that the amount of capital internally supplied by each member (e.g., the balance in his or her internal account) is independent of his or her membership rights. The amount of capital externally supplied by sources of external financing is, of course, separate from and independent of membership rights. The idea is to have that same separation between membership rights and internal financing — as if it were external financing — not to eliminate the internal financing. The internal funding, represented by the internal capital accounts, will still differ from external financing in that the internal accounts must be readjusted every fiscal year to reflect the positive or negative retained earnings.

In a properly structured workers' cooperative corporation, the membership rights are not only separated off from the property rights to net book value, they are also transformed into personal rights attached to the workers' functional role. Since the membership rights remain coupled to the property rights to the net book value in a statutory workers' cooperative, the membership rights remain essentially as property rights. Membership in a statutory workers' "cooperative" is still considered as a question of ownership, i.e., as a property right. In the Yugoslavian worker-managed firm, the membership rights (in a slightly attenuated form) are indeed treated as personal rights, but only at the cost of altogether eliminating the property rights to the net book value (which are considered as "social property"). Any net value of the fruits of the workers' labor that is retained in the firm is automatically forfeited by the workers. The best known example of a system of workers' cooperatives, which both treats the membership rights essentially as personal rights and maintains the members' property rights to most of the net book value through a system of internal accounts, is the Mondragón system of industrial cooperatives (Johnson and Whyte, chap. 8). Many new workers' cooperatives in America, such as those assisted by the Industrial Cooperative Association, have internally restructured the legal shell of a conventional corporation or a statutory cooperative corporation (e.g., by creating the internal accounts) so as to create the model structure for a workers' cooperative corporation.

NOTES

1. Equivalent formulas for the total value of the corporate shares may be found in Merton H. Miller and Franco Modigliani, "Dividend Policy, Growth, and The Valuation of Shares," *The Journal of Business of the University of Chicago,* 34 (October 1961): 411-33.
2. These complications and other details are treated in the model bylaws and other explanatory literature of the Industrial Cooperative Association, 2161 Massachusetts Avenue, Cambridge, MA 02140.
3. Vanek, Jaroslav, *The Labor-Managed Economy* (Ithaca: Cornell Univ. Press, 1977), pt. 4.
4. *Ibid.,* p. 186.

16

How the Old Coops Went Wrong
Paula Giese

ORIGINS IN STRUGGLE

You pull down our wages, shamefully to tell;
You go into the market, say you can't sell;
When that we do ask when these bad times will mend,
You quickly give answer, "When the wars are at end."
Ye tyrants and tradesmen, your race is soon run;
We'll bring you to account for the wrongs you have done.
            —*Lancashire weavers' union organizing song, 1838*

People's cooperatives have their origins in working-class struggles in the nineteenth century. The first coops represented a peaceful attempt to build an alternative, people-controlled system of goods distribution, an attempt which often looked beyond that to an entirely people-controlled political economy. Most of the present coops see themselves that way, too, not only providing a little help in individual struggles for survival, but actively working for an end to exploitation, profiteering — and the hostilities and wars a system based on this generates.

It is important, in these struggles, not to forget the realities of power. There is a local reminder of this that all coop people should remember. Matt Eubanks, a North Minneapolis black activist, helped to organize a coop for local black people; it was quite a success, as it really met some community needs. It was such a success

Paula Giese was Assistant Professor of Humanities, University of Minnesota, at the time she wrote this article; in 1972 she was fired by the University for her political activism. After several years of paralegal work for political prisoners, she became a licensed private investigator. She now works for legal defense, rights, and environmental issues cases, doing investigation, research and legal briefs.

Reprinted with permission from *North Country Anvil,* nos. 11, 12, 13.

that it was firebombed and destroyed in December 1970. Matt was hounded and harrassed by the police and never got it going again.

Although that bombing occurred in the midst of several political and weirdo bombings (like the bombing of a used-car lot), which the Right and Liberal press screamed meant "the breakdown of civilization," there was no press attention or public outcry about this destruction of an institution in the black community, little support from "radical" whites, and no offers of assistance in rebuilding from white people's coops. "Struggle for change" cannot be conducted wholly by running cut-rate services, even if they are people-controlled. There is also the question of mutual defense.

Some historical understanding seems necessary for building such defenses, because the first several waves of coops were either destroyed or so thoroughly co-opted as to have become parts of "the system." Yet these often started with strong, hardworking people who well understood the nature of the struggle and had considerable ideological unity among themselves, so were not subject to internal splits, or weakened by internal red-baiting.

The coop movement started in early nineteenth-century Britain. It developed out of industrialization and the forcing of small farmers from "the common lands," which were enclosed and claimed by the wealthy. It accompanied and sometimes provided the center for labor union and political power struggles. By the start of World War II, so "successful" was this movement that coops controlled fully one-sixth of all British retail trade. The coops owned a bank, which lent money, held savings, financed new coop ventures, etc., that was next in size to the Bank of England. But these British coops were just another bunch of chain stores by that time, which is also what happened in the U.S. in Minnesota. Yet they started with a lot of ideological unity, and with good common agreement about how that would translate into practice. Let's look at this common ground:

> First: That labor is the source of all wealth; consequently the working classes have created all wealth.
>
> Second: That the working classes, although the producers of wealth, instead of being the richest are the poorest of the community; hence they cannot be receiving just recompense for their labor.
>
> Third: That they shall form a mutual protection society, which aims at independence for its members by common effort and common capital shared by them all.
>
> Last: By living in community with each other, on the principles of mutual co-operation, united possessions, equality of exertions, and of the means of enjoyments, shall these members become not

merely financially bettered but happy and at peace each with all.
[Ripponden Co-operative Society Bylaws, 1833 (pre-Marx)]

In the early nineteenth century, the small farmers who were not making it, propertyless workers, unemployed exfarmers, and small craftsmen were struggling to organize themselves — to become a self-conscious class — and to survive. Women were in the forefront in struggles around food. Marches, demonstrations, and "bread riots" at marketplaces were common, and were commonly led by women. The working class strove to bargain collectively with employers (though often they did not have a clear idea that this is what they were struggling for). Women sought ways to use collective purchasing power to feed and shelter their families without paying huge profits to landlords, owners, grain millers, and middlemen.

Early strikes by stillborn unions were easily broken, because there were large numbers of unemployed people near starvation who would work, or send their children to work, in the mines, cloth mills, and factories. Political action and petitions to government were ignored. Militant demonstrations, marches and attempts to destroy factory machinery to force employer bargaining brought heavy repression. Soldiers shot or sword-slashed demonstrating workers and their families. Many were killed in these "riots"; those identified as leaders were arrested and imprisoned, deported (often to Australia), or executed. Government spies were everywhere.

At the end of an unsuccessful weavers' strike in 1843, twenty-seven men and one woman (Ann Tweedale) found themselves black-listed; they could not get any kind of work. They formed a collective discussion group, "The Equitable Society of Rochdale Pioneers," which spent months discussing how their political beliefs could best be translated into action.

From Ann, the suggestion came that, if they could not organize producers to bargain for living wages, perhaps they could organize them as consumers of food and other necessaries, to obtain these, at least, at a better price. From such a beginning, a more effective and sweeping change might grow.

The group was ideologically diverse: Owenites, Chartists, Socialists, Radicals, religious dissenters. They did not arrive at an ideology all could agree upon. But they did agree on a program. Starting with $140 and a shabby store, (the "Ow'd weaver's hut in Toad Lane"), they established an organization which has grown into a worldwide movement, though not the way they hoped it would.

We should look closely at their organization. Virtually every coop which has grown and flourished has organized itself around the Rochdale Principles. Those which have not done so have either failed or remained very tiny bodies, providing small, limited services to a few hundred people at most.

First, the collective purposes for which the group would try to grow:

> The establishment of a store for the sale of provisions, clothing, etc.
>
> The building, purchasing, erecting of a number of houses in which those members desiring to assist each other in improving their domestic and social conditions may reside.
>
> The manufacture of such articles as the society may determine, to provide employment of such members who may be without employment, or who may be suffering the consequences of repeated reductions in their wages.
>
> The purchasing or rent of land which shall be cultivated by members who may be out of employment or whose labor is badly paid.
>
> And further: as soon as is practicable, this society shall arrange powers of production, distribution, education, and government — in other words to establish a self-supporting colony of united people, and assist other societies in establishing such colonies. [Rochdale Equitable Society, 1843]

By "colony," they meant a politically and economically independent group within the mother country. They meant also to grow and join with others, until the mother country's economy and rulership "withered away." Their goal was a people's state, whose economy was democratically controlled by those whose work produced its wealth. The means to this end — the immediate operating principles — they set down in three "first principles"; experience soon led to others:

1. Democratic control — one vote per member no matter how much capital he puts up or how many stock shares he holds, and no proxy voting.

2. Returns on invested capital of members shall not be more than the prevailing bank interest rates; dividends do not fluctuate; and coop stock is not to be speculatively traded.

3. The Patronage Refund. After operating expenses are paid, and reserves for member education and expansion are set aside, the remainder of earnings is paid out to patrons as a percentage of how much they have bought at the coop. This principle is generally considered the most important in the success of presently existing large coops.

Of the "secondary" principles, three are particularly important in terms of financial success. They had been drawn from bitter experience of an earlier Christian Socialist coop movement, which had grown to several hundred stores, then failed:

a. Business for cash only — no credit.

b. Current market prices shall be charged — no price-cutting.

c. Adequate reserves for depreciation, expansion, and unforeseen difficulties shall be regularly set aside.

The *patronage refund* principle and the three secondary financial principles all have slightly different rationales, but all stem from the same basic problem which faced coops then, as it does now: how can a poor, weak and undercapitalized enterprise survive under capitalism?

Cash-only business derived from the trouble coops got into when they expanded credit: they piled up debts they couldn't pay out of accounts receivable they were unable to collect. Rarely could coops rely on the means of the establishment to extract payments from the poor to whom they extended credit. Coops that gave credit, therefore, went under. They still do.

The *market-value pricing* policy was an attempt to avoid two dangers. One danger was price wars, which the under-capitalized coops always lost. Large enterprises could always undercut them and wait them out. The second danger of lower-than-market prices (immediate savings for member-customers) was setting prices too low because of inexperience to cover actual costs.

The *adequate reserves* priniciple was an attempt to plan for unexpected costs. What is "adequate" is hard to determine, especially if you are trying to expand. But "unforeseen events" might include having your store smashed up by police or burned by a mob led by a government agent. It might include having all your goods stolen, or being cheated on your orders or payments by merchants out to get you. All of these things frequently happened to the early coops.

This also supported the patronage refund method of operation, because that allowed coops to hold the sales revenues and "profits" long enough to tell what true expenses would be, and to have some cash reserves in case of emergency. It also led to an expansion principle: Where possible, coops "shall combine their strengths in democratic association for the purposes of wholesaling, manufacturing, and providing services too large to be undertaken by local organizations."

Yet if a coop is to expand, it must draw in new members and not alienate potential supporters, whatever their politics. So another principle was added, the principle of *political neutrality*. As we shall see, in Minnesota, this was a double-edged weapon. Neutrality is a political concept; it favors the existing social order.

The Consumer Co-operative League of America (educational arm of National Co-operatives, Inc. [NCI]), an umbrella organization of all kinds of coops, believes these principles are economic-political necessities for any successful coop.

The success of coops organized in accordance with them has been considerable in some ways. Coops affiliated with NCI have millions of members and do several billion dollars worth of business yearly. They include supermarkets, rural electric companies, Land O'Lakes Creameries, and the National Credit Union. The St. Paul Farmers Union Co-operative, started on less than $1,000 raised by members in 1927, distributed to its members in 1970 more than $13,000,000 in patronage refunds from savings made by collective purchase of farm supplies.

Evidently, the Rochdale weavers were onto something, in terms of success as defined by growth and money. But something got into the coop movement which drained it of all its early militancy and idealism, and which now casts doubt on whether coops can be a force for social change at all.

The large establishment coops are surely not such a force. Their own literature makes this plain. They repeatedly assert that coops are part of "the free-enterprise" system, not opposed to it. NCI coops are madly opposed to "communist subversion." During the early Cold War years, Minnesota's commissioner of agriculture praised coops to the legislature. He called them a "bulwark against Socialism and Communism." That is what they are now.

If coops aren't bulwarks for the ruling class, they get offed in time-honored ways.

The early coops certainly didn't start out to be bulwarks against socialism, but to be peaceful means of bringing it about. But they became nearly indistinguishable from the institutions they were supposed to replace. A closer look at the American — and particularly Minnesota — record helps to show why. The purposes of the Rochdale workers — for whom coop operating principles were to be a means to the end of a people-controlled economy and society — those purposes were forgotten entirely, or actively denied.

THE NONPOLITICAL COOPS

Toiling millions now are waking,
  See them marching on;
All the tyrants now are shaking,
  Soon their power is gone.
Storm the fort! Ye Knights of Labor,
  Battle for our cause;
Equal Rights for every neighbor,
  Down with tyrant laws!
          — *1880 original song of "Knights of Labor"*

The first important American coop movement was started by a secret society of farmers and flourished in the agricultural depression that followed the Civil War. At first an illegal, underground society, it was called The Patrons of Husbandry, better known as the Grange.

Minnesota was one of the first states to have a Grange coop; in 1869, an exchange was established for buying and selling farm goods. The national Grange coop and political movement grew for a few years, then halted and slid backward into a social group. There are several reasons for this.

Politically, the Grange had little internal unity. There was nothing like the visionary statement of purposes of the Rochdale society, and there was no thought of building a society around collective ownership of the means of production and distribution. Grange farmers were highly individualistic. Grange marketing coops were simply a more efficient way than individual marketing to sell produce, providing some chance of more equal footing in dealing with rail and mill robber-barons.

As for collective buying of supplies and other needs, there appear to be two financial reasons for the Grange failure. The Grange coops did not follow the Rochdale principle of delayed patronage refund; they passed on savings immediately in lower prices. Grange stores and warehouses were undercapitalized and had no reserves, so they could not survive price-cutting and other attacks launched by well-heeled capitalists.

Too, several Grange organizations moved into direct manufacture of farm equipment before they were able to handle the technical, financial, or organizational parts of such a venture. Bankruptcies weakened the whole organization and destroyed many farmers' confidence in it.

Finally, much energy and militance was drawn off into the political Non-Partisan League, started in 1917 locally, a promising organization that kept on promising and never delivering until most of its members went into the new Farmer-Labor Party, still hopeful.

The next large venture into coops was made by urban labor. In the late nineteenth century, America's first industrial union was formed — the Knights of Labor. Its song was originally the militant one quoted above. By 1918, the song had degenerated into the better-known:

> Hold the fort, for we are coming,
>   Union men be strong.
> Side by side we battle onward,
>   Victory will come.

Perhaps this reflects what happened to the Knights: they were smashed.

The Knights were the first union not organized on a craft basis. Like the later Industrial Workers of the World (IWW), they had a broad, utopian, socialist vision, and an ultimate goal of economic and political power for the working class. At the height of their growth, in 1885, the Knights had a million members, and, in midwest urban elections, could call out a much larger vote to support the candidates they favored, who were generally populists. (According to most academicians, populists in America have been rural, antitechnology, anti-industry, and conservative. This is false.)

The Knights had set up both producers' and consumers' coops. The producers' coops were intended to give jobs to laid-off and striking workers; the stores sold at a discount to union members. Profits made in sales to nonmembers went into the union strike fund. There were about 300 stores and about 200 small factories in 1885, as the Knights entered the battle to force the steel industry to recognize the rights of workers. The coops were seen by the union — and unfortunately, also by Big Steel and Big Rail — as an integral part of the struggle.

Demonstrations and wildcat strikes were met by troops, arrests, lockouts, imprisonment, blacklisting, and murders by the capitalist opposition. By the end of the century, the Knights of Labor had declined to a small group of aging men. Their coop stores and factories had been burned out, bombed out, wrecked by company agents, forced out economically, or abandoned.

A similar story could be told of the cooperative ventures attempted by the United Mine Workers of Illinois (UMW) between 1913 and 1923. Their coops were to include cooperatively run housing to replace the miserable company shacks; health insurance, hospitals, and schools were also envisioned. A UMW coop chain store venture was the start. It was deliberately smashed by financial maneuvers, with an occasional burned-out store, especially in the southern Illinois areas where there had been an attempt to build black-white cooperation through the stores in order to strengthen the union.

The third American wave of cooperatives — the one which lives on in the National Co-operatives, Inc. group, with its "circle pines" emblem — began in the Midwest, with some of its strongest, deepest roots in Minnesota. Farmers and Iron Rangers started this movement. Unlike the Grange and Knights movements, it did not begin with a large national organization which had broader purposes, but with small groups of people.

There were two kinds of coops. One kind — to be discussed in a separate section later — tied itself initially to left political thought and action. The other kind — the type of group that has flourished — was primarily interested in economic advantage (or survival) for its members. This second sort of group avoided ideology and politics, and saw coops as a means of using the capitalist economic system, not as a means of changing it. Farmers' marketing and supplies purchase coops were mostly of this type. Let's look at the growth of two such coops: Midland Oil and Farmers' Union Central Exchange-Grain Terminal Association.

In 1921, a group of farmers in Cottonwood, Minnesota, organized a gas station coop, selling oil and gasoline from a rickety pump at a back-street location. The gas coop was able to return about 20 percent of the purchase price to its members. The idea of gas-oil coops instantly took hold among midwestern farmers. Gas, oil, and fertilizer (around which a battle was also being fought, mainly in Indiana) are the main farm operating expenses, aside from such capital expenses as farm machinery.

As the small gas-oil coops spread, the oil wholesalers began refusing to deal with them. The oil monopolies — which had not really been broken up in the federal "trust-busting" actions — were quite arrogant and open about their reasons for not dealing with "those bunches of farmers." But their arrogance provided a spur for the otherwise individualistic farmers to get together: they got mad. In 1926, a county agricultural agent, E.G. Cort, organized thirteen oil coops into Midland Co-operative Oil Association, the first wholesale

TABLE 16.1 GROWTH OF MIDLAND CO-OPERATIVE OIL ASSOCIATION, 1927-1934

Year	No. of coops	Sales volume	Patronage refund
1927	13	$ 269,863	$ 3,436
1928	—	417,956	1,938*
1930	138	598,750	11,811
1934	275	1,751,007	44,799

*A bank they kept their cash in failed.

distributor for gas, oil, kerosene, and grease. Its pre-World War II growth is shown in table 16.1. Midland did the largest volume of gas-oil business in Minnesota.

Unfortunately, Midland (and other gas-oil coops, such as Union Oil of Kansas City) soon showed up a weakness in the percentage-patronage refund principle of operation: it favored the larger purchasers at the expense of the smaller and poorer ones. Not only was this true because the larger purchasers (the bigger farmers) got back bigger refunds; it was usually also true that the larger farmers could afford to wait until year-end for their savings in the form of refunds. The smaller farmers were often in desperate straits and could have used the immediate savings of lower prices. Sometimes they had to have credit.

Thus, the gas-oil coops, with their very rapid growth, became a factor favoring the growth of large, highly mechanized farms, and the decline, failure, and loss of smaller, "less efficient" ones. The gas-oil coops fitted slickly into the network of economic forces in capitalism which concentrate ownership of the means of production. Far from opposing these trends, they were part of them. This may have accounted for their immediate success.

Nonetheless, these "independent oil distributors" are under heavy attack now from the giant oil monopolies, and the recent maneuverings and manipulated shortages have put a considerable number of independent distributors out of business. In the next few years, most of the remaining ones will have been pushed under.

With the sort of growth exhibited by Midland Oil, there was no possibility — and little pretense — of a "democratic coop society." Professionalized management became an immediate necessity, and there was a rapid, sharp separation between the owner-consumers and management. This was all right with most of the farmer-cooperators. They weren't looking for utopian societies; they wanted cheap gas and oil. They were uninterested in running the coops as long as the coops delivered.

The Farmers Union Central Exchange (FUCE) — a coop purchasing outfit which stocked oil, fertilizer, and other farm supplies — and the Grain Terminal Association, a collective grain marketing outfit allied with FUCE, were started on the remnants of the earlier Grange movement, abandoned during the political struggles around the Non-Partisan League.

In 1927, the Farmers Union Terminal Association, which marketed livestock, set aside $1,000 to get the wholesale Central Exchange going. In 1929, it had 20 member associations, sold 425 tank-carloads of gasoline, and 31,875 gallons of lubricating oil. By 1935, it had 227 member coops, was selling 4,150 tank cars of gasoline, 1,144,604 gallons of oil, and $137,936 worth of tractor tires.

Again, the patronage refund principle favored large farmers, farmers who didn't need credit, farmers who weren't operating on such close margins that they needed immediate lower-price savings and weren't able to wait for year-end refunds.

The Grain Terminal Association (GTA) became the biggest part of the St. Paul Farmers Union Central Exchange. It was a collective marketing group, originally mostly for Minnesota wheat farmers; other grains (rye, corn, soy) were added as these became economically important in the state. The advantages of collective grain marketing at first were considerable for all farmers. When the railroads owned the elevators, and the giant local milling-baking capitalists Pillsbury, Washburn-Crosby, and General Mills controlled the entire grain-marketing system, farmers were always in debt:

Farmer is the man, farmer is the man.
Buys up on credit until fall.
Then they take him by the hand
And they lead him off his land.
And the merchant is the man that gets it all.
[Depression song (1923)]

It didn't matter whether there was overproduction (which presumably lowers prices) or underproduction (which is supposed to raise them); the market was controlled, and the farmer got just enough to get by on, if that. (Even now, the farmer gets only eight cents of each food dollar and that must cover all his costs.)

So cooperative marketing, which gave farmers control of some grain-storage elevators and better bargaining positions with shippers and millers, was a help.

Nevertheless, the FUCE-GTA tended to be a conservative organization, even given the social limits of what the coop movement can be expected to do. The farmers had collective marketing, storage, and shipping arrangements. They benefited a great deal from these, and, in some cases, were able to cut out certain middleman entirely. Why not go the next step and set up coop milling and baking enterprises, controlled by farmer-producers, or perhaps jointly with consumers, who were working back toward the origins of production by organizing their stores into regional associations and larger wholesalers? Many of the FUCE-GTA farmers saw this as a logical next step. Producers and consumers could between them have organized at least the food production sector of society without middlemen, and controlled it by themselves.

The leadership of GTA tried to turn them away from this logical step and succeeded, with constant statements such as this one:

> That [setting up a mill] isn't the producer's job. When we take our grain to market, our job as producers is finished. We shall welcome the day when the consumers reach the point where they come out here and build a flour mill next door to us. But it is up to the consumers themselves to take this step. [1938]

Why? Well, there were quite a few reasons. One reason was the FUCE and GTA leadership got to be pretty tight with Pillsbury-General Mills leadership. Another reason was structural, and would operate whether or not there were personal linkages.

The producer coops sold to everyone, and the farmers produced in such volume that consumer coops and small enterprises were only a small part of their market. Mainly, they sold to the giants who could do national and international selling. And the giants were always out to get them. They couldn't rock the boat too much, or they'd be thrown overboard. Their small gains, and small challenges to capitalist power, placed them under constant attack.

For example, the National Taxpayers' Equity Association (NTEA) had been organized by mill-industry hireling Ben McCabe of Minneapolis. NTEA was always bawling to the state (and national) legislatures about the "unfair" tax breaks coops were getting — namely, not having to pay corporate taxes on the "profits" coop members saved by collective buying and by using their own labor. NTEA directed a lot of its attention to the FUCE-GTA, until some deals were made.

The main deal was made on the federal level. This was legislation setting up two categories of coops. One category is *non-profit, tax-exempt*. Such coop memberships are limited to farmers only, mostly large ones at that. The other category is *nonexempt* coops, which have nonfarmer members (as most consumer coops do) and have to pay tax on "corporate profits" — a tax which further reduced the savings refunded to members.

These laws form a permanent barrier to producer-consumer market organizing that cuts out capitalist middlemen. The criteria in existing legislation are — and are intended to be — mystifying, even to insiders. For instance, a nonexempt coop, which is given certain small advantages over a "for profit corporation," is defined as "a business operating in a cooperative manner." The mystifications and complications leave plenty of room for big deals, via legalistic interpretation. Even for the tax-exempt farmer coops, the legalistic and tax advantages go to the larger farmers and dairymen, at the expense of the smaller ones.

I talked to a survivor of those early, nonpolitical farmer coops. She and her husband were still small dairy farmers, still belonged to a small coop several levels up in the hierarchy. Their coop is affiliated with Land O'Lakes Creamery.

"Did you find the coop an advantage?" I asked. She said:

> At first it was. But the bigger ones took over very quickly. Now, in our coop, about all we have to cooperate on is paying for the truck which picks up from all of us. We have nothing to say about prices or policy.
>
> Recently there have been some rulings about the kind of storage tank you have to have to be "Class A," which you have to be if you are going to sell milk at all. The requirement is for a very big storage tank — it would hold three times what we produce.
>
> We just bought our new storage tank three years ago. It isn't paid for yet. We can't afford the new tank, which is much bigger than we would ever need. And so we are quitting.

And so they have. Like Midland, FUCE-GTA and other farm marketing coops have been important factors in centralizing production on fewer, larger farms, forcing out smaller farmers.

The new wave of sixties and seventies coops is made up of mostly little stores, with an emphasis on healthy foods of various kinds. (This was also an emphasis of Ann Tweedale's plans for the Rochdale cooperative; she was particularly annoyed with the dangerous habit of stretching and whitening flour with chalk and lime.)

Nevertheless, many new wave folks have their eyes on "extending back" to the land — to becoming, or joining with, producers. The unpolitical coops discussed in this section should be studied, and people should try to figure out ways of gaining volume savings and collective market power without building in structural features that lead to bigness and centralization. It is not at all clear how this can be done, or if it can be. Well-organized attacks on existing (hostile) regulatory and tax legislation are essential.

THE POLITICAL COOPS

A feudin' and a fussin' and a fightin'
That is a wrong that needs a rightin'.
Hurry up and get the funeral over, and then
We can start up our feudin' again.
       — *Appalachian mountaineer song, Left theme song*

We've seen that the unpolitical coops, which had no vision of broad social change and no principles except "buy cheap, sell dear," were co-opted almost from the very outset. Counter-culture cooperators may feel confidence in their collective commitment to building for change as a protection from co-optation. I think this confidence is wholly unwarranted for any local coop I know about; in general, the Rochdale British cooperators had a clearer view of what they were trying to do than do modern local folks. Their principles were agreed on, written down for everybody to see and work toward, not merely tacitly understood as vague ideals springing from "life-style."

Clarity did not protect them. In fact, pretty early, they faced the need to "grow or die." This led to their adding the principle of *political neutrality* that would make it possible for anyone to join without being turned off by politics. They added a lot of stuff about internal education, because they hoped to convert member-supporter-customers into political-supporter-activists. Status quo neutrality won out, because it's not really neutral. Let's look at Minnesota Depression-era coops that were explicitly activist, at first, and see what happened there.

Around the turn of the century, there was a wave of Scandinavian immigration. Swedes, Norwegians, and Finns settled in Minnesota, Wisconsin, Northern Michigan, and Northern Illinois, where they were employed at first in logging and mining, then in small-farming the poor, logged-over lands.

The Finns, especially, brought with them strong beliefs in unions and in consumer coops, both of which had lightened their oppression in Czarist-controlled Finland. They also brought strong commitments to the achievement of socialism. Oppressive conditions in mining, logging, small farming, and urban labor strengthened these commitments. Coop stores, housing, and community halls were set up in northern Minnesota and the Iron Range. The first coop — as best we know — was organized in 1903 in Nashwauk, Minnesota. It was named the Elanto Company, after the semi-underground, repressed and harassed Elanto Society of Finland. (The 1903 Finnish Elanto was connected in some way — it is not clear how — with Lenin.)

Many of the coops were associated with Workers Halls or Socialist Halls, set up as places for social get-togethers and discussions to develop political consciousness. Class struggle was well understood by these miners, farmers and workers. But they were an ethnic and linguistic minority, having relatively little contact with others in the state. The main newspaper of this group, *Tyomies,* was very radical, as many will tell you, but unless you could (can) read Finnish — one of the most difficult languages in the world for Indo-European language speakers — *Tyomies* was (is) closed to you.

(There are interesting parallels between the radical — and isolated — Finns and movements sparked by radical Jews immigrating in large numbers to the east coast from Slavic countries about the same time. A real understanding of the structural forces of capitalism and their effects on "conscious" socialist groups probably will require systematic exploration of these parallels, which have received no attention from academics.)

In 1917, representatives from nineteen small Minnesota and Wisconsin coops met at Superior, Wisconsin. Private wholesalers and merchants were combining to attack them, refusing to sell to their stores, cheating them, raising prices. So the group decided to fight back by forming their own wholesale.

A collection from those present raised $15.50, starting capital for the Central Co-operative Wholesale (CCW), which used space, labor help, and some financial donations from the Communist Party, whose members were well represented in the small coops. Printing was done by the *Tyomies* newspaper staff, at first on an informal basis and later by a formalized arrangement providing that *Tyomies* would set and print the CCW newspaper, *The Cooperative Builder,* which was written in English.

Before we get into some of the unhappy stuff, let's take a look at a

TABLE *16.2* GROWTH OF CENTRAL CO-OPERATIVE WHOLESALE, 1917-1934

Year	Members	Customers	Sales	Surplus	Net Worth
1917	15	15	$ 25,574	$ —	$ 748
1918	25	50	132,423	—	6,351
1920	48	100	409,591	4,223	21,911
1924	60	99	613,215	5,896	33,370
1929	90	128	1,755,627	15,492	134,412
1934	97	124	1,787,556	22,154	308,922

happy growth chart, table 16.2. ("Customers" in this table means stores that weren't members of CCW, and sometimes weren't coops.)

The table tells us several things. First, growth was pretty steady. There was no big change at the time of the 1929 Wall Street stock-market crash. Farmers and miners were hard up before and after that. The farm depression started in 1929; the crash affected mainly people who write analyses. Even city workers were hard up before the crash. The coops, meanwhile, were growing organically, not in response to periodic crises.

Another thing we can see from the table (which becomes even more marked for later years) is that net worth was climbing quite a bit faster than surplus, in proportion to sales increase. Basically, that means CCW was plowing most of its collective buying savings into capital expansion: trucks, storage facilities, equipment, and so on. That's how it was able to grow so fast. Unfortunately, just as it started to grow, it started to split along political lines.

By 1920, CCW was doing almost half a million dollars worth of business. This was the point at which the serious split began. A few people who remember the fight are still around, but it is obvious that their accounts of it are still highly partisan. I am unable to unravel the connections between the coop movement, with its communist-socialist-opportunist splits, and the internal turmoil which eventually destroyed the left direction of the Farmer-Labor Party in the late 1930s. It is evident that there are many interconnections.

It is clear that the Communist Party (CP) controlled or partly controlled many of the small coops. Its membership was fairly large in northern Minnesota, where it was vigorous and respected as an organizer among miners (the IWW seems to have won many loggers). The CP had given CCW much support over its first critical years: office space, loans, labor. It is not clear whether loans were repaid, but apparently no payment was contemplated by CCW for office space and other services. Now come two versions of the split.

From Erick Kendall, an anti-Communist, red-baiter, and former editor of the CCW newspaper *The Cooperative Builder,* comes this version:

> In 1929, the CP demanded a $5,000 loan from CCW. This was refused; it was contrary to the Rochdale Principles to involve the co-ops in this kind of direct politics, as opposed to the political implications of 'economic democracy,' which are inherent in their existence and nature. The demand was defeated by those who well understood that it was destructive. Then the CP demanded 1% of the gross (which would have been about a $10,000 donation from CCW to them). They tried to pack the boards and vote this through, but we defeated them.

In 1930 at its annual meeting, CCW declared itself for "neutrality."

From a former CP member who was involved comes this version:

> When the wholesale was just getting started, we were very much a part of it all. As they started to succeed, we were forced out, amid a lot of accusations that we had "infiltrated" that which we had started ourselves. At first we saw the co-ops, and they saw themselves, as part of the general class struggle. If it had not been for our support and our work, there would have been no CCW. When they grew successful, the bourgeois opportunists moved in fast. They engaged in smear tactics, packed board meetings and attempted to split the younger people from the older ones, saying theirs was "the new way, the American way, not the old country way." We were pressed financially, especially for legal defense funds, our people were getting arrested all the time. We thought they might repay us at a time when we needed it as much as they had at the start when we helped them.

Kendall, incidentally, made a sort of career of coop red-baiting for a while. He used the English language newpaper to lay out a line that coops were defenders of the free enterprise system, would fight the Communists, etc., etc. A favorite tactic, proudly admitted by him, was to attend a meeting of a fairly left, together coop and bait members into making various statements to the effect that they were Communists and proud of it. He would then print selected versions of these in the newspaper, warning that the Commies were trying to take over. Since CCW also forced *out* of the wholesale all the "Communist dominated" cooperative stores, those tended to not be doing so well financially. So Kendall would do a number on how the "free enter-prise" coops were succeeding, the Communist ones failing. There-fore, free enterprise was right, Communism wrong.

The conflict was very bitter and sometimes violent. It divided families, especially on old (radical) versus young (conservative) lines. The language difference contributed to the degeneration of the once-radical Farmer-Labor Party (F-L), which was gaining electoral strength enough to frighten off an alliance between the two capitalist parties, before they discovered the much more fruitful strategy of merging one capitalist party with the F-L. During the conflicts in the coops, Communists, fellow travelers, and some red-white-and-blue reds were "purged." At the end of World War II, the purge was completed. The CP, in the meantime, was purging itself of "bourgeois opportunists." Since there were an awful lot of them around, as always, that left it greatly weakened numerically. At the same time, the CP was cuddling up to Big Liberal Bourgies in their Popular Front, anti-Fascist strategy.

While the sectarian battle was going on — in all likelihood encouraged and perhaps financed by capitalist representatives — the capitalists were taking hostile note of the coop movement and getting it on to get it off.

One entire volume of Minnesota statutes, laws regulating coops (vol. 20A), was passed, unnoticed, while the left and the sort-of-left were fighting each other. Additional legislation, since passed, fills two more volumes. Minnesota is one of the worst states in which to incorporate a coop, from the point of view of legal restrictions.

This bewildering legislation, passed while left groups were fight-ing among themselves and fighting red-baiting liberals, favors big-ness and professional management. It sets various standards for some things which most groups would not want to meet (for instance, phony health regulations which can be obeyed only with expensive equipment). There was no unified fight against this legislation; none is shaping up now. So extensive and complex is existing legislation that it amounts to a total weapon which can be used against new wave coops if they ever grow enough to be seen by food capitalists as a real or potential economic threat. Member-customer consciousness-raising, and unified plans of political action, would seem to be a must, if the new wave coops are to escape the fates of the old ones.

We should not be contemptuous of those who went before us. Often they seem much more together than we are. Yet, the political coops that survived the infighting, purges, and economic assassination have become supermarkets indistinguishable from Red Owl, except that they have member-directors, and each year refund a percentage of sales-slip totals to members who save their receipts.

I have been a member of one of these coop supermarkets since 1958; I joined as a student in Chicago, and have kept up in order to get the weekly paper. The coop charges the going rate for food, exploits its employees, peddles junk, poisons, gadgety trash ("Whatever the customers want"). Big money is spent on advertising, costs are passed on in prices. The main difference from capitalist supermarket chains is the makeup of its board. Generally broken-down do-gooder liberals, who were Left Youth in the 1930s but have since made good, these are the people who "won" the struggle the left lost then. They retain a few rags of social consciousness from their poor days, so they mandate their coop to do a little social program, such as summer camp for "disadvantaged" children, whose ghetto parents cannot buy on the coop's no-credit policy.

Hyde Park Community Coop, the one I belong to in Chicago, has been publishing its "history" in its weekly newspaper: it's up to 1938 now, and it's sad, sad reading. There is the original store, started in somebody's apartment. There is the first "store, store" with homemade wooden counters. The proud day they can afford to buy a cooler. The long debates about not exploiting their own workers, stockboys, and such. The arguments about whether to take milk delivery service that is union and white or non-union and black. The old photos — they look like us.

Recent newspapers have told a "today" coop story. At a membership meeting, a vote was taken to handle only United Farm Worker (UFW) grown lettuce. The meeting was attended by 180 people. (This was an unusually large number — average attendance at membership meetings is 25, average mail-vote on board positions is 300.) The manager complained that his was nonneutrally "political," and furthermore violated the rights of 12,820 people who didn't attend the meeting, who just wanted the cheapest and best lettuce they could get (or he could get for them). He caved in when threatened with UFW support pickets, which would have included an alderman, a banker and several famous professors. (Poor thirties people, they made good.)

So UFW lettuce went into the coolers; the Aztec Eagle from the crates was proudly displayed. Not only did customers not complain, but people came from all over Chicago to buy the only "pure" UFW lettuce in town.

Then the local UFW support committee was tipped off by some drivers that they were bringing in Teamster lettuce. Two men from the support group went down to the loading-storage area in the coop's basement to see the crates, but were stopped on the way down by manager Gib Spencer. They pushed by him, and he began screaming for help. They saw Teamster, Bud Antle, crates all over the place; scab lettuce was going into the eagle-decorated coolers. Meanwhile, manager Spencer was calling a coop guard, who was armed only with a club and handcuffs, and a shopping center guard, who had a gun. While the guard held a gun on them, the two UFW organizers were handcuffed and shoved around by Spencer and the coop guard.

So there was an emergency meeting. The board decided that the 13,000 members would have to decide the lettuce question somehow. They felt it was maybe a little deceptive of manager Spencer to put scab lettuce in eagle-decorated coolers. Guns, like the guard's are horrid, too. But they were terribly upset about the "violence" of the UFW organizers. So: latest word from a struggling thirties coop. Weird to read about this on the front pages of the newspaper, then go through the early, hopeful history reprinted on the back pages. A kind of double vision that brought on vertigo and nausea.

Coops cannot be politically neutral, for there is no such thing. Nor can they make revolution — or any kind of significant change — merely by existing and growing. It is important to recognize the criticism made clear back in the eighteenth century by pre-Marx British Levelers: namely, it is not possible to build an alternative society quietly and peacefully, wholly outside the mainstream society, for the latter's rules control most of the wealth and the means of producing new wealth (land, minerals, energy supplies, factories, tools). If an alternative looks likely to threaten this, they fight it. If you cannot defend your alternative, they win.

Struggles for control must go on inside existing institutions, where most of the resources are located and most of the people are working. People's coops can be small utopian models, and survival centers for such struggles. But the food industry will not become people-controlled by the building of coops. Not while there exists the A&P (world's largest retail network), the U.S. Defense Department, Tenneco (oil, factory, farms conglomerate), Pillsbury, General Mills, General Foods, Green Giant, Ralston Purina, International Minerals and Chemicals, IT&T, International Harvester, etc. Coop people should ask themselves how they can best aid struggles within such power-controllers as those corporate giants. This may lead to more fruitful strategies which would achieve the Rochdale pioneers' purpose: Not a people's store, but a people's world.

For all the disappointments and sell-outs, still a good old song, good end:

> Arise, ye prisoners of starvation,
> Arise, ye wretched of the earth.

> For justice thunders condemnation,
> A better world's in birth.

> No more tradition's chains shall bind us,
> Arise, ye slaves, no more in thrall!

> The earth shall rise on new foundations,
> We have been nought, we shall be all.

> *Chorus:*
> It is the final conflict,
> Let each stand in his place.
> The International working class
> Shall free the human race.

> We want no condescending saviors,
> To rule us from a judgment hall.
> We workers ask not for their favors:
> Let us consult for all.

> To make the thief disgorge his booty,
> To free the spirit from its cell,
> We must ourselves decide our duty,
> We must decide and do it well.

17

Workers' Cooperatives:
Remedy for Plant Closings?
Frank Lindenfeld

The organization of workers' cooperatives, based upon employee and community ownership and democratic management, promises a partial solution to unemployment created by plant closings. Many factories slated for shutdown by their corporate owners could be made economically viable if reorganized as workers' cooperatives. Examples of such cooperatives both in this country and abroad have demonstrated that they can be efficient and effective, can encourage the creation of new jobs through reinvestment, and increase both the income and the job satisfaction of their members.

The problem of plant closings affects every part of the United States, although the industrial Northeast has perhaps suffered most severely. There, a continuing wave of factory shutdowns over the last two decades has resulted in considerable unemployment and added to the severity of urban problems, as businesses desert not only central cities, but the entire area. In Pennsylvania alone, some 5,000 factories closed between 1969 and 1975, with a resultant loss of some 66,000 jobs. New service jobs absorbed some of the resulting unemployment, but many of these jobs required lower skill levels and paid less.

Corporations have moved plants to the "sunbelt" and out of the country in their search for lower costs, especially lower wages in nonunion areas. Others they have closed down altogether. The reasons for the shutdowns have been diverse. Some are divestitures by corporate conglomerates that have, in their zeal to expand, swallowed too much too fast, or businesses milked of profits for five to ten

This article includes portions of "Workers' Cooperatives as a Partial Solution to the Problem of Plant Closings," *Pennsylvania Journal of Urban Economic Development,* October 1978, and "Workers' Cooperatives: A Model for Economic Democracy," *WIN,* 24 November 1977.

years by their new owners and then discarded.

Still others are closings of functioning units that do not return "enough" profit. The Sperry Rand library furniture factory in Herkimer, New York, for example, did not measure up to the corporation's standard of a 22 percent return on invested capital and was slated for closing (Whyte 1978a). In other cases, foreign competition or other factors may depress an entire industry; in these ailing industries — steel is an example — continued operation of shutdown factories is usually not feasible without some form of government subsidy. As Alperovitz and Faux have shown, the giant Campbell steel works in Youngstown, Ohio, could have been reopened under worker-community ownership with adequate federal loan guarantees and a promise to purchase some of the steel (Alperovitz and Faux, chap. 18).

Workers' cooperatives are owned either by their employees, or jointly by the workers and members of the community. Since stock ownership is a known and accepted part of the existing American economy, this aspect of workers' cooperatives is not likely to be controversial. Since the 1960s, employee stock-ownership plans (ESOP's) have been adopted by hundreds of American firms. There are today an estimated 1-3,000 ESOP's in the United States. Most allow only for minority stock ownership by workers, but, in fifty or more cases, the workers own a majority of the stock, giving them at least formal control of their companies (Select Committee on Small Business, U.S. Senate 1979). Very few of these firms, however, have a democratic management where the workers exercise any power in the day-to-day operation of the workplace.

Workers' cooperatives go beyond mere stock ownership to give those who work in an enterprise a say in its policies and operation on the basis of one worker, one vote. This includes the power to determine what services or products will be produced, to determine how the surplus they have created will be allocated, to hire and fire managers, and to approve or disapprove new plant investment. Cooperatives are usually a much wider attempt to maximize the well-being of their workers — this includes good working conditions, adequate pay, and job security — as well as that of the community within which they are located. An important aspect of the latter is the creation of new jobs.[1]

Workers' cooperatives are potentially viable for a number of reasons. Employee satisfaction is usually higher than in stockholder corporations — a number of studies have found a direct connection between job satisfaction and degree of participation in decision-making. Productivity is higher, because workers feel they own a piece of the company and are more motivated to cut waste and inefficiency and maintain high quality service or production. The cooperatives can be more efficient and less costly than contemporary corporate management with its high supervisory personnel salaries, waste in production, worker apathy, and absenteeism. They do this through information and skill sharing, so that members are able to do more than one job, and by using fewer supervisors and foremen. When work needs to be done, it is accomplished in a cooperative spirit, in place of the more usual "that's not my job" attitude found in many businesses.

As the case of the American plywood cooperatives shows, average income can be higher than in similar privately-owned businesses, because of increased productivity. At the same time, wage differentials tend to be low, increasing the organization's cohesion.

Finally, the cooperatives can aim for reasonable profits instead of the highest possible profit levels sought by many corporations.

On the negative side, workers' cooperatives may not find it easy to survive in an economy geared to corporate capitalism. Further, the same difficulties and weaknesses that contributed to the original shutdown may, in some cases, continue to plague a successor company. Successful coops may change imperceptibly as they grow in size and stability until they resemble their corporate counterparts in practically every respect, including personnel relations and marketing and pricing policies. Also, cooperatives may all too easily adopt a "workers' capitalist" mentality in which the firm becomes insensitive to consumers and the community, seeking profit first and foremost like any other business concern.[2]

CONVERSION OF CLOSING PLANTS
TO WORKERS' COOPERATIVES

A number of shut-down firms have been bought up by workers and community members in the last ten years in efforts to preserve jobs. Many have used Employee Stock Ownership Plans (ESOP's) to effect the changeover. The cases include: Bates Fabrics Co.; Chicago and Northwestern Railroad; Jamestown Metal Products; Mohawk Valley Community Corporation; Pacific Paperboard Products; Saratoga Knitting Mills; South Bend Lathe; and Vermont Asbestos Group (Whyte 1978a). In 1979, a group of workers in McKeesport,

Pennsylvania, were trying to reopen a steel foundry as a worker-owned firm. Almost every instance involved a change in *ownership* without any break with traditional systems of managerial *control*. Nevertheless there is a greater likelihood that worker-community-owned firms will evolve democratic management structures than that traditionally owned companies will do so.

The largest attempted conversion of a closed plant to worker-community ownership was the 1977-79 drive to reopen the Campbell Steel Works, spearheaded by local religious leaders organized as the Ecumenical Coalition of the Mahoning Valley. At stake were the jobs of some 4,000 persons laid off when the plant was closed in September 1977. The plant was formerly a part of Youngstown Sheet and Tube Company, a company purchased by the Lykes conglomerate in 1969. Since the closing, Lykes merged with another conglomerate, LTV, with the approval of the Carter administration. The merger made their combined steel operations into the third largest steel manufacturers in this country.

The Ecumenical Coalition sponsored a feasibility study which indicated the plant could successfully reopen if the government supplied several hundred million dollars in loan guarantees, and agreed to purchase only a small fraction of its output (see chap. 18). The new company, to be known as Community Steel, Inc., was to have a fifteen-member board of directors, with six members elected by the company's workers, six by outside investors and other purchasers of stock, and three by a community corporation designed to represent the broad interests of the local community. The community corporation would include in its membership interested area-residents as well as representatives of labor, business and industry, and local government. Thousands of residents, including many former workers at the plan, pledged savings to a fund to purchase the factory. The coalition applied for a $15 million federal grant and initial loan guarantees of $245 million. The loan guarantee was rejected by the Carter administration in 1979, however, effectively stopping the plan to reopen the plant under worker-community ownership.

As yet, there are few examples in this country of successful transformations of shut-down firms into workers' cooperatives with *both* worker-community ownership *and* democratic management. Some can be found in the plywood industry, where seven of the cooperative firms in the Pacific Northwest grew out of conglomerate divestitures. More recently, a national organization, the Federation for Economic Democracy, was established to help launch worker-owned, democratically managed firms where companies have been closing and laying off workers. Because of lack of funds, the national office closed in 1977 after two years of operation, though local offshoots have been actively trying to reorganize closed plants as producers' cooperatives.

The cooperative plywood factories are notable as the only workers' cooperatives in this country that date back to the 1920s and 1930s. About thirty plywood coops were established, though only half survived through to 1982. The plywood plants are noteworthy both as the oldest extant examples of workers' cooperatives in this country and as illustrations of the benefits of this organizational form.

The plants average in size between 100 and 300 workers. The Board of Directors is elected by the workers, each of whom has one vote. Each worker originally put in $1,000-2,000 to buy a share of the company. Wage rates are high, and average take-home pay is above union standards. In a few plants, all the workers receive the same (high) wages.

According to Berman (chap. 7), productivity in these plants is higher than in comparable privately owned plywood firms. She attributes the superior productivity in these firms to the fact that members work harder and more carefully because they have a stronger motivation, reinforced by both the participatory atmosphere and the incentive of direct financial gain. The cooperatively owned plywood firms do have managers (chosen by elected directors) to enforce labor discipline, but the cooperative structure has eliminated the need for some positions because the workers themselves carry out many supervisory, executive, maintenance and plant-improvement functions, and they are versatile, able, and willing to shift around and do a variety of production jobs.

The level of participation varies within and across the plywood firms. Many members do take advantage of the opportunity to influence enterprise decisions, and members are paid for attending membership and committee meetings. Decisions of managers and of the Board of Directors can be appealed to the entire membership which has the ultimate say.

Recent Examples

The record of failing businesses in America bought out by their employees recently has not been very impressive. Most employee buy-outs have not included any significant degree of workers' self-management, and the economic problems that plagued their predecessor organizations have often continued.

One foundering company purchased by its workers in 1980 was Rath Meat Packing in Waterloo, Iowa. This meat packing plant, with over 2,000 workers, lost $22 million over five years in the 1970s. It was rescued through the initiative of officials of Local 46 of the Amalgamated Meat Cutters Union, who arranged a worker buy-out through an Employee Stock Ownership Plan (ESOP).

The Rath ESOP structure is unusual in that, in theory, it provides for democratic control of the stock on a one worker, one vote basis. The employees contributed a total of about $8 million to buy the company, in the form of temporary wage and benefit reductions. Under the Rath ESOP, employees will own a majority of the stock within three years and in addition, the union local was given the power to name a majority of members of the Board of Directors as soon as the plan was approved. The new equity contributed by the workers enabled the company to qualify for a $4.5 million plant modernization loan from the United States government (Gunn 1981).

The company hired a new chief executive officer, but kept on most of the previous managers. The union president and several workers sit on the Board of Directors, but so far there have been few changes in traditional hierarchical management policies. Absenteeism has dropped and productivity has increased. Nevertheless, some workers are grumbling, and there has even been talk about going on strike. It remains to be seen whether workers' ownership and formal control of the Board of Directors will be turned into a truly democratic management structure at all levels, whether the workers will retain their overall stock control in the future, and indeed whether the company will even survive. Rath earned a profit in 1980, but by 1981 it was once again losing money, reflecting in part difficult market conditions that led to the closing of 10 percent of American slaughterhouses during 1980 and 1981, according to the *Wall Street Journal* (2 December 1981).

There have been several recent attempts to reopen shut-down plants specifically as workers' cooperatives. Most of them have not met with success, however. In Clinton, Massachusetts, the Colonial Cooperative Press was set up in 1978 with the help of the Boston-based Industrial Cooperative Association (ICA). The new press was established to reemploy some of the former workers at the shut-down Colonial Press Printing Company. The old press had once been the largest employer in town, providing jobs for 1,800 persons. But in

1974 it was acquired by a conglomerate and started the decline that led to its 1977 shutdown. Started with the help of three of the company's unions, the new organization employed some twenty workers for two years before it failed.

The Colonial Press and Rath Meat Packing examples are interesting because they had the cooperation of local union leaders. An obstacle to the spread of the workers' cooperatives in this country until the present has been the conservatism of the labor unions. To a large degree, trade unions in the United States form a self-interested aristocracy within the working class. Unions have garnered higher wages and better working conditions for their members but have rarely questioned the so-called prerogatives of management; rather, unions are actually a stabilizing influence that allows management to increase predictability, control, and profits. The early Knights of Labor and the Industrial Workers of the World (IWW) were exceptions; the ideology of the IWW, especially, was one of class struggle and direct action by workers to take over the workplace (Foner 1965). Little of this militance remains today in the business unionism of the United Auto Workers, Teamsters, American Federation of Teachers, and others. Even such "left" unions as the United Farm Workers have chiefly stressed bread-and-butter issues and rarely extend their demands to include workers' self-management. The challenge of plant closings, however, could make economic democracy a real issue for unions, because it is an alternative to management's laying off their members.

In Willimantic, Connecticut, when Menorah Kosher Poultry closed in 1976, some 75 persons (primarily minority women) lost their jobs. After two years of persistent effort by the Connecticut Federation for Economic Democracy group, a new processing company, International Poultry, was formed. The financial package that enabled the chicken plant to reopen was developed with the aid of the ICA. It included a $100,000 interest-free loan from the Campaign for Human Development of the Catholic Church, two $30,000 no-interest loans from the federal Community Services Administration and from interested individuals, and a $50,000 loan from the U.S. Small Business Administration. After funding was secured, International Poultry hired a new manager, and friends and prospective workers put in many hours of volunteer effort to renovate the building and install necessary equipment.

The new plant opened in 1979 with eleven workers, but the business was short-lived. By the following year, it was having difficulty staying open in the face of heavy competition. It had not been able to capture and retain any substantial share of the institutional market which would have guaranteed its success.

The Community Ownership Organizing Project in Oakland, California, tried to help its former workers take over the closed Hubbard Company, manufacturers of hardware used by electric utilities, but the banks which were owed money by Hubbard were uncooperative (COOP 1977). In Boston, the ICA tried to help reopen Kasanoff's Bakery. That effort faltered, in part because of interunion rivalries and the objections of a neighbor to bakery renovations.

The Philadelphia Association for Cooperative Enterprise (PACE), which has been doing educational work and providing technical assistance to cooperatives for several years, has recently been helping officials of the local Retail Clerks union in their bid to reopen a number of A & P supermarkets closed in 1982. After being acquired by a West German conglomerate, A & P closed 19 stores in the Philadelphia region. The President of the Retail Clerks union, Wendell Young, has been actively promoting cooperatives as a means of creating jobs for the 2,000 workers laid off with scant notice. There are still numerous business hurdles to clear, however, before any of the stores reopen under cooperative ownership and management.

English Cooperatives

For other illustrations of conversions of closing plants to workers' cooperatives, we must turn abroad. In England, several cooperatives were formed in 1975 to provide jobs for workers in companies being closed. The most notable of these is Triumph-Meriden Motorcycle Works. The workers took over the cycle factory after its parent company decided to close it down (Edelstein, chap. 9; Carnoy and Levin 1976). Almost half of the 1,750 workers occupied the plant and refused to leave. In place of closing the factory, a worker-managed cooperative was proposed. After lengthy negotiations, the Labor government extended a large loan that enabled the workers to buy the plant.

Initially, all workers at Triumph including top managers received the same pay, £50 per week. Policy decisions are made by a council of the directors, including a majority of eight elected by the workers (Carnoy and Levin 1976). Several years later, this egalitarian structure has been maintained, though pay is up to £68. Voluntary overtime and bonuses stretched this out to some £85 per week by 1979, with numerous fringe benefits. The shop-floor atmosphere is still relaxed and friendly, and job rotation, rather than strict division of labor, is the rule. The workers have compromised with their original egalitarian philosophy to the extent of hiring five nonmember professional employees at higher salaries. The new cooperative is apparently more efficient in production than the previous company. By 1978, it was the only remaining motorcycle factory in Britain (Carnoy 1979). Marketing difficulties and competition from Japanese cycles helped place the fledgling coop in financial difficulty by 1979, with the only hope of rescue, a further government loan, most likely to be denied by the Tory government.

NECESSARY INGREDIENTS FOR SUCCESSFUL CONVERSIONS

A number of elements are necessary for the successful transformation of closing firms to workers' cooperatives. These include: leadership; an adequate business plan; availability of financing; a supportive political climate; a suitable marketing strategy; and an organization to educate workers and managers for democratic management.

Leadership

Dedicated leadership is vital to accomplish the transition to a workers' cooperative and to make a success of the new firm. In the crucial time period after a plant closing is announced, organizers are needed to promote the idea of workers' ownership and democratic management, and to coordinate the many tasks that must be accomplished if there is to be a reopening of the closed facility under worker-community control. Such leadership may initially be supplied by a supporting organization along the lines used by unions to promote organizing drives, but, for the success of the project, it is vital that former workers and union officials be brought into the planning, organizational and decision-making process early, and that they take an active part in any plant reopening committee.

In the next stage, when it becomes apparent that the effort to reopen the plant may lead to success, it is important to find and train a key manager or managers who can work in a cooperative, participatory atmosphere and who have the necessary technical skills.

Business Plans

To insure the success of the proposed new firm, adequate business plans must be formulated by any committee to reopen. These include an initial feasibility study, production and marketing plans, and a financing package to enable the workers to buy out the previous owners. Some thought must also be given to the proposed internal control and management structure of the organization to maximize the probability of continuing democratic management.

The purpose of the feasibility study is to analyze whether the new organization would be able to produce and sell enough of a service or product at prices that would enable it to continue in business. Although each case will be different, efforts to reopen a plant will probably be most fruitful in situations where:

1. The industry is relatively labor intensive, to minimize total capital required.

2. The product or service is a consumer item for which there is a genuine need to maximize the possibility of political marketing and community support.

3. The organization is medium size (30-300 workers?), large enough to have an impact on the community but small enough to maximize the effectiveness of democratic management.

4. There is some government support.

If the results of the initial study are encouraging, a committee can begin to launch the new workers' cooperative. The feasibility study must be conservative to avoid taking over "lemons" that have low prospects of success under *any* form of ownership or management.

Financing

A major difficulty in converting shutdown plants to workers' ownership and management is obtaining the money to buy out the old firm. Where plant closings involve severance pay, it may be possible to use such funds to purchase the company. Also, local development corporations can be set up to apply for loans or loan guarantees from the U.S. Small Business Administration or other government agencies. At some point, we will have to recognize the plant-closing phenomenon as a political problem that affects our entire society and the industrial Northeast especially. In this light, it is entirely appropriate to use government funds to help workers in economically depressed areas to buy out plants that are threatening to move, either directly, in the form of grants or loans to community development corporations, or indirectly, in the form of federal or state loan guarantees.

Another resource that may eventually be tapped for this purpose is the billions of dollars in union and government pension funds (Rifkin and Barber 1978). Still another avenue would be opened by the establishment of community development credit unions and similar financial institutions. Money saved by the public today is used by banks to finance large corporations. These same funds could be withdrawn by middle- and lower-income depositors and placed in lending institutions that support self-managed firms. A model for such a lending institution is the Caja Laboral Popular in the Basque region of Spain, which functions like a credit union. With over 190,000 depositors, the Caja is a key element in the success of a network of 65 workers' cooperatives that has created some 18,000 jobs in twenty years (Oakeshott 1978; Johnson and Whyte, chap. 8).

Political Climate

The availability of capital to finance worker-community purchases of closing plants is partly a reflection of the prevailing political climate. In this country, the government has helped business for a long time. Lockheed received a quarter-billion dollars' worth of government aid when that corporation was going bankrupt in 1971. In 1979, Chrysler Motors sought $1.5 billion of government financial help to remain in business. The Carter administration's decision *not* to support the proposed worker-community steel plant in Youngstown was based as much on politics as economics.

Similarly, in England, a key factor in launching several workers' cooperatives in 1975 was a sympathetic Labor government willing to grant loans or loan guarantees. The election of a Tory government in 1979 means that the cooperative Triumph-Meriden factory may not be able to obtain the financial help it needs to stay in business. The lesson is that the movement for workplace democracy must be part of a wider political movement that supports the use of public resources to aid cooperatives. A political climate that supports workers' cooperatives may also help them with their marketing problems.

Marketing

The political marketing strategy proposed for community development groups by Hampden-Turner (1975, chap. 6) may also be appropriate for workers' cooperatives. Hampden-Turner suggests that Community Development Corporations sell more of their products to middle-class consumers by appealing to their political sympathies. Similar approaches could work equally well for a federation of workers' cooperatives. This might be facilitated by an educational campaign directed toward liberal consumers showing them how they can vote for a better society with their purchase dollars. Such an effort would be similar to the "buy union" campaigns of some unions such as the International Ladies' Garment Workers Union and the United Farm Workers Union. Political marketing would encourage consumers sympathetic with the objective of building a better society through workers' cooperatives to buy as much as possible from them. Such a campaign could stress the importance of buying products or services of worker-managed firms, even when they cost a little more than competing brands, to keep jobs within the local community.

Organizational Structure

In plant-closing situations, the first thought is to preserve jobs; this issue may overshadow the equally important one of enhancing the quality of those jobs by creating an organization that is not only *owned* by workers and community members, but *controlled* by them as well.

A number of simple mechanisms would ensure a democratic control of the new organizations. Instead of control based on voting proportional to the number of shares owned, workers' cooperatives are based on the principle of one worker, one vote. The legal structure of workers' cooperatives could be similar to that of traditional corporations, even to the extent of often having two classes of stock; the *voting* stock would be held only by those who work in the firm, usually on the basis of one worker, one vote (this includes managerial personnel as well). Ownership of voting stock actually serves as a form of membership and would have to be surrendered on leaving employment; workers' cooperatives cannot be "owned" by stockholders in the same sense as private corporations (Ellerman, chap. 15).

Democratic control of the firm can also be embodied in a stock trust, where all the voting stock is held by the trust, and each worker has the right to an equal vote for the trustees. With either of these mechanisms, voting stock need represent only a nominal fraction of the total equity. Nonvoting stock could be held by government agencies, unions, banks, and private investors as well as by the workers themselves. (Additional needed funds would be obtained through debt financing.)

Many other variations would be consistent with democratic control. For example, those who work in a firm might have the right to elect two-thirds of the governing board, with the other third selected by unions, municipalities or state governments. Alternatively, workers could select half of a company's Board of Directors, and consumers the other half.

Workers' cooperatives need a structure that guarantees democracy not only at the top policy levels, but also at the operational middle and lower levels of the organization. One way to accomplish this is through a two-tier structure, where the basic building blocks are service or production teams of five to twenty persons. Each team would be responsible for organizing its own work. The organization would consist of a number of teams, with "link-pin" representation from team leaders forming a managerial council. Such a council would hire and fire the top management and meet with them regularly.

The question of size is difficult: how big can an organization grow and still maintain a degree of democratic participation and control by the membership? No clear answers exist, though organizations with hundreds of members seem more manageable than those with thousands.[3] A practical limit for the two-tier structure is around 500 persons. But most workplaces don't really need thousands of workers. For example, 95 percent of all manufacturing industries in this country had a total of no more than 250 white- and blue-collar workers per plant in 1970 (Stein and Hodax 1976).

THE NEED FOR SUPPORTING ORGANIZATIONS

The presence of a supporting organization can be crucial in the development of worker-community owned and democratically managed firms. The plan to reopen Campbell Steel would not have gotten as far as it did without the help of the Mahoning Valley Ecumenical Council. If the Philadelphia A & P stores reopen as workers' cooperatives it will be partly because of effective technical help supplied by PACE. The functions of such organizations include: providing leadership in the promotion of local workers' cooperatives; education; banking; encouraging economic development of an area; providing technical services to workers' cooperatives; and coordination of the local movement for self-management as it grows.

A supporting organization can take an initiatory role, identifying businesses that are in danger of closing yet are economically viable. Once such target businesses are identified, organizers from the supporting organization could go out and talk with the workers (and their union representatives) to discuss the possibility of their buying out the firm and running it themselves.

The educational function is important partly because the idea of self-management is relatively unknown in this country. One by-product of outreach efforts may be that the word gets around that there is an organization willing to help employees convert firms to worker-community ownership and self-management, and some may come asking for such help. Also, at the beginning stages of workers' cooperatives, internal education will be very important for success. A whole new outlook is needed. It is difficult to get rid of old habits of mind, like "let the boss worry about it." These attitudes need to be replaced with a sense of responsibility, where workers feel it's their company, that they can and should have a say, and that the results of their efforts will benefit themselves.

The supporting organization, through an affiliated financial institution, can act as a bank or community holding company. Actual title to buildings and machinery can rest in the supporting organization, which then leases them to the workers' cooperatives (Cornell Self-Management Working Group 1975). The supporting organization or its bank affiliate "owns" the assets and receives interest payments. The workers' cooperative controls the use of the assets. A major portion of the surplus can be reinvested as a means of building up the budding system of self-managed enterprises and to help create additional firms. Much of the surplus can be kept in the name of individual workers as pension funds that may be withdrawn at a future date, but invested through the banking affiliate. Where there are several workers' cooperatives in a given area, a major advantage of such external financing is the diversification of investments so that the failure of one of the businesses would not necessarily destroy the pension savings of individual workers.

The accumulation of a substantial investment fund by such a supporting organization can also lead to an entrepreneurial function of actively promoting new workers' cooperatives in promising lines of endeavor to promote a balanced economic development of the community. This would obviously be allied with a research and development branch that would search out new technologies. These functions are performed in Spain by the Caja Laboral Popular on behalf of a network of 65 workers' cooperatives (Johnson and Whyte 1977; Oakeshott 1978; chap. 8).

A supporting organization could also provide for various specialized technical services affiliated with the workers' cooperatives in addition to research and development. These services would include legal and accounting services, business consulting, and trouble-shooting in the area of interpersonal relations.

Finally, a supporting organization could help coordinate the efforts of various self-managed firms in a given region, to provide linkage of the cooperatives with each other. It might help in promoting trade between self-managed firms and in advertising and marketing to the general public. It could develop a brand label for goods or services provided by democratically organized firms, similar to the union label, that would encourage sales and counteract competition. The supporting organization could, perhaps, also perform a certifying function, so that the public would be more confident that a business that calls itself a workers' cooperative is one in fact.

CONCLUSION

Workers' cooperatives formed to fight plant closings may help point the way toward the development of an entire self-managed sector of the economy coexisting with the present private and public sectors. The growth of such a third-sector network would be enhanced by increasing political consciousness and the development of a political movement in support of economic democracy, decentralization, and increasing production for local consumption.

It is difficult to assess the prospects of workers' cooperatives at this time. Properly organized, they could save many jobs where plants are closing. Such cooperatives may be given a boost by the new Consumers Cooperative Bank, which can use up to 10 percent of its funds for loans to producers' cooperatives, and by legislation to establish a loan fund especially to help reopen closed plants. Providing government loans to cooperative firms would probably be perceived by the public as preferable to adding to the welfare rolls, creating new make-work jobs, or federal takeover of the industry. A state such as Pennsylvania, that has provided over $200 million in support for the German VW firm, might do at least as much for self-help groups of its own taxpayers!

A caution: workers' cooperatives are not a panacea. Like other businesses, they need capable management, adequate capital, and good marketing strategies. Not all plant closings may be suitable for reopening under any auspices. It is sobering to remember that neither International Poultry nor Colonial Cooperative Press lasted very long. Of the three British companies reorganized as producers' cooperatives in England in 1975, two again folded by 1979, and the third, Triumph-Meriden Motorcycles, was in financial difficulty (Edelstein, chap. 9).

The idea of workers' cooperatives is relatively unknown in the United States and may be resisted because it is unfamiliar. It may encounter opposition from labor-union leadership that sees a threat to its present power, from corporations afraid of the threat of potential competition, and from workers conditioned to accept the traditional hierarchical structures. Nevertheless, with the default of private industry, conversion of closing plants to workers' cooperatives may become an increasingly attractive alternative to federally sponsored make-work programs as a means of saving and creating jobs. Workers' cooperatives can provide an antidote to unemployment, and also a means of returning to workers a sense of dignity, pride in achievement, craftsmanship, and control over their work and the fruits of their labor.

NOTES

1. Like other small businesses, small or medium-size cooperatives are more likely to create jobs than giant companies. During the 1970s, the 1,000 largest corporations in the United States generated less than 1 percent of the new jobs in the private sector (Subcommittee on Antitrust, Consumer and Employment, U.S. House of Representatives 1978).
2. To guard against this, it may be helpful to build in some form of comanagement, where publicly appointed or elected representatives vote on the firms' boards of directors.
3. The Youngstown project was probably too large. It involved several thousand workers in an industry where the capital costs per worker are relatively high. Quite aside from the issue of size as it may limit organizational democracy, the need to raise hundreds of millions of dollars may have doomed this project from the outset.

18

The Youngstown Project

Gar Alperovitz
Jeff Faux

The Lykes Corporation acquired Youngstown Sheet and Tube Company in 1969. After milking profits from its steel operations for almost a decade, the conglomerate closed down the big Campbell Steel Works, laying off 4,100 workers.

Local religious leaders organized the Ecumenical Coalition of the Mahoning Valley, which launched an impressive campaign to reopen the plant. The coalition sponsored the Alperovitz and Faux feasibility study with the National Center for Economic Alternatives (NCEA), excerpts from which are printed here.

Alperovitz and Faux suggested reopening the Campbell plant as a worker-community-owned enterprise; this plan was supported by the Ecumenical Coalition and local steelworkers. The proposal was stopped by the Carter Administration, however. The government turned down the loan guarantees requested by the coalition to help reopen the plant. It furthermore approved the merger of Lykes with another conglomerate, LTV Corporation (that had swallowed Jones and Laughlin Steel) which formed a new steel giant. One of the first actions of the new company was to close yet another of its steel plants in the Youngstown area.

— The Editors

Gar Alperovitz and *Jeff Faux* are Codirectors of the National Center for Economic Alternatives, based in Washington, D.C., with offices in Boston, Massachusetts, and Augusta, Maine. The Center is developing proposals for restructuring the United States economy over the rest of this century. Its work stresses democratic planning, balanced development, and the creation of economic conditions to support values of community and human growth. They have coauthored *Rebuilding America* (Simon and Schuster, 1981).

This study was supported by grants from the U.S. Department of Housing and Urban Development and the Community Services Administration.

INTRODUCTION

On 19 September 1977, the Youngstown Sheet and Tube Company suddenly announced its intention to close a major portion of its huge steel mill in Campbell, Ohio, and permanently lay off some 4,100 employees. The decision produced one of the largest single steel-industry shutdowns in modern United States history.

The announcement came as a severe shock to the people of the Youngstown-Campbell-Struthers area of the southern Mahoning Valley in Ohio. At least another 3,600 jobs were estimated to be lost through the secondary multiplier effect on suppliers, retail businesses, and others. The projected impact on the local public sectors was severe. The shut-down mill, for example, provided roughly 65 percent of the property-tax revenues to the city of Campbell; total tax losses were expected to be in excess of $7 million in the first three years.

Lykes is a New Orleans-based conglomerate which acquired the Youngstown Sheet and Tube Company in 1969. Local sentiment condemned Lykes for channeling Sheet and Tube's cash flow into further conglomerate acquisitions and into service of the debt incurred by Lykes in acquiring Sheet and Tube, rather than into steel-industry investment required to keep Sheet and Tube competitive.

Concerned about the effect of the steel shutdown on the community, a group of religious leaders, representing the Catholic, Protestant, Orthodox, and Jewish faiths in the area, formed the Ecumenical Coalition of the Mahoning Valley to help create a solution to the unemployment crisis. Because the problem had sprung from an alteration in the fundamental base of the Youngstown area economy, the members of the coalition understood that a positive response would require more than the social welfare approach in which many religious leaders had traditionally been involved. It would require an immediate strategy for economic redevelopment.

Moreover, it would require a strategy that went beyond the conventional approaches to redevelopment. For example, Lykes had already tried to sell the Campbell Works to other foreign and domestic steel companies, but found no takers. And the alternative of bringing in other outside industries to fill the gap left by the layoffs was, at best, a long-term prospect. In an era of economic stagnation, the intense competition between cities and states for the small number of firms seeking to expand or relocate, plus the long lead times involved, made it unlikely that diversification alone could solve the immediate problem.

Thus, it seemed that any effort to reemploy the laid-off workers in the foreseeable future would have to center on a reopened mill, but it also seemed that no existing steel company was prepared to undertake the venture. In this situation, the religious leadership of the Valley committed itself to explore a form of enterprise directly accountable and responsible to the community: worker-community ownership. The idea was first suggested by local steelworkers. It embodied concerns for jobs rather than welfare, for self-help and widespread participation rather than dependence on absentee decision-makers.

The Ecumenical Coalition sponsored a feasibility study with the National Center for Economic Alternatives. Its initial purpose was to determine the structure and feasibility of reopening the Campbell Works under some form of local community- and employee-controlled arrangement.

At the outset, it was clear to all parties that the issue in Youngstown was not simply a steel industry problem, but was also an issue of urban decay like that facing many parts of the country in an era of slower economic growth. The sudden large job losses were like a severe heart attack to the economic functioning of a city like Youngstown, but elsewhere — throughout the Northeast, the Midwest, and in other regions — smaller plant closings were a slower form of disease weakening the economic base of urban areas. The Secretary of HUD, Patricia Harris, in announcing the feasibility study contract with the center, stressed the need for new models of community involvement to solve these problems.

As is evident from the following, the general finding of the center's research team is that a reopening of the Campbell site, though difficult, is technically feasible — that is, it can result in an economically viable worker-community-owned steel company. The reopening will require some special assistance from the federal government which, we believe, is well within its present authority. On the basis of the public sector costs and benefits involved, this assistance is clearly justifiable. The fact that recent federal government actions have contributed to the difficulty of reopening the Campbell Works is an additional justification for federal help (see below). Further, there is an opportunity to transform the Campbell Works into a national showcase demonstration project which aims to develop and test new self-help, urban policy, productivity, energy conservation, and environmental protection policies. Given these larger goals, the project's significance extends far beyond the community of Youngstown; it addresses critical issues of the economy (e.g., productivity) and fundamental questions facing communities confronting plant closings throughout the nation.

PRELIMINARY FINDINGS (APRIL 1978)

On 11 April 1978, two months prior to decisions relating to the major national steel merger we shall review subsequently,[1] the National Center for Economic Alternatives issued a preliminary analysis. At that point, the study team concluded that "given certain reasonable actions on the part of the community and the Federal government, the Campbell Works can be reopened and operated as a profitable basic steel manufacturer under worker-community ownership."

The study analyzed numerous technical and financial strategies. The analysis showed that several of these strategies could result in profitable operations.

The most important of the variables tested in the analysis were:

1. Technology (separate installations of (a) a conventional Basic Oxygen Furnace (BOF), (b) an electric furnace, and (c) the so-called Super-BOF developed by Mr. Albert Calderon).

2. Markets (sales of approximately 1.4, 1.5, and 1.7 million tons per year).

3. Productivity gains from greater worker participation (assumption of no gains and gains of 1-2 percent per year for initial ten years).

4. Price of the facilities ($10 million — scrap value; and $50 million — the amount taken by the Lykes Corporation as a tax write-off).

The alternatives analyzed assumed, as a limiting case, start-up in the first quarter of 1979 with an initial hiring of 2,000 workers, an additional hiring of 1,500 workers in 1980, maintenance of existing steel industry wage-rates and fringe benefits including pensions, and — to test the worst case first — a debt-equity ratio of nine to one (with government loan guarantees).

The initial study addressed the question of reopening what was considered the closed portion of the Campbell Works; that is, the entire works — including the blast furnaces and coke ovens of the Campbell Works — less the ongoing pipe mill. The blast furnaces and the coke ovens had a limited remaining life of two to three years. However, they were crucial to the costing and provision of hot metal in the first two years of operation, prior to new steelmaking equipment being installed.

The initial financial analysis of the "base case" — roughly a simple reopening of the Campbell Works with *no* major changes in technology — showed large negative rates of return over a twenty-year period. The projections changed for the better, however, with the introduction of certain technical and marketing assumptions.

The most important finding was that, with proven technology (the electric furnace), a modest increase in sales above a conservatively estimated market share of 1.4 million tons, and a modest rise in productivity, the analysis revealed a profitable firm over the twenty-year time horizon contemplated.[2]

In the opinion of the project's consultants, the assumptions of the model and the key variables were reasonable. They also defined the challenges facing the effort. Although a private firm might seek other investments which might bring a higher return, the rates of return were deemed sufficient to warrant the investment when considered in addition to the other benefits to the community. It is also important to remember that not all of the key assumptions needed to occur to the extent assumed in the analysis in order to create a profitable enterprise; many combinations were possible. An explanation of the more important variables follows:

Technology

The electric furnace and the conventional BOF are proven and tried technologies. Estimates of the cost of producing steel under these two technologies were consistent with industry figures.

At that point (in April 1978), the center had not yet completed its technical analysis of the Super-BOF. This analysis concluded that the technology was untried, and that the high productivity claims for the Super-BOF were unproven. This left the electric furnace as the most sensible choice of technologies.

Markets

The base market of 1.4 million tons was a relatively conservative figure representing simply a continuation of the Campbell Works' historic share of the commercial market for steel in the United States.

The 1.4 million-ton market estimate included roughly 200,000 tons which, before the closing, were sold internally to other subsidiaries within the Lykes Corporation. With the closing of the Campbell Works, Lykes would have to get the steel somewhere. Since that internal market had previously been supplied from Campbell, it was reasonable to expect that it would be in Lykes's best interest to continue this practice.

In addition, NCEA did an analysis of the potential of public procurement markets which might be available to a unique worker-community-owned firm representing a model or "demonstration" strategy for the solution of similar problems faced by other urban areas in America.

Even if commercial sales of the Campbell Works were not increased, it was concluded that an additional sale of 100,000 to 300,000 tons in federal-related procurement was a reasonable goal *if,* as the statements of the secretary and undersecretary of HUD indicated, the importance of the project as a new self-help urban model were accepted. The amounts needed were estimated as 2-6 percent of federal-related purchases (and probably less), i.e., roughly 0.001 to 0.003 of overall annual United States steel sales. None of the procurement strategies required purchases at noncompetitive prices or subsidization. As indicated above, even modest additions of federal procurement significantly increased rates of return on the model.

Financing

The estimates of capital needed ranged from $525 million for the electric furnace assumption to $730 million for the Calderon Super-BOF technology. The 10 percent equity contribution, therefore, ranged from $52 million to $73 million.

The following potential sources of equity capital were identified:

Mahoning Valley Residents
employees
Mahoning Valley organizations (churches, labor unions,
    businesses, community organizations)
national church groups
Urban Development Action Grants (UDAG)
private investors outside the Valley
Lykes/LTV Corporation (through transfer of assets at
    low or zero prices)
potential suppliers of equipment.

The following were identified as potential sources of loans and loan guarantees and grants:

U.S. government loan guarantees (programs such as those administered by the Economic Development Administration, U.S. Department of Commerce)
State of Ohio loan guarantees
State of Ohio direct loans
private sector debt placement
Environmental Protection Agency grants (new control technology)
Department of Energy grants (energy conservation)
Lykes/LTV Corporation
equipment suppliers.

Raising the necessary sums of money from these sources appeared feasible, although not easy. In the center's judgment, the necessary financing package could be put together only if the Campbell Works were seen, in the eyes of the federal government, national churches, and other interested outsiders, as a *unique* project of special relevance to other communities. Hence, it would be worthy of a unique and special effort as a national showcase demonstration site.

Productivity

The assumptions of new productivity were an increase above the trend of 2 percent for the first three years, 1.5 percent for the next two years, and 1 percent for the next four years, and zero thereafter. The figures used in the model were tentative, but there is considerable evidence that the participation of employees in the ownership of a private enterprise can result in substantial productivity increases. The testing of this possibility in large-scale industry — and its significance for the overall economy in a national context of failing productivity and cost inflation — emerged as an important aspect of any demonstration effort.

From the experiences of American corporations with worker ownership and worker participation, a consistent, if not overwhelming, pattern emerges. In several parts of the country, estimates of productivity increases resulting from increased participation of workers in ownership and decision-making range to 20 percent and above (in contrast with the more modest estimates used in the study). Furthermore, experience in the steel industry itself and interviews with present and former steelworkers and management personnel at the Campbell Works and Brier Hill mills suggest the potential for productivity improvement at a reopened Campbell Works.

In the most extensive survey to date on the performance of worker-owned companies in the United States, the Institute for Social Research of the University of Michigan, in a 1977 report, concluded that thirty worker-owned companies for which performance data was available showed a *higher level* of profit than did similar conventional firms in their respective industries. In the same report, managers at ninety-eight worker-owned companies were interviewed. The managerial respondents stated that the industrial relations climate in worker-owned firms was good, and that worker ownership was having a positive effect on productivity and profits.

There are a number of remarkable performances within individual companies. For example, the worker-owned plywood cooperatives in the Pacific Northwest have consistently outperformed conventionally owned plywood companies. In a study conducted in the 1960s, worker-owned firms averaged 30 percent higher productivity than conventionally owned firms. In the South Bend Lathe Corporation, a worker-owned effort financed in part by the Economic Development Administration, productivity increases reached 25 percent in the first twelve months. The Chicago and Northwestern Transportation Company, a midwestern railroad with 14,800 employees, has been worker-owned since 1972. The company has earned profits in five out of the last six years, while two of its main competitors, the Chicago, Rock Island and Pacific Railroad, and the Chicago, Milwaukee, St. Paul, and Pacific Railroad, have filed for bankruptcy.

A number of American corporations in recent years have increased workers' participation within their factories with positive results. Comprehensive studies of these experiences have reached the conclusion that increases in worker participation generate significant improvements in productivity. A National Science Foundation-funded study in 1975 determined that positive productivity changes resulted in 80 percent of the workers' participation cases it studied.

The report of the U.S. Department of Health, Education, and Welfare, *Work in America* (HEW 1973), concluded:

> It is imperative then, that employers be made aware of the fact that *thorough* efforts to redesign work — not simply "job enrichment" or "job rotation" — have resulted in increases in productivity from five to 40 percent. In no instance of which we have evidence has a *major* effort to increase employee participation resulted in a long-term decline in productivity.

Several experiences with labor-management productivity committees in the steel industry have demonstrated the viability of worker participation. In a Kaiser Steel continuous-weld pipe mill in Fontana, California, a labor-management committee was established to prevent a shutdown of the mill. Within three months, productivity increased 32 percent and the plant was saved. At the Youngstown Metal Products Company, a metal fabricating plant in Youngstown, Ohio, a labor-management productivity committee led to productivity improvements of 5.5 percent, a decline in average delays from 10 percent to 3 percent, and a decline in absenteeism from 15 percent to 7 percent.

Most labor-management committee efforts which do not involve ownership participation, however, have failed. In part, this is because of suspicions of steelworkers, right or wrong, that management was using the committees as a way of instituting "speed-ups" and similar strategies. There is also some complaint in general that management has been uninterested in employees' suggestions. Obviously, the center is in no position to judge precisely what happened in all past efforts. But, on the basis of experience elsewhere and a number of discussions with steelworkers as well as with steel managers, it was concluded that if, because of their ownership position, the workers had confidence that management was not working against their interest, significant improvement in efficiency could be forthcoming.

REFINING THE PRELIMINARY FINDINGS
(MAY-JULY 1978)

Financing Package

After the preliminary analysis, NCEA studied alternative ways of financing the electric furnace option — roughly $525 million over an eight-year period.

Four alternative financing packages were developed, but only one of them was found to be feasible. Approximately 75 percent of the financial package in this alternative is debt, and 25 percent is a combination of direct equity, tax loss sale, and grants — a three-to-one debt-equity ratio. Under this circumstance, the investment-banking community felt that the United States guaranteed long-term bonds were marketable. They felt that once the United States loan package was committed, it would be reasonable to assume that the remainder of the funding would be obtained.

This means that, in terms of the essential costs and benefits involved, the federal government could even make an equity contribution of $75 million which earns *no cash dividends* and still earn 9 percent for the public sector on its investment because of the projected increase in tax revenues alone.

Except on rare occasions, of course, the federal government does not purchase stock in private corporations. But the analysis did underscore that the indirect federal investment reflected in the financial package falls well within the cost-benefit considerations that apply in this situation. The $20 million in UDAG grants is considerably below the $75 million equity investment that the tax revenue increases alone would justify. And, while the loan guarantees in theory may represent some indirect subsidy, they are, in any event, quite small compared with the return to the public sector.

The above analysis probably understates the benefits of a reopened Campbell Works. It focuses almost exclusively on the increased tax revenues to be gained, and does not include the costs, for example, of forced migration in search of work. Secondly, it does not include as benefits the research and demonstration testing for urban policy and industrial-productivity strategies.

Market

The study team concluded that, with a creative marketing plan, an aggressive sales force, and an improved product, plus retention of some existing captive Lykes Corporation markets currently served by Campbell Works, the retention of a 1.4 million-ton-share commercial market was a reasonable assumption.

A second market area to which the team devoted additional attention was government procurement. The preliminary report identified government or government-influenced steel purchases at about 9.2 million tons per year. The Northeast-Midwest Institute report identified ways in which a limited amount of this procurement could be directed towards a reopened Campbell Works.

Worker-community Ownership and Community Participation

Since its initial proposal by steelworkers in the Mahoning Valley, the concept of widespread ownership of the new facility by workers and members of the community has been a central feature of the Youngstown demonstration effort. It was also one of the key issues the National Center for Economic Alternatives was specifically mandated to investigate.

The NCEA found —

> some form of worker ownership was necessary to achieve the above-average productivity gains called for;
>
> some form of community ownership was essential in order to maintain local control of the steel mill;
>
> given the large amounts of federal aid contemplated, some form of public accountability was essential;
>
> widespread local investment would be maximized if the corporate structure assured that the company would operate in the public interest and in the interest of maintaining stability *in the local economy.*

Given these basic conditions, the center examined a wide variety of possible corporate structures, many of which were taken from actual worker-community enterprises in the United States.

Out of this analysis, five representative models were selected and then subjected to a number of criteria. The criteria included:

> local control
>
> ease of financing
>
> ease of implementation
>
> ability to attract management
>
> ability to retain the union's role and to encourage productivity
>
> tax advantages
>
> simplicity
>
> degree to which returns on public investment in Campbell Works could be used to further other Mahoning Valley economic development efforts.

When subjected to the criteria, one of the structures seemed, on initial analysis, to be superior to the others. For the sake of focusing analysis and getting feedback from the community, this structure was designated the "recommended model."

The recommended model was a for-profit operating corporation, with one-third of the board of directors to be selected by individual common stock shareholders, one-third by a community corporation, and one-third by an Employee Stock Ownership Plan (ESOP) representing current employees of the new corporation. The corporation was also to issue nonvoting preferred stock to be sold to outside institutions, such as national religious organizations and labor unions.

The major advantages of this structure were:

1. Control of the corporation remains in the Mahoning Valley no matter who might end up owning the common shares after resale, etc.

2. Cumbersome restrictions on resale of shares and the need for bureaucratic controls are avoided.

3. The ESOP provides tax advantages and an incentive for worker productivity.

4. Local public accountability provides a vehicle for federally assisted financing.

5. Local investments are maximized through the issuance of one class of voting common stock and one class of preferred stock.

6. The for-profit structure of the operating company is attractive to qualified management.

Although there are numerous examples of direct worker-ownership, with certain exceptions, most of these are of smaller scale than the Youngstown project. Further, although several successful worker-owned firms have been financed with federal assistance, again, none of these is of the scale or has the potential implications of the Youngstown effort. It became clear that, in situations where large-scale public investment or loan guarantees are contemplated, no simple form of worker ownership seems advisable. Rather, some form involving the lodging of accountability and benefits in a wider public or quasi-public institution appears to be essential.

On 26 and 27 July 1978, the preliminary recommendations for a worker-community ownership structure at a reopened Campbell Works were presented to representatives of the Youngstown community by NCEA consultants.

At the conclusion of the two community meetings, the set of eight criteria used for evaluation of the five structural models was approved by a consensus vote of the community representatives. The four criteria considered to be most important were: (1) maintaining local control; (2) obtaining maximum financing; (3) maintaining the role of the labor union and encouraging workers' participation; and (4) attracting qualified management.

The recommended structure for worker-community ownership was approved by a consensus vote of the community representatives, with three qualifications. The three qualifications, supported by a sizable percentage of the audience, were:

1. The role of the community corporation should be limited to something less than the recommended 33 percent equity participation. The community representatives, however, concurred that the community corporation should function as a conduit for government funds and charitable contributions directed to the operating company, should represent the community on the board of directors of the operating company, and should aid in broad-ranged economic development programs for the Mahoning Valley.

2. The selection of a board of directors for the community corporation should be made by a broad-based group of community interests, rather than solely by political representatives.

3. The role of individual investors in the operating company should be increased, while at the same time safeguarding local control with stock restrictions and high shareholder vote requirements.

The revised plan called for 40 percent of the stock to be held by an employee stock trust, 40 percent by outside investors, and 20 percent by the community corporation. Decision-making was to be by two-thirds vote.

In addition to the meetings on corporate sturcture, on 27 June 1978, a meeting was held at the union hall of Local 1418 of the United Steelworkers of America in Campbell, Ohio. The meeting was called to discuss the opportunities for increased workers' participation and high productivity at a reopened Campbell Works. Some eighty steelworkers currently or formerly employed at the Campbell Works attended the meeting.

The consensus among the steelworkers at the meeting was that productivity could be improved significantly at a reopened Campbell Works with a worker-community ownership structure. A minority of the steelworkers believed that the shut-down plant had been operated efficiently and that few gains could be expected in a reopened plant.

The steelworkers asserted that morale at the Campbell Works had been low under Lykes Corporation management; and that the highly skilled work force had not been supported adequately with machinery and tools. They also stated that suggestions for productivity improvements had often been ignored. As one worker stated, "If they had to spend money for new equipment, they wouldn't listen. They would only listen if it would eliminate a man or two."

PUBLIC EDUCATION AND THE SAVE OUR VALLEY CAMPAIGN

An important aspect of the public education process involved the launching by the Ecumenical Coalition in February of the Save Our

Valley Campaign (SOV). This created a process which, in addition to encouraging the opening of accounts, developed widespread public discussion of the goals of the study, worker ownership in general, and the larger questions of community self-help, national urban policy, and the future of Youngstown's industrial base. The Ecumenical Coalition produced a saturation TV, radio, and billboard campaign that reached almost every resident of the Mahoning Valley. Numerous interviews, articles, talk shows, and public meetings gave residents an opportunity to discuss the future of the Campbell Works, the developing plan for reopening, and the economic future of the people of the Valley. NCEA staff and consultants participated in many of these public discussions, religious convocations, and media briefings. By the end of July, the Save Our Valley Campaign, with the active participation of virtually all representatives of the local savings-and-loan and banking community, had encouraged the opening of 6,000 SOV accounts by individuals, local labor unions and churches, and national religious denominations. The total amount in these accounts as of 1 September was nearly $4 million.

The Youngstown layoffs are viewed generally as a symbol of a larger national economic sickness affecting many American communities; the powerful local religious leadership and the participatory model the Ecumenical Coalition has proposed suggests a way for church people to get involved in finding fundamental solutions to economic problems. The Ecumenical Coalition's pastoral letter, *A Religious Response to the Mahoning Valley Steel Crisis,* has become an important document in the development of a theology of social action for American churches in a time when communities and family life are threatened by industrial shutdowns and runaways and other economic crises.

IMPACT OF THE MERGER DECISION
(MAY-SEPTEMBER 1978)

The decision of Attorney General Griffin Bell on 21 June 1978 to approve the merger between Lykes and LTV corporations, and to do so without specific conditions attached to facilitate the community effort, altered the progress of the project.

Although there is still disagreement as to the full impact of the merger decision, in effect, the merger created a new steel company — Youngstown Sheet and Tube *and* Jones and Laughlin — which is now in a position to absorb markets and facilities that would have been available to a reopened Campbell Works had there been no merger. The fear of many antitrust experts that merging the seventh and eighth largest steel companies would produce another giant which could directly weaken competition was realized explicitly and directly in the effects on this project: without the merging of the two giants, the prospects for another competitive, but smaller, firm were much higher; with the merger, the prospects for retaining sufficient markets to maintain competition by a smaller firm are weakened.

Before the announcement of its intent to merge with LTV, the Lykes Corporation was willing to sell that portion of the Campbell Works which included the blast furnaces and coke ovens to any willing buyer. The prospect of the merger changed Lykes's position on this point, since the coke ovens and blast furnaces were of economic value to LTV. Had the merger been disallowed, it appears likely that Lykes would once again have been willing to sell the same facilities it was willing to part with before it began merger negotiations with LTV. Self-evidently, of course, conditions could also have been attached to the merger requiring the sale of the coke ovens and the blast furnaces to a new firm at the Campbell Works.

Lykes/LTV's present unwillingness to commit to purchase steel for internal markets takes 200,000 tons away from the base assumption of 1.4 million tons in the feasibility analysis. But, even more important, should the customer lists be not only unavailable but in the hands of a new competitor, the assumption that Campbell Works could recapture the rest of its former markets would be weakened. Clearly, the obvious locational advantages of the Campbell Works would permit recapture of some of the customers, but, without the lists, there is no way of knowing precisely what the gap is.

Lykes/LTV is also unwilling to sell the Campbell Works to a community group for either a nominal fee or for its scrap value. The corporations have indicated, however, that they may be willing to sell the idled portion of the Campbell Works at a reasonable price representing less than the market value of the facilities as a going enterprise.

CONCLUSIONS

Had there been no merger, or had the merger contained the conditions necessary to secure the Campbell Works and access to its former markets, our recommendations would have been to move the reopening to the next stage by forming a corporation, beginning to raise the money for the purchase of the plant, starting a search for the core management, and beginning work immediately on the next stage planning questions.

One option, of course, was to abandon the effort completely, to declare the reopening of the Campbell Works "unfeasible," and to accept as inevitable long-term unemployment and severe social problems in the community.

The key to the situation was obviously the role of the federal government. The actions of the government in the decision of the Attorney General caused specific damage to the prospects for reopening the mill; the Ecumenical Coalition, local steelworkers, and the political leadership of the Valley felt they had reason to ask that the federal government undo this new damage. (For instance, targeting of a relatively minor percentage of overall government-related procurement can offset even the maximum estimates of the market loss caused by the merger.)

The justification for a major demonstration project in Youngstown was *both* local and national. The justification was not the commercial and economic advantage of one community alone, but the need throughout the nation to develop new strategies to preserve jobs, increase productivity, test new technologies, and help urban communities facing economic decay. This requires a partnership of responsibility — and a joint leadership role — in the next stages of an undertaking with purposes which extend beyond the local community. The community alone can take the project no further. The government could have helped facilitate purchase of the facility. In 1978, the government had two broad options: to withdraw any further participation from the project or to move forward.

The government chose the former course. By not approving the $15 million action grant and an associated $245 million loan-guarantee package, and by allowing the merger of Lykes and LTV to form a new giant steel company, the Carter Administration killed the plan to reopen the Campbell Steel Works under worker and community ownership. The situation was aggravated by subsequent announcements of further steel-plant closings in the Youngstown area, adding to the already immense problems of unemployment there.

The role of the federal government in projects of this size is crucial. Without firm government backing, the proposed community steel company could not succeed. The administration has thus condemned Youngstown and its surrounding communities to continuing economic stagnation.

NOTES

1. On 21 June 1978, the Attorney General of the United States overruled the recommendation of the Department of Justice's Antitrust Division and personally approved a proposed merger of the Lykes Corporation and the LTV Corporation — the parent company of Jones and Laughlin Steel. In doing so, he ignored the request of the Ecumenical Coalition, the United Steelworkers of America, and the key local political leaders that, if any merger were approved, certain specified conditions be included which would facilitate the reopening of the Campbell Works. The Department of HUD had also asked that consideration be given to the request for such conditions. Because of the importance of the merger decision to the prospects for success, and because the merger approval took place at the end of our study, as the following pages indicate, a full understanding of the project requires that the question of feasibility be judged both before and after the Attorney General's act.

2. One of the major objections often raised to reopening basic steel production in the Youngstown area concerns the cost and difficulties of bringing ore and coal into the area. However, the electric furnace option — which operates largely on scrap — does not encounter this objection. The Youngstown area is in the heart of major scrap markets in the United States and has certain advantages in this respect.

19

Building Participatory Democracy within a Conventional Corporation

Rosabeth Moss Kanter
Barry A. Stein
Derick W. Brinkerhoff

INTRODUCTION

Rosabeth Kanter's *Men and Women of the Corporation* (1977) described the constraining effects on organizations which limit the opportunity and power of their workers, adding to an already long list of sociological critiques of modern industrial bureaucracies. But what, if anything, can be done? This paper looks at change potential using a case study.

We address the question of what kinds of vehicles make it possible for industrial workers to reform their own work by considering work and quality of work life (QWL) in the context of organization structure reform. We use Kanter's perspective on the critical elements

Rosabeth Moss Kanter is Professor of Sociology and Professor of Organization and Management, Yale University, and Chairman of the Board of Goodmeasure, Inc., a Cambridge, Massachusetts, organizational consulting firm. She has authored seven books, including *Men and Women of the Corporation,* winner of the 1977 C. Wright Mills Award.

Barry A. Stein is President of Goodmeasure, Inc. He is active in helping organizations understand how they can enhance both their quality of work-life and their productivity.

Derick W. Brinkerhoff is an independent management consultant. Currently, he is an Associate with Practical Concepts Inc., organizing management training seminars for public sector management. In addition, he is engaged in research on management problems related to the implementation of social service delivery projects.

Revision of a paper presented at the 74th annual Meeting of the American Sociological Association, Boston, Mass., 27–31 August 1979. Originally titled "Building Blocks for Participatory-Democracy within a Conventional, Hierarchical Corporation: First Steps in a Quality of Work Life Project in an Electronics Factory." Reprinted by permission of Goodmeasure, Inc.

in people's involvement in work, and demonstrate a systematic approach to building a new kind of organization — a parallel organization — within a traditional factory-division of labor and hierarchy. It is through the parallel organization that people have access to the opportunity and power denied to them, or at least difficult for them to obtain, in the conventional operations of the factory.

By describing a case in detail, we hope to contribute to sociological practice as well as sociological theory. We will describe the theoretical framework informing the QWL project we designed (with Barry Stein as Project Manager), the factory background and setting, the five stages of the project, the immediate results within the context of the factory, and the larger theoretical and practical significance of the *parallel organization* concept.

THEORETICAL FRAMEWORK

The approach to QWL that was adopted in this project has as its organizing principle Kanter's structural theory of organizational behavior (1977). Key aspects of this theory are:

1. Individual effectiveness in a job is, in part, a function of the structural characteristics of that position — its location in the system — as well as a result of individual abilities.

2. Behaviorally, the most relevant aspects of a position within the organization are (a) the level of opportunity, and (b) the amount of power available to someone occupying that position. Opportunity, in addition to its standard definition as "access to advancement," means challenge and the chance to grow, to increase competence and skills, and to contribute to the central goals of the organization. Power means access to resources, the capacity to mobilize them, and knowledge of the tools to accomplish tasks efficiently. (See Kanter 1977, 1979 for specific indicators of opportunity and power.)

3. People whose positions provide them with opportunity are highly motivated to perform; as a result, they tend to develop and use their skills and knowledge productively. People who are empowered are more effective performers; they tend to support and empower their subordinates, and are strongly committed to the organization and its goals.

4. Conversely, those without opportunity withdraw; they tend to devalue their skills and lower their aspirations. Those in positions of relative powerlessness become petty tyrants, resistant to change and innovation; they supervise their subordinates closely, preventing them from acquiring skills and confidence.

Based on these sociological, rather than psychological, principles, the project aimed at altering organizational structures. The focus was not on job satisfaction nor the content of tasks *per se,* but on providing workers with access to opportunity for career advancement and growth, and to decision-making power. Thus, what the project made possible, with the guidance provided by a consulting team, was a new set of *organizational* relationships. In contrast to other QWL efforts, any specific work reforms were made by the workers themselves. The parallel organization created served as the primary vehicle for changing industrial work conditions, rather than technology, job design, or labor negotiations.

BACKGROUND AND SETTING

Compu Corp. (not its real name) is a large producer of high-technology electronic equipment, with seventeen plants world-wide and well over a billion dollars in annual earnings. Although known as a fast-growth company with almost unlimited potential, Compu Corp. recently experienced changing market-conditions that necessitated some reorientation within the firm. In response to the market, Compu Corp. considered the possibility of limiting staff increases, establishing stricter guidelines for hiring and promotion, and centralizing and standardizing production procedures. Anticipating the impact of these changes, the company wanted to reexamine its management practices in general, and, as a specific starting point, to improve the administrative capacity and effectiveness of its supervisors at the production level. At this point, Compu Corp. brought in a group of outside consultants, headed by the senior author, and requested a pilot project to achieve these goals in one of the company's plants, the Chestnut Ridge factory (a non-union facility).

THE PROJECT AT COMPU CORP.

The project at the Chestnut Ridge plant proceeded through five stages: planning and orientation; gathering information and structural diagnosis; planning action; implementation; and integration and diffusion of results.

Stage 1

The overriding goal of the first stage, *planning* and *orientation,* was to generate understanding and support for the project on the part of corporate and plant management and staff. We conducted a set of individual interviews followed by several group discussions and seminars. At these latter meetings, Kanter's structural framework was presented, and its relevance to organizational effectiveness at Chestnut Ridge discussed. Consultants and seminar participants then collaboratively explored what might be done.

Some people expressed doubts about the feasibility of a project which seemed to rely excessively upon the as-yet-untested skills of those at the lower levels of the organization. These doubts were dealt with openly, and, despite discomfort over the possibility of failure, these exploratory sessions led to a decision to proceed.

In addition to providing a forum for educational discussion, we also created a Project Advisory Group composed of senior manufacturing and personnel managers in order to provide a formal base of support for the activities to be undertaken. This supplied knowledgeable counsel for decisions needed for implementation, legitimacy for participation by plant people, and high-level linkages to prevent the project from floating, unconnected to the rest of Chestnut Ridge and Compu Corp.

Stage 2

The second stage saw the gathering of *information* and *diagnosis,* with feedback to the members of the plant. To supplement what information we had already collected from informal interviews and observation, we used a formal questionnaire which measured the information, flexibility, opportunities, and problems that people had in their jobs. Three slightly different versions of the questionnaire were developed in collaboration with the advisory group and members of plant management and staff, one each for supervisors, work coordinators, and direct labor.

The questionnaire was completed by 25 percent (100) of those in direct labor, 66 percent (15) of work coordinators, and 66 percent (28) of supervisors. Data analysis took place in several stages, but we made preliminary results available quickly to everyone who had participated in any way. Findings were presented through short memos distributed to employees and through voluntary discussion sessions.

The provision of written and oral feedback was an important step in convincing people in the plant that the project represented something potentially useful. Based on past experience, many employees were quite skeptical that any kind of follow-through would succeed the initial enthusiasm.

Stage 3

At the start of the third stage, we devised in-plant structures to translate Kanter's theory, the questionnaire information, and the experience of the project participants into *action*. These structures consisted of: (1) a project steering committee representing product management, production supervisors, employee relations, and members of the outside consulting group; and (2) three pilot groups of supervisors representing three different product lines. These structures bypassed, but paralleled, the internal hierarchy of the plant. The strategy here was to create a setting for experimental action that was loose enough to allow for flexibility and some trial-and-error, yet similar enough to the existing organization so that the lessons learned there could easily be seen as relevant to the larger setting.

The steering committee was intended to gradually take over responsibility for managing the project, thereby decreasing the need for external consultation. Its members were drawn from a diagonal slice through the plant, cutting across vertical hierarchies and horizontal functional areas. For the pilot groups, the committee chose the most interested people from among the plant's eight production units.

Following the guidelines of the Chestnut Ridge Research and Development (R&D) Committee, which had budgetary authority for any in-plant experimental programs, each of the three pilot groups set about drawing up a proposal and plan for an action project relevant to its particular business unit. The groups successfully presented their proposed projects directly to the R&D Committee for approval.

Stage 4

In the fourth stage, the pilot groups began *implementation* of their projects. The groups' own initiative and commitment shaped the implementation process; they were free to make the key decisions about how to organize themselves, to involve direct labor, and to maintain current production levels. Pilot group members developed specific plans and objectives, educated themselves about the topic of their particular projects, gathered more information about Chestnut Ridge relevant to their projects, explored the resources available at Compu Corp., and coordinated with each other and the steering committee as they sought to follow through on their proposals.

Pilot group 1 tackled the redesign of jobs on one of the few assembly lines in the plant. This was particularly important because that unit was intended to serve as a model for changes expected to follow within Chestnut Ridge. However, in the course of gathering data on themselves and their group, the members of pilot group 1 had come to recognize that there was considerable dissatisfaction with work on the assembly line, and a related recognition that it was not particularly efficient. In discussion, people also decided that something could be done to improve both situations.

Pilot group 2 elected to work on career-planning development. Two related issues were, they felt, particularly important: (1) the need for a more systematic and effective entry process for new members of a production group (whether they were internal transfers or new hires), and (2) the need to help people understand the career options open to them, with access to appropriate counseling. The issue of entry was recognized during the earlier diagnostic phase as particularly critical, since the data and discussion showed that people needed much too long to learn how to "work the system," and that, given the turnover in the production groups (and the plant in general), learning had to be faster. But this was also clearly linked to inadequate knowledge of opportunity and careers overall, both for direct labor and supervisory personnel.

Pilot group 3 worked on the resolution of procedural inconsistencies among the eight production units at Chestnut Ridge. They recognized, in the course of their discussions about the data, that there was only nominal consistency in coordination and communication among the production units (which were independent as to tasks, but were dependent on a common support system and the movement of people among them). To attack this problem, the members of the group even developed a questionnaire for people in other production units, subsequently carrying out a series of interviews. (They ultimately suggested holding a forum for all supervisors in the plant, something that had never happened.)

Pilot group 3 investigated a second kind of inconsistency, namely, differences in the training of supervisors and its timing. This turned out to be an issue of access to training that would be relevant to supervisors as they were learning their job. In particular, people were concerned that the programs available at Compu Corp., though of high quality, were not always designed to teach them what they felt they needed, nor were the programs necessarily available when that help was needed. Accordingly, pilot groups developed information on a more appropriate set of training courses and their arrangement. This group also worked closely with members of the personnel and training staff, who were, of course, responsible for designing and carrying out such programs.

Stage 5

In the fifth stage, the two processes of *integration* and *diffusion of results* emerged as the central activities. The steering committee undertook presentations to others at Chestnut Ridge to inform them of project activities. Project participation was incorporated into new job descriptions and was made an integral part of participants' performance evaluations. The products of the three pilot groups were applied to the problems for which they were designed.

In addition, the parallel structure embodied in the steering committee and the pilot groups was made a permanent part of the Chestnut Ridge factory. A plant charter states that the committee represents "an opportunity for people of all levels within Chestnut Ridge to participate in the experimentation of managing change. Also a forum in which ideas toward improving processes are developed." Thus, the parallel organization continues as an ongoing mechanism to solve problems beyond those originally identified by this particular project.

IMMEDIATE RESULTS

The obvious results from the project are the products that emerged from the efforts of the three pilot groups:

1. A set of strategies to increase job effectiveness on the assembly line through the use of flexible teams, and to increase product quality by reducing defect rates.

2. A career counseling and development package made up of modules that can be combined in a variety of ways to suit the needs of various users. These modules include performance-appraisal training for supervisors, new-hire orientation, career path planning, and employee development.

3. A report on production group procedural inconsistencies that impede work coordination, and suggestions and options for action. Based in part on this report, management, with collaboration by supervisors and direct labor, developed options for reorganization of production operations.

4. A procedure for evaluating and modifying supervisory training. The information generated by this project has been used as a resource in the design of better programs for the development of supervisors.

Besides these specific products, there is another set of results from the project that has not only had an immediate impact, but also has the potential for more far-reaching effects. This set contains the results of project involvement for the participants. Chestnut Ridge management and labor identified the following outcomes: improved managerial capacity, increase in planning skills, less concern for own job and more for Chestnut Ridge and Compu Corp. as a whole, increased motivation on the job, decrease in stereotypic views of both labor and management personnel, better use of plant resources, and others.

In short, people in the factory who participated in the project gained important new skills, became more productive, and, in the process, were more satisfied with their jobs. As one participant said, "My own personal involvement with this project has helped me a lot in developing the skills I need as a supervisor...I wish more supervisors could be given the opportunity to work on the same type of project." These participants were not atypical employees; statistical tests on background data for participants and nonparticipants showed no significant differences. The parallel structure instituted by the project provided a mechanism for the Chestnut Ridge factory to tap the potential contained within its human resources.

THE THEORETICAL AND PRACTICAL SIGNIFICANCE OF PARALLEL STRUCTURES

The project's immediate results are, in a sense, less significant than the new parallel structure the project brought into being. The function of the immediate results was not to serve as scientific evidence in the sense of proving that the intervention generated positive change; indeed, we cannot offer any such proof, partly because of the dynamic nature of the oganization in which the project took place. Seeking a verdict of success based on immediate outcomes diverts attention from a major problem facing work-reform projects: ensuring lasting results. The whole point of QWL efforts should be to create ongoing parallel organizations with the capacity to solve continuing series of new problems and to provide a steady stream of new opportunities, rather than to carry out "one-shot" reforms whose concrete results can be measured in the short term, but whose impact on the organization is purely transient.

Instead, the true function of the immediate results just outlined was to give company decision-makers enough evidence of the merit and potential of the parallel organization to justify institutionalizing and extending it as a formal structure in the plant. The *real* result of the project, then, was to create a parallel operating structure, and to show that it could function side by side with the existing mechanistic, bureaucratic, hierarchical factory structure. The parallel structure can provide an alternative vehicle for generating and more broadly distributing opportunity and power. (See fig. 19.1 for a contrast between these two forms.)

The concept of a parallel organization has been used occasionally and casually by those engaged in promoting quality of work life. It has not been used, however, systematically nor with a true understanding of its significance for either QWL practice or organization theory. The specific elements of our project were not unique in and of themselves; most would be endorsed by a variety of organizational theorists and change schools, such as the socio-technical systems analysts. The unique contribution and sociological significance of the project reported here is the conceptualization surrounding it. This conceptualization, we feel, makes clear just what can make democratic reform effective.

The opportunity-power framework shows the importance of certain ways people are involved in an organization, namely, their location in career and resource-distribution structures. And the parallel organization emerges as the vehicle for creating new ways of grouping people flexibly, providing challenge and learning possibilities, and opening access to resources, support, and recognition. It cuts across the hierarchy and existing functional distinctions. It is the *creation* of a parallel structure that constitutes the central reform and the major change. It is not the immediate results of the parallel organization's members' efforts that are most significant, though they do represent useful changes in specific areas — e.g., the team assembly or new communication vehicles or more open career access methods that are often equated with work reform. It is, rather, the existence of the parallel structure. QWL experience is often described in terms of new technology and team assembly, but those are just two specific manifestations of a variety of organizational, structural changes that involved decentralization and creation of parallel problem-solving and decision-making vehicles (Gyllenhammar 1977; Kanter and Stein 1979).

The parallel-organization concept also suggests some revisions in organization theory. Our experience with the creation of a parallel organization shows that it may be possible for a *mechanistic* and an

FIG. 19.1 Contrast between conventional line hierarchy and participatory-democratic parallel organization

CEG
—HIJ advise

ABDF   ABCCE   BCDDA

PARALLEL ORGANIZATION

- problem solving — high uncertainty
- focused primarily on "organization"
- expandable "opportunities" (e.g., appointment to a task force)
- flexible, rotational job-assignments
- developmental assignments
- short chain-of-command
- objectives top-down also bottom-up
- rewards: learning
  recognition
  contribution
  bonus
- diagonal slices—mixed functions
- leadership develops anywhere

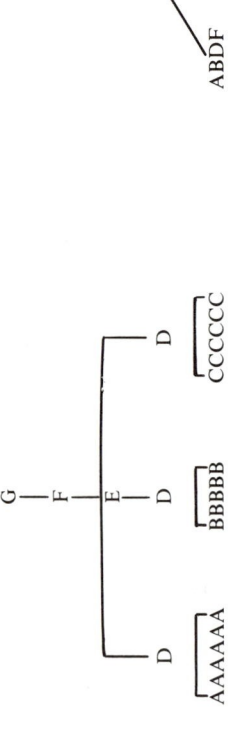

G
F
E
D   D   D
AAAAAA   BBBBB   CCCCC

CONVENTIONAL LINE ORGANIZATION

- routine operation — low uncertainty
- focused primarily on "production"
- limited "opportunities" (e.g., promotion)
- fixed job-assignments
- competency established before assignment
- long chain-of-command
- objectives usually top-down
- rewards: pay, benefits

- functionally specialized
- leadership correlates with level

organic organization to exist side by side, carrying out different but complementary tasks. These two organization types are not opposites, then, but are different vehicles for involving people in tasks and in the organization.

The mechanistic organization is the operating hierarchy defining job titles, pay grades, one set of reporting relationships, and one set of formal tasks. In the mechanistic organization, opportunity has a tendency to be limited to formal promotion paths, and power a tendency to be limited to the contacts and resources inherent in a specifically defined job. The main function of the mechanistic organization is the maintenance of production and the system that supports it — that is, the continuing routinization of useful procedures.

The organic organization, on the other hand, is embodied in the parallel structure. Here, people are grouped in a number of different ways, each appropriate to the problem-solving tasks at hand, with contact across the hierarchy. A different set of decision-making channels and reporting relationships is in operation, and the whole organization is flexible and flat. In the parallel, more organic structure, opportunity and power can be expanded far beyond their zero-sum limits in the old, mechanistic organization. The main function of the parallel organization is to provide for continued reexamination of routine, exploration of new options, and development of new tools, procedures, and approaches — that is, the institutionalization of change.

This idea is not really encompassed by any of the current thinking about organization structure. It suggests the potential for people to be simultaneously involved in a work organization in two different ways and through two different *equally formal* structures. This is not a matrix (which primarily deals with reporting relationships and expands the mechanistic structures without modifying their properties), although it shares the notion of multiple vehicles of authority and accountability. This is not an example of project organization, since it also involves a bureaucratic form for continual self-extension and self-modification, although it shares the notion of temporary task teams. And this is not an informal organization, since it is official, acknowledged, and possessed of its own management structure with linkages to the rest of the organization.

The parallel organizational form may be a significant answer to the problem of how to reform industrial and other organizational work. The workers, including managers and professionals, do it themselves through their participation in the parallel organization.

The lessons of the organic organization are thus brought back to the mechanistic organization, but without replacing it. *Both* come to function side by side. The issue is not, then, how to change entrenched hierarchical bureaucracies; that problem has proven to be so recalcitrant as to appear nearly impossible to solve as stated (Berg et al. 1978). But, through the creation of parallel structures, *alternatives* to bureaucracy can be fashioned alongside it. That is the point. A second formal structure that is oriented to quality of work life can be erected not on the ruins of the first, but on its living capacity to do what it does best, with its mission and tasks gradually becoming appropriate to its form.

This notion has the potential to influence both organization theory and change efforts in organizations.

20

The Labor Movement and Worker Management

C. George Benello

In assessing the possibilities for self-management in the United States, it is necessary to understand the role of organized labor within the capitalist system; it is difficult to see how self-management could develop significantly without at least the acquiescence, if not the positive support, of organized labor. Organized labor today is very much a product of its historical origins so that it is impossible to understand the constraints within which it operates without understanding something of its history. American labor has been shaped by its immigrant origins and by the possibilities of both industrial and geographic expansion. During its formative period, the American society was never forced to face the effects of its own dedication to nonplanning and pell-mell industrialization; there was always an open frontier to the west, with land to spare. Those who found the rapidly industrializing East too constricting for their ambitions could always journey westward.

Moreover, the ethnic variety of the immigrant groups was a factor which further impeded the development of worker solidarity and class consciousness, and was indeed used to maintain the divisions within the working class (Aronowitz 1974). Organized labor, divided from the start, has never been able to do more than try to keep pace with the growth of capitalism in a society able to industrialize with few of the traditional restraints derived from older institutions. The technological and organizational transformations attendant on capitalist development have created further divisions within labor. As blue-collar workers became organized into labor congresses — a

C. George Benello is Coordinator for the Five College Project on Economic Participation and Self-Management. He is an Adjunct Professor, School of Social Science, Hampshire College. He is also a Board Member of the Industrial Cooperative Association, and does consulting work on self-management.

phenomenon which itself is only twenty-five years old — the demand has shifted to white-collar workers, who were, until recently, unorganized. The increasing Taylorization of work has created severe status differences between skilled and unskilled labor, blue collar and white collar, so that these groups have never developed overall solidarity (Braverman 1974; Stone 1975). White-collar workers have resisted being organized into blue-collar unions. Added to this are the divisions resulting from racial as well as ethnic differences. As a result, the organized sector of American labor, approximately 23-28 percent, depending on whether one includes the teachers' unions, is significantly smaller than its European counterparts.

Since the thirties, organized labor has formed an increasing part of the national consensus. In the early part of this century, in contrast, American labor possessed a radicalism which, for reasons which will become evident, has disappeared. It sought to implement workers' control, setting up producers' cooperatives in the early 1900s and proposing a plan to take over failing railways through a national corporation which would be run by the workers, shortly after World War I. However, in addition to the strength of the mythology of the "land of opportunity," backed by continuing industrial growth and the access of the worker to middle-class status, two important causes can be listed for the siphoning off of labor militancy into economistic demands, and the consequent integration of the labor movement into the corporate capitalist system.

The first cause historically, and the most important, was the successful channeling of labor militancy into acceptable and legally defined forms of conflict which agreed to the basic rules of the capitalist game (Domhoff 1971, chap. 6). The legislation of the 1930s, including the Wagner Act, the National Labor Relations Board, and Social Security, was, as Domhoff (1971) has shown in an important study, the product of initiatives taken by the liberal wing of the ruling class, often in the face of strong labor opposition. This legislation essentially involved a bargain which Samuel Gompers, then the leader of the American Federation of Labor (AFL), accepted. The bargain amounted to an agreement that, in return for labor's right to organize and obtain government recognition, it would restrict its activity to economistic demands and foreswear overtly political activity and attempts to challenge the capitalist system.

In 1900, the National Civic Federation (NCF) was formed, containing members from a third of the 300 largest corporations in the country, as well as some of the AFL leadership. It developed social legislation, preempting the field from the labor unions, and served as mediator in labor disputes. In similar fashion, the American Association for Labor Legislation (AALL), a group whose leadership overlapped to a large extent that of the NCF, had a major hand in obtaining legislation in the areas of industrial health, safety, health insurance, and unemployment insurance. An organization also dominated by members of the upper classes, it was largely successful in foisting on labor, despite its opposition, legislation which, while benefiting labor, also assured its further integration into the capitalist system. Even Gompers eventually resigned from the AALL.

The conventional historical approach has always been that the social legislation which benefited labor has been proof of pluralism in the United States, since it indicates a victory of the forces of labor over big business. This argument could be made because the conservative business groups represented best by the National Association of Manufacturers (NAM) did, in fact, oppose such legislation. But so did organized labor; it was the liberal wing of the ruling class which was farsighted enough to grasp the possibility that organized labor could be integrated into the capitalist system, and that, when it was, it could be a vehicle for the social control and discipline of the workers, while at the same time strengthening the ideology of pluralism.

Perhaps the best evidence of the passive or oppositional role of labor in social legislation affecting it is the Wagner Act (Domhoff 1971, chap. 6). Often called "labor's bill of rights" because it guarantees the right of collective bargaining and sets up government mediating mechanisms, it was passed at a time when organized labor was at almost an all-time low. From a union strength of 12 percent of the labor force in 1920, it declined to 6 percent in 1933. The Wagner Act was passed in 1935. It was passed because, while the Great Depression had weakened organized labor drastically, labor militancy had risen, and there was fear that it would take radical political expression. The need was seen to strengthen organized labor, to assure that no organized movement would develop. With the help of the leadership of organized labor and the liberal wing of big business, the Wagner Act was finally passed, after a long fight with the conservative NAM wing of big business. This, too, has been mistaken as a conflict between labor and business; instead, it is the product of a phenomenon which has often been experienced on the American scene: the successful siphoning off of radical protest into reformist channels. Management's current, though half-hearted, attempts to siphon off the discontent of the rank and file through job enrichment programs and other gimmicks is simply the latest in a long line of successful efforts to bypass organized labor. If the efforts are weak, it is because the leadership of organized labor has by now thoroughly made its peace with the system.

The second factor that served to guarantee a nonradical and economistically oriented labor movement was the role of Communism in the movement. The depression of the thirties gave rise to the hope that the capitalist system was at last experiencing its predicted downfall, and Communism took hold within the labor movement. With the success of the New Deal and, above all, of World War II in bailing out the capitalist system, the Communists, by now entrenched in the labor leadership, maintained their belief in the eventual collapse of the system but simply postponed the date. Paralleling to a marked degree the behavior of the *Conféderation Général du Travail (CGT)** in the May Days of 1968 in France, they foreswore radical tactics and, instead, concentrated on building union strength within the context of the accepted ideology of collective bargaining. Moreover, in line with the policy of Popular Frontism, they aligned themselves with the Democratic Party in the effort to become respectable, while continuing to work for positions of power within the unions. With the development of the Cold War and McCarthyism, and also as a result of the Smith Act, the unions successfully purged themselves of Communist elements. As proof of their newly won status as junior members of the power elite, union leaders outdid big business in espousing Cold War ideology; the AFL-CIO cooperated actively with the Central Intelligence Agency (CIA) in helping to assure that the Latin-American labor movement would not become infected with left-wing ideologies.

What had happened was that the ruling groups within government and big business made it clear that the condition for continuing to enjoy the benefits of acceptance and protection through collective bargaining, and for continuing to be a junior partner of the power elite was the renunciation, once and for all, of alien ideologies. Labor must accept the official definitions which equated freedom with the free enterprise system. It was all right to struggle for higher wages and for protective legislation — after all, business also seeks its own protective legislation and higher profits — so long as one accepted the basic rules of the free-enterprise game. Ideological struggle was not permissible, even if the form it took was hardly revolutionary. This further clarification of what was required of organized labor in order

*The *CGT* is the Communist Party-affiliated French labor union — *Eds.*

to maintain its status as one of the organized groups within the ruling circles completed the assimilation and integration of labor into the American consensus. By the time it happened, the leadership of organized labor had already enjoyed status as members of government commissions, and in many cases, were friends with members of the ruling class. Big labor had the experience of working closely with big business, and had found it was possible to establish a modus vivendi.

The result of this continuous and forced process of integration of organized labor into the role of junior member within the capitalist system has been to fatally narrow its scope, and in the process, render it vulnerable to the demands of its own rank and file. It could not question the authority of management to control the workplace, or to determine the goals of production and profit levels. Hence, management was able to pass on wage raises to the consumer, often with a handsome increment of profit thrown in. For every dollar of wage increase the United Auto Workers (UAW) wrung out of General Motors, GM was able to raise the price by three-and-a-half dollars (Bell 1973, p. 127). The result has been that the leadership of organized labor has been unable to meet the growing demands of the rank and file for improved conditions of work. And, with respect to the 75 percent of those outside the ranks of organized labor, it has become more and more an exclusionary interest-group, dividing the interests of those within from those outside its doors. The spate of wildcat strikes, work stoppages, and so on, and, more recently, the organization of black and women's caucuses are proof of the decreasing capacity of the leaders of organized labor to maintain their control of the rank and file while continuing to follow the demands imposed on them as "responsible" members within the American consensus (e.g., Brecher 1972).

If a movement for self-determination and freedom in work arises, it will have to arise outside the institutions of organized labor. For, behind the rigidity and autocracy of the AFL-CIO leadership, there are the power-political facts of life which that leadership understands far better than do the young dissidents within the rank and file. The history of American labor is a living illustration of the power of the capitalist system to both accommodate and integrate dissent into its own social and political definitions of reality. Organized labor is now, at a time when hundreds of thousands of workers are losing their jobs, finding itself unable to safeguard those jobs and unable to make its demands keep pace with the rising cost of living for those who remain at work. It is hardly a time for labor to extend its demands; moreover, since the recession, labor insurgency has gone down in the face of threatened jobs. Beyond a very few and unsuccessful attempts, such as the UAW's attempt to develop community unions of the unemployed in the sixties, organized labor has mostly been interested in protectionist policies which furthered the capitalist aim of maintaining a continuing pool of the unemployed to discipline the working force.

But the American corporate system is itself in trouble. Having lost its monopolistic position in the work economy, and faced with increasingly organized cliques controlling vital resources that are in short demand, it can no longer be the guarantor of the American Dream. The degeneration and delegitimation which is manifesting itself at the base of the society does not take a glaring or startling form. Yet, each year, the statistics of social pathology grow, and, with this growth, alienation and unrest increase. For those able to find work, the dichotomy between expectations and the realities of increasingly depersonalized work in large organizations grows. During the period of World War II affluence, with a new generation of workers who had not experienced the Great Depression, there developed a search for something more meaningful than the rate race. But the system is unable to provide anything beyond subsistence-level living and unemployment or subemployement for an increasing number, somewhere between 25 and 50 percent of the population, depending on where the poverty line is drawn. Here expectations enter in as well: if work cannot be intrinsically rewarding, at least it must be capable of buying the standard consumer package which represents membership in the middle class — a car, appliances, TV, a house in the suburbs.

At present, the United States is suffering from the competition of organized and disciplined work forces abroad working for lower wages — the example of Japan immediately comes to mind — and the pressure to exact more productivity out of the worker is great. This was the cause of the famous Lordstown strike: the speed-up of the assembly line in order to build compact cars that could compete with the European and Japanese imports. Since the profit margin on compacts is smaller than that on the inflated, full-size cars Detroit was wont to produce, the attempt was to restore the profit margin by a rationalization of the assembly line that exceeded anything so far attempted. But the attempt backfired and led to the most explicit demands for humanized working conditions that had yet been heard.

Moreover, the workers were young, and, despite the hot denials of the UAW leadership that there is any difference between younger and older workers, it is among the young workers that the work stoppages, the wildcat strikes, the contract refusals are predominantly found. The new values of the youth culture have united students and blue-collar workers, and, in both cases, the success ethic, with its demand for drudgery and deferred gratification, is being questioned.

Lordstown is also an example of the community of union-management interests. The union leadership recognized the need to tread a delicate line between the pressures generated by the rank and file and its basic desire to translate the demands of the Lordstown workers into manageable economistic terms of wage demands that could successfully be negotiated. The GM management maintained secret communication with union leaders throughout the strike, and lent the UAW $30 million to help meet the UAW strike insurance expenses (Herman 1975). This underlines the extent to which the union movement has become a functional part of the overall system, needed to maintain discipline among the work force. In many cases, strikes have originated from issues which involved work floor control or the lack of it. But the union leadership, having accepted the manager's right to manage, have continuously and, for the most part, successfully translated demands that involved issues of control into economistic demands for higher wages.

At present, the capacity of the unions to continue to raise wages is significantly reduced. The United States suffers from a growing trade deficit (the weakening of the dollar abroad which seems so far unable to reduce the deficit) and a continuing inflation at home. The inflation bears most heavily on four necessities — energy, food, housing, and health care. These, because they are necessities, affect all workers. Foreign competition continues, despite the deflation of the dollar, and the effect of this is to maintain a steady and high level of unemployment. Although there is evidence that the automation of jobs is slowing down, or at least not rising, since, in the period of present business stagnation, companies cannot afford the capital costs of automation, the growth of conglomerates and multinationals has caused many jobs to move overseas or into areas of unorganized labor in this country, largely the South. As suggested, unions are powerless to affect this trend.

The loss of jobs to other areas provides an opportunity for the development of worker management which may just possibly affect the attitude of unions toward it. An example is the textile workers' unions in the Northeast. For several decades, textile mills have been moving south to areas of lower labor cost. The garment industry, in particular, has also suffered from foreign cheap imports, and the result has been the devastation of towns like Fall River, Massachusetts, which have become poverty areas. Recently, while working with the Federation for Economic Democracy, we approached the local of the International Ladies' Garment Workers Union (ILGWU) in connection with the possible reopening of a mill in a small, northern New York town. Local officials were, at best, lukewarm to the idea of opening the mill as a worker cooperative. However, when we approached officials at the state level, they both indicated interest and offered help. At this level of the union hierarchy, there was a recognition of the breadth and seriousness of the problem, and officials at this level were not threatened as they were at the local level.

There is evidence from the work that has gone on both through the Federation for Economic Democracy and in the decentralized local groups that followed from it that the chief problem, at least in the initial stages of developing worker-managed enterprises, rests with local union officials. Experience with attempts to reopen a shut-down bakery indicated that local business agents saw their jobs threatened by the possibility of a workers' cooperative; they realized all too quickly that, if the workers could obtain direct control over the surplus — what is traditionally defined as the profits of the enterprise — they would have no need of business agents to bargain for them.[1] We countered this by pointing out that the union could serve other functions, to be discussed below, and, in the case of the bakery, which had a total of three unions, the response from two of the unions ended up being positive, while the third remained strongly intransigent. We later learned that this particular business agent was out of favor with his own union leadership, which was rather hoping that we would find ways of getting rid of him.

The existence of three unions points to another serious defect of the present union structure in dealing with the issues of worker management and worker control. To discuss it, it is necessary to be clear what we are talking about. The efforts of the Federation for Economic Democracy and of the local groups associated with it have been based on the assumption that efforts to implement worker management would have to proceed outside of the context of the labor movement, and, only when it could be proved that jobs could be saved and that worker cooperatives were viable economically, would it be possible to interest the labor leadership in the work involved, and contacts have been, for the most part, on the local level. This brings up the distinction between *worker management* and *worker control*. Proposals for worker control have been developed by writers such as G.D.H. Cole, Anton Panekoek, and Antonio Gramsci in the last century and in the early part of this. More recently Andre Gorz has urged workers to develop a strategy of encroaching control.

However, none of these writers saw labor unions as the originators of such a movement, feeling that, even in the case of the European labor movement, the unions were too hierarchical and bureaucratic to react in any way but negatively to the idea of worker control (Gorz 1967; chap. 21). *Worker control* in this context has been understood to mean direct efforts by workers to organize councils and assemblies in the workplace in order to carry on struggles for control over the conditions of work. Such struggles have taken place in several European countries, notably in the north of Italy, but have never reached the point where the actual control and ownership of an enterprise fell into the hands of the workers, although the possibility existed briefly at the Fiat automobile plant in Turin, and workers did succeed in operating the LIP watch factory for a period in France.

Worker management, although it is a broad term covering all aspects of the operation of an enterprise controlled and owned by workers, has come to refer, in practice, to those enterprises, notably in Yugoslavia, but existing also in Great Britain, Spain, and elsewhere in Europe, which are totally controlled by workers. These enterprises have, in almost all cases, developed either as the result of government policy, as in the case of Yugoslavia, or as the result of a start-up or changeover to a system of worker management where outside ownership either did not exist or voluntarily gave over control to the workers. Hence, whatever the strategic implications, the fact remains that the existing examples of worker-managed enterprises have not arisen out of workers' struggles for control, but rather as a result of conscious decisions on the part of either governments, entrepreneurs, or founders to develop such enterprises. This suggests the truth of the organizational axiom, expressed by Kenneth Boulding amongst others, that it is a lot easier to start a new organization from scratch than it is to try to radically alter the structure of an existing organization.

In the United States, the strategy has been to attempt to develop worker-managed enterprises largely out of plant shut-downs, since the work force was in place, and the workers obviously wished to continue working. In a number of cases, it was evident that the plant had failed to show a profit because of serious mismanagement. A contributory factor was the fact that, in the case of conglomerate or multinational ownership, a portion of the expenses of the head office was charged as a cost of the plant, and this cost, in one case amounting to millions, was clearly the difference between a net profit and a net loss. In these cases, workers, who often have ways of finding out the true state of financial affairs in the company, felt strongly that, if they were given a chance to run the plant, they could do better than the previous management. In the case of the internal operation of the plant, this was probably true. But what the workers lacked was expertise in financing and sales, for the external side of production is almost always relegated to the domain of management.

To return to the subject of organized labor, the case of the bakery illustrates a problem that those who attempt to create worker management will continue to encounter when dealing with organized labor. The bakery had two bakers' unions within the plant, involved in a jurisdictional dispute; the two unions were significantly divided along color lines, with one union being mainly black and the other white. A third union had jurisdiction over the one hundred or so trucks which delivered the bread. While this case may be extreme for a relatively small operation of some two hundred workers, the structure of organized labor in the United States is such that, in the case of large plants, several unions are represented, often with different contracts and different pay scales. Moreover, pay is determined by seniority, and the prospect of any equalization of the pay scale or the introduction of other criteria for income is resisted.

In short, unions are structured to represent workers' interest, or some of them, within the capitalist system. The organization of unions along trade lines (and, in Europe, along party and religious lines), the exclusive focus on economistic issues, and the acceptance of managerial definitions of the scope and nature of the job and the reward scale are contrary to the demands for worker organization under self-management (Gorz 1973; chap. 21; Pannekoek 1975). Unions could serve in several important roles under a system of self-management, but, to do so, they would have to be organized so as to represent a single enterprise as a whole, and, while some of their present functions would become irrelevant, other functions would have to be extended and still other new functions developed. At the present time, with the prospect of continued stagflation and continued unemployment, there are incentives for unions to encourage job creation and counteract plant shutdowns by at least accepting the idea of worker-management, even if they do not take an active role in bringing it about. But, for this to happen, it is necessary for the advocates of worker management to answer the question posed by one high UAW official, who accepted the idea that worker management could save jobs but wanted to know the role his union could play.

It is possible to envisage the role of unions vis-a-vis a movement for worker management in terms of a number of stages. Only the initial stages are based on experience at this point, but, in view of the history of organized labor in this country, the experience so far seems to lead to cautious optimism. Because the core of union demands at the local level centers around wages, those unions that we have dealt with have insisted that, whether the enterprise became worker managed or not, the existing wage levels must be kept. This creates a number of problems for a worker-managed enterprise: In the first place, who is the wage contract to be made with? Secondly, the requirement that the existing wage contract be maintained means that the enterprise loses the opportunity to lower the income level in the event that business is bad and the earnings are insufficient to pay income to the workers at the contract level. The workers may well wish to continue without resorting to the conventional solution of layoffs. For, in a worker-managed enterprise, the concept of wages no longer applies; as owners, the workers earn income, and should be free to set the level for themselves, either lower or higher than their previous wage level.

However, it is important to realize that, if the basis of the union contract is eliminated as the very first step in the transition to worker management, it is unlikely that the union will continue to support the project. At the same time, it is a general practice of worker-managed enterprises to choose to lower overall income in the case of a business downturn rather than to lay off working members, who, after all, have a share in the business. The solution allows the union to maintain the centrality of the wage contract, while, at the same time, it allows the workers to reduce income in the event that earnings dip. A wage contract is made out and a wage level set, according to the union's wishes. It is a contract between the union representatives and the board of the enterprise, elected by the workers. The enterprise is so structured that individual worker accounts are set up, representing the worker earnings at decided-upon income levels to reflect differences in skill level, seniority, work time, and so on. (The decision on income differentials is a separate problem which also must be worked out.)

The accounts, in the case of surplus earnings beyond those needed to meet the decided-upon income level, operating expenses, and a portion set aside for reinvestment and growth, will receive, at the worker's option, a portion of that surplus — a dividend on their work, so to speak. In the event that earnings are insufficient to pay the worker's income at the agreed-upon wage level, the difference between what is actually paid out and what is agreed upon simply becomes a debt to the accounts, to be paid later, when earnings warrant it. Since there is some flexibility in determining costs to the enterprise, and it is the workers who determine these costs, they may, when they so decide, reinvest their earnings in such things as advertising, market expansion, operating equipment, or other items, while debiting their accounts in the event that it is impossible to both make these investments and pay themselves income at the contracted wage level.

The incentive for a union to go along with such a scheme is that the union can maintain dues-paying members. In several cases, workers have been reluctant to consider continued union membership for that very reason, feeling that the union did little enough for them before, and would do less in the event that they became worker-managed. However, it is possible to negotiate with a union an arrangement that part of the dues goes into a fund to assist workers in other enterprises to buy out their company in the event that it is to be shut down. There have been discussions with a large union about the possibility of allocating a portion of the strike fund toward buying out companies; in the case of a sneaker manufacturer in Connecticut, which threatened to shut down if workers continued to press for a wage hike, this provision would have allowed the workers to continue pressing their demands, offering to buy the company if the owners threatened to pull out.

Union pension funds are an enormous source of potential capital if they could be used to buy out enterprises. But, in most cases, these funds are under the control of trustees made up of management and banking figures, with, at best, a minority of union representation. Unless unions were willing to make efforts to gain control over their pension funds, which, given the management contribution, is unlikely, it is impossible to conceive of pension funds as a source of capital. However, worker-managed enterprises could set up pension funds under their own control, and these could finance the growth of worker management. Unions have at various times set up credit unions, health clinics, and consumer unions. Self-managed enterprises could encourage unions to perform these services which are both in the union tradition and close to the tradition of worker cooperatives.

If unions came to accept the validity of self-management, which they might well do if faced with the existence of a number of such enterprises created from plant shutdowns, they could, perhaps, be induced to leave the matter of wages to the internal decision of members of the enterprise, and concentrate instead on such matters as industry-wide standards and on the role of arbiter in disputes between a worker or groups of workers and the management of the enterprise, representing the workers as a whole. This would correspond to their traditional function of being responsible for grievance procedures, and would prevent the danger of the tyranny of the majority over individual members. Moving beyond this, they could take up the idea suggested by some advocates of self-management of developing a workers' bill of rights covering hiring and firing procedures and workers' rights on the job.

Before the American labor movement became successfully integrated into the capitalist system, unions at various times sponsored workers' cooperatives which either failed or, more often, were crushed by industry groups such as the NAM. It is unlikely that the labor movement of today will show any interest in repeating these experiments. But, if others help develop workers' cooperatives, it is in the unions' self-interest to admit them to the union movement. If these cooperatives were capable of growing with anything like the dynamism shown by the Mondragón system of cooperatives in northern Spain, the union movement would then be forced to take serious notice of worker management, and this might possibly help introduce something of the older union spirit by demonstrating that there existed an alternative to being a junior partner in the capitalist system. However, all this is in the realm of pure speculation. What is far more evident is the fact that the union leaders, or at least some of them, fully recognize that, as things stand, they are powerless in the face of loss of jobs, and they are willing, albeit cautiously, to help when workers seek to maintain their jobs under conditions of worker management.

On the national level, organized labor could serve as an important lobbying force to introduce legislation favoring worker management as a solution to unemployment. Several cities in the New

England area, having recognized the uselessness of relying on private industry to create jobs in the center city, have called on community development corporations, and, in two cases, on the Federation for Economic Democracy, to assist in creating enterprises which would operate under different mixtures of community and worker control. The new cooperative bank explicitly includes worker cooperatives in its purview. Legislation is being planned to allow federal funds equivalent to a small percentage of unemployment insurance to be used for investment in worker-owned enterprises as an answer to plant shutdowns. So far, organized labor has not been involved in any of these efforts. But the health of organized labor has depended on an expanding economy and the possibility of real wage gains for its members. Now, with stagflation a continuing feature of the economic landscape, any program which gives promise of successfully creating jobs or of preventing the flight of jobs abroad and to nonunion areas must, of necessity, be attractive to organized labor. However, worker management has a long way to go before it can fulfill that promise.

NOTES

1. For a complete account of the attempt to maintain the bakery under worker ownership, see "How the Workers Almost Pulled it Off," *Boston Phoenix,* 26 April 1977.

21

Workers' Control Is
More Than Just That

André Gorz

When we speak about *workers' control,* we usually have some very different things in mind. Some see workers' control as an end in itself, i.e., as something that can and must be won within the framework of the capitalist system, to improve the situation of the working class. Others look at workers' control as something that will never be won as long as capitalism exists, and that must be championed for precisely that reason. According to this second view, which I personally share, workers' control is not an end in itself. It is mainly a means or method, a means whose true significance can be understood only if we place it in a strategic perspective of social and political revolution.

A few factual examples may illustrate why and how the issue of workers' control has become so relevant in recent class conflicts all over Europe, and also to show why long-drawn-out struggles for control have never and nowhere led to complete success.

There were times when the working class could act on the assumption that there were heaps of ready cash in the bosses' safes or the corporations' banks. Traditional union action rested on the hypothesis that the employer, if pressed hard enough, would eventually give in and grant higher wages and better working conditions. Traditional working-class action assumed the corporations' finances and the system as a whole to be flexible. But this assumption no longer holds true. Flexibility has been organized away and replaced

André Gorz, who also writes under the name Michel Bosquet in *Le Monde,* is the author of *Strategy for Labor* and other works. His latest book, *Ecology as Politics,* was published by South End Press.

Reprinted from *Participatory Democracy in Canada,* edited by Gerry G. Hunnius, © 1973 Black Rose Books, by permission of the publisher.

by rigid planning of all the factors on which production depends.
Thus —

> the quickened pace of technological innovation calls for advance
> planning of the corporation's future investment;
> the greater weight of fixed capital compels long term financial
> planning of amortization, depreciation, reserves, and finan-
> cial costs;
> increased international competition prevents unforeseen higher
> costs from being offset by higher prices;
> rigid financial planning also calls for rigid predetermination of
> labor costs.

This overall rigidity of modern management policies tends to
jeopardize the traditional bargaining power of labor unions. Wages
nowadays tend to be predetermined, and not only wages, but also the
working process itself. Therefore, management tends to react very
sharply to unforeseen wage demands that would jeopardize the corporation's financial planning. Unplanned wage demands tend to be
considered as a direct attack on the logic and balance of the capitalist
system. Both management and the state tend to fight such demands
by accepting a trial of strength and meeting the working class in
head-on clashes.

Of course, if we fight hard enough, we can force the corporation
to give us a little more than they would like; we can temporarily throw
the capitalist system out of balance and make small inroads into the
plans and profits of corporate capital. But experience has taught us
that this kind of success can be only temporary. Within a relatively
short time, one of two things will happen:

1. Capitalists may consider that the profits which the new wage
rates leave are not attractive enough and that they, the capitalists, do
not have sufficient power to take away from the working class what it
has just won. In such a situation, the bourgeoisie will close down the
plants, fire part of the workers, organize a recession; capital will go on
strike and wait until the working class is sufficiently weakened to
become submissive again.

2. The alternative to this extreme solution is more common:
within a relatively short time, capitalists will restore what they consider to be attractive rates of profit by taking away at least part of the
wage increases which we have won.

There are various ways of taking them away from us. For
example:

rising prices reduce our real wages;

work is intensified and part of the workers laid off;

those who remain have to work faster and harder;

the work process is not only speeded up, it is "rationalized," which means new equipment is installed, skilled work is replaced by unskilled work, and the evaluation of jobs and skills is made according to new criteria.

In short, workers are made to pay dearly and heavily for their increased wages. Their subjection to so-called scientific organization of the work process becomes more and more rigid.

As you know, the new time-and-motion measuring-systems break down the act of working into minute motions, and no longer allow for individual variations in work speed, nor for any kind of significant individual bonuses. Wage rates are negotiated when the system is introduced and are not open to revision. Management is intent on making long-term deals with the union and on using the union as a kind of police force to see to it that the workers fulfill their part of the bargain. Wage increases are planned in advance as part of the deal, and shop-floor rebellion against working conditions tends to be answered by lockouts.

Thus, scientific management closes the trap on the workers. We are now learning that the laborer's subjection to the work process had something artisanlike in the past: work speeds and piece rates could be tampered with to a certain extent. But no longer. Management policy has become global, and so has the subjection of the workers. Working conditions are rigidly predetermined and can no longer be influenced by individual meddling.

Workers thus will remain at the complete mercy of despotic and arbitrary managerial decisions unless they win sufficient power on the factory floor to refuse new work rules, work speeds, new definitions of skills and of rates, and so on — unless, in other words, they win direct power over the work process. That is what workers' control is mostly about, at first sight. We need control for strictly economic reasons, so as to counteract the power of management to burden us with more and more exhaustion work and with deteriorating working conditions in exchange for some meager wage raises. But, if this is so, then it also must be quite clear to us that the struggle for control will be even fiercer, even more merciless, than the struggle for wages. The struggle for control, even more than the struggle for increased wages, aims at checking the profit which capital can make on our labor.

Therefore, management will fight demands for control with all overt or covert means at its disposal. Just as management will grant us higher wages when it can't help doing so, only to try and take them away from us at a later stage, so management may grant us, at certain moments, power of control — only to try and destroy these powers at a later stage, be it by force or by deception. Control is not something that can be won once and forever. It is something which, once we have won it at least partly, will have to be defended in ceaseless battles, or else we shall lose it to capitalist management, however enlightened it may pretend to be, because genuine workers' control attacks at its very source the domination and exploitation of labor by capital.

This you probably know from experience, although some may have had different experience in certain advanced factories which try to introduce so-called job enrichment. This is something which we will discuss later. In my view, the important point, for the moment, is that the struggle for workers' control is necessarily an extremely bitter struggle which cannot be won and which cannot even be *waged* within the traditional framework and ideology of the unions.

To make this point clear, I'd like to submit to you a few critical considerations about the history and the limitations of the union movement. Originally, the unions developed out of the workers' need for self-defense and self-organization. In their early stages, when they were still genuine organs of workers' self-organization, unions tended to be quite radical. We still witness this radicalism whenever a new union is built up from scratch through the initiative of rank-and-file militants who get together and try to do things as they see them and fight for demands they deeply feel, no holds barred. This is something which happened in recent years in Detroit, for example, with the League of Revolutionary Black Workers.

This type of revolutionary union movement, however, has become something exceptional. Overall, the big national unions are now *institutions* which see it as their task not to overthrow or even to question the capitalist system, but rather to defend the interests of the working class within the framework of that system. This change of attitude, of course, can be historically explained: for decades, there was no concrete prospect of a proletarian revolution in the West. The working class proved incapable of overthrowing the system. Top union leaders understandably felt that it was pointless to insist on revolutionary demands that could not be achieved in the absence of a revolutionary situation. Though some of them did not completely discard the hope that such a situation might arise again, they thought it was realistic, in the meantime, to fight for things that could be won right away, such as better wages and other improvements. The more intelligent capitalists openly or discreetly encouraged this realistic attitude: bargaining over demands is cheaper than fighting over them. Fundamentally, then, corporate capital was reconciled to the existence of labor unions and showed willingness to recognize them officially, but on two conditions:

1. Unions must voice only demands that are realistic, that do not call capitalism into question, that are *negotiable*.

2. Once an agreement has been bargained out, unions must stick to it and prevent the workers from breaking it.

Wherever these two conditions were accepted, labor unions turned into permanent institutions holding legal rights and responsibilities: they became permanently structured and therefore hierarchical and bureaucratic organizations; they held tremendous bargaining power, but they also held the power to discipline and to police reluctant workers. As institutions holding institutionalized power within the capitalist state, union bureaucracies, of course, showed less and less inclination to jeopardize their self-interest by stimulating demands and aspirations that were incompatible with the logic and the power structure of the capitalist system. Demands that could not be won by bargaining and by juridically defined forms of action were considered pointless. Demands that had no chance of being accepted by capitalist managers were thus eliminated from the outset. They were eliminated because top union leadership could not engage in risky and losing battles. Realism thus led union leaders to translate all demands that sprung up from the rank and file into propositions that would prove acceptable and negotiable to the representatives of capital. The objective function of labor unions has thus become a function of ideological and political mediation, and union leadership has become a conservative force.

Now, the question we must ask ourselves is: can this type of centralized and bureaucratic unionism wage an effective struggle for workers' control? The answer is an emphatic "No." Labor unions that feel responsible to the capitalist managers for keeping the factories going; labor unions that commit themselves not to strike as part of the bargain they have entered; in a word, labor unions that behave as institutional mediators within the capitalist society are inherently incapable of leading an effective struggle for rank-and-file demands for control — except if control itself can be institutionalized and subordinated to regulations that will make it ineffective. This is a point which has been well documented in Western Europe as well as in the United States.

Of course, some people will object that labor unions' leadership has become conservative and timid only because the working class itself is apathetic. Union bureaucrats everywhere, particularly in my country, Canada, like to assert that the masses would not understand and accept a more aggressive and combative union policy. Facts prove these assertions to be false. The truth is that the bureaucratic machines of institutionalized labor unions are very much afraid of losing control over the working class, since the unions draw their institutional strength and bargaining power from their ability to keep the laboring masses under control. Most top union leaders are frightened of the wild and uncontrollable demands and outbursts that would explode from the rank and file if the workers were free at any moment to gather, discuss, and decide what their grudges are, what they wanted to do about them, and how. And this is precisely what would happen if genuine workers' control were fought for on the shop floor, i.e., if demands and actions could be decided permanently *from below* without control and mediation *from above*.

At present — and as long as the centralized and bureaucratic structure and organization of the big unions persist — it is practically impossible to know how the working class really feels about its condition in the factories, in the offices, and in society. The impressive number of wildcat strikes which has developed in recent years does, however, point to the fact that an untapped potential of combativeness and radicalism exists, a poential which the traditional structure of labor unions tends to repress. Let me give you a few examples of this.

In Great Britain, for example, more than 80 percent of all strike action in recent years was wildcat. These strikes were and are called by shop stewards, not by the unions themselves, on issues relating to wages and to workers' control. Some people, of course, will say that these issues are always specific and do not prove great radicalism and class consciousness. Quite true: after all, more than half of the British working class votes Conservative.

The question we must ask, however, is: what political and class consciousness would the working class have if its national organizations were as democratic and as aggressive as the elected and revocable militants on the shop floor? We have no idea about this, but there is an interesting story which I'd like to tell you about the dangers of taking so-called working class apathy at face value.

In the early sixties, a British professor of sociology by the name of Goldthorpe made an extensive investigation of the Vauxhall workers at Luton. He wanted to find out what class consciousness they had left, how they felt about their work, about wages, about life generally — and what chances there were that acute conflicts would break out in a well-managed and advanced big factory. Professor Goldthorpe had about 80 percent of the Vauxhall workers interviewed individually. His investigation lasted two years. His conclusions were optimistic: he found the Vauxhall workers to be completely integrated into the system. They had, so he said, no deeply felt grudges. They were rather satisfied with their wages. They neither liked nor disliked their work; they looked at it as a rather boring but inevitable part of their life. They didn't want to give it much thought. Their general attitude toward work, according to Professor Goldthorpe, was to perform it so as to get rid of it; they wanted to forget about it at the end of the working day, to go home, watch television, grow vegetables in their garden, fiddle around in their home. Their working life was rather marginal to them and what really mattered to them was their life at home, which was their real life. Therefore, Professor Goldthorpe concluded that class consciousness was practically nonexistent at Vauxhall, that the workers were behaving according to middle-class patterns, and that class struggle belonged to the past.

The Goldthorpe report was still at the printer's when a few militants got hold of a résumé of Professor Goldthorpe's conclusions. They had this résumé mimeographed and handed out a few hundred copies. A week or so later, the *Daily Mail* printed a report on Vauxhall's profits. The net profit for that year amounted to about £900 per worker, and this net profit had been sent back to General Motors in the United States. This piece of news was also circulated among the workers. The next day, something happened which the *Times* reported as follows:

> Wild rioting has broken out at the Vauxhall car factories in Luton. Thousands of workers streamed out of the shops and gathered in the factory yard. They beseiged the management offices, calling for the managers to come out, singing the "Red Flag" and shouting "string them up!" Groups attempted to storm the offices and battled the police which had been called to protect them.

The rioting lasted for two days.

Now, this is what happened in an advanced factory where the

union was strong and where 80 percent of the workers had been interviewed and been found to lack class consciousness. What does it all mean? Does it mean that Professor Goldthorpe was stupid? It certainly means that Goldthorpe made a major mistake: he interviewed each worker separately and found each worker to be individually *resigned to,* if not *reconciled with,* his condition. He concluded that all these thousands of individual resignations made for a collective apathy. And then something happened which he had not thought of: all these workers who had said individually "That's how life is, there is nothing much that can be done about it," all these workers started to discuss things among themselves. They started to discuss them because the conclusions of Mr. Goldthorpe were circulated in the factory. And, as they discussed things, they found out that they all felt alike: they felt apathetic but frustrated; they *were* apathetic because, as individuals, in their individual isolation and loneliness, no one could do anything to change things. But, when people start talking about their loneliness, their frustration, their powerlessness, they cease to be isolated and powerless. They start melting into a group which holds immeasurably greater power than the individual power of all those who compose it.

In other words, the very investigation of Mr. Goldthorpe about the lack of class consciousness helped tear down the barriers of silence and isolation that rendered the workers apathetic; the Goldthorpe investigation itself stimulated an explosion of class consciousness and combativeness.

This is by no means an isolated example. As a matter of fact, wherever extensive interviews and investigations have been made inside factories, they have been followed within a very short time by violent outbreaks and spontaneous strikes. What happened at the Vauxhall works in Luton also happened at the Firestone plant in Oslo, Norway. It also happened at the Ford plant near Cologne, Germany, where the head of the local union had complained for years that wages, working conditions, and labor relations were so good that there was nothing much that the union could do in the factory. In this case, it so happened that the head of the Ford union died and was replaced by an inquisitive young militant. The new man decided to have a more thorough look at things. He handed out questionnaires, inviting the workers to say freely how they felt about a variety of issues: about working conditions, about working speeds, about piecework, about the foremen, etc. The replies were devastating. The immense majority of workers complained bitterly about working speeds, monotony, nervous exhaustion, lack of breaks, despotic behavior of the foremen, and so on. A summary of the replies was circulated. And a week later, when management announced that the assembly lines would have to be speeded up provisionally, just for two days, the whole factory broke out into a strike for the first time in fifteen years.

The same kind of story could be told about the Alfa Romeo car factory in Milan, Italy, about the shipyards at Genoa, about the Pirelli tire factory at Turin, about the steelworkers at Dunkirk, France. What does it all mean? First of all, it shows that, when workers are given a chance to discuss and decide among themselves — in open gatherings — the grudges and the claims which they want to voice, their demands and their methods always prove more radical than what top union leadership had expected. Free discussion and exchange within the rank and file about factory life almost inevitably lead to violent outbursts of protest and unforeseen strike action.

What lesson are we to draw from this? The lesson, I suggest, is that a potential of frustration and of revolt lies permanently dormant within the working class and that, in so-called *normal* periods, no one knows how deeply the working class feels oppressed, exploited, frustrated, and dominated. *No one* knows about it normally: neither the union leadership, nor the workers themselves. We do not know about it because there are no words to convey and to make clear how we feel. We have no words to speak about our oppression, our distress, our bitterness, and our revolt against the exhaustion, the stupidity, the monotony, the lack of meaning of our work and of our life; against the contempt in which our work is held; against the despotic hierarchy of the factory; against a society in which we remain the underdogs and in which goods and enjoyments that are considered normal by the other classes are denied to us and are parceled out to us only reluctantly, as though we were asking for a privilege. We have no words to say what it is and how it feels to be workers, to be held in subjection, to be ordered around by people who have more and who pretend to know more and who compel us to work according to rules *they* set and for purposes that are *theirs,* not ours. And we have no words to say all this because the ruling class has monopolized not only the power of decision-making and of material wealth; they have also monopolized culture and language. They are not only taking away from us our strength, our health, our labor and the meaning of work; they also take away from us the means to communicate; including the words, the language we speak. There is no language available to say how we feel because we are never given a chance to say things and be heard. There are no papers, no movies, no books about factory work and life. The work and life in the factories — and also in the huge offices — is something this society doesn't want to hear about. For decades, the ruling class has sentenced the working class to be prisoners not only of rules and laws that cannot be discussed or questioned, but also to be prisoners of an estranged language, of a language which is pervaded with values and with an ideology in which there is no room for what we feel and want.

It is because the working class is silenced that explosions of discontent always come as a surprise and always are violent. It is because we have no words to say what we want and no means to make it come true that we have to resort to violence as a way of saying: enough is enough, we won't play by the rules any longer, we won't take any more of it. Violence is the first and necessary step by which the oppressed refuse their oppression. Violence expresses effectively a total and immediate refusal of the established order and its discourse. But sporadic violence remains a substitute for the effective destruction of this order. Last year, after days of violent strike action and street riots, the Fiat automobile workers at Turin invented a magnificent slogan. It said: "What do we want? Everything." All right: we want everything right away, we want to overthrow capitalism, abolish all inequality, build a society of equals; we want to change life. But how do we go about it? Outbursts of violence are but the first and indispensable step toward it. But they are not enough. They liberate us momentarily but they don't change things. Changing things requires effective and sustained action, and sustained action requires a method and an overall view of the ends and means of struggling.

So, then, we have to ask again: what are we really fighting for? What does workers' control really mean to us? I submit that it means much more than improving working conditions in this or that factory without changing anything else. To make this clear, let us assume that we work in plants and offices that produce napalm for the war in Vietnam, miniature radio transmitters for the CIA, canned food containing chemical additives that may damage people's health, pornographic magazines, and the like. Are we capable of saying something like, "I don't mind producing napalm and pornography as long as it pays and as long as the job is not too hard?" I suggest none of us is capable of *saying* such a thing, though many of us are actually engaged in doing such things. How can this be explained?

The explanation, I submit, lies with the division of labor. Labor is divided both socially and technically. It is divided socially insofar as there are those who have wealth, power, and higher education — and who make the decisions; there are those who have only a higher education and who loyally serve the powerful, thereby getting certain privileges; and then there is the mass of those who have no wealth and no education (or a technical and specialized training only), and who fulfill the sharply defined and rigidly predetermined tasks which they are given. There can be no question about not fulfilling the task; you have to take it or leave it. You are compelled to do it not because someone is ordering you to do so, but because the process of production has been organized in advance to give each laborer one precise and narrowly limited job to do, without any possibility of doing something different or of doing his job in an unprescribed way. This sharp limitation and narrow specialization of jobs does not mean that they hold no initiative and responsibility. They may call for inventiveness, hard thinking, and sustained concentration. But things are organized such that no one knows enough about the other aspects of the process of production to be able to wonder what the heck he is really doing; things are organized so that no one is capable of taking initiatives and making decisions on the job that would call the overall process of production into question. In other words, every job-holder is a cog in the machine; every job-holder is responsible only for the work that is assigned to him and not for the overall product that will grow out of it. Responsibility for the overall product lies with a handful of top managers only; and, once they have made their decisions, they organize and divide the work process into thousands of fragmented and predetermined little tasks, forcing everyone to comply with their decisions without really knowing what they are all about.

In a word, the technical division of labor, i.e., the way in which the jobs are parceled out, is not only an organization of production: it is also a technique of domination, a device to keep workers ignorant and to keep them in subjection. This is ever more true nowadays than fifty or a hundred years ago. Nowadays, the tremendous increase in the productivity of labor and the potentialities of automation make virtually possible a total and radical transformation of the work process: repetitive jobs could be abolished in most places; where they cannot yet, they could be performed alternatively and only for short periods, by everyone; multilateral training and comprehensive education could be made accessible to all; the barriers between manual and intellectual work could be torn down; rotation of jobs, collective debate on and responsibility for the methods of production and the quality of products could be made the rule. Free time could be tremendously increased and become socially creative if waste, parasitism and militarism were eliminated. All over the advanced capitalist world, the working class as a whole and each worker individually have much more insight, skill, knowledge, know-how, and creative capacities than they are allowed to show in their jobs. All over the advanced capitalist world, an unbearable discrepancy develops between the stupidity, fragmentation, and irresponsibility of jobs and the actual or potential creativity of job-holders. It is an obvious fact that capitalist management cannot call upon the creativity of the working masses: this would be incompatible with the right of hiring and firing people, to which management clings. Why should the masses put their creative capacities at the service of bosses who will make the workers unemployed if they become more efficient and thus more productive? Why should reduced costs and increased efficiency be our concern if what we produce is wasted, if there aren't enough jobs for all, if our right to earn a living is made dependent on our willingness to make useless and destructive things like weapons, tailfins, and moon rockets? Why should we want to be creative in our work if it does not serve the needs of the people but only the needs of capital for growing profits?

Capitalist management dare not call upon the creativity of the masses for fear of having all these questions explode. To prevent them from exploding, the division of labor is organized to make people feel more ignorant and incompetent than they are, to keep them in subjection, and to divide them by arbitrary barriers and differentiation of status and salary. The difference between skilled and unskilled workers, between workers and technicians, between technicians and engineers, is arbitrarily created as a technique of domination and of fragmentation of the working class. Every one of us knows from experience that this hierarchic division is irrational and senseless, that there is no such thing as a hierarchy of competence, that the competence of the workers is not smaller but only different from the competence of a technician, that wage differentiation does not rest on merit, on performance, on efficiency, but on *social* criteria, and that education serves much less to increase a man's competence in production than it serves to breed *social attitudes* and conformity to the values and ideology of capitalist society.

So then, in my view, when we speak of workers' control, we speak of the capability of the workers to take control of the process of production and to organize the working process as *they* think best. To organize the work process in such a way as to stop it from being oppressive, mutilating, soul-destroying, and health-destroying; to organize it to allow for the maximum display of each worker's initiative, responsibility, creativity; to organize it to replace forced labor and authoritarian division of labor by free cooperation.

Ultimately, there is no difference between workers' control and workers' power. Workers' control is one step, a first and partial step toward seizing power within and over the process of production. The struggle for workers' control is a struggle for power, and therefore it can be waged effectively only if it demonstrates in itself our capability of exercising power over the process of production. To demonstrate this capability, we need not wait for anyone's approval or agreement. We had some recent examples, in France and Italy, where workers started rotating and swapping jobs which they considered to be interchangeable, though fourteen different wage rates were applied to these jobs. And they demanded equal pay for all. We've had the famous example of the Pirelli tire factory at Turin where the 5,000 workers of a huge complex plant established new work-speeds without any technician's or engineer's help and had the whole factory run at varying speeds, just to prove that they were capable of making it function smoothly their own way and that piece rates were nonsense. And we also had the important "reverse strikes" in Western France and in Japan, where public transport workers went "on strike" by making public transport a free service.

In all these and many other instances, the workers did not demand control as something that can be granted to them by the bosses; they struggled for control by simply taking control of the factory or of the shop and by having it function their way. Indeed, control is not something we can ask for and be given: it is something we have to take and that will be given to us because we have taken it already and won't give it up. Therein lies the great superiority of struggles for control over traditional trade unionism. A strike for control is different from all other strikes because strike action in itself is already an exercise in workers' power. It is different from traditional strikes because the workers don't go home and wait until their spokesmen have made a bargain with management. In a strike for control, the masses themselves, i.e., the workers' assembly, decide what can and must be done here and now.

Such strikes are exercises in workers' democracy, in workers' self-government and self-determination. They produce their organs of self-government, workers' councils and workers' committees, committees that are responsible only to the general assembly of the workers, delegates that can be recalled at any moment. All forms of bureaucracy, of representative democracy, of delegation of power are liquidated in these moments of self-organization and of direct democracy. In such moments, repressed needs and aspirations explode; the working class experiences its capability of self-rule and of mastering and modifying the work process. It experiences the possibility of refusing domination by management and by the state, as well as by union or party bureaucracies. It undergoes, in a word, a revolutionary experience; and, if action lasts long enough; if it is not stifled by bureaucratic control from above; if the workers who gather and debate freely in open assemblies have time to produce new leaders and vanguards, workers' councils will spring up, i.e., the specific organs of collective, revolutionary self-organization and of collective power.

But neither the workers' councils, nor the factory or shop committees, nor the workers' power they stand for can prevail unless the political power of capitalism is broken, unless the capitalist state itself is overthrown and the capitalist relations of production and division of labor are abolished. The struggle for workers' control must either develop an all-out attack against all forms of hierarchy, against all forms of monopolization of power and of knowledge, against all forms of domination and bureaucracy, including the so-called socialist state bureaucracy, or else whatever power the workers have won in action within the factories will be broken and rendered meaningless in a very short time.

The workers' councils and committees that spring up during mass action and wield effective power over the production process cannot become lasting organs of dual power within the present system. They cannot coexist for long with the power of capitalist management and of the capitalist state. They can coexist with them only antagonistically, in periods of acute struggle that must take the form of a trial of strength. If such a trial of strength is not rapidly won by the working class; if it is not carried forward by political vision and organization; if it does not transcend itself into a generalized all-out offensive for a completely new society, then the organs of workers' power or workers' control must inevitably degenerate.

As we have again seen recently in Italy, there can be no protracted draw, no uneasy truce between organs of workers' power and the power of capitalist management. There can be no coexistence between these two opposed and unreconcilable powers because their trial of strength, if it is not won all-out by the working class, must end up in bargaining and settlement. But a settlement will only be accepted by management if its terms fit into the logic of capitalism and allow management to win back undisputed power. Moreover, settlements are necessarily compromises, compromises must be negotiated, and negotiations cannot be conducted by the workers themselves, but only by delegates speaking on their behalf. These delegates may win some improvements and some new rights for the workers. They may win *token* rights of control *on behalf* of the workers. But the right of workers' control *by the workers themselves* will never be won within the present system. It will never be won because, as I said above, the present division of labor splits up the workers of any factory, differentiates them hierarchically, isolates each group from all the others, prevents the free flow of communication, plunges each individual into harassed loneliness. All the capitalist firm may be willing to grant is control by appointed delegates on behalf of the workers. But *delegated* power of control is something totally different from *direct collective* power. Delegation gives rise to a new group of mediators who will tend to be offered privileges, bureaucratic and institutionalized status, to keep the workers *under their* control. This is exactly what happened in Sweden.

You may ask, then: what is the point of fighting for workers' control if we can't get it? Or if we could get it only in a different social system? The answer is twofold:

1. As Max Weber said, it is only by pursuing the impossible that we will make what is possible come true. It is only by fighting for genuine workers' power as *we* see it that we will corner management into granting us rights and conditions that would never have been granted if we kept asking for them politely and reasonably. Token rights of control are better than nothing if we are able to use them to keep the fight going for full and genuine rights. Improvements such as job enrichment are better than nothing if we are able to use them to keep questioning and fighting the division of labor everywhere. And they are better than nothing also because workers who are not intellectually, morally, and nervously destroyed by work will be ready for more advanced struggles involving our way of life inside or outside the factories.

2. And an even more important point: the results of the struggle for workers' power cannot be measured by its immediate outcome. The main result of this struggle is that it changes people, it changes ourselves. It is something like a self-educational process. Through it, we discover, or rather we invent, the working class's capability of self-organization, of self-determination, of control over the production process. We discover that workers are by no means as incompetent as the division of labor wants to make them feel, that competence is, to a large extent, a myth maintained by those who rule us and by an educational system which is instrumental in differentiating people, not in educating them.

Every struggle for workers' power that involves large numbers of people; every struggle that results in the formation of workers' councils and committees, in open assemblies, in free debate, in the exercise of direct democracy and of collective power; every such struggle prepares the working class to become the ruling class and to abolish all extraneous forms of power from above.

Of course, the genuine organs of workers' power that spring up during struggles will not and must not outlast every struggle. They will wither away when the battle is over, when a compromise has been made. But they will spring up again more powerfully at the next opportunity. They will have formed new militants and new natural leaders. They will be indispensable organs of dual power during and after a Socialist revolution. They will be necessary if we want to build a Socialism in which the state withers away, in which political power is checked and balanced by the direct democracy of the councils.

All this, of course, leads us far beyond the question of workers' control proper. But I think we have to look beyond and put the struggle for control in a strategic perspective. Without such a perspective, without a political instrument that will link the struggle for control to the struggle for workers' power in and over society, this struggle cannot go beyond the stage which it has reached in Great Britain, for example, and in which it has been blocked for years: i.e., an uninterrupted chain of wildcat strikes which effectively paralyze production and effectively weaken British capitalism, but which do not succeed in changing the pattern of production and the class nature of society.

If we want to go beyond this stage, we need a political, strategic, and theoretical vision. And we need an instrument for producing it and for coordinating our struggles.

References

Achtenberg, Ben. 1975. Reports. *Working Papers for a New Society* 2 (Winter): 5–8.

Adizes, Ichak. 1971a. *Industrial democracy Yugoslav style: the effect of decentralization on organizational behavior.* New York: Free Press.

———. 1971b. Role of management in democratic (communal) organizations. *Annals of Public and Cooperative Economy* 42: 399–420.

Agenor: European Review. 1969. *Industrial democracy.* No. 13 (Nov.): 28–40.

Albert, Michael, and Hahnel, Robin. 1981. *Socialism today and tomorrow.* Boston: South End Press.

Aldrich, Howard, and Stern, Robert. 1978. Social structure and the creation of producers' cooperatives. Paper presented at the Ninth World Congress of Sociology, Uppsala.

Almond, Gabriel A., and Verba, Sidney. 1963. *The civic culture: political attitudes and democracy in five nations.* Princeton: Princeton University Press.

Alperovitz, Gar, and Faux, Jeff. 1975. The economy: what kind of planning? *Working Papers for a New Society* 3 (Autumn): 67–73.

Alvarado-Greenwood, William, et al. 1978. *Organizing production cooperatives: a strategy for community economic development.* Berkeley, Calif.: National Economic Development and Law Center.

Anderson, Charles H. 1971. *Toward a new sociology — a critical view.* Homewood, Ill.: Dorsey Press.

Argyris, Chris. 1954. *Human behavior in organizations.* New York: Harper & Row.

———. 1964. *Integrating the individual and the organization.* New York: John Wiley and Sons.

———. 1974. Alternative schools: a behavioral analysis. *Teachers College Record.*

Aronowitz, Stanley. 1974. *False promises: the shaping of the American working class consciousness.* New York: Seabury Press.

Bart, Pauline B. 1977. Seizing the means of reproduction: a feminist illegal abortion collective — how and why it worked. Paper presented at the Meeting of the American Sociological Association, Chicago.

_____. 1978. Review of *In Necessity and Sorrow: Life and Death in an Abortion Hospital* by Magda Denes. *Sociology and Social Research* 63 (Oct.)

Bart, Pauline B., and Frankel, Linda. 1980. *The student sociologist's handbook* (3rd ed.). Glenview, Ill.: Scott Foresman.

Bates, F.L. 1970. Power behavior and decentralization. In *Power and organizations,* ed. Mayer Zald, pp. 175–76. Nashville: Vanderbilt University Press.

Beer, Stafford. 1966. *Decision and control: the meaning of operational research and management cybernetics.* London: John Wiley and Sons.

Behn, William et al. 1976. *Educational requirements for industrial democracy.* Palo Alto, Calif.: Center for Economic Studies.

Bell, Daniel. 1973. The subversion of collective bargaining. In *Workers' control: a reader on labor and social change,* ed. Gerry G. Hunnius et al. New York: Vintage Books.

Bellas, Carl J. 1972. *Industrial democracy and the worker-owned firm: a study of twenty-one plywood companies in the Pacific Northwest.* New York: Praeger.

Bendix, Reinhard. 1962. *Max Weber: an intellectual portrait.* Garden City, N.J.: Anchor Books.

Benello, C. George. 1975. Implementing self-management in the United States: the funding and educational development organization. Mimeographed. Ithaca, N.Y.: FEDO.

Bentley, Walter L. 1925. Organization and procedures of the American Cast Iron Company. Master's thesis, Department of Commerce and Administration, University of Chicago.

Berg, Ivar; Freedman, Marcia; and Freeman, Michael. 1978. *Manager and work reform: a limited engagement.* New York: Free Press.

Bergnéhr, Bo. 1975. Secrecy regulations under the new act of collective bargaining. Mimeographed. Remarks delivered at the Symposium on Swedish Collective Bargaining Legislation, 8–9 October, at Institute of Industrial Relations, University of California, Los Angeles.

Berman, Katrina V. 1967. *Worker-owned plywood companies: an economic analysis.* Pullman: Washington State University Press.

Bernstein, Harry. 1974. Democracy on the job: grand goal in Sweden. *Los Angeles Times.* 9 November, pp. 1, 21, 25.

Bernstein, Paul. 1973. Existing democratized enterprises in the U.S. and Britain. In *Democratizing the workplace: from job enrichment to workers' control.* Cambridge, Mass.: American Friends Service Committee, pp. 1–13.

———. 1974. Worker-owned plywood companies of the Pacific Northwest. *Working Papers for a New Society* 2 (Summer): 24–34.

———. 1975. A preliminary model of the internal dynamics of workplace democratization. *Social Sciences Work Paper* #85, pp. 1–60. University of California, Irvine.

———. 1976. *Workplace democratization: its internal dynamics.* Kent, Ohio: Kent State University Press.

Bernstein, Paul, and White, Marianne. 1973. Democratic mentality in the Czechoslovak reform movement. Mimeographed.

———. n.d. An overlooked alternative: the Czechoslovak alternative and its implications for social change in America. Available from the authors, Irvine, California.

Bettelheim, Charles. 1974. *Cultural revolution and industrial organization in China: changes in management and the division of labor.* New York: Monthly Review Press.

Blau, Peter. 1970. Decentralization in bureaucracies. In *Power and organizations,* ed. Mayer Zald, pp. 150–74. Nashville: Vanderbilt University Press.

Blauner, Robert. 1964. *Alienation and freedom.* Chicago: University of Chicago Press.

Bloss, Esther. 1938. *Labor legislation in Czechoslovakia.* New York: Columbia University Press.

Blum, A.A. 1971. The office employee. In *White-collar workers,* ed. A.A. Blum. New York: Random House.

Blum, Fred H. 1968. *Work and community: the Scott-Bader Commonwealth and the quest for a new social order.* London: Routledge and Kegan Paul.

Blumberg, Paul. 1973. *Industrial democracy: the sociology of participation.* New York: Schocken Books.

Blumenthal, W. Michael. 1956. *Co-determination in the German steel industry.* Princeton, N.J.: Princeton University Press.

Bowles, Samuel, and Gintis, Herbert. 1976. *Schooling in capitalist America.* New York: Basic Books.

Brager, George. 1965. The indigenous workers: a new approach to the social work technician. *Social Work* (April): 33–40.

Brannen, P.; Batstone, E.; Fatchett, D.; and White, P. 1976. *The worker directors: a sociology of participation.* London: Hutchinson.

Brant, Irving. 1964. *The Bill of Rights: its history and meaning.* New York: Collier.

Braverman, Harry. 1974. *Labor and monopoly capital.* New York: Monthly Review Press.

Brecher, Jeremy. 1972. *Strike.* San Francisco: Straight Arrow Books.

Brinton, Maurice. 1970. *The Bolsheviks and workers' control, 1917–1921: the State and counter revolution.* London: Solidarity.

Brom, Thomas, and Kirschner, Edward. 1974. Buying power: community-owned electric systems. *Working Papers for a New Society* 2 (Summer): 46–55.

Brown, Douglass V. 1958. Problems under the Scanlon Plan: summary-management session. In *The Scanlon Plan: a frontier in labor-management cooperation,* ed. Frederick G. Lesieur, pp. 81–82. Cambridge: MIT Press.

Business Week. 1970. Getting at the root of a labor crisis. 17 October, pp. 56–59.

_____. 1971. Swedish worker directors. May.

_____. 1975. Managing Alberta's oil money. 31 March, pp. 76–77.

Campbell, Alastair, et al. 1977. *Worker owners: the Mondragón achievement; the Caja Laboral Popular and the Mondragón cooperatives in the Basque provinces of Spain.* London: Anglo-German Foundation for the Study of Industrial Society.

Carnoy, Martin. 1979. A tale of two sit-ins. *Working Papers for a New Society* 6 (Mar./Apr.): 12–16.

Carnoy, Martin, and Levin, Harry M. 1976. Workers' triumph: the Meriden experiment. *Working Papers for a New Society* 3 (Winter): 47–51, 54–56.

Čekota, Anthony. 1964. Thomas Bat'a — pioneer of self-government in industry. In *The Czechoslovak contribution to world culture,* ed. Miroslav Rechcigl, pp. 342–49. The Hague: Mouton.

Clark, Peter B., and Wilson, James Q. 1961. Incentives systems: a theory of organizations. *Administrative Science Quarterly* 6: 129–66.

Clegg, Ian. 1971. *Workers' self-management in Algeria.* New York: Monthly Review Press.

Coleman, James. 1970. Social inventions. *Social Forces* 49: 163–73.

Conference Board, The. 1971. Job design for motivation. New York.

COOP. 1977. Outline of efforts to establish a Hubbard Company worker cooperative. Oakland: Community Ownership Organizing Project.

Cornell Self-Management Working Group. 1975. Toward a fully self-managed industrial sector in the United States. *Administration and Society* 7 (May).

Craft, Carl. 1974. New managerial work programs, old issues, and the vision of workers' control. In *Democratizing the workplace: from job enrichment to workers' control.* Cambridge, Mass.: American Friends Service Committee, pp. 1–5.

Crozier, Michael. 1964. *The bureaucratic phenomenon.* Chicago: University of Chicago Press.

Dachler, H.P., and Wilpert, B. 1978. Conceptual dimensions and boundaries of participation in organizations: a critical evaluation. *Administrative Science Quarterly* 23: 1–40.

Dahl, Robert A. 1970. *After the revolution: authority in a good society.* New Haven: Yale University Press.

Das, Napagopal. 1964. *Experiments in industrial democracy.* Bombay: Asia Publishing House.

Davis, L., and Cherns, A. 1975. *The quality of working life,* vol. 2. New York: Free Press.

Denes, Magda. 1976. *In necessity and sorrow: life and death in an abortion hospital.* New York: Penguin Books.

Dennison, George. 1972. Politicizing the free school movement. *New Schools Exchange Newsletter* 77 (30 Apr.): 2–3.

Derber, Milton. 1970. *The American idea of industrial democracy, 1865–1965.* Chicago: University of Illinois Press.

Deutsch, Karl W. 1963. *Nerves of government: models of political communication and control.* Glencoe, Ill.: The Free Press.

Dolgoff, Sam. 1974. *The anarchist collectives.* New York: Free Life Editions.

Domhoff, G. William. 1971. *The higher circles.* New York: Vintage Books.

Douglas, Paul H. 1921. Shop committees: substitute for, or supplement to, trade unions? *Journal of Political Economy* 29 (Feb.): 89–107.

Duberman, Martin. 1972. *Black mountain: an exploration in community.* New York: E.P. Dutton.

Dunn, William. 1973. The economics of organizational ideology. In *International sociological conference on participation and self-*

management 6: 195–212. Zagreb: Institute for Social Research.

Eccles, Tony. 1976. Kirkby Manufacturing and Engineering. In *The new worker co-operatives,* ed. Ken Coates, pp. 141–69. Nottingham: Spokesman Books.

Economist. 1975. The world of cooperation. 3 May, pp. 82–83.

Edelstein, J. David. 1976. The Scottish Daily News. *Working Papers for a New Society* 3 (Winter): 52–53.

Edelstein, J. David, and Warner, Malcolm. 1976. *Comparative union democracy: organization and opposition in British and American unions.* New York: John Wiley and Sons.

Elden, J. Maxwell. 1976. Democracy at work for a more participatory politics: worker self-management leads to political efficacy. Ph.D. dissertation, Department of Political Science, University of California, Los Angeles.

Emery, Frederick E., and Trist, Eric L. 1969. Socio-technical systems. In *Systems thinking,* ed. F. E. Emery, pp. 281–96. London: Penguin Books.

Emery, Frederick E., and Thorsrud, Einer. 1976. *Democracy at work.* Leiden: Martinus Nijhoff Social Sciences Division.

Equity Shoes Limited. 1966. *Rules of Equity Shoes Limited.* Leicester.

Espinosa, Juan G., and Zimbalist, Andrew. 1978. *Economic democracy: workers' participation in the management of industrial enterprise in Chile 1970–73.* New York: Academic Press.

Etzioni, Amitai. 1961. *A comparative analysis of complex organizations.* Glencoe, N.Y.: Free Press.

Etzkowitz, Henry. 1978. The liberation of technology. *WIN Magazine* 14.

Farrow, Nigel. 1964. John Lewis Partnership: the profit in worker-ownership. Reprinted in *Co-ownership, co-operation, and control,* ed. Paul Derrick and J. F. Phipps, pp. 83–91. London: Longman's Green, 1968.

————. 1965. Scott-Bader Commonwealth, Ltd. Reprinted in *Co-ownership, co-operation, and control,* ed. Paul Derrick and J. F. Phipps, pp. 95–100. London: Longman's Green, 1968.

Fein, Mitchell. 1972. Motivation for work. In *Handbook of work, organization, and society,* ed. Robert Dubin. Chicago: Rand McNally.

Ferree, Marx. 1976. Working-class jobs: housework and paid work as sources of satisfaction. *Social Problems* 23 (Apr.): 431–41.

Fine, Keitha S. 1973. Workers' participation in Israel. In *Workers' control: a reader on labor and social change,* ed. Gerry Hunnius et al., pp. 226–67. New York: Vintage Books.

Finifter, A. W. 1972. *Alienation and the social system.* New York: John Wiley and Sons.

Flaes, Robert M. B. 1973. Yugoslavian experience of workers' self-management. In *International sociological conference on participation and self-management* 6: 113–22. Zagreb: Institute for Social Research.

Flanders, A.; Pomeranz, R.; and Woodward, J. 1968. *Experiment in industrial democracy.* London: Faber and Faber.

Fleet, Ken. 1976. Triumph Meriden. In *The new worker co-operatives,* ed. Ken Coates, pp. 88–108. Nottingham: Spokesman Books.

————. 1978. KME fights for life. *Workers' Control Bulletin,* New Series, no. 6 (Dec.): 22–23.

Foner, Philip S. 1965. History of the labor movement in the United States. Vol. 4, *The industrial workers of the world, 1905–1917.* New York: International Publishers.

Freire, Paulo. 1970. *Pedagogy of the oppressed.* New York: Seabury Press.

Frieze, Irene H.; Parsons, Jacquelynne E.; Johnson, Paula B.; Ruble, Diane N.; and Zellman, Gail L. 1978. *Women and sex roles.* New York: W. W. Norton.

Fromm, Erich. 1968. *The revolution of hope.* New York: Bantam Books.

Frost, Carl, et al. 1973. *The Scanlon Plan for organizational development.* East Lansing: Michigan State University Press.

Gardner, Richard. 1976. *Alternative America.* Privately published.

Glaser, Barney, and Strauss, Anselm. 1967. *The discovery of grounded theory: strategies for qualitative research.* Chicago: Aldine.

Glenn, E. N., and Feldberg, R. L. 1977. Degraded and deskilled: the proletarianization of clerical work. *Social Problems* 25: 52–65.

Gorupić, Drago, and Paj, I. 1971. Workers' participation in management in Yugoslavia. *International Institute of Labour Studies Bulletin* 9: 129–72.

Gorz, André. 1967. *Strategy for labor.* Trans. M. Nicolaus and V. Ortiz. Boston: Beacon Press.

Gouldner, Alvin. 1954. *Patterns of industrial bureaucracy.* Glencoe, N.Y.: Free Press.

Graubard, Allen. 1972. *Free the children.* New York: Pantheon Books.

Gunn, Christopher. 1981. The fruits of Rath: a new model of self-management. *Working Papers for a New Society* 8 (March/April): 17-21.

Grayson, D. 1979. Business as usual. *Labour Leader* 71 (Apr.): 5.

Guerin, Daniel. 1970. *Anarchism: from theory to practice.* New York: Monthly Review Press.

Gurdon, Michael A. 1978. The structure of ownership: implications for employee influence and organizational design. Ph.D. dissertation, Cornell University.

Gustavsen, Bjorn. 1973. Environmental requirements and the democratization of industrial organizations. In *International sociological conference on participation and self-management* 4: 5-22. Zagreb: Institute for Social Research.

Gyllenhammar, Pehr. 1977. *People at work.* Reading, Mass.: Addison-Wesley Publishing.

Hackman, J.R. 1975. *Improving the quality of work life: work design.* U.S. Department of Labor Monograph.

Hage, Jerald. 1965. An axiomatic theory of organizations. *Administrative Science Quarterly* 10: 289-320.

Hage, Jerald, and Aiken, Michael. 1970. *Social change in complex organizations.* New York: Random House.

Hall, Richard. 1963. The concept of bureaucracy: an empirical assessment. *American Journal of Sociology* 69: 32-40.

Hammer, Tove Helland, and Stern, Robert N. 1980. Employee ownership: implications for the organizational distribution of power. *Academy of Management Journal* 23 (no. 1): 78-100.

Hampden-Turner, Charles. 1975. *From poverty to dignity.* New York: Doubleday.

Hawley, Willis D. 1974. The possibilities of nonbureaucratic organizations. In *Improving the quality of urban management,* ed. Hawley and D. Rogers, pp. 371-425. Beverly Hills: Sage Publications.

Heller, F. A., and Rose, J. B. 1973. Participation in decision-making reexamined. In *International sociological conference on participation and self-management* 4: 123-24. Zagreb: Institute for Social Research.

Henry, Jules. 1965. *Culture against man.* New York: Vintage Books.

Herman, Peter. 1975. In the heart of the heart of the country: the strike at Lordstown. In *Root and branch,* ed. Root and Branch. New York: Fawcett Publications.

Herzberg, F. 1966. *Work and the nature of man.* Cleveland: World Publishing.

HEW. 1973. *Work in America.* U.S. Department of Health, Education, and Welfare. Cambridge: MIT Press.

Hindus, Maurice. 1947. *The bright passage.* New York: Doubleday.

Holloway, Mark. 1966. *Heavens on earth: utopian communities in America.* New York: Dover Publications.

Huckfield, Leslie. 1974. Riding it out at Meriden. *Personnel Management* (Sept.), pp. 26–29, 41.

Hunnius, Gerry G. 1973. Workers' self-management in Yugoslavia. In *Workers' control: a reader on labor and social change,* ed. Gerry G. Hunnius et al., pp. 268–321. New York: Random House.

Hunnius, Gerry G.; Garson, David; and Case, John, eds. 1973. *Workers' control: a reader on labor and social change.* New York: Random House.

International Labor Office. The Bat'a Boot and Shoe Factory. In *Studies on Industrial Relations, Series A,* no. 33: 217–63.

Israel, J. 1971. *Alienation: from Marx to modern society.* Boston: Allyn & Bacon.

Jenkins, David. 1973. *Job power: blue- and white-collar democracy.* Garden City, N.Y.: Doubleday.

Jones, Derek. 1979. Producer cooperatives in the U.S.: an examination and analysis of socioeconomic performance. Department of Economics, Hamilton College.

Kanter, Rosabeth Moss. 1972a. *Commitment and community.* Cambridge: Harvard University Press.

––––––. 1972b. The organization child: experience management in a nursery school. *Sociology of Education* 45: 186–211.

––––––. 1977. *Men and women of the corporation.* New York: Basic Books.

––––––. 1979. Access to opportunity and power: measuring institutional racism/sexism inside organizations. In *Social indicators of institutional discrimination: management and research tools,* ed. Rudolfo Alvarez. San Francisco: Jossey-Bass.

Kanter, Rosabeth Moss, and Zurcher, Louis, Jr. 1973. Concluding statement: evaluating alternatives and alternative valuing. *Alter-*

native Institutions, a special issue of the *Journal of Applied Behavioral Science* 9: 381–97.

Kanter, Rosabeth Moss, and Stein, Barry A., eds. 1979. *Life in organizations.* New York: Basic Books.

Karlsson, Lars Erik. 1973. Experiments in industrial democracy in Sweden. In *International sociological conference on participation and self-management* 3: 71–102. Zagreb: Institute for Social Research.

Kaye, Michael. 1972. *The teacher was the sea: the story of Pacific High School.* New York: Links Books.

King, B.T., and Janus, I.L. 1956. Comparison of the effectiveness of improvised versus non-improvised role playing in producing opinion changes. *Human Relations* 1: 177–86, as cited in Reissman.

Kinkade, Katherine. 1974. Power and the utopian assumption. *The Journal of Applied Behavioral Science* 10: 402–14.

Kirkham, Mavis J. 1973. Industrial producer co-operation in Great Britain: three case studies. Master's thesis, Sheffield University.

Kleiber, Nancy, and Light, Linda. 1978. *Caring for ourselves.* Vancouver: School of Nursing, University of British Columbia.

Knight, Peter. 1975. New forms of economic organization in Peru: toward workers' self-management. In *The Peruvian Experiment,* ed. Abraham Lowenthal. Princeton: Princeton University Press.

Kolaja, Jiri. 1960. *A Polish factory: a case study in workers' participation.* London: Lexington.

———. 1965. *Workers' councils: the Yugoslav experience.* London: Tavistock.

Kozol, Jonathan. 1972. *Free schools.* Boston: Houghton Mifflin.

Kunin, T. 1955. The construction of a new type of attitude measure. *Personnel Psychology* 8: 65–78.

Lawler, E.E. 1977. Reward systems. In *Improving life at work,* ed. J.R. Hackman and J.L. Suttle. Santa Monica, Calif.: Goodyear Publishing.

Leavitt, H.J. 1964. *Managerial psychology.* Chicago: University of Chicago Press.

Lesieur, Frederick G., ed. 1958. *The Scanlon Plan: a frontier in labor-management cooperation.* Cambridge: MIT Press.

Lichtheim, George. 1969. *The origins of socialism.* New York: Frederick A. Praeger.

Likert, Rensis. 1961. *New patterns of management.* New York: McGraw-Hill.

Lipset, S.M.; Trow, Martin; and Coleman, James. 1962. *Union democracy.* New York: Anchor Books.

Litwak, Eugene. 1961. Models of bureaucracy which permit conflict. *American Journal of Sociology* 67: 177–84.

Locke, E. A., and Schweiger, D. M. 1978. Participation in decision-making: one more look. In *Research in organizational behavior,* ed. B. M. Staw, vol. 1. Greenwich, Conn.: JAI Press.

Long, R. J. 1977. The effects of employee ownership on job attitudes and organizational performance: an exploratory study. Ph.D. dissertation, Cornell University.

Lynd, Staughton. 1974. No supervision without representation. *Working Papers for a New Society* 2 (Summer): 16–22.

McCauley, Brian. 1971. Evaluation and authority in radical alternaive schools and public schools. Ph.D. dissertation. Department of Education, Stanford University.

Macciocchi, Maria. 1972. *Daily life in revolutionary China.* New York: Monthly Review Press.

Maccoby, Michael. 1975. Changing work: the Bolivar project. *Working Papers for a New Society* 3 (Summer): 43–55.

McEwan, John D. 1971. The cybernetics of self-organizing systems. In *The case for participatory democracy,* ed. C. George Benello and Dimitrios Roussopoulos, pp. 179–94. New York: Viking Press.

McGregor, Douglass. 1958. The Scanlon Plan through a psychologist's eyes. In *The Scanlon Plan,* ed. Frederick G. Lesieur, pp. 89–99. Cambridge: MIT Press.

Mackie, Allister. 1976. The Scottish Daily News. In *The new worker co-operatives,* ed. Ken Coates, pp. 109–40. Nottingham: Spokesman Books.

McKitterick, T.E., and Roberts, R.D. 1953. *Workers and management: the German co-determination experiment.* London: Gallancz.

Mansbridge, Jane. 1973. Town meeting democracy. *Working Papers for a New Society* 1: 5–15.

———. 1977. Acceptable inequalities. *British Journal of Political Science* 7: 321-36.

Mao Tse-Tung. 1963. *Selected works.* Peking: Foreign Languages Press.

Marieskind, Helen Isabel. 1976. Gynecological services: their historical relationship to the womens' movement with experience of self-help clinics and other delivery modes. Unpublished Ph.D.

dissertation, University of California, Los Angeles, School of Public Health.

Maslow, Abraham. 1954. *Motivation and personality.* New York: Harper & Row.

Melman, Seymour. 1969. Industrial efficiency under managerial vs. cooperative decision-making: a comparative study of manufacturing enterprises in Israel. *Studies in Comparative Development.* Beverly Hills: Sage Publications.

Michels, Robert. 1959. *Political parties.* New York: Dover Publications.

Miller, George A. 1967. Professionals in bureaucracy: alienation among industrial scientists and engineers. *American Sociological Review* 32: 755–68.

Mohr, James C. 1978. *Abortion in America.* New York: Oxford University Press.

Mommsen, Wolfgang. 1974. *The age of bureaucracy: perspectives on the political sociology of Max Weber.* New York: Harper & Row.

Mouzelis, Nocos. 1968. *Organization and bureaucracy: an analysis of modern theories.* Chicago: Aldine.

Mulder, Mauk. 1971. Power equalization through participation? *Administrative Science Quarterly* 16 (Mar.): 31–40.

———. 1973. The learning of participation. In *International Sociological Conference on Participation and Self-Management* 4: 219–28. Zagreb: Institute for Social Research.

Myrdal, Jan. 1970. *China: the revolution continued.* New York: Pantheon Books.

National Industrial Conference Board. 1919. *Research Report #21: Works councils in the United States.* Boston: NICB.

———. 1922. *Research Report #50: Experience with works councils in the United States.* New York: Century Co.

———. 1933. *Collective bargaining through employee representation.* New York: Century Co.

NDP Ottawa Report. 1973–1975. (Occasional publication of the New Democratic Party) Ottawa, Ontario: Office of the Federal Leader.

Neill, A.S. 1960. *Summerhill.* New York: Hart Publishing.

New schools exchange directory. 1967; 1973. Santa Barbara: New Schools Exchange.

NICB. See National Industrial Conference Board.

Norcross, Derek. 1975. Worker participation. *Los Angeles Times,* 9 March.

Nordhoff, Charles. 1875. *Communistic societies of the U.S.* New York: Dover Publications, 1972.

Norton, John H. 1974. Caveats on workers' control. Mimeographed. Cambridge: Harvard University Business School, March.

Nunnally, J.C. 1967. *Psychometric theory.* New York: McGraw-Hill.

Oakeshott, Robert. 1978. *The case for workers' coops.* London: Routledge & Kegan Paul.

Obradović, Josip. 1970. Participation and work attitudes in Yugoslavia. *Industrial Relations* 9 (Feb.): 161–69.

Olson, Mancur, Jr. 1968. *The logic of collective action.* New York: Schocken Books.

———. 1969. Two categories of political alienation. *Social Forces* 47: 288–99.

O'Toole, James, ed. 1973. *Work and the quality of life.* Cambridge: MIT Press.

Pannekoek, Anton. 1975. Workers' councils. In *Root and Branch: the rise of the workers' movement,* ed. Root and Branch. Greenwich, Conn.: Fawcett Publications.

Papanek, Jan. 1946. *Czechoslovakia.* Boston: Appleton.

Parsons, Talcott. 1942. Ages and sex in the social structure of the U.S. *American Sociological Review* 7: 604–6.

Participation and self management. 1972–1973. 6 vols. Zagreb: Institute for Social Research.

Pateman, Carole. 1970. *Participation and democratic theory.* Cambridge: Cambridge University Press.

Pearl, Arthur. 1964. Youth in lower class settings. Paper presented at Fifth Symposium on Social Psychology, p. 5, as cited in Reissman.

Perrow, Charles. 1971. *Complex organizations: a critical analysis.* Englewood Cliffs, N.J.: Prentice-Hall.

———. 1976. Control in organizations: the centralized-decentralized bureaucracy. Paper presented at the annual meeting of the American Sociological Association, New York.

Perry, Stewart. 1978. *San Francisco scavengers: dirty work and the pride of ownership.* Berkeley and Los Angeles: University of California Press.

Potvin, Raymond H. 1958. *An analysis of labor-management councils in Belgian industry.* Washington, D.C.: Catholic University of America Press.

Puckett, Elbridge. 1958. Measuring performance under the Scanlon Plan. In *The Scanlon Plan,* ed. Frederick G. Lesieur, pp. 65–79.

Cambridge: MIT Press.

Reissman, Frank. 1965. The helper therapy principle. *Social Work* (April): 27–32.

Remington, Robin. 1969. *Winter in Prague: Czechoslovak Communism in crisis.* Cambridge: MIT Press.

Richman, Barry. 1967. *Industrial society in Communist China.* New York: Random House.

Rifkin, Jeremy. 1977. *Own your own job.* New York: Bantam Books.

Rifkin, Jeremy, and Barber, Randy. 1978. *The North will rise again: pensions, politics and power in the 1980's.* Boston: Beacon.

Rothschild-Whitt, Joyce, 1976a. Conditions facilitating participatory-democratic organizations. *Sociological Inquiry* 46: 75–86.

———. 1976b. Alternative institutions as collectively controlled workplaces: some dilemmas. Paper presented at the 71st Annual Meeting of the American Sociological Association, September.

———. 1978. Organizations without hierarchy: a comparative study of collectivist-democratic alternatives to bureaucracy. Ph.D. dissertation, Department of Sociology, University of California, Santa Barbara.

Rus, Veljko. 1972. The limits of organized participation. In *International sociological conference on participation and self-management* 2: 165–88. Zagreb: Institute for Social Research.

Salancik, G. R. 1977. Commitment and the control of organizational behavior and belief. In *New directions in organizational behavior,* ed. G. M. Staw and G. R. Salancik. Chicago: St. Claire Press.

Satow, Roberta Lynn. 1975. Value-rational authority and professional organizations: Weber's missing type. *Administrative Science Quarterly* 20: 526–31.

Schuchman, Abraham. 1957. *Codetermination: labor's middle way in Germany.* Washington, D.C.: Public Affairs Press.

Schumacher, E. F. 1973. *Small is beautiful: economics as if people mattered.* New York: Harper & Row.

Scottish Daily News. (n.d.) Discussion document. Mimeographed. Glasgow.

Scottish Daily News Enterprises Limited. 1975. *Prospectus.* Glasgow.

Seeger, Murray. 1975. Socialists in Sweden plan third step. *Los Angeles Times,* 16 November, pt. 9, p. 1.

Select Committee on Small Business, U.S. Senate. 1979. The role of the federal government and employee ownership of business.

29 January. Washington, D.C.: U.S. Government Printing office.

Shearer, Derek. 1974. North moves left: politics in British Columbia. *Working Papers for a New Society* 2 (Spring): 49–56.

Šik, Ota. 1971. *Plan and market under Socialism.* White Plains, N.Y.: International Arts and Sciences Press.

Smith, Arthur. 1978. Meriden faces a long hard ride. *Financial Times,* 20 January.

Smith-Rosenberg, Carroll. 1975. The female world of love and ritual: relations between women in nineteenth-century America. *Signs* 1 (Autumn): 1–29.

Sorey, G. K. 1975. (Profit-sharing consultant) Personal communication, March.

Sprague, Blanche. 1932. Bat'a, chief figure in the world's shoe industry. In *Facts and figures in economic history,* pp. 276–303. Cambridge: Harvard University Press.

Stein, Barry A. 1974. *Size, efficiency and community enterprises.* Cambridge, Mass.: Center for Community Economic Development.

Stein, Barry A., and Hodax, Mark B. 1976. *Competitive scale in manufacturing.* Cambridge, Mass.: Center for Community Economic Development.

Stern, R.N., and Comstock, P. 1978. *Employee stock ownership plans (ESOPs): benefits for whom?* Key Issue No. 23. New York State School of Industrial and Labor Relations, Cornell University.

Stern, Robert N., and Hammer, Tove Helland. 1978. Buying your job: factors affecting the success or failure of employee acquisition attempts. *Human Relations* 30: 1001–17.

Stone, Katherine. The origin of the job structures in the steel industry. In *Root and Branch,* ed. Root and Branch. New York: Fawcett Publications.

Stradal, Karel. 1969. Choosing the general manager: democratization of the SKODA-Plzen Metallurgical Works. In *Czechoslovak Life* (Sept.): 30–33.

Sturmthal, Adolf. 1964. *Workers' councils: a study of workplace organization on both sides of the iron curtain.* Cambridge: Harvard University Press.

———. 1969. Workers' participation in management: USA. *International Institute of Labour Studies Bulletin* no. 5: 149–86.

Subcommittee on Anti-Trust Consumers and Employment, U.S.

House of Representatives. 1978. Future of small business in America. 9 November. Washington, D.C.: U.S. Government Printing Office.

Swidler, Ann. 1976. Teaching in a free school. *Working Papers for a New Society* 4: 30–34.

———. 1979. *Organization without authority: dilemmas of social control in free schools.* Cambridge: Harvard University Press.

Szulc, Tad. 1972. *Czechoslovakia after World War II.* New York: Viking Books.

Tabb, J. Yanai, and Goldfarb, Amira. 1970. Workers' participation in management: Israel. *International Institute of Labour Studies Bulletin* no. 7.

Taylor, Frederick W. 1947. *Scientific management.* New York: Harper & Row.

Taylor, Rosemary C. R. 1976 . Free medicine. *Working Papers for a New Society* 4: 21–3, 83–94.

Theobald, Robert. 1970. *Alternative America II.* Chicago: Swallow Press.

Therborn, Goren. 1974. (Faculty of Sociology, University of Lund, Sweden) Personal communication, September.

Thompson, James D. 1967. *Organizations in action.* New York: McGraw-Hill.

Thompson, James D., and Tuden, Arthur. 1959. Strategies, structures, and processes of organizational decision. In *Comparative Studies in Administration,* ed. J. Thompson, chap. 12. Pittsburgh: University of Pittsburgh Press.

Torbert, William. 1973. An experimental selection process for a collaborative organization. *Journal of Applied Behavioral Science* 9: 331–50.

Trist, Eric L. 1963. *Occupational choice: the loss, rediscovery and transformation of a work tradition.* London: Tavistock.

Vanek, Jaroslav. 1970. *The general theory of labor-managed market economies.* Ithaca, N.Y.: Cornell University Press.

———. 1971. *The participatory economy: an evolutionary hypothesis and a development strategy.* Ithaca: Cornell University Press.

———, ed. 1975. *Self-management: economic liberation of man.* Baltimore, Md.: Penguin Books.

Vernon, Raymond. 1971. *Sovereignty at bay: the multinational spread of U.S. enterprises.* New York: Basic Books.

Vroom, V. H. 1964. *Work and motivation.* New York: John Wiley and Sons.

Warner, A. L., and Low, J. O. 1947. *The social organization of the factory.* New Haven: Yale University Press.

Webb, C. 1912. *Industrial cooperation: the story of a peaceful revolution.* Manchester: Cooperative Union.

Weber, Max. 1946. *From Max Weber: essays in sociology,* trans. and ed. Hans Gerth and C. Wright Mills. New York: Oxford University Press.

———. 1947. *The theory of social and economic organization,* trans. A. M. Henderson and Talcott Parsons. New York: Oxford University Press.

———. 1954. *Max Weber on law in economy and society.* Cambridge: Harvard University Press.

———. 1968. *Economy and society,* ed. Guenther Roth and Claus Wittich. New York: Bedminster Press.

Whyte, Martin King. 1973. Bureaucracy and modernization in China: the Maoist critique. *American Sociological Review* 38: 149–63.

Whyte, William Foote. 1978. Employee-community ownership to save jobs when firms shut down. *Congressional Record* 124, no. 94 (19 June).

Wild, R. 1976. *Work organization: a study of manual work and mass production.* London: John Wiley and Sons.

Williams, A. 1913. *Co-partnership and profit-sharing.* New York: Henry Holt.

Wilson, Harold B. 1974. *Democracy and the workplace.* Montreal: Black Rose Books.

Wood, James R. 1978. Legitimate leadership in voluntary organizations: the controversy over social action in Protestant churches. Monograph, Department of Sociology, University of Indiana, Bloomington.

Woodward, Joan. 1965. *Industrial organization: theory and practice.* Oxford: University Press.

Zald, Mayer N., and Ash, Roberta. 1964. Social movement organizations: growth, decay, and change. *Social Forces* 44 (May): 327–41.

Zwerdling, Daniel. 1974. Looking for workers' control. *Working Papers for a New Society* 2 (Autumn): 11–15.

———. 1975. Shopping around: nonprofit food. *Working Papers for a New Society* 3: 21–31.

———. 1980. *Workplace democracy: a guide to workplace ownership, participation and self-management experiments in the United States and Europe.* New York: Harper & Row.

INDEX

Abortion collective, illegal, 139-53; membership of, 140; negative experiences in, 149-50; origin of, 139-41; self-identity changes in, 42, 139-53; structure of, 140-42; study method of, 143-44

Abrahamsson, Bengt, 22n

Absenteeism, 5, 9

Achtenberg, Ben, 77

Adequate reserves principle, 319

Adjudication. *See* Arbitrators; Disciplinary procedures

Adizes, Ichak, 70

Adler, Warren (legal collective), 247

Advancement: in bureaucracies, 30; in collectives, 30-31. *See also* Career advancement

Adversary relationship and incentives, 76

Affected interests principle, 303

Age: of shareholder and success, 169; and union discipline, 389

Agglomerates, scavenger, 119-20, 121

Aiken, Michael, 48 n. 8

Aitken, Sir Max. *See* Beaverbrook

Albert, Michael, 7

Aldabaldetrecu, F., 197 n. 6

Aldrich, Howard, 47 n. 1

Alecoop, 179, 181, 183. *See also* Mondragón System

Alfa Romeo, mentioned 405

Alienation: in face-to-face meetings, 127, 130; factors in, 88-89; in illegal abortion collective, 142; in industrial democracy, 90, 91, 100, 101, 105, 106; and job dissatisfaction, 5; measurement of, 98

Allen, George (IGP): on committees, 233; on participation, 240

Almond, Gabriel A., 73

Alperovitz, Gar: 79, 294, 338; on Youngstown Project, 353-69

Alternative organizations: defined, 24; in real systems, 288. *See also* individual types

Alvarado-Greenwood, William, 2

Amateur-factotum, 35

American Association for Labor Legislation, 385

American Federation of Labor. *See* Capitalism and AFL

Anarchist Amazons, 137 n. 5

A&P conversion to cooperative, 344

Apathy: and control, 402-4; and oligarchization, 12

Apprenticeship(s): on alternative newspaper, 36; as equalizer, 45; in illegal abortion collective, 142; and oligarchization, 13; in scavenger companies, 119, 120; at Triumph-Meriden, 213

Arbitrators in workplace democracy, 68, 395

Argyris, Chris, 49 n. 10, 88

Aronowitz, Stanley, 383

Arizmendi, Father José María, 179-82, 194

Arrieta, Jose Letona, 197 n.1

Ash, Roberta, 142, 151, 297 n. 1

Assemblies. *See* Meetings

Associated Plywood Mills, Inc. *See* Olympia Veneer

Attitude, work. *See* Work attitude

Austin Community Project, 272, 274, 276 n. 2; mentioned, 244

Authoritarian structure: effects of, 88; of *Scottish Daily News,* 207

Authority: attitudes toward, in free school, 263-64; in bureaucracy, 45; in collectives, 2, 6, 26-27; delegation of, 263-64; in free school, 263; in limited participation, 5; in workplace democracy, 3, 7. *See also* Control

Autonomy: in teams, 286-87; work-group, 52

Bailey, F. G., 136 n. 1

Baker, Jake: on Seattle Workers' Brigade, 244, 279-89

Barber, James, 136 n. 1

Barber, Randy, 346

Baroja, Julio Caro, 197 n. 3, n. 6

Bart, Pauline B.: 14, 49 n.15, 77, 151, 152; on self-identity in collectives, 139-53

Basque cooperative. *See* Mondragón

Bates, F. L., 29

Beaverbrook, Sir Max Aitken, 218 n. 2

Beaverbrook newspaper chain, 200, 218-19 n. 2. *See also Scottish Daily News*

Beer, Stafford, 66
Behn, William, 63
Bell, Daniel, 387
Bell, Griffin, Attorney General, 366, 368, 369 n. 1
Bellas, Carl J., 173 n. 1, 174 n. 7, n. 10, n. 12, 175 n. 15, 195
Bendix, Reinhard, 23, 136 n. 1
Benello, C. George: 78, 197 n. 7, 295; on labor movement, 383-96
Benn, Anthony Wedgwood, 200
Berg, Ivan, 382
Bergnehr, Bo, 64
Berle, Adolf, 81 n. 11
Berman, Katrina: 56, 59, 61, 65, 68, 74, 81 n. 6, 89, 90, 123 n. 12, 157; on plywood cooperatives, 161-75, 173 n. 1, 174 n. 7, 195, 341
Bernstein, Paul: 4, 6, 21, 22, 34, 42; on participation in decision-making, 51-81, 53, 56, 62, 63, 64, 65, 66, 68, 73, 79, 89, 90, 173 n. 1
Bettleheim, Charles, 4, 48 n. 7, 78, 80 n. 1
Bhudeva. *See* Meacham, Bill
Black Mountain (school), 44-45
Blasingame, Karen (legal collective), 247
Blau, Peter, 29
Bloss, Esther, 68
Blue-collar worker. *See* Worker, blue-collar
Blum, A. A., 101
Blum, Fred H., 63, 68, 79
Blumberg, Paul, 9, 42, 49 n. 10, 52, 73, 85, 109, 178, 193
Blumenthal, W. Michael, 64
Bookchin, Murray, 136 n. 4
Bosquet, Michel. *See* Gorz, André
Boston Phoenix, The, 49 n. 12, 396n
Boston Women's Health Book Collective, 139n
Boulding, Kenneth, 391
Bowles, Samuel, 41
Brager, George, 146
Brannen, P., 88
Brant, Irving, 66
Braverman, Harry, 5, 101, 384
Brecher, Jeremy, 387
Breman Enterprises, 297 n. 2
Brinkerhoff, Derick W.: 295; on participation (QWL Project), 371-82
Brinton, Maurice, 66, 77
British cooperatives: early, 316-20; modern producers', origin, structure, and problems of, 199-219. *See also*

Rochdale principles; individual names
Brom, Thomas, 78
Brown, Douglas V., 75
Bureaucracy: advancement in, 30; and collectives, 23-47; decision-making in, 28; incentives in, 31; goal of, 151; parts of, 21; recruitment in, 30; role differentiation in, 35, 36-38; rules in, 28; social control in, 28; social relations in, 29-30; social stratification in, 33-34; workplace democracies within, 295. *See also* Corporation(s)
Bureaucratic personality, 41
Bureaucratization, 12
Business plans for conversion, 345-46
Business Week, 63
Buy-outs. *See* Plant closings

Caja Laboral Popular: entrepreneurial function of, 193, 194-95; function of, 184, 185-87, 347; origin of, 179, 180-81
Campbell, Alastair, 11
Campbell Steel Works. *See* Youngstown Sheet and Tube
Capital: in Breman Enterprises, 297 n. 2; in Kirkby, 217, 218; in plywood cooperatives, 168-69; in Triumph-Meriden, 214-15; in workplace democracy, 7, 121; in Youngstown Proposal, 294. *See also* Financing
Capital gains in scavenger companies, 115
Capitalism: and AFL, 384; and AFL-CIO, 387; and blue-collar workers, 383-84; and collectives, 288; and cooperatives, 324, 339; and farmers' markets, 325, 326; and gas-oil cooperatives, 324; and labor, 383-88; and Seattle Workers' Brigade, 288; and unions, 392, 401; and wage demands, 397-99; and workers' control, 288, 399-400, 407-8, 410-11
Capitalist corporation defined, 299
Career advancement: in collectives, 30; in organizational behavior theory, 373; in QWL Project, 373, 376, 377; in illegal abortion collective, 148; in Weberian system, 51
Carnoy, Martin, 214, 344, 345
Carr, Kurt (IGP), 238
Case, John, 136 n. 3
Cash-only business, 319

Caucus, premeeting, 128, 131, 132

C. C. Grains (Cooperating Community Grains): and Seattle Workers' Brigade, 280, 281; separation of, from Seattle Workers' Brigade, 279, 285–86, 287

Central Co-operative Wholesale, 329, 330–32

Chapman, John, 136–37, n. 4

Cherns, A., 88

Chestnut Ridge. *See* QWL Project

Chicago and Northwestern Railroad, 339, 360

China, workplace democracy experiments in, 4, 34, 48 n. 7, 68

Clark, Del (IGP), 234–35

Clark, Peter B., 31

Clegg, Ian, 4, 66

Codetermination, 4, 57, 59

Cole, G. D. H., 391

Coleman, James, 47

Coleman, John C., 123 n. 14

Collective (s): auto repair shop, 243, 244; and bureaucracies (*See* Bureaucracy); bylaws of, 67; characteristics of, 2–3, 26–38, 48 n. 8; community (*See* Austin Community Project; Ownership, worker-community; Seattle Workers' Brigade); constraints on (*See* Constraints); Control in (*See* Control); and cooperatives, 272–74; creating (*See* Entrepreneurial function; Plant closings, conversion of, to worker-management); education in (*See* Education); egalitarianism in, 34; growth of, 47 n. 1; health (*See* Abortion collective, illegal; Free clinic); ideal-typical model of, 23–47; incentive structures in (*See* Incentives); and industrial democracy, 2–3; law practice (*See* Law collective; Santa Barbara Legal Collective); number of, 2; origin of, 1–2; purpose of, 26; recruitment in, 30–31; significance of, 245; school *(See* Black Mountain; Free school; Pegasus; Summerhill West): and small entrepreneur, 48 n. 6; worker criticism of, 273–74. *See also* Cooperative(s)

Collective Bargaining: and capitalism, 386; by early British cooperatives, 317; issues of, 56, 87–88

Collectivist personality: characteristics

of, 49 n. 10, 232–33; lack of, 41–42; in illegal abortion collective, 42

Colonial Cooperative Press, 342–43; mentioned, 351

Comanagement, 8, 13, 352 n. 2; in free school, 265–67

Commitment: in collectives, 3, 31, 39, 88–89; at IGP, 222–23; in illegal abortion collective, 141, 151; in industrial democracy, 105, 106; measurement of, 97–98; in plywood cooperatives, 168, 169, 172; of Mondragón workers, 182–83; in producers' cooperatives, 203; in scavenger companies, 112–14; in Seattle Cooperating Community, 280–81; and share ownership, 90; in Summerhill West, 258

Committee of the Chapel, 204

Committee(s): at Equity Shoes, 208–9; as face-to-face assemblies, 136 n. 4; at IGP, 233; nonowning worker on, 88; for participation, 59; significance of, 410

Communication in cooperatives: in Seattle Workers' Brigade, 287; as success factor, 174 n. 9

Communist Party, the: and Central Cooperative Wholesale, 329, 330–32; and cooperatives, 320; and labor movement, 386

Community: conflict, face-to-face, 125–26; and cooperatives, 13, 296 (*See also* C. C. Grains; Ecumenical Coalition; Plant closings; Seattle Workers' Brigade); ownership (*See* Ownership, community; Ownership, worker-community); in workplace democracy, 7, 13, 22; in Yugoslavia, and cooperatives, 13

Community Development Corporations, 347

Community Furniture Company, study of, as industrial democracy, 93–108

Community Ownership Organizing Project, 344

Community relations assembly (IGP), 227, 229, 233

Community Steel, Inc. See Youngstown Sheet and Tube

Competence: in collectives, 35, 36; in illegal abortion collective, 141–42, 144–46, 150

Compu Corp. See QWL Project

Comstock, P., 107

Conféderation Général du Travail, 386

Conference Board Report, 88

Conflict: fears of, in face-to-face meetings, 129, 131–36, 136 n. 2; in illegal abortion collective, 150; protection from, in face-to-face meetings, 125–26; structuring, 133–35. _See also_ Tension

Connecticut Federation for Economic Democracy, 343

Consciousness training, 132–33

Consensus defined, 27. _See also_ Decision-making

Constraints on collectives: emotional intensity as, 40–41; environmental, 43–44; homogeneity as, 39–40; individual differences as, 44–45; lack of collectivist personalities as, 41–42; record-keeping as, 12, 43, 44, 268 n. 2; time as, 38–39 (_See also_ Meetings)

Consumer: bureaucratization of, groups, 12; representation in workplace democracy, 13. _See also_ Cooperatives, consumer; Cooperatives, food

Consumers United, 240 n. 1. _See also_ IGP

Consumer Co-operative League of America, 320

Consumers Cooperative Bank, 351

Control: at alternative newspaper, 33; in bureaucracies and collectives compared, 33, 38–45; in collectives, 267; community-worker, 302–3; delegated, 411; direct, 303; in free schools, 262–69; hierarchical, 1; indirect, 303; and job dissatisfaction, 1; in Kirkby, 204; management, 5–6, 77; by nonowning worker, 87–89; in plant closings, conversion of, to worker management, 340; in plywood cooperatives, 341; in Rath Meat Packing conversion, 342; in Rochdale Principles, 319; in _Scottish Daily News,_ 202–4; by shareholder, 90, 107–8; structures, 4; struggle for, 334; in Summerhill West, 258, 259; traditional, 87–88; in Wheatsville Food Co-op, 274–75. _See also_ Authority; Hierarchy

— community-worker, 273, 275, 302–3; in cooperative corporation, 303; in free school, 265–66; structures for, 266–68; in Youngstown Sheet

& Tube Proposal, 363–65

— social: in bureaucracy, 28; in collectives, 29; in illegal abortion collective, 151; in law collective, 29;

— worker: in Breman Enterprises, 297 n. 2; of decision-making, 53, 57–61; definitions of, 1, 4, 397; direct collective, 411; in Equity Shoes, 212–13; as gauge of success, 10; at IGP, 222, 230, 231; in illegal abortion collective, 151–52; as job enrichment, 52; meaning of, 397–412; and members' control, 268–69 n. 3; and ownership, 87–89, 105; in plant closings, conversion of, to worker management, 348–49; purposes of, 399–400; in _Scottish Daily News,_ 202–3; strategies for, 397–412; strike for, 409–10, 412; struggle for, 409–12; token, 411; and success in plywood cooperatives, 171–72; and worker management, 391–96; of work process, 399–400; in Yugoslavia, 244

COOP, 344

Cooperating Community, problems of, 280–81, 287. _See also_ C. C. Grains

Cooperative Builder, The, 329, 331

Cooperative(s): black, 315–16; bombings of, in Minnesota, 315–16; British, 158 (_See also_ British cooperatives); bylaws (_See_ Discussion Document; Ripponden Co-operative Society; Rochdale Principles); and collectives, 272–74; community service, and member, 273–74; corporation (_See_ Corporation, cooperative); defined, 8; creating (_See_ Entrepreneurial function); failures of, 311–12; federation, 14, 172, 244–45, 268 n. 3, 350–51; gas-oil, 323–25; growth of, 24–25; issues in, 56; nonpolitical, 321–28; origins of, historical, 173 n. 3; 315, 316–34; political, 328–32; schools (_See_ Black Mountain; Free school; Pegasus; Summerhill West); supermarket, 333–34; United Mine Workers, 323; viability of, 338–39

— consumer: Knights of Labor, 322; vulnerability of, 244

— food: 12, 31, 32, 295; control in, 268–69 n. 3; hybrid form of, 274–76

— producers': British, 199–219; defined, 8; degeneration of, 177–78;

favorable characteristics of, 166–69; of Knights of Labor, 322; strawberry growers, 2; plywood companies as, 161–73; problems of, 201; viability of, 166; and worker share-ownership, 90
— service: assessing, 10; scavenger companies as, 109–24
Coordinators in free school, 35
Copreci, 191–93
Corner Green Grocery, 283–84
Corporate operating committee at IGP, 226
Corporate system, 388
Corporation(s): benefits in, 87; and co-operatives, 352; ownership of, 303–5; participatory democracy within (*See* IGP: Industrial democracy; QWL Project); rights in, 299–300
— cooperative, restructuring as, 299–313; evaluation of, 310–13; workers' rights in, 300–1
Cornell Self-Management Working Group, 350
Cort, E. G., 323
Coser, Lewis, 136 n. 1
Craft, Carl, 56
Credit unions, 44, 347. *See also* Caja Laboral Popular
Crisis center, face-to-face meetings in, 123–31, 132, 133–34; structure of, 129–30
Crozier, Michael, 45, 136 n. 2
Councils: in Belgium, 62; at *Scottish Daily News,* 201, 206–7; nonowning worker on, 88; representative, 59; social, in Ulgor, 189; workers, 68, 410
Culture, factor of, 21–22, 43

Dachler, H. P., 88
Dahl, Robert A., 77, 136 n. 1
Das, Napagopal, 74
Davis, L., 88
Decision-making: delegation of, 272; in free schools, 262; structure and, 271–77; at Summerhill West, 259, 260; in Wheatsville Food Co-op, 276
— consensual: and delegation, 262–64; and majority voting, 264–65; in Seattle Workers' Brigade, 280, 283
— participatory: bias in, 81 n. 6; in collectives, 2, 26–27, 28, 34; competition and, 81 n. 5; consultation

as, 4, 57, 59; control of, 57–61; in cooperatives, 56; defined, 60–61; elements in, 51–80; fears in face-to-face, 125–36; goal of, 61; homogeneity and, 48–49 n. 9; at IGP, 225–30; individual rights in, 66–67; issues in, 53, 56, 80 n. 2; in job enrichment, 52; kinds of, 53–61; in plywood cooperatives, 171–72; protection of workers in, 65–67; reduction of, 61; in scavenger companies, 111; size and, 47 n. 3; success criteria of, 80 n. 3; and tension, 41; union collective bargaining and, 53, 56, 59–60; in workplace democracy, 6–7
DeFall, Emily (legal collective), 247
Democratic consciousness, 22, 42, 69–73
Democratic theory of government in co-operatives, 301, 302
Demystification: as equalizer, 45; in illegal abortion collective, 140, 142, 148–49; as internal education, 2; and role differentiation, 35
Denes, Magda, 142
Dennison, George, 17
Derber, Milton, 65, 68
Deutsch, Karl W., 66
Díaz-Plajá, Fernando, 183, 197 n. 5
Disciplinary procedures: in China, 68; in kibbutz, 68; and participation, 67–69; in plywood cooperatives, 165–66, 341; in Summerhill West, 258
Discussion Document, 201, 202–3, 218
Dividends: in scavenger companies, 115; in worker-owned firms, 123 n. 12
Division of labor: in China, 48 n. 7; significance of, 407–8, 411, 412. *See also* Head and handwork; Scientific management; Taylorism
Dolgoff, Sam, 3, 66, 68, 73
Domhoff, G. William, 384, 385
Duberman, Martin, 45
Dunn, William, 81 n. 7

Economist, 77
Ecumenical Coalition, 340, 349, 354–55, 365–66, 368, 369 n. 1
Edelstein, J. David: 47 n. 3, 158; on British producers' cooperatives, 199–219, 344, 351
Eden, Dov, 110, 122 n. 2
Education: and attitude, 102; in collectives, 2, 45, 49 n. 10, 152, 288–89; for consumers, 347–48; in plant clos-

ings, conversion of, to worker management, 349–50; at IGP, 236–37; in industrial democracy, 3, 105; in legal collective, 249–50; of Mondragon, 178–79, 180, 183; in plywood cooperatives, 172; public, in Youngstown Sheet and Tube Proposal, 365–66; workers' need for, 12–13, 14, 63, 107–8

Efficiency: assessing, in workplace democracy, 10; in authoritarian organizations, 88; in Chile, 9; of kibbutz, 9; of scavenger companies, 120–21; and scientific management, 51; size and, 9–11

Eiden, Richard (legal collective), 247n

Elanto Company, 329

Elden, J. Maxwell, 42

Elitism, 271–72

Ellerman, David: 124 n. 22, 197 n. 7, 295, 297 n. 2; on legal structure of cooperatives, 299–313, 348

Emery, Frederick E., 52, 88

Employee. *See* Worker

Employee Stock Ownership legislation, 22

Encounter training, use of, 133

England. *See* British

Entrepreneur, small, and collectives, 48 n. 6

Entrepreneurial functions: of cooperatives, 163, 352 n. 1; of Mondragon, 185–87, 193, 194–95; of Seattle Workers' Brigade, 283–84; of supporting institutions, 350. *See also* Expansion

Environment and collectives, 43–44, 49 n. 13

Equitable Society of Rochdale Pioneers, 317. *See also* Rochdale Principles

Equity Shoes Ltd., 200n, 208–13; cooperative advantages of, 213; management of, 208–9; structure of, 209–11

Escuela Politecnica Professional, 180

ESOP. *See* Share(s)

Espinosa, Juan G., 3, 8, 9

Etzioni, Amitai, 29, 31

Etzkowitz, Henry, 43

Eubanks, Matt, 315–16

Evaluation in limited participation, 5

Expansion: of modern cooperatives, 328; in Rochdale Principles, 318, 319–20. *See also* Entrepreneurial functions

Expertise: in bureaucracy, 45; in collectives, 45; and job rotation, 64–65; in kibbutz, 65; managers', 64–65; and oligarchization, 12–13. *See also* Demystification; Specialist

Factory shutdowns. *See* Plant closings

Farmers and cooperatives, 323–28

Farmer-Labor Party, 322

Farmers' Union Central Exchange-Grain Terminal Association, 323, 325, 326, 327

Farrow, Nigel, 77, 79

Fathers of the Chapels Committee, 204–5

Faux, Jeff: 72, 294, 338; on Youngstown Project, 353–69

Feasibility study: for plant closing, conversion of, to worker management, 345–46; of Youngstown Sheet and Tube Proposal, 355–61

Federation for Economic Democracy, 340–41, 390, 396

Fein, Mitchell, 76

Feldberg, R. L., 101

Feminism: in C. C. Grains, 285; of collective workers, 139–53; in illegal abortion collective, 146–48; in Seattle Workers' Brigade, 284–85; and workers, 137 n. 5

Ferree, Marx, 145

Fibich, 70

Finance committee at IGP, 230–31

Financial: autonomy, 14–15, 44; constraints on collectives, 43–44; rewards in scavenger companies, 115; risk of worker-owner, 98–100; success factor in cooperatives, 174 n. 12

Financing: federal assistance for, in cooperatives, 340, 342, 343, 345, 346; internal and external, in cooperatives, 312–13; in Mondragón System, 186, 194

— problems: of cooperatives, 311–12, 347; of free school, 266; of Grange, 321; of Menorah Kosher Poultry, 343; of Pegasus, 262; of plant closings, conversion of, to worker management, 342, 346, 347, 350; of Rath Meat Packing, 342; of Seattle Workers' Brigade, 284; of Summerhill West, 259–60; of Triumph-Meriden, 218, 219 n.5, 344, 347; of workplace democracy, 14, 121; of Youngs-

town Sheet and Tube Proposal, 294, 340, 347, 356, 358–59, 361–62. *See also* Capital
Fine, Keitha, 65, 67, 68, 74, 78, 123 n. 15
Finifter, A. W., 92
Firing. *See* Disciplinary procedures; Hiring
Flanders, A., et al. 63, 66, 98
Food Co-op Handbook, The, 272, 275–76, 277 n. 4
Formal rationality, 23
Frankenberg, Ronald, 136 n. 1
Frankfurt, Jo Anne (legal collective), 247n
Free clinic: compensations in, 33; economic constraints on, 43–44; motivation in, 31, 32; recruitment in, 30; role differentiation in, 35, 36; wages in, 34
Freeman, Jo, 276 n. 1
Freire, Paulo, 63
Free school(s): antiauthoritarian attitudes in, 263–64; control in, 257–69; coordinators in, 35; decision-making in, 262; financial problems of, 266; growth of, 24–25; hiring in, 265; legal constraints on, 43, 268 n. 2; parents and, 265–66; role differentiation in, 35; rules in, 27–28; social stratification in, 49 n. 14; structure of, 263; students and, 265, 266, 267–68. *See also* Black Mountain; Pegasus; Summerhill West
Frieze, Irene H., 145
Fromm, Erich, 51
Fruits of labor, 301–2, 306

Galbraith, John Kenneth, 80 n. 2
Gans, Herbert, 123 n. 13
Gardner, Richard, 25, 47 n. 1
Gas-oil cooperatives, 323–25
Geico and IGP compared, 220–30
Gershowitz, Harold, 123 n. 11
Gibbons, James P.: on business, 223; on education, 236; as founder of IGP, 159, 223; on leadership, 234; on self-management, 225, 233, 238; workers' attitude toward, 230, 235, 237, 238–39
Giese, Paula: 295; on history of cooperatives, 315–35
Gintis, Herbert, 41
Glaser, Barney, 25
Glenn, E. N., 101
Goals: of Austin Community Project,

272; of Knights of Labor, 322; of movement organizations, 151; and oligarchization, 12; in Rochdale Principles, 318; of workplace democracies, 7, 13
Goffman, Erving, 123 n. 13
Gold, Raymond, 123 n. 13
Goldfarb, Amira, 65
Goldthorpe, Professor, and Vauxhall strike, 403–4
Gompers, Samuel, 384, 385
Gorupić, Drago, 63, 64, 66, 74
Gorz, Andre: 56, 293, 391, 392; on workers' control, 397–412
Gouldner, Alvin, 27, 28
Grain Terminal Association, 325–26, 327
Gramsci, Antonio, 391
Grange cooperatives, 321
Graubard, Allen, 43
Gray, J., 197 n. 6
Great Britain. *See* British
Greenwood, Davydd, 183, 197 n. 2
Guerin, Daniel, 26
Gurdon, Michael A.: 14, 86, 92, 95; on worker ownership, 87–108
Gurich, Juan Leibar, 197 n. 1
Gyllenhammer, Pehr, 379

Hackman, J. R., 88
Hage, Jerald, 48 n. 8
Hahnel, Robin, 7
Hall, Richard, 48 n. 8
Hammer, Tove Helland: 14; on worker ownership, 87–108
Hampden-Turner, Charles, 78
Harris, Patricia, 355
Hawley, Willis D., 264
Hawthorne Western Electric, 5
Hayden, Tom, 17, 294
Hayward school. *See* Pegasus
Head and handwork, 5, 51. *See also* Division of labor; Scientific Management; Taylorism
Health collectives. *See* Abortion collective, illegal; Free clinic
Heaps, Fran (IGP), 240
Henry, Jules, 41
Herbst, 88
Herman, Peter, 389
Herzberg, F., 88
Hess, Karl, 273, 277 n. 7
HEW, 52, 85, 89, 360
Hierarchy: in collectives, 6, 26; in bureaucracies, 34, 381; in face-to-face conflicts, 125–26; in illegal abortion

collective, 140, 149, 151–52; in Rath Meat Packing, 342; in Wheatsville Food Co-op, 275; in workplace democracy, 381. *See also* Stratification
Hiring: in free school, 261, 265; at IGP, 227–28; in Wheatsville Food Co-op, 274–75. *See also* Nonowning worker
Hochner, Arthur, 110, 122 n. 5
Hodax, Mark B., 349
Hodge, Robert M., 123–24 n. 18
Holistic work roles. *See* Role differentiation
Holyoake, George Jacob, 121, 124 n. 21
Homogeneity: in bureaucracies, 28, 39; in collectives, 29, 39–40; in decision-making, 48–49 n. 9; in face-to-face conflict, 135; in illegal abortion collective, 151; in IGP, 240
Hours of work: in bureaucracy, 87; in legal collective, 254; as patronage credits, 174 n. 8; in plywood cooperatives, 169
Hubbard Company, 344
Huckfield, Leslie, 213
HUD, 369 n. 1
Hughes, Everett C., 123 n. 13
Humanizing: as goal of participation, 61; of lawyers, 255
Human needs, 10. *See also* QWL Project
Hunnius, Gerry G., 78, 79, 80 n. 1
Hyde Park Community Cooperative, 333

IGP (Interational Group Plans), 158–59, 221–240: Decision-Making Model, 228; education at, 236–37; financial decisions at, 230–31; homogeneity at, 40; origins of, 223–25; political environment and, 237–38; protection of worker in, 230 n. 2; self-management problems of, 222–23, 231–36, 239–40; structure of, 223–24; union and, 232; worker attitude at, 229–30; workers in, 222; mentioned, 16
ILGWU (International Ladies' Garment Workers Union), 348, 390
Illegal abortion collective. *See* Abortion collective, illegal
Incentives: in alternative newspaper, 31, 32–33; in bureaucracies, 31; in collectives, 31–33; failures of conventional, 76; in food cooperatives, 31, 32; in free clinic, 31, 32; in legal collective, 32
Income: in conventional and scavenger companies compared, 115–16; corpo-

rate net, 307; form of, in worker-owned firms, 123 n. 12; and job stigma, 123 n. 16; legal terms for, 306–7; in Kirkby, 216; retained net, 309; in scavenger companies, 119–20; in workplace democracy, 7. *See also* Wages
— ratio: in China, 34; in collectives, 3, 34; in corporations, 3; in Mondragón, 180; in plywood cooperatives, 162; in Ulgor, 180
Individual differences: in bureaucracy, 44; in collectives, 44–45, 49 n. 16
Individual rights: in kibbutz, 67; in participation, 65–67, 68; in unions (anarchist Spain), 67
Industrial Cooperative Association, 313 n. 2, 342, 343, 344
Industrial democracy: attitudes toward participation in, study of, 87–108; characteristics of, 3; and collectives, 2–3; education in, 107; financial risk of worker-owner in, 98–100; management, role of, in, 106–7; occupational interest groups in, 92–93, 102–6; ownership, worker-management-community in, 89–91, 93–95; share ownership in, effects of, 87–89, 90–91, 107–8; status in, 91–92, 100–2; study method of, 95–98
Industrial Workers of the World. *See* IWW
Information-sharing; in collectives, 152; and industrial secrecy, 64; in participation, 62–65, 75–76; in Sweden, 64; in Yugoslavia, 63
Institutional supports: of plant closings, conversion of, to worker management, 350; of Mondragón, 178–79, 195–96; of workplace democracy, 14–15, 21–22
Institutionalization, 11–12
Internal capital accounts, 308, 309, 310, 311
International Group Plans. *See* IGP
International Ladies' Garment Workers Union. *See* ILGWU
Interviews as method of study, 143–44
Investment, membership, in cooperatives, 307–9. *See also* Share(s)
Investors Council at *Scottish Daily News*, 201–2
Iron Rangers, 323
Israel, J., 90, 101
Israel. *See* Kibbutz
IWW, 343; mentioned 322

Jack, James, 201–2
Jackall, Robert, 246n
Jamestown Metal Products, 339
Jane. *See* Abortion collective, illegal
Jenkins, David, 6, 51, 52, 53, 63, 75, 76
Job(s): creating, in workplace democracy, 7, 352 n. 1; distribution in Wheatsville Food Co-op, 275; enlargement, 52; enrichment, 400, 411
— evaluation: in Copreci, 191–93; in Mondragón, 189–90
— redesign: in General Foods, 6; in QWL Project, 375–76
— rotation: on alternative newspaper, 36; in collectives, 2, 45; at Equity Shoes, 211; in illegal abortion collective, 141–42; in industrial democracy, 3; at IGP, 227; in legal collective, 249, 250–51; and oligarchization, 12–13; in plywood cooperatives, 341; at *Scottish Daily News,* 205; in Summerhill West, 259; at Triumph-Meriden, 345; for workers' expertise, 64–65
— satisfaction: in industrial democracy study, 105; lack of, 1, 5; measurement of, 97; need of, 245; and ownership in plywood cooperatives, 172; and participation, 88; in QWL Project, 378; in scavenger companies, 117–18
— security: in plywood cooperatives, 168; in scavenger companies, 115; in workplace democracy, 7
— skills: in illegal abortion collective, 141; myth of, 4–5; in QWL Project, 376–77
— stigma: measurement of, 124 n. 19; of scavengers, 117, 123 n. 16
— turnover: and alienation, 5; in Mondragón, 187
Johnson, Ana Gutiérrez: 34, 42, 44, 90, 157; on Mondragón System, 177–97, 197 n. 4, 313, 347, 350
Joint management, 4, 57, 59
Jones, Derek, 219 n. 7
Jones and Laughlin Steel. *See* LTV
Juarez Scavenger Company, 116
Judiciary. *See* Disciplinary procedures

Kadi justice, 28
Kanter, Rosabeth Moss: 24, 31, 41, 44, 295; on participation (QWL Project), 371–82, 372, 379
Kasanoff's Bakery, 344
Katz, Sue, 137 n. 5

Kaye, Michael, 30
Kazan, Nick, 123 n. 9
Kendall, Erick, 331–32
Kibbutz, 3–4, 65, 67, 68, 78
King, Alan. *See* Baker, Jake
King, B. T., 152
Kinkade, Katherine, 263
Kirkby Manufacturing and Engineering: control of, 204; demise of, 158; need of, for capital, 217; origin of, 200n; structure of, 219 n. 4
Kirkham, Mavis, 308, 212–13
Kirschner, Edward, 78
Kleiber, Nancy, 142, 143
Knight, Peter, 4
Knights of Labor: cooperatives, 172, 173 n. 3; and self-management, 343; song of, 321
Kolaja, Jiri, 66
Kozol, Jonathan, 43
Kunin, T., 97

"Labor's bill of rights," 385
Labor movement: and the Communist Party, 386 (*See also* Communist Party); history of, 383–85; and white-collar workers, 384; and worker-management, 383–96. *See also* Union(s)
Labor theory of property, 301–2, 306
Lancashire Weavers song, 315
Lapworth, Bill (Triumph-Meriden), 214
Law collective: incentives in, 32; low wages in, compensation for, 33; recruitment in, 29; wages in, 32, 34. *See also* Santa Barbara Legal Collective
Lawler, E. E., 88, 90
Layoffs. *See* Job security; Plant closings
Leaders, control by, at IGP, 228, 239
Leadership: of Arizmendi, Father José María, 179–82; and democratic consciousness, 70; Gibbons on, 234; in plant closings, conversion of, to worker management, 345; of supporting institutions, 349
League for Education and Culture, 179
League of Revolutionary Black Workers, 400
Leavitt, H. J., 38
Legal title, 77
Legal workers, 250–51
Legislation and unions, 384–85, 395–96
Lesieur, Frederick G., 58, 59, 60, 74, 76
Levin, Harry M., 214, 344
Light, Linda, 142, 143
Likert, Rensis, 58, 59

Lindenfeld, Frank: 244; on free school, problems of control in, 257–69, 295; on plant closings, conversion of, to worker management, 337–52; on workplace democracy, 1–18

Link-pin, 11, 349

Lipset, S. M., 26

Litwak, Eugene, 46

Locke, E. A., 88, 107

Long, R. J., 92

Lordstown strike, 388–89

Los Truckaderos, 273, 277 n. 6

Low, J. O., 92

LTV, 340, 366–67, 369 n. 1

Lykes Corporation, 353, 354, 366–68, 369 n.1

Lynd, Staughton, 56, 66

MacCauley, Brian, 48 n. 5

Macciocchi, Maria, 74

Maccoby, Dr. Michael, 238

McEwan, John D., 66

Mackie, Allister *(Scottish Daily News)*, 204, 207, 208, 219 n. 3

McReynolds, David, 274, 277 n. 8

Management: collaborative, 88–89; communication with, 174 n. 9; and information sharing, 62–65; and limited participation, 106–7; in Mondragón, 188; professional, 324; of *Scottish Daily News*, 201. *See also* Self-management

Manager(s): in bureaucracy, 21, 264; in free school, 264; at IGP, 228, 233–35; as interest group, 92–93; middle, 105–6; owners, 103–6; professional, 12, 345; at Triumph-Meriden, 345; worker-community, ownership, 89–91

Managerial committee, 11

Mandators, 21

Mansbridge, Jane J.: 34, 40, 85; on fears in face-to-face meetings, 125–37

Mao Tse-Tung, 70

Marieskind, Helen Isabel, 142–43

Market(s): and collectives, 243; and conversion to cooperative, 347–48, 351; farmers', 325–26; in IGP, 223; for Mondragón System, 187; and plywood cooperatives, 167; and *Scottish Daily News*, 208, 218; and Triumph-Meriden, 202, 215, 218, 345; and workplace democracy, 14; in Youngstown Sheet and Tube Proposal, 356, 357–58, 362

Market-value pricing, 319

Marx, Karl, on ownership, 89, 90; on worker-ownership, 121, 124 n. 20

Maslow, Abraham, 70, 88

Maxwell, Robert, 202, 207, 217

Meacham, Bill (Bhudeva), 276 n. 3

Means, Gardiner, 81 n. 11

Meara, Hanna, 123 n. 13

Mechanistic organization, 380–82

Meetings: fears in face-to-face, 125–37; general, for participation, 59, 68; paid attendance at, 341, 174 n. 10; plenary, 11; shareholders, 166; study, 249–50; time taken by, in collectives, 38–39, 171–72, 233

Melman, Seymour, 9

Member(s): of corporation, 299; multiple, 304

Membership: certificates, 308, 309, 310; of collectives, 2; of illegal abortion collective, 140; in corporation and other organizations compared, 304

— rights: in corporation, 299, 305, 307; and net book value, 312–13; in restructuring corporation, 302, 308

Mendocino free school, 262, 266

Menorah Kosher Poultry, 343–44

Michels, Robert, 12

Midland Co-operative Oil Association, 323–24

Miller, George, 98

Miller, Merton H., 313 n. 1

Minnesota cooperatives, 320, 321–32

Modigliani, Franco, 313 n. 1

Mohawk Valley Community Corporation, 339

Mohr, James C., 142

Mommsen, Wolfgang, 47–48 n. 4

Mondragón System, 157, 177–97, 395; bank in, 15; collectivist personalities in, 42; components of, 178–79; cultural base of, 182–83; economic base of, 182; financial autonomy in, 44; growth of, 9–10, 183–87; income ratio in, 3, 34; internal accounts in, 313; and plywood cooperatives compared, 158; significance of, 193–97; size of, 10; social gains of, 187–88; social problems of, 188–91; workplace restructuring in, 191–93 (*See also* Copreci); mentioned, 7, 14, 15

Morale in workplace democracy, 9

Morris, David, 273, 277 n. 7, 283

Motivation: factors in, 88–89; in illegal abortion collective, 152; and participation, 88; in plywood cooperatives, 168; political, 248, 252–53; in scaven-

ger companies, 118; and share ownership, 90
Mouzelis, Nocos, 24
Mulder, Mauk, 70
Myrdal, Jan, 74

National Association of Manufacturers (NAM), 385, 395
National Center for Economic Alternatives (NCEA) and Youngstown Sheet and Tube Proposal, 355, 356, 358, 361–65, 366
National Civic Federation (NCF), 384–85
National Commission on Productivity, 123 n. 10
National Co-Operatives, Inc. (NCI), 320, 323
National Cooperative Bank, 15, 17, 21–22, 243, 245, 294, 396
National Credit Union, 320
National Industrial Conference Board, (NICB), 56, 63, 68
National Science Foundation, 360
National Taxpayers' Equity Association, 326
Nationalization as transfer of ownership, mentioned, 77
Neill, A. S., 258
New School for Democratic Management, The, 14; mentioned, 243
Newspaper, alternative: incentives at, 31; homogeneity in, 39; legal constraints on, 43; structure of, 49 n. 11; task-sharing on, 36; time priorities at, 39; wages on, 32–33, 34. See also Scottish Daily News
Newton, Gary H.: 244, 268 n. 3; on structure and decision-making, 271–77
Nonowning worker(s): control by, 87–89; in plywood cooperatives, 164, 170–71; in scavenger companies, 118–20, 171
Non-Partisan League, 322
Notes and retained net income, 309
Nunnally, J. C., 97

Oakeshott, Robert, 197 n. 6, 347, 350
Occupational-interest groups, 92–93, 96–97, 102–6
Office workers: attitudes of, 105–6; as nonmember workers, 170; as owners, 101; unions and, 384
Oligarchization, 12–13
Olson, Mancur, Jr., 91, 96, 98

Olympia Veneer Company, 162, 174 n.5
Organic organization, 381–82
Organizational behavior theory, 372
Ownership: and control, 89; of corporation, 299, 303–5; effects of, 91; of fruits of labor, legal, 301–2; and job stigma, 123 n. 16; of kibbutz, 78; in limited participation, 5; in Marxian theory, 89, 90; measure of, 96; in Mondragón, 195; nonprivate, 77; in plant closings, conversion of, to worker management, 340; sense of, 97, 105; status, 91, 92; transfer of, for self-management, 76, 77, 78–79; of cooperative corporation, 304–5, 311;
— community, 13, 78 (See also Ownership, worker-community); nonprivate, 78–79; in statutory cooperative corporation, 311
— worker: alienation and, 100, 101; and attitudes toward participation, study of, 87–108; benefits of, 91; in Breman Enterprises, 297 n. 2; and control, 87–89; degeneration of, 109; and employee ownership compared, 306–7; financial risk of, 95–96, 98–100; Holyoake on, 121; at IGP, 223–24; and job satisfaction in plywood cooperatives, 172; Marxian view of, 121; of means of production, 7; and occupational interest groups, 92–93; in plywood cooperatives as motivation, 172, 341; purchase for, 77; rewards of, in scavenger companies, 109–22; and status, 91–92, 100–2; and work attitudes in scavenger companies, 2, 116–18; in Yugoslavia, 78, 79
— worker-community, 89–91, 340; and plant closings conversion, 348–49; study of, 93–108; in Youngstown Sheet and Tube Proposal, 362–65

PACE (Philadephia Association for Cooperative Enterprise), 344, 349
Pacific Paperboard Products, 339
Paj, I., 63, 64, 66, 74
Panekoek, Anton, 391, 392
Parallel organizations, 295. See also QWL Project
Parsons, Talcott, 42
Participation: characteristics of, 6; as continuum, 4; in corporation (See Industrial democracy; QWL Project); in decision-making (See Decision-

making); education for (*See* Education); at Equity Shoes, 209–10; limited, 4–6, 106–7; necessity of, 239–40; origins of, 4–5; at Procter & Gamble, mentioned, 225; requirements for, 232; retreat from, 5–6; rewards of, 109–22; and worker performance, 88

Pateman, Carole, 42, 49 n. 10, 107

Patrons, worker-owner as, 174 n. 8

Patrons of Husbandry, 321

Patronage refund, 320: in Farmers Union Terminal Association, 325; in Rochdale Principles, 318–19; in St. Paul Farmers Union Co-operative, 320; weakness of, in Midland Oil, 324

Pearl, Arthur, 152

Pearson, Peg, on Seattle Workers' Brigade, 244, 279–89

Pegasus (free school): demise of, 262; origin of, 261; parents' participation in, 261–62; roles in, 261; structure of, 261–62

Pennock, J. Roland, 136–37 n. 4

Pension funds: as capital, 394–95; in conventional firm, 87; shares held in, 108

Personal Justice Committee (IGP), 226–27

Pepper, S. W., 209–11

Perrow, Charles, 28, 29

Perry, Stewart, 34, 42, 110, 122 n. 3

Peterson, 142

Philadelphia Association for Cooperative Enterprise. *See* PACE

Plant closings: and community, 16, 296, 390; reasons for, 337–38. *See also* Unions

— conversion of, into worker management, 294, 295, 337–52, 391–92; necessary ingredients for, 345–49; plywood cooperatives as, 340, 341 (*See also* Plywood producers' cooperatives); supporting institutions and, 349–51; unions and (*See* Unions). *See also* Kirkby Manufacturing; *Scottish Daily News;* Triumph-Meriden; Youngstown Sheet and Tube

Plywood producers' cooperatives, 157, 161–73; control in, 341; demise of, 172, 175 n. 15; disciplinary procedures in, 68, 341; expertise of workers in, 65; and Mondragón compared, 158; financing of, 162,

163–64; history of, 161–64, 341; income ratio in, 3, 34; information sharing in, 64; issues of decision-making in, 56; job rotation in, 341; job security in, 10; meetings in, 341; names of, 173 n. 2; nonowners in, 164; operation of, 164–66, 173 n. 4; productivity in, 157, 341, 360; reduced number of, 169–70, 172, 175 n. 15; return from surplus in, 74; self-management in, 166–73; size of, 3, 341; share ownership problems in, 15, 16; structure of, 341; wages in, 10, 123 n. 12, 341; mentioned, 221, 243, 339

Polaroid Corporation, 5–6

Political: alienation and share ownership, 90, 91; criticism of cooperatives, 273; defined, 17; democracy and workplace democracy compared, 65–66; emphasis in Seattle Workers' Brigade, 284, 287–88; expression in worker-managed business, 288; growth and feminism, 145–48, 150–53; instability of authoritarian firms, 88; as motivation in legal collective, 248, 252–53; signficance of workplace democracy, 294; strength and cooperatives, 111, 315–16, 334–35

— climate: and alternative institutions, 22, 43, 293, 347; of British producers' cooperatives, 217; and IGP, 237–38

— neutrality: and cooperatives, 328; in Rochdale Principles, 320

Politics of function, 17

Politics of struggle, 17

Pomeranz, R., 98

Potvin, Raymond H., 62

Power. *See* Control

Prestige: in bureaucracies, 33–34; in collectives, 34

Production process: in China, 48 n. 7; in cooperatives, labor theory and, 301–2, 306; coordinating, in QWL Project, 376–77; in Mondragón, 178; in plywood cooperatives, 173 n. 4; workers' control of, 407–9

Productivity: in conventional firm, 361; in Kaiser Steel, 361; in plywood cooperatives, 341; as success factor, 167–68; in South Bend Lathe, 360; and worker-ownership, 359–61; in Youngstown Metal Products Company, 361; in Youngstown Sheet and

Tube feasibility study, 356, 359–61
Professional attitude in legal collective, 248–49
Profit(s): in cooperative corporation, 306–7, 308; in corporation, 76, 299, 307; economic, 299, 300, 307; as limiting factor in Mondragón, 194–95; in workplace democracy, 7. *See also* Return from surplus
Project Advisory Group in QWL Project, 374
Property rights, 299
Protection of worker: in American Cast Iron Pipe Company, 65; in IGP, 230 n. 2; in decision-making, 65–67
Psychological health: in authoritarian organizations, 88; and participation, 88; of scavengers, 117–18. *See also* QWL Project
Puckett, Elbridge, 76
Punishments. *See* Disciplinary Procedures
Pyramid. *See* Stratification

QWL (Quality of Work Life) Project, 371–82; information gathering in, 374; implementation of, 375–77; results of, 377–78; significance of, 378–82; theoretical framework of, 372–73

Radicalism. *See* Cooperatives, political
Rainwater, Lee, 123 n. 13
Record-keeping: and bureaucratization, 12; as constraint in collectives, 43, 44, 268 n. 2; in scavenger companies, 111
Recruitment: in bureaucracies, 30; in collectives, 29, 30–31
Refuse collectors. *See* Scavenger companies
Reissman, Frank, 146
Reports as information-sharing, 63
Return on investment in Rochdale Principles, 318
Return of surplus: in Breman Enterprises, 297 n. 2; at IGP, 224; as information, 75–76; in Mondragón, 180, 184; in plywood cooperatives, 165, 174 n. 7; in Ulgor, 184
— in participation, 81 n. 9, n. 10; forms of, 74; guaranteed, 73–76; guidelines for, 74–76; as information-sharing, 75–76; in Scanlon Plan, 74
Rewards of ownership. *See* Scavenger companies
Reward structure in limited participation, 5
Rifkin, Jeremy, 17, 109, 346
Ripponden Cooperative Society, 316–17
Riptide, 245
Roberts, Norman (legal collective), 247n
Rochdale Principles (Equitable Society of Rochdale Pioneers), 318–20, 328, 331n
Role(s): in community meetings, 125; in illegal abortion collective, 141–42; worker's, legal significance of, 300
— differentiation: in bureaucracy, 35, 36–38; in collectives, 2–3, 35–36; minimizing, 36, 142
Rossi, Peter H., 123–24, n. 18
Rothschild-Whitt, Joyce: on workplace democracy, 1–18, 6, 12, 16, 21, 22; on collectivist organization, 23–49, 47 n. 2, 86n, 139n, 142, 149, 150, 151, 152, 244, 297 n.1
Roy, Jimmy *(Scottish Daily News)*, 205, 206
Rubyfruit Mills, 285
Rucci, Jeannie (legal collective), 247n
Rule(s): in bureaucracies, 28; in collectives, 27–28; infractions (*See* Disciplinary procedures)
Rus, Veljko, 73
Russell, Raymond: 10, 11, 14, 85, 122 n.5; on rewards of participation, 109–24, 123–24 n. 3, 17, 18

St. Paul Farmers Union Central Exchange, 320, 325
Salary. *See* Wages
Salancik, G. R., 95
Sales-agency agreement, 163
Sanders, Jerry, 122 n. 6
Santa Barbara Legal Collective, 247–56; attitude in, 248–49; benefits of, 255–56; clients of, 252–53; defined, 247; education in, 249–50; meetings in, 249–50; members of, 247n; motivation for, 248, 253–54; origin of, 248; problems in, 253–55; wages in, 250
Saratoga Knitting Mills, 339
Savas, E. S., 123 n. 10
Save Our Valley Campaign, 365–66
Scanlon Plan, 60, 74
Scavenger companies: assessment of, 114; collectivist personalities in, 42; cost reductions in, 119; financial

rewards in, 115; financial structure of, 119–20, 121; formation of, 110–11; growth of, 118; income ratio in, 3, 34, 243; institutionalization of, 11; job stigma and, 123 n. 16; nonowner workers in, 118–20; share ownership in, 16; study of, 110–22; work of worker-owner in, 110–18

Schlesinger, Melinda Bart, 85; on self-identity in collectives, 139–53

Schools. *See* Black Mountain; Free school; Pegasus; Summerhill West

Schumacher, E. F., 34, 196

Schweiger, D. M., 88, 107

Scientific management, 51–52, 399; in Mondragón, 188. *See also* Taylorism

Scott Bader, 77, 199, 218 n. 1; income ratio in, 34

Scottish Daily News: demise of, 158, 207–8; financing of, 202; origin of, 199–201; philosophy of, 203–4; marketing problem of, 218; structure of, 201–3, 206; unions in, 204–6

Seattle Workers' Brigade, 279–89: and Cooperating Community, 287; dissolution of, 286–87; entrepreneurial action of, 283–84; feminism in, 284–85; issues in meetings of, 283; origin of 280–81; political emphasis of, 284; problems of, 283, 284; sexism in, 284–85; teams in, 281–83, 285–87; wages in, 243, 284

Seeger, Murray, 77

Select Committee on Small Business, 338

Self-help model, 142–43; and political growth, 145–46

Self-identity changes in collectives, 42, 139–53

Self-management: defined, 6, 8; goal of, 225; of IGP, 221–40; labor movement and, 383–96; in legal collective, 254; in plywood cooperatives, 166–73; problems of, at IGP, 231–36; structure and, 271–77; transfer of rights for, 77; and unions, 343

Sexism, 254–55, 284–85

Shares: in corporation, legal significance of, 299, 307, 338; as membership certificates, 310; in pension funds, 108; transfer of, 77–78, 79, 115, 119, 165, 169–70; at Triumph-Meriden, 214; working, in plywood cooperatives, 164–65

— -holder: age factor of, 169; alienation of, 90, 91; contribution of, in plywood cooperatives, 165; control by, 90, 107–8; rights of, 300, 310–11; in scavenger companies, 110–11; status of, in industrial democracy, 91, 92; wages of, in plywood cooperatives, 123 n. 12

— ownership: as control, 90, 108; deficiencies of, 15; at IGP, 224; limiting, 16; need for, in cooperatives, 295, 338; and plant closings, conversion of, to worker management, 89–108, 330–39, 342, 348, 363–64; of plywood cooperatives, 162, 169; at *Scottish Daily News,* 201–2; in Vermont Asbestos Group, 15; workers, and producers' cooperatives, 90

Shutdowns. *See* Plant closings

Siegel, Paul W., 123–24 n. 18

Sik, Ota, 79, 81 n. 5

Simmel, George, 136 n. 1

Size: and decision-making, 264, 271; and efficiency, 9–11; and face-to-face conflict, 125–26, 133–35; limit for participation, 349; of plywood cooperatives, 341; of Wheatsville Food Co-op, limit of, 276; of workplace democracies, importance of, 2–3, 10–11, 12, 47 n. 3, 167; in Youngstown Proposal, 294, 352 n. 3

Small Business Administration, 169

Smith-Rosenberg, Carroll, 147

Social capital, 275–76

Social change: cooperatives as force of, 320; as motivation, 248, 251–53; parallel structures and, 378–82; requirements for, 406; workplace democracy and, 10, 293–412

Social relations: in bureaucracies, 29–30; in collectives, 30, 35; problems of, in legal collective, 253–55; as social cost in collectives, 40–41

Solomon, Richard (legal collective), 247n

Sorey, G. K., 76

South Bend Lathe, 339, 360

Specialist: in bureaucracy, 35; in illegal abortion collective, 140; in Mondragón, 186; wage at *Scottish Daily News,* 206; workers' hiring, 65

Spencer, Gib (supermarket manager), 334

Status: ownership, and attitude, 100–2;

in scavenger companies, 120; of shareholder in industrial democracy, 91, 92
Stefanelli, Leonard, 111, 122–23 n.7
Stein, Barry A.: 10, 295, 349; on participation (QWL Project, 371–82, 379)
Stern, Robert N.: 14, 47 n. 1, 86; on worker ownership, 87–108, 90, 92, 95, 101, 107, 108
Stone, Katherine, 384
Stratification: minimizing, 7; income, 3 — social: in alternative newspaper, 34; in bureaucracies, 33–34; in collectives, 34; in free clinic, 34; in free school, 49 n. 14; in legal collective, 34
Strauss, Anselm, 25
Strike(s): in British cooperatives, 317, 412; in Fiat factory, 406; in Ford plant (Germany), 404–5; by Knights of Labor, 322; Lordstown, 388–89; in Mondragón, 188, 190–91; at Pirelli tire factory, 405, 409; reasons for, 402-5; reverse, 409; as struggle for control, 409–10; in Ulgor, 188, 190–91; at Upper Clyde Shipbuilders, 200; wildcat, and social change, 412; in workplace democracy, 5, 9
Strikers, wildcat, and legal collective, 253
Strongforce, 245, 268–69 n. 3
Structure: of alternative newspaper, 49 n. 11; commonalities of collective, 25, 26–38; flaws in cooperative, 311; legal, for cooperative corporation, 295, 299–313; for plant closings, conversion of, to worker management, 348–49; of plywood cooperatives, 341; and self-management, 271–77; two-tier, 349; in QWL Project, 375; in Youngstown Sheet and Tube Proposal, 363–65. See also Teams
Sturmthal, Adolf, 53, 59, 68, 74
Substantive rationality for model of collectives, 23–47
Suggestion box, 59, 268–69 n. 3
Summerhill West: decision-making in, 258, 260; disciplinary problems in, 258–59; financial problems of, 259–60; goal of, 258; origin of, 257; parents' control in, 258–59; reorganization of, 260; student participation in, 258, 260; wages in, 259–60
Sunset Scavenger Company, 111, 112–113, 114, 115, 118, 122–23 n. 7
Swidler, Ann, 29, 42, 49 n. 14
Szulc, Tad, 73

Tabb, J. Yanai, 65
Task-sharing: on alternative newspaper, 36; and equality in collectives, 35, 45, 142; in industrial democracy, 3; as internal education, 2; and oligarchization, 13; problems of, 13; in scavenger companies as incentive, 112–114
Taxes: and farmers' cooperatives, 326–27; and IGP, 224; and plywood cooperatives, 165, 174 n. 13; in restructuring corporation, 307, 310
Taylor, Frederick W., 5, 51
Taylor, Rosemary C. R., 42, 136 n. 3, 142
Taylorism: in Mondragón, 191, 196–197; reasons for, 4–5; and status, 384
Teachers as workers. See Summerhill West
Teams: autonomy of, in Seattle Workers' Brigade, 283, 286–87; control by, at IGP, 226–28; and plant closings conversion, 349; in QWL Project, 377
Teamsters Union, 343
Technological change: as constraint in Ulgor, 192–93; as success factor in plywood cooperative, 167; in Youngstown Sheet and Tube Proposal, 356, 357, 369 n. 2
Tension, avoidance of, 40–41; in collectives, 40–41; in face-to-face meetings, 125–37; at IGP, 233, 235; in scavenger companies, 118; of worker-owner in industrial democracy, 102
Theobald, Robert, 70
Thorsrud, Einer, 88
Thompson, 48–49 n. 9
Time: and face-to-face conflict, 134; as social cost in workplace democracy, 38–39, 149, 171–72, 233
Torbert, William, 30, 42
Tricot Knitting Mill, study of, as industrial democracy, 94–108
Trist, Eric L., 52, 88
Triumph-Meriden Motorcycle cooperative: demise of, 158; financing problems of, 218, 219 n. 5, 347; marketing problem of, 202, 218; as producers' cooperative, 200–1, 213–15, 344–45; structure of, 213–14, 219 n. 4; wages in, 206, 219 n. 6; mentioned, 77, 203, 351
Trivelli, Pablo, 197 n. 6
Tuden, Arthur, 48–49 n. 9
Tufte, Edward J., 136 n. 1
Tweedale, Ann, 317, 327
Tyomies, 329

Ularco, 185, 188, 190–91

Ulgor: income ratio in, 180; management board of, 188; return of surplus in, 184; Social Council in, 188–89, 190; strikes in, 188, 190–91; workplace structure in, 192–93; mentioned, 181, 185

Union(s): as arbiter in self-managed plants, 395; as bureaucracies, 401; buy campaign of, 348; and capitalism (*See* Capitalism); and cooperatives, 174–75 n. 14, 352n; and co-operative supermarket, 333–34; as client of legal collective, 253; and decision-making, 53, 56, 59–60; in Equity Shoes, 210; historical role of 400–1; at IGP, 232; individual rights in anarchist, 67; information-sharing and, 63; as institutions, 400–2; issues controlled by, 87–88; and legislation, 384–85, 395–96; as lobby for worker management, 395–96; origin of, 400; pension funds as capital, 394; and plant closings, conversion of, to worker management, 295–96, 343, 345, 346, 390, 392–96; in plywood cooperatives, 164; radicalism of new, 400; in Rath Meat Packing conversion, 342; of scavenger companies, 120; at *Scottish Daily News,* 203–6, 208; structure, problem of, 390, 392; in Triumph-Meriden, 213–14; in Sweden, 63; wage and return to shareholders compared, 174 n. 7; and wages, 387, 389, 398–99; wage contracts, 393; and white-collar worker, 384; and worker management, 295–96, 343, 389–96. *See also* names of unions

United Auto Workers, 343, 387, 388, 389

United Farm Workers: buy union campaign of, 348; and cooperative supermarket, 333–34; and workers' self-management, 343

United Mine Workers, 322–23

United Steelworkers of America, 369 n. 1

Universal PROUTist Youth Federation, 277 n. 5

Value-rationality, 23

Vanek, Jaroslav, 6, 7, 80, 90, 121, 197 n. 6, 311–12, 313 n. 3

Vauxhall workers, 403

Verba, Sidney, 73

Vermont Asbestos Group, 15, 77, 108, 221, 339

Vernon, Raymond, 57

Voting rights: in cooperatives, 301, 308; in cooperative corporation, 300–1; in corporation, 299–300; and membership, 169; in plant closings, conversion of, to worker management, 348

Vroom, V. H., 95

Wage(s): as advances, 174 n. 8; in British cooperatives, 219 n. 6; in collectives, 32–33, 243; control of, in conventional firm, 87; in cooperative corporation, 300, 306–7, 308; equal as success factor in plywood cooperatives, 168, 169, 171, 341; at Equity Shoes, 211; hours of work and, 169; as income, 123 n. 12; inflation and, 389; in legal collective, 250; low, compensation for, in collectives, 33, 250; lowering, in plywood cooperatives, 168; for meeting attendance, 171; of nonmember workers in plywood cooperatives, 171; as patronage dividends, 174 n. 8; in scavenger companies, 115; in *Scottish Daily News,* occupational structure and, 206; in Seattle Workers' Brigade, 243, 284; in Summerhill West, problems of, 259–60; at Triumph-Meriden, 206, 213, 214, 216, 219 n. 6, 344; structure in Mondragón, 189–90

Wagner Act, 385

Walsh, Edward, 123–24 n. 14, n. 18

Warner, A. L., 47 n. 3, 92

Webb, Beatrice, 122 n. 1

Webb, C., 90

Webb, Sidney, 122 n. 1

Weber, Max, 23–24, 28, 35, 45, 47–48 n. 4, 51, 411

Weberian theory: of legitimate domination, 47–48 n. 4; of organizations, 28; of rational administrative system, 51

Wheatsville Food Co-op, 244, 274, 275–76

White, Marianne, 79

White-collar workers. *See* Worker(s), white-collar

Whyte, William Foote: 17, 34, 42, 44, 48 n.7, 90, 157; on Mondragón System, 177–97, 313, 338, 347, 350

Wild, R., 88

Williams, A., 90
Wilson, Harold (Prime Minister), 207
Wilson, James Q., 31, 61
Wolff, Kurt H., 136 n. 1
Women in producers' cooperative, 170.
    See also Feminism; Sexism
Woodward, J., 98
Work attitudes: communication of, 402–
    6; at IGP, 229–30, 232, 234, 235–36; in
    industrial democracy, 105–8; in legal
    collective, 248–49; in Mondragón,
    182–83; in organizational behavioral
    theory, 372; in QWL Project, 378; in
    scavenger companies, 116–18; in Se-
    attle Workers' Brigade, 288–89
Worker(s): accounts, 393–94; autonomy,
    88–89; as beneficiaries at Triumph-
    Meriden, 214; in bureaucracy, 21; and
    capitalist mentality, 339; coin-
    fluence, 4; information-sharing of,
    62–65; interests, 13, 244; legal, 250–51
— blue-collar: as interest group, 92–93;
    and white-collar worker, 51–52
— management: in Europe, 391; in
    Spain, 391; and worker control,
    distinction between, 391–96
— white-collar: and blue-collar worker,
    51–52; as interest group, 92–93; self-
    management by (See IGP); and
    unions, 384
Worker-Owned Plywood Association,
    172
Workplace democracy: assessing success
    of, 10; American attitude toward,
    293–94; characteristics of, 6–8,
    21–80; and communities, similari-
    ties of, 125–26; constraints of, 38,
    39–40, 41–44; within conventional
    bureaucracies, 295 (*See also* Indus-
    trial democracy; QWL Project);

corporate divestitures and growth
    of, 16–17; decline of, in Equity
    Shoes, 211–13; efficiency of, 9–11;
    experiments in, 3–4; external
    factors in, 21–22; forms of, 11; fu-
    ture of, 296; goal of, 1, 6, 18, 81
    n. 7, 293; government and, 13; iso-
    lation of, 14; judicial systems in,
    67–69; legal forms of, 15–16; move-
    ment for, 16–18; ownership of, 76–
    79 (*See also* Ownership); and polit-
    ical democracy, 65–66; politics of,
    17; popularity of, 17; research
    methods for, 24–25; social costs of,
    38–41; worker participation in,
    need for, 239–40

Yarrow, Sarah. *See* Peg Pearson
Young, Wendell, 344
Youngstown Sheet and Tube: impact of
    closing of, on community, 354; sig-
    nificance of closing, 355–56, 366,
    368
— proposal for conversion, 340, 353–69;
    feasibility study of, 355–65; financing
    problems of, 347; reasons for demise
    of, 352 n. 3; Save Our Valley Cam-
    paign and, 365–66; mentioned, 8, 13,
    16, 294, 338
Yugoslavia, workplace democracy in,
    3, 7, 13, 63, 78, 79, 244, 313, 391

Zald, Mayer N., 142, 151
Zimablist, Andrew, 3, 8, 9
Zurcher, Louis, Jr., 24
Zwerdling, Daniel: 6, 65, 107, 158; on
    IGP (International Group Plans),
    221–40, 268–69n

ABOUT THE EDITORS

Frank Lindenfeld is Professor of Sociology, Cheyney State College, and a member of the Board of Directors of the Philadelphia Association for Cooperative Enterprise (PACE). He is currently engaged in a study of the Jamaican sugar workers' cooperatives. He is the author of "Problems of Power in a Free School," chapter 12, and "Workers' Cooperatives: Remedy for Plant Closings?" chapter 17 of this volume.

Dr. Joyce Rothschild-Whitt is a member of the faculty of Sociology at the University of Louisville where she is developing a special graduate program on changing patterns of work and labor. Previously she served on the faculty of the Industrial and Labor Relations School at Cornell University, helping to coordinate the New Systems of Work and Participation program. She is the author of "The Collectivist Organization: An Alternative to Bureaucratic Models," chapter 1 of this volume, as well as two forthcoming books, *Dilemmas of Organizational Democracy* (with Allen Whitt) and *Worker Ownership and Control in the U.S.* (with William Foote Whyte).